MEDIEVAL DUBLIN XI

This volume is dedicated
by the Friends of Medieval Dublin
to the memory of

Gerry O'Flaherty

(1933–2019)

Requiescat in pace

Medieval Dublin XIX

Seán Duffy

EDITOR

FOUR COURTS PRESS

Typeset in 10.5 pt on 12.5 pt Ehrhardt by
Carrigboy Typesetting Services for
FOUR COURTS PRESS LTD
7 Malpas Street, Dublin 8, Ireland
www.fourcourtspress.ie
and in North America for
FOUR COURTS PRESS
c/o IPG, 814 N Franklin St, Chicago, IL 60610.

A catalogue record for this title is available
from the British Library.

ISBN 978–1–84682–967–3 hbk
ISBN 978–1–84682–966–6 pbk

This book is published with the active support of
Dublin City Council/Comhairle Chathair Átha Cliath.

Dublin City
Baile Átha Cliath

Printed in England
by CPI Antony Rowe, Chippenham, Wilts.

Contents

Abbreviations

AFM — *Annála ríoghachta Éireann: annals of the kingdom of Ireland by the Four Masters, from the earliest period to the year 1616*, ed. J. O'Donovan, 7 vols (Dublin, 1851)

AH — *Analecta Hibernica, including the report of the Irish Manuscripts Commission* (IMC, Dublin, 1930–)

AI — *The annals of Inisfallen (MS Rawlinson B. 503)*, ed. S. Mac Airt (DIAS, Dublin, 1951)

ALC — *The annals of Loch Cé: a chronicle of Irish affairs from AD 1014 to AD 1590*, ed. W.M. Hennessy, 2 vols (RS, London, 1871; repr. IMC, Dublin, 1939)

ATig — 'Annals of Tigernach', ed. W. Stokes in *Revue Celtique*, 16 (1895) 374–419; 17 (1896) 6–33, 119–263, 337–420; 18 (1897) 9–59, 150–97, 267–303; reprinted in two vols (Felinfach, 1993)

AU — *Annála Uladh ('Annals of Ulster'), otherwise Annála Senait ('Annals of Senat'): a chronicle of Irish affairs AD 431 to AD 1540*, ed. W.M. Hennessey and B. MacCarthy, 4 vols (Dublin, 1887–1901); *The annals of Ulster (to AD 1131)*, ed. S. Mac Airt and G. Mac Niocaill (Dublin, 1983)

BL — British Library, London

Bradley et al. (eds), *Dublin in the medieval world* — John Bradley, Alan J. Fletcher and Anngret Simms (eds), *Dublin in the medieval world: studies in honour of Howard B. Clarke* (Dublin, 2009)

Cal. S.P. Ire. — *Calendar of state papers relating to Ireland, 1509–73 [etc.]*, 24 vols (London, 1860–1911)

CARD — J.T. Gilbert (ed.), *Calendar of ancient records of Dublin*, 19 vols (Dublin, 1889–1944)

CCD — *Calendar of Christ Church deeds*, ed. M.J. McEnery and Raymond Refaussé (Dublin, 2001)

CCR — *Calendar of the close rolls* [...], *1272*–[*1509*], 47 vols (PRO, London, 1892–1963)

CDI — *Calendar of documents relating to Ireland, 1171–1307*, ed. H.S. Sweetman and G.F. Handcock, 5 vols (PRO, London, 1875–86)

CGG — *Cogadh Gaedhil re Gallaibh*, ed. and trans. James Henthorn Todd (London, 1867)

CIRCLE — Peter Crooks (ed.), *A calendar of Irish chancery letters,* c.*1244–1509* (available at http://chancery.tcd.ie/)

Civil Survey — *The Civil Survey, AD 1654–56*, ed. R.C. Simington, 10 vols (Dublin, 1931–61)

CJRI — *Calendar of the justiciary rolls of Ireland*, ed. James Mills et al., 3 vols (Dublin, 1905–56)

Clarke et al. (eds), *Ireland and Scandinavia* — H.B. Clarke, Máire Ní Mhaonaigh and Raghnall Ó Floinn (eds), *Ireland and Scandinavia in the early Viking Age* (Dublin, 1998)

Clarke, *Dublin, Pt 1* (IHTA) — H.B. Clarke (ed.), *Dublin, part I, to 1610*, IHTA, no. 11 (RIA, Dublin, 2002)

CPL — *Calendar of entries in the papal registers relating to Great Britain and Ireland: papal letters* (London, 1893–)

CPR — *Calendar of the patent rolls* [...], *1232–[1509]*, 53 vols (PRO, London, 1911)

CPR Ire., Hen. VIII–Eliz. — *Calendar of the patent and close rolls of chancery in Ireland, Henry VIII to 18th Elizabeth*, ed. J. Morrin (Dublin, 1862)

Crawford and Gillespie (eds), *St Patrick's* — John Crawford and Raymond Gillespie (eds), *St Patrick's cathedral, Dublin: a history* (Dublin, 2009)

CS — *Chronicum Scotorum*, ed. W.M. Hennessy (London, 1866)

CStM — *Chartularies of Saint Mary's abbey, Dublin*, ed. J.T. Gilbert, 2 vols (RS, London, 1884–6)

DGMR — Philomena Connolly and Geoffrey Martin (eds), *Dublin guild merchant roll* (Dublin, 1992)

DHR — *Dublin Historical Record*

DIB — *Dictionary of Irish biography*, ed. J. McGuire and J. Quinn, 9 vols (Cambridge, 2009)

Extents Ir. mon. possessions — *Extents of Irish monastic possessions, 1540–1541* [...], ed. N.B. White (IMC, Dublin, 1943)

FAI — Joan Newlon Radner (ed.), *Fragmentary annals of Ireland* (Dublin, 1978)

Gilbert (ed.), *Hist. & mun. docs* — J.T. Gilbert (ed.), *Historic and municipal documents of Ireland, AD 1172–1320, from the archives of the city of Dublin* (RS, London, 1870)

Gillespie and Refaussé (eds), *Medieval manuscripts* — Raymond Gillespie and Raymond Refaussé (eds), *The medieval manuscripts of Christ Church cathedral, Dublin* (Dublin, 2006)

Griffith (ed.), *Cal. inquisitions*
Margaret C. Griffith (ed.), *Calendar of inquisitions formerly in the office of the chief remembrance of the exchequer prepared from the MSS of the Irish Record Commission* (IMC, Dublin, 1991)
IHS *Irish Historical Studies*
IHTA Irish Historic Towns Atlas (RIA, Dublin, 1986–)
IMC *Coimisiún Láimhscríbhinní na hÉireann* (The Irish Manuscripts Commission)
JRSAI *Journal of the Royal Society of Antiquaries of Ireland*
Mac Niocaill, *Buirgéisí*
Gearóid Mac Niocaill, *Na Burgéisí, XII–XV aois*, 2 vols (Dublin, 1964)
Milne (ed.), *Christ Church*
Kenneth Milne (ed.), *Christ Church cathedral Dublin: a history* (Dublin, 2000)
NAI National Archives of Ireland
NLI National Library of Ireland, Dublin
PRIA *Proceedings of the Royal Irish Academy*
Reg. Alen *A calendar of Archbishop Alen's register,* c.*1172–1534*, ed. C. McNeill (RSAI, Dublin, 1950)
Reg. All Hallows
Registrum prioratus Omnium Sanctorum juxta Dublin, ed. R. Butler (IAS, Dublin, 1845)
Reg. St John *Register of the Hospital of S. John the Baptist without the New Gate, Dublin*, ed. Eric St John Brooks (IMC, Dublin, 1936)
Reg. St Thomas *Register of the abbey of St Thomas, Dublin*, ed. J.T. Gilbert (London, 1889)
Rep. DKPRI *Reports of the deputy keeper of the public records in Ireland* (Dublin, 1869–)
RIA Royal Irish Academy
RLC *Rotuli litterarum clausarum, 1204–24 [etc.]*, ed. T.D. Hardy, 2 vols (London, 1833–44)
SGAC Elizabeth Boyle and Liam Breatnach (eds), '*Senchas Gall Átha Cliath*: aspects of the cult of St Patrick in the twelfth century' in John Carey, Kevin Murray and Caitríona Ó Dochartaigh (eds), *Sacred histories: a festschrift for Máire Herbert* (Dublin, 2015), pp 22–55
Stat. rolls Ire. Edw. IV, i
Statute rolls of the parliament of Ireland: 1st to 12th of King Edward IV, ed. H.F. Berry (Dublin, 1914)
Stat. rolls Ire. Edw. IV, ii
Statute rolls of the parliament of Ireland: 12th & 13th to 21st & 22nd of King Edward IV, ed. James Morrissey (Dublin, 1939)

Stat. rolls Ire. Hen. VI
Statute rolls of the parliament of Ireland: reign of King Henry VI, ed. by H.F. Berry (Dublin, 1910)

Stat. rolls Ire. Ric. III to Hen. VIII
Statute rolls of the Irish parliament: Richard III–Henry VIII, ed. Philomena Connolly (Dublin, 2002)

TNA The National Archives of the United Kingdom [including former PRO], Kew

Contributors

BRUCE M.S. CAMPBELL is emeritus professor of medieval economic history at Queen's University, Belfast.

JENNIE COUGHLAN is an osteoarchaeologist with Irish Archaeological Consultancy Ltd.

PAUL DUFFY is associate director and senior project manager with Irish Archaeological Consultancy Ltd.

LENORE FISCHER is an independent scholar and holds an MA in medieval history from the University of Limerick.

RENÉ GAPERT is currently the coordinator for the National Missing Persons Helpline and holds a PhD in forensic anthropology and anatomy from University College Dublin.

JOSEPH HARBISON is associate professor in medical gerontology at Trinity College Dublin and a consultant physician in St James's Hospital, Dublin.

RUTH JOHNSON is the city archaeologist at Dublin City Council and holds a PhD in medieval history from Trinity College Dublin.

RANDOLPH JONES is an independent scholar, based in England, who has an interest in medieval Ireland.

TERENCE KILLEEN is a research scholar at the James Joyce Centre, Dublin who has published widely on Joyce-related matters.

GRACE O'KEEFFE holds a PhD in medieval history from Trinity College Dublin and is on-line editor at *History Ireland* magazine.

CATHERINE SWIFT lectures in medieval and Irish studies at Mary Immaculate College, University of Limerick.

MAEVE TOBIN is senior archaeological consultant and osteoarchaeologist with Irish Archaeological Consultancy Ltd.

BERNADETTE WILLIAMS is an independent scholar who holds a PhD in medieval history from Trinity College Dublin.

Editor's preface

The preceding volume in this series, *Medieval Dublin XVIII*, was launched by the Minister for Heritage, Mr Malcolm Noonan TD, during the 2021 Medieval Dublin Symposium, an event which sadly took place exclusively online because of the pandemic. It was exciting therefore to be able to return in 2022 to in-person events. The Friends of Medieval Dublin, in addition to holding its annual symposium in person in the Long Room Hub at Trinity College Dublin on Saturday 8 October 2022, also cooperated with Dublin City Libraries on a very special event. On 25 February 2022, we marked the 850th anniversary of Henry II's visit to the city, and of his charter granting Dublin to Bristol, by holding a half-day seminar in the Wood Quay Venue, an event at which we were honoured to be joined by the incumbent Deputy Lord Mayor of Dublin, Counsellor Joe Costello, and the Lord Mayor of Bristol, Steve Smith. The editor of this volume, along with Dr Grace O'Keeffe, Professor Marie Therese Flanagan and Professor Nicholas Vincent explored the historic connections between medieval Ireland and Britain. They explored the shared history of Dublin and Bristol through the lens of conquest, trade, politics and the famous charter which made Dublin for a brief period in the late twelfth and thirteenth centuries a colonial appendage of the merchants of Bristol. For those who missed it, the proceedings of the day can be viewed on the Dublin City Public Libraries & Archive YouTube channel (https://www.youtube.com/watch?v=Vpns5B8ryVA).

Along with our now traditional walking tours of medieval Dublin during Heritage Week 2022, the Friends of Medieval Dublin, including our Secretary Dr Caoimhe Whelan, contributed two articles on the development of the medieval port in Dublin to the 'Ports, Past and Present' project (University College Cork, Aberystwyth University, University of Wales Trinity Saint David and Wexford County Council). The Project considers five ports and their communities on either side of the sea: Dublin Port, Rosslare Harbour, Holyhead, Fishguard and Pembroke Dock. You can access the articles on the medieval port of Dublin and much other interesting matter at https://portspastpresent.eu/items/.

In addition, we offer you this volume of studies stretching from Dublin's Hiberno-Norse period all the way to the Tudors, split fairly evenly between history and archaeology, including among the latter that important subgenre, osteoarchaeology. Three papers in the latter sphere occur in the pages that follow in which specialists in the field report the findings of their examination of the skeletal remains of ancient Dubliners unearthed at three important church sites in the vicinity of the medieval walled town – the hospital of

St John the Baptist and the abbey of St Thomas the Martyr (both in Thomas Street) and the parish church of St Peter de la Hulle (at the corner of Aungier Street and Longford Street Great). Paul Duffy also reports below on the findings of his excavation at the latter site, where commendable efforts have been made to preserve some of the fabric of the surviving structures beneath the floor of what is now a branch of Lidl!

The papers arise in the main from our annual symposia which enjoy capacity audiences of up to 200 members of the public, admission being entirely free, thanks to the contribution to costs by the Department of History, Trinity College, to whom the editor is exceedingly grateful. Similarly, it has only proved possible to publish this nineteenth volume in the *Medieval Dublin* series because of the ongoing commitment to the project by Dublin City Council. Here it is a pleasure to acknowledge the support of the Chief Executive, Mr Owen Keegan, the City Heritage Officer, Charles Duggan, and the ceaseless encouragement of the City Archaeologist, Dr Ruth Johnson. The latter provides below a detailed study of an extraordinary find – a decorated slate uncovered at excavations at 124–8 The Coombe: it illustrates the cover of the present volume and we are indebted to the excavators, Aisling Collins and Kevin Weldon, for all of their assistance in this regard.

The entire series has been published by Four Courts Press for whose collaboration the Friends of Medieval Dublin remain most grateful and the editor would like to thank Martin Fanning for the meticulous attention to detail which has characterized his work on the papers below.

Since the appearance of the last volume, the death has occurred of that quiet gentleman Gerry O'Flaherty, who was an unobtrusive observer and benign enthusiast of the activities of the Friends over many years and it is an honour for us to dedicate the volume to his memory.

SEÁN DUFFY
Chairman
Friends of Medieval Dublin

Gerry O'Flaherty
(1933–2019)

'He loved literature, he loved Dublin, and most of all he loved his family.' This was all that Gerry O'Flaherty, who has died aged 86, allowed as eulogy at his strictly Latin Mass funeral. Touching as it is, it falls some way short of describing his impact in the first two areas mentioned. He didn't just love literature, he actively served and promoted it, especially the work of James Joyce. (It was typical of this complex man that while a very devout and observant Catholic, he had absolutely no problem with any aspect of Joyce's work, except perhaps some of the denser parts of *Finnegans Wake*, with which he sometimes allowed himself to express impatience.)

Gerry was one of the principal organizers of the First International James Joyce Symposium, held in Dublin in 1967, a crucial moment in the promotion of Joyce's work both here and globally. With none of the principal Irish academic bodies particularly interested, Gerry and a small band of fellow enthusiasts took it upon themselves to set up this venture; it was largely thanks to him that it happened where it needed to happen, in Dublin, and not in, say, Tulsa, Oklahoma, as it very easily might. And even though the symposium received mixed reviews, at best, in the Irish media, Dublin's foundational importance in Joyce's work had been fully established. He was also heavily involved in organizing the next symposium, in 1969, again in Dublin, thus establishing it as a biennial event, which it remains.

Then, in the early 1970s, Gerry was a founder member of the James Joyce Institute of Ireland, the first body in the city dedicated to the study and promotion of Joyce's works. It gathered weekly in Newman House on Stephen's Green (later in the James Joyce Centre) where a band of enthusiasts applied themselves diligently, but also with much laughter, to the texts of the master. Noted – and genuine – Joyce scholars such as Roland McHugh and Vincent Deane found it a nurturing environment where they could develop their interests in a receptive setting. And to those who were setting off on an involvement in the Joycean world, Gerry was encouraging and supportive – not just morally but with active assistance. His backing and belief were hugely inspiring. The James Joyce Institute still exists, now based in the James Joyce Centre, and its survival – going on to 50 years – is a testament to the depth of Gerry's love for this quintessentially Dublin author.

Again, to say he loved Dublin is a considerable understatement. His knowledge of the city and its history was encyclopaedic and formidable. This was befitting for someone born in Crampton Court, in the very heart of the city. Many books of annotations of Joyce's work owe their Dublin material – where it is right – almost entirely to Gerry's input. (Where it is wrong they obviously didn't bother to ask.)

The late Gerry O'Flahery, photographed by Robert Nicholson at the James Joyce Summer School, 2007

He is thanked for assistance as far back as Richard Ellmann's famous biography, which first appeared in 1959. He produced a book, *The book of the Liffey: from source to the sea*, with Elizabeth Healy and Christopher Moriarty, in which he managed to incorporate many Joyce references. An active member of the Old Dublin Society, he gave talks and contributed to their journal, the *Dublin Historical Record*. He was also involved with the *Dublin Magazine*, being assistant to the editor, Rivers Carew.

In later years, Gerry's love of literature, Joyce and Dublin received a new outlet when, with the encouragement of former head of news Ed Mulhall, he began broadcasting on RTÉ. With his beautifully modulated Dublin voice, he first took part in a series of radio programmes based on the rebroadcasting of RTÉ's celebrated reading of Ulysses. In these, he discussed episodes of the book with his friend Fritz Senn, the eminent Zürich-based Joycean, now in his 96th year. He then broadcast several pieces about Dublin on RTÉ television in a series called *Capital D*, later folded into *Nationwide*, following the *Six One News*. These included a programme on the Dublin institution of Mount Jerome Cemetery. He also took part in a programme dedicated to the friendship between him and Fritz. It included footage of Gerry for the first time at Joyce's grave in Zürich (he didn't seem to mind having to travel to Zürich to see it) and it was a moving moment. The poet Thomas Kinsella, a fellow Dubliner to whom the city greatly mattered and who has also recently left us, was the subject of a programme with Gerry which delivered special insights into the poet and his world.

Gerry combined all these interests with an active career in publishing, editing and the civil service, in the then An Foras Forbartha. But there is no doubt that the three concerns mentioned at his funeral were indeed the dominating motifs of his life. Gerry's life was exemplary in his dedication to all three. And the importance to him of the third of them, his family – his wife Lelia, his children Owen and Ellen – was very evident, despite the innate reserve of this very private man. 'Dublin made me.'

TERENCE KILLEEN

(This appreciation first appeared in the *Irish Times* on 27 January 2020; the Friends of Medieval Dublin wish to record their gratitude to the latter and to the author for permission to reprint it here.)

Norwegian *scing*-traders and other skinners in early Dublin

CATHERINE SWIFT

Que vers la cort li cuers me tire,
Qui ja estoit tote essemblee.
De mainte diverse contree
I ot contes et dus et rois,
Normanz, Bretons, Escoz, Irois;
D'Angleterre et de Cornuaille
I ot mout riche baronaille,
Et des Gales jusqu'en Anjou,
Ne ou Mainne ne an Poitou
N'ot chevalier de grant afeire
Ne riche dame debonaire
Que les meillors et les plus gentes
Ne fussent a la cort a Nantes …[1].

> My heart draws me toward the court, now completely assembled. There were counts, dukes and kings from many different countries: Normans, Bretons, Scots, Irish; there were very powerful nobles from England and Cornwall, and from Wales to Anjou, in Maine and in Poitou, there was no knight of great importance and no attractive lady of high birth of whom the best and most engaging were not in the court at Nantes.[2]

Chrétien de Troyes was a poet at the court of Louis VII's daughter in Champagne and was subsequently patronized by the guardian of Louis's son, Philip Augustus. He is thought to have written his earliest Arthurian tale, *Érec et Énide*, sometime in the early 1170s, although the precise dates are disputed.[3] It has been suggested that his description of these ceremonies held at Nantes may be a literary reflection of events organized by Henry II of England – an element in the latter's political manoeuvrings to impose his son Geoffrey as duke of Brittany. Henry had forced the previous incumbent to resign and had married his son to the five-year-old heiress before having Geoffrey installed as duke.[4] Whether or not it is true that Chrétien was inspired by real-life events

1 Chrétien de Troyes, *Erec et Enide: edition critique d'après le manuscript B.N. fr.1376*, ed. Jean-Marie Fritz (Paris, 1992), pp 500–2. 2 Chrétien de Troyes, *Arthurian romances*, trans. D.D.R. Owen (London, 1993), p. 88. 3 Douglas Kelly, 'Chrétien de Troyes' in Glyn S. Burgess and Karen Pratt (eds), *The Arthur of the French: the Arthurian legend in medieval French and Occitan literature* (Cardiff, 2006), 135–86, p. 135. 4 Ibid., p. 137; Nicolas Prouteau (ed.), *Les Plantagenets dans les pays de la Loire* (Nantes, 2021), p. 23.

in the above depiction of the mythical court of King Arthur, his reference to Irishmen at Érec's coronation reminds us that, by his day, Ireland had been drawn into the motley collection of western European dominions linked together through political allegiance to Henry II and his wife, Eleanor of Aquitaine, as suzerains.[5]

Ireland's status as the landmass on the furthest western edge of the known world may have represented an exotic and largely unknown curiosity to a French poet but it was one which was clearly hovering in Chrétien's consciousness as he compiled *Érec et Énide*. In addition to the Irish presence at the coronation with which the tale ends, the poet included a short description of Garras de Corque, *uns rois mout fiers*, 'a most proud king', who, along with five hundred knights, the king of Scotland, the count of Gloucester and various leaders of apparently imaginary kingdoms, attended Eric's marriage.[6] It was the king of Cork (Cormac Mac Carthaig of Desmond) who was the first Irish king to swear allegiance to Henry II on his arrival into Ireland in 1171 according to Gerald of Wales, and this may say something more significant about the south Munster over-kingdom and its contemporary status in French-speaking circles than historians have appreciated.[7] On the other hand, it is hard to imagine that Chrétien's subsequent description of Orguelleus de la Lande, taking part in a tourney on a fabulous Irish steed, is anything other than a fantastical localization in a far distant land.[8]

If Chrétien's description of the events at Nantes is indeed reflective of contemporary Plantagenet courts, it is worth noting the importance which he ascribes to royal generosity in assembling the king's supporters. King Arthur is said to have knighted over four hundred aristocratic sons at Nantes, bestowing on each of them three horses and rich clothing. Chrétien was quite specific about the latter:

> Mout fu li rois poissanz et larges:
> Ne dona pas manteax de sarges,
> Ne de coniz ne de brunetes,
> Mes de samiz et d'erminetes,
> De vair entiers et de dyapres,
> Listés d'orfrois roides et aspres.[9]

5 As a comparison, as Count of Mortain, Henry's son John issued a charter for the men of Bristol in 1188, which was addressed to *omnibus hominibus et amicis suis Francis et Anglicis, Walensibus et Hibernensibus presentibus et futuris* ('to all men and to his friends, French and English, Welsh and Irish, present and to come'): N. Dermott Harding (ed.), *Bristol charters 1155–1373*, Bristol Record Society Publications I (1930), pp 8–9. 6 Owen, *Arthurian romances*, pp 26–7. 7 A.B. Scott and F.X. Martin (eds), *Expugnatio Hibernica: the conquest of Ireland by Giraldus Cambrensis* (Dublin, 1978) pp 92–3. 8 See the description of the king of Connacht's difficulty in riding a *destrier* in 1210 in *Histoire des ducs de Normandie et des rois d'Angleterre*, printed in Seán Duffy, 'King John's expedition to Ireland 1210: the evidence reconsidered', *IHS* 30 (1996), 22–4. 9 *Erec et Enide*, ed. Fritz, p. 502.

> The king displayed great opulence and liberality; he did not give cloaks (*manteax*) made of serge or rabbit fur or brown cloth but of velvet and ermine, whole *vair* (spotted) furs and flowered silk bordered with hard, stiff gold braid.[10]

Examples of heavy embroidered silks imported from Byzantium and the Near East still survive in western Europe. The most famous is the coronation cloak embroidered with camels and lions in gold thread which was made for Roger II of Sicily in the first half of the twelfth century and which became part of the regalia of the Austro-Hungarian empire. Rather nearer to Nantes, the cloak of St Mexme is still kept in the Musée d'Art et d'Histoire at Chinon and is decorated with horizontal rows of paired felines in chains, interspersed with trees and birds. Its precise origin and date is debated but Byzantine silks were traded through Pavia and Rome from at least the ninth century while gold-embellished robes, both secular and lay, are well documented in English and French sources from the eleventh and twelfth centuries.[11]

While there is no surviving evidence from Ireland for anything as exotic as these cloaks, some silks of rather less quality reached Dublin by the tenth century where excavations have produced evidence for silk incorporated into various styles of head coverings. These include scarves and caps as well as tassels and decorative fringes.[12] Comparable silk caps to those found at Dublin have been found at York, Lincoln and London and they too are of tenth- to early eleventh-century date. The precise origin of these silks is not clear: they may have been woven in Byzantine territories, in Spain or possibly even in Egypt.[13] In the absence of other information and given the parallels in form, it seems probable that they were brought to Ireland by English merchants rather than representing an indigenous trade with the Mediterranean.

An international European trade in exotic furs was also of long standing by the latter twelfth century, beginning perhaps during the Roman empire. The famous account of Ohthere, visitor to the late ninth-century court of King Alfred of Wessex, describes how he brought furs, walrus ivory and feathers rendered by the *Finnas* (Sami?) of the Arctic north to Kaupang on Norway's south coast.[14] Christian Keller has suggested that it was the prospects of the profits from such trade that inspired some of the earlier Icelandic settlers (many of whom came from northern Norway) to establish the Greenland and Labrador colonies.[15] By the twelfth century and the emergence of Norwegian

10 Owen, *Arthurian romances*, p. 88. 11 C.R. Dodwell, *Anglo-Saxon art: a new perspective* (Ithaca, 1982), pp 175–85. 12 Elizabeth Wincott Heckett, *Viking age headcoverings from Dublin*, Medieval Dublin Excavations 1962–81, Series B 6 (Dublin, 2003), pp 4–6, 64, 67, 93. 13 Ibid., pp 49–52, 105–8. 14 *Ohthere's Voyages: a late ninth-century account of voyages along the coasts of Norway and Denmark and its cultural context*, eds Janet Bately and Anton Englert, Maritime Culture of the North 1 (Roskilde, 2007), pp 44–6; P.H. Sawyer, *Kings and Vikings* (London, 1982), pp 64–5, 71–2. 15 Christian Keller, 'Furs, fish and ivory:

royal dynasties in contemporary historical documentation, it appears that the furs gathered from the northern territories were being increasingly brought under royal control. *Historia Norvegiae* states that

> on the borders of Norway is an immense wilderness which divides the country along all its length and separates the Norwegians from the heathens … In that region there live vast numbers of animals including bears, wolves, lynxes, foxes, sables, otters, badgers and beavers … In Finnmarken there are also very large numbers of squirrels and ermines. From all these animals' pelts the people pay a large tribute every year to the Norwegian kings who are their overlords.[16]

Interesting details about the manner in which such furs might be exported from Norway can be found in *Tristrams saga ok Ísöndar*, a Norse version of the story of Tristan and Isolde written at the court of King Hákon Hákonarson by a Brother Robert in 1226. King Hákon's support base was in western Norway and in the merchant city of Bergen, and an intriguing facet of Brother Robert's text is the amount of detail it provides on Norwegian and other traders in the western Atlantic. Indeed, according to *Hákonar saga Hákonarsonar*, Hákon's fame in the west was such that, in 1263, the Irish asked him to come to Ireland, take over the island and eject their English overlords.[17]

The story of Tristan's initial capture, begins with the arrival into a Breton harbour of a *mikit hafskip*, 'a large seagoing vessel':

> It carried a large cargo and Norwegian traders who had been driven there by long-lasting, northerly storms. There were lots of grey and white pelts (*mikil grávara ok hvítskinn*), beaver skins and black sable (*bjórskinn ok svartr safali*), walrus tusks and bear skins (*tannvara ok bjarnfeldir*), goshawks, grey falcons, and lots of white falcons, wax, skins of cattle and goats (*húðir, bukkaskinn*), dried fish, tar, whale oil, sulphur and all kinds of Norwegian goods.[18]

The author goes on to say that, as *Norrœnir* (Norwegians), the merchants did not speak either Breton or French but the precocious Tristan was able to speak with them in their native tongue. The merchants decided to kidnap him for future sale as a slave but, although they had intended to return to Norway,

medieval Norsemen at the Arctic fringe', *Journal of the North Atlantic*, 3 (2010), 1–23; Alf Ragnar Nielsson, *Landnåm fra Nord: Utvandringa fra det nordlige Norge til Island I vikingtid* (Stamsund, 2012). 16 *Historia Norwegie*, ed. Inger Ekrem and Lars Boje Mortense, trans. P. Fisher (Copenhagen, 2003), pp 59–61. 17 Colmán Etchingham, Jón Viðar Sigurðsson, Máire Ní Mhaonaigh and Elizabeth Ashman Rowe, *Norse-Gaelic contacts in a Viking world: studies in the literature and history of Norway, Iceland, Ireland and the Isle of Man* (Turnhout, 2019), pp 97–104. 18 Marianne E. Kalinke (ed.), *Norse romance I: the Tristan legend*

storms drove them to Cornwall where they decided to abandon Tristan as he had brought them bad luck.

It is notable here that the Norse word used to describe both the furs of wild animals and the hides of domestic goats is *skinn*. This was subsequently borrowed into Middle English, as an alternative to the Anglo-Saxon words *hyd* and *fell* which had the same meaning. Qualifiers attached to *skinn* in Middle English indicate that, in its English guise, it too could be used for both domestic and wild animals, but the word is also frequently found in the thirteenth century as an occupational byname: Scynnere, Skenner, Sckinir or Skinner.[19] Two such thirteenth-century examples are Walterus Sckinir and Hugo le Schinnere de Carmefichet, listed under the years 1257–8 and 1261–2 respectively in the *Dublin guild merchant roll*.[20] In a previous paper in this series, Paul Duffy has drawn attention to a thirteenth-century Dublin poem indicating that at least some Dublin skinners were actively engaged in processing animal skins and that this was seen as a dirty and smelly job:

> Hail, you skinners with your poisonous vat! Whoever smells it is much distressed. When it thunders you may void excrement therein. Misfortune on your manners, you cause the whole street to stink![21]

The processes involved in preparing animal skins, whether for leather or fur, are fairly similar although the tanning acids used to denude hides of all hair (as opposed to simply making pelts supple) are rather stronger. At a recent symposium on St Thomas's abbey, Paul Duffy illustrated a wide variety of pits of various shapes and sizes from the north side of the precinct, suggesting that skins being treated there were of different size and, presumably, undergoing a variety of different processes. Linguistic evidence, for example, indicates that medieval tanners could be *barkers*, who used the bark of oak trees as a major tanning agent or *whittawers* who tended to use alum and salt to produce paler leather.[22] The Thomas Street site produced a considerable amount of horn and animal bone, which divided fairly evenly between cattle and sheep, suggesting that these may have been the main animals being treated in that particular area. Duffy's suggestion was that the tanning in these pits may have been designed

(Cambridge, 1999), pp 50–1. **19** *Middle English compendium*, at https://quod.lib.umich.edu/m/middle-english-dictionary/dictionary/MED40696/track?counter=1&search_id=19433208 (accessed 4 August 2022); *Oxford English dictionary online*, s.v. 'skinner'. **20** *DGMR*, pp 99, 104. **21** Paul Duffy, 'Saints and skinners: excavations along the northern precinct of the abbey of St Thomas the Martyr, Dublin' in Seán Duffy (ed.), *Medieval Dublin XVIII* (Dublin, 2021), pp 194–242, at p. 228, quoting Angela M. Lucas, *Anglo-Irish poems of the Middle Ages* (Dublin, 1995). **22** Elspeth M. Veale, 'The emergence of the London skinners' in her *The English fur trade in the later Middle Ages* (London, 2003), pp 35–56 (*British History online*, at http://www.british-history.ac.uk/london-record-soc/vol38/pp 36–56 [accessed 30 August 2022]).

to produce softer leather products such as the vellum used in book production, gloves and shoes.[23] In this context, it is worth remembering that Ireland was also known in the thirteenth century for its export trade in furs, especially pine marten and squirrel. A 1207 charter granted to Rouen by Philip Augustus, for example, stated that every ship coming from Ireland should pay a tax of forty pine marten skins.[24] It seems likely that such furs could also have been treated and prepared for export somewhere within the wider suburbs of Dublin city.

As discussed elsewhere,[25] these thirteenth-century references are by no means the earliest references to *skinn* in an Irish context. The word also appears as an Irish borrowing (*scing*) in pre-Anglo-Norman texts, most notably in the eleventh-century poems on royal gifts dispersed by the Uí Briain kings of Thomond. Paralleling the actions of King Arthur in Chrétien's description of the ceremonies at Nantes, the Uí Briain cemented their alliances with lesser kings and leaders with gifts of weapons, clothing and other precious goods. Among these were ten *sgingi* given to the king of Osraige, another ten to the king of Leinster and ten to the king of Dubthrian (Dufferin, Co. Down). The small numbers involved indicate that these were valuable pelts rather than simply hides of cattle, sheep or even horse. Similarly, a reference in the Annals of Inisfallen in 1180 lists *scingeda* amongst *ór ⁊ arget, scingeda ⁊ bruttu ⁊ matlu* ('gold and silver, furs and cloaks and mantles').

An intriguing question is whether such eleventh- and twelfth-century *scingeda* were brought to Ireland directly by Scandinavian merchants or whether they simply represent Irish trade with English or Continental middlemen. (It is assumed here that the fact they are called by a Norse loanword indicates that they are foreign imports.) The Norse text *Gunnlaugs saga ormstungu* implies that the situation was, in all likelihood, a complex one: this describes how an Icelandic poet visiting the court of London received a cloak lined with fur from the hands of the English king. He subsequently travelled to Dublin in company with merchants and there received another cloak from King Sigtrygg, also lined with fur.[26]

Another Icelandic text, *Eyrbyggja saga*, mentions a merchant vessel trading between Dublin and Iceland ostensibly at the beginning of the eleventh century:

23 Paul Duffy, 'The sacred and the profane: preliminary results of archaeological excavations at 30 & 32–36 Thomas Street', podcast available https://soundcloud.com/history-hub/sets/the-abbey-of-st-thomas-the-martyr-symposium (accessed 30 August 2022). 24 Gilbert (ed.), *Hist. & mun. docs*, p. xxxiii, quoting Jean Duchesne, *Historiae Normannorum scriptores antiqui* (Paris, 1619), p. 1063; Alain Sadourney, 'L'époque communale (1204–début due XIVe siècle)' in Philippe Wolff (ed.), *Histoire de Rouen* (Toulouse, 1979), pp 75–98 at pp 76–8. 25 See Catherine Swift, 'Taxes, trade and trespass: the Hiberno-Norse context of the Dál Cais empire in *Lebor na Cert*' in Kevin Murray (ed.), *Lebor na Cert: Reassessments*, Irish Texts Society Subsidiary Series 25 (London, 2013), pp 34–61, at pp 50–2. 26 Ibid., pp 53–4.

> In the summer that Christianity was adopted by law in Iceland, a ship from Dublin (*Dyflin*) put in at Snaefell Ness. Most of the crew came from Ireland and the Hebrides but there were some Norwegians too (*Voru þar á írskir menn og suðureyskir en fáir norrænir*). They lay at Rif for a good part of the summer, then with a fair wind sailed up the fjord to Dogurdar Ness, where a number of people from the neighbourhood came to trade with them.[27]

The same saga also refers to Icelanders such as Þóroddur who had travelled west to Dublin in the time of Jarl Sigurður Hlöðvésson of Orkney (who died at Clontarf in 1014) and Guðleifur Guðlaugsson who went on a trading voyage to Dublin in the time of St Olaf (who died in 1030). If we could take these dates at their face value, this could be evidence for trading contact between Dublin and Iceland in the eleventh century but it would certainly suggest that Dublin ships were known in Iceland in the thirteenth century when the saga was compiled. In a similar vein, *Egils saga* refers to a well-established trading route from Iceland to Dublin and speaks of outfitting a *kaupskip … med kaupeyri* ('a merchant ship … with items for exchange') with instructions to travel south to Dublin because *sú er nú ferð frægst* ('that is a journey which is highly regarded').[28] Archaeological deposits from Christchurch Place and Fishamble Street in Dublin have produced walrus skulls and even whale-bone showing evidence of North Atlantic imports into Dublin, substantiating the textual evidence for such trade routes.[29]

A recent study of the DNA of walrus remains found in western European contexts has shown that these divide into two main types, identified as a western and an eastern clade. Modern walrus belonging to the western clade have only been identified in Greenland and North America whereas those belonging to the eastern clade have been found in Greenland but also in the Barents Sea, off the northern coasts of Norway and Russia. Excavated samples from Dublin's St John's Lane and Fishamble Street and belonging to the date-range AD 900–1125, which were included in this study, produced one example of western walrus and two of eastern type.[30] The authors calculate that, in the period covered by the Dublin samples, it is statistically unlikely that Greenland was the exclusive source of European walrus ivory and this suggests (though it

27 *Eyrbyggja saga*, eds Einar Ól Sveinsson and Mattias Þórðarson, Íslensk Fornit iv (Reykjavik, 1935); see H.B. Clarke, '"Go then south to Dublin; that is now the most praiseworthy voyage": what would Brynjólfr's son have found there?' in A. Mortensen and S.V. Arge (eds), *Viking and Norse in the North Atlantic: select papers from the proceedings of the Fourteenth Viking Congress, Tórshavn, 19–30 July 2001* (Annales Societatis Scientiarum Færoensis, Supplementum XLIV, Tórshavn, 2005), pp 441–5. 28 *Egils saga* ed. Bjarni Einarsson, Viking Society for Northern Research (London, 2003), p. 45. 29 Patrick F. Wallace, *Viking Dublin: the Wood Quay excavations* (Dublin, 2016), pp 365–6. 30 Bastiann Starr, James H. Barrett, Agat T. Gundek and Sanne Boessenkool, 'Ancient DNA reveals the chronology of walrus ivory trade from Norse Greenland', *Proceedings of the Royal Society:*

cannot be proven) that Dublin was in trading contact with both Norse Greenland and the Barents Sea in the tenth and eleventh centuries.[31] Such links may have been indirect; Insular-style penannular brooches and other metalwork (which can only be attributed to generalized Irish Sea contexts) have been found at the southern Norwegian trading site of Kaupang where, as noted above, Ohthere traded his northern goods.[32]

Apart from walrus and whale bone, we know that Iceland was exporting arctic fox and seal-skins while in his *Topographia Hibernie* Gerald of Wales stated that Iceland produced and exported *girofalcones et accipitres grandes et generosos* ('large and noble gerfalcons and birds of prey').[33] We also know that polar bears were being trapped in Greenland and Robert Bartlett notes the gift of the pelts of polar bears by Henry II to his monks at Grandmont.[34] These large and dangerous animals could also be exported as live animals and we know that they were kept as curiosities at the courts of various rulers including the Holy Roman Emperors Henry III and Frederick II as well as at the Norwegian and Danish courts, which we might expect to have greater contact with Iceland. The Norwegian king Hákon Hákonarson (or Hákon IV) famously sent a gift of a polar bear to Henry III of England who provided his London sheriffs with instructions that they were to 'support our White Bear in our Tower of London; and to provide a muzzle and iron chain to hold him when out of the water; and a long strong rope to hold him when he was fishing in the Thames'.[35]

The Icelandic sagas do not, unfortunately, provide precise details as to the nature of northern trade goods that might have arrived in Ireland. An unsubstantiated claim in *Orkneyinga saga* that Earl Thorfinn of Orkney held lands in Ireland might suggest one route by which arctic furs from Norway (possibly ultimately arriving from Iceland and Greenland) may have reached the west.[36] The twelfth-century chronicle *Morkinskinna* states that the Norwegian king Magnús Berfoettr conquered Dublin and then appointed *gæzlumenn* or royal administrators to rule the city for him at the very beginning of the twelfth century while he himself was away, visiting with Muirchertach Ua Briain in the west.[37] This Norwegian interest in Dublin is normally assumed to be due to Dublin's fame as an international port, and the existence

Biological Sciences, 285 (2018), 1–9, Suppl. Table 1. 31 Ibid., 4–5. 32 Egon Wamers, 'Continental and Insular metalwork' in Dagfinn Skre (ed.), *Things from the town: artefacts and inhabitants in Viking Age Kaupang*, Kaupang Excavation Project Publication series 3 (Aarhus, 2011), pp 80–8. 33 'Topographia Hibernica' in *Geraldi Cambrensis Opera*, ed. James F. Dimock et al., 8 vols (Rolls Series, London, 1861–91), v, p. 96; Bruce E. Gelsinger, *Icelandic enterprise: commerce and economy in the Middle Ages* (Columbia, 1981), pp 12–16. 34 Robert Bartlett, *England under the Norman and Angevin kings 1075–1225* (Oxford, 2000), p. 575. 35 T.J. Oleson, 'Polar bears in the Middle ages', *Canadian Historical Review*, 31 (1950), 47–55. 36 *Orkneyinga Saga: the history of the earls of Orkney*, eds Hermann Pálsson and Mathias Þórðarson (London, 1978), p. 71. 37 *Morkinskinna: The earliest Icelandic chronicle of the Norwegian kings (1030–1157)*, ed. Theodore M. Andersson (Ithaca

of a Norse-speaking community in Dublin of at least eleventh-century date is indicated by the use of dotted runes on a cattle scapula found at Christchurch Place in a mid-eleventh-century context. Such dotted runes appear to have become widespread in Scandinavia only in the early eleventh century. (The other Dublin runic inscriptions, while lacking diagnostically datable runic symbols, were all found within archaeological layers dating to the period AD 950–1125.)[38]

An alternative possibility would be to look to Danish merchants trading Norwegian goods through England in the light of the enhanced links between Denmark and England during the eleventh century. In Schleswig town laws of *c.*1200, the local skinners paid either a mark of silver annually to the Danish king or presented him with one thousand 'skins' when he came to town – an arrangement which strongly suggests both a royal interest in the trade and the likelihood that it was a profitable one.[39] According to the twelfth-century *Vita* of St Knud Lavard, the town of Schleswig was under constant attack by Wendish pirates.[40] Such dangers highlight the extent to which the town's fortunes were tied to the Baltic trade routes, including the import of furs from Novgorod and the Rus to the west.[41] *Knýtlinga saga*, a mid-thirteenth-century account of early Danish kings, tells, for example, how the Danish king decided to send the merchant Viðgautr as an envoy to Novgorod and how the man promised to bring back eight thousand pelts to the king.[42]

While we cannot know whether ships bearing furs came to Dublin directly from territories under Norse control or via middlemen in Britain or elsewhere, the Norse *Tristams saga ok Ísöndar* provides us with a literary account of how such traders might have fared in Ireland. When it was decided to send him to Dublin to ask for Isolde's hand in marriage, Tristan announced that *Kunnigt er mér Írland ok írska manna siðir* ('I am familiar with Ireland and with the customs of the Irish') and he decided that they would call themselves merchants or *kaupmenn*. Twenty of the king's *hirðlið* or retinue were equipped 'with sufficient food, good drink and money enough and they loaded [their

New York, 2000), p. 310. **38** Michael P. Barnes, Jan Ragnar Hagland and R.I. Page, *The runic inscriptions of Viking Age Dublin*, National Museum of Ireland Medieval Dublin Excavations 1962–81, Series B 5 (Dublin, 1997), pp 5–6, 13, 30–3. **39** Nils Hybel and Bjørn Poulsen, *The Danish resources* c.*1000–1550: growth and recession*, The Northern World series, 34 (Leiden, 2007), pp 263–4. **40** Thomas K. Heebøll-Holm, 'Between pagan pirates and glorious sea-warriors: the portrayal of the Viking pirate in Danish twelfth-century Latin historiography', *Viking and Medieval Scandinavia* 8 (2012), 141–70 at 153. **41** Anton Englert, *Large cargo ships in Danish waters 1000–1250: evidence for specialized merchant seafaring prior to the Hanseatic period* (Roskilde, 2015); James Howard-Johnston, 'The fur trade in the early middle ages' in Jacek Gruszczyński, Marek Jankowiak and Jonathan Shepard (eds), *Viking age trade: silver, slaves and Gotland* (London, 2020), pp 102–25. **42** Thomas S. Noonan and Roman Kovalev, 'The furry forties: packaging pelts in medieval Northern Europe' in Janusz Duzinkiewicz, Myroslav Popovych, Vladyslav Verstiuk and Natalia Yakovenko (eds), *States, societies and cultures east and west: essays in*

ship] with good wheat, flour and honey, wine and all sorts of the finest drink'.[43] Archaeological and textual finds make it clear that wine was certainly imported into thirteenth-century Dublin while murage grants attest to a trade in wheat, flour and honey through the city although such sources do not make it clear whether these were Irish products or goods imported from abroad.[44]

On arrival into *Dyflinisborg*, Tristan's group cast anchor, lowered their boat (*bát*) and sent two men on horseback to obtain permission from the king to sell their goods. They told the king:

> We are merchants [*kaupmenn*] and travel with goods from country to country … We loaded our ship in Brittany [*Bretland*] and intended to sail to Flanders but when we got out to sea a storm came up and drove us for a long time with great tossing about until we came to this harbour. We just heard that provisions are difficult to come by in Ireland and, for that reason, we travel here laden with goods. If we could receive your permission to sell in peace our wine and our provisions, then we will bring up our ship in the harbour and offer our goods for sale. But if you do not wish it to be, then we will sail to other countries.

Having received permission, they returned to their ship, sailed up into the harbour, moored the ship and erected their tents.[45]

This is an interesting description. Howard Clarke has noted that manmade harbours are relatively rare in medieval Ireland and the norm was to use the riverbanks along which towns were situated. Excavated evidence in Dublin shows the reclaiming of land and the building of wooden revetments along Wood Quay to try and improve the docking facilities.[46] If the above quotation is a factual description of Dublin's arrangements, it may be that the harbour described here was the natural shelter of the Black Pool but, more importantly, this description indicates that merchants and their ships remained at some distance from the settlement before being granted permission to come into the urban area of the walled town. Later thirteenth-century descriptions of Dublin's merchant customs indicate that there were royal tolls taken of goods coming into the port and that distinctions were then drawn between goods arriving by ship and goods arriving on horseback or carried on a man's back.[47]

It is also interesting that this story told by Tristan to mislead the Dublin authorities stresses the effects of weather, the need to adjust plans mid-route and the constant search to seek out new markets. This chimes very much with

honour of Jaroslaw Pelenski (New York, 2004), pp 653–82, at p. 661. 43 Kalinke, *The Tristan legend*, pp 94–5. 44 Gilbert (ed.), *Hist. & mun. docs*, pp 53, 76, 96–7, 124; Clare McCutcheon, *Medieval pottery from Wood Quay, Dublin: the 1974–6 Waterfront excavations*, National Museum of Ireland Medieval Dublin Excavations 1962–81, Series B 7 (2006). 45 Kalinke, *The Tristan legend*, pp 96–7. 46 Wallace, *Viking Dublin*, pp 155–68. 47 Gilbert (ed.), *Hist. & mun. docs*, pp 128–30; *CARD*, i, pp 232–4.

the accounts of merchant activity in the Icelandic sagas in general. The phrase 'trading routes' implies that ships went back and forth on a regular basis between fixed points but perhaps a more valid approach to conceptualizing merchant navigation in this period is the nineteenth-century concept of 'tramp steamers', ships which went, often on speculative journeys, to source goods which they knew to be valuable and to markets where they could offload them. We have no attested Irish equivalent to the story of the twelfth-century merchant from La Rochelle, Alexander Auffredi, who was said to have sent ships to Africa and gone bankrupt awaiting their return, only to be miraculously restored to wealth by their reappearance seven years later. Auffredi won the hearts of his fellow citizens by using the profits to build a hospital for his town. Dublin also had men willing to invest in building hospitals and churches and we know that, like their contemporaries elsewhere, its merchants and sailors faced many dangers up to and including having their ships impounded by Plantagenet kings.[48] An incident in the *Vita* of St Lorcán Ua Tuathail (Laurence O'Toole), for example, tells how a leading citizen of Dublin, in danger of drowning at sea, was persuaded by the archbishop to promise a new church dedicated to the Virgin Mary.[49]

* * *

Merchant activity in Dublin in the first half of the thirteenth century is almost uniquely attested through the fortuitous survival of the *Dublin guild merchant roll* (*DGMR*), still in possession of the city authorities. This list has been analysed by John Bradley, Robin Frame and others,[50] and, using the evidence of names qualified by *de* + place-name, has been interpreted as showing an influx of people who came to Dublin, in the main, from Bristol and the southwest of Britain. This builds on the earlier work of John J. Webb who in 1929 (long before the more recent edition of the *DGMR*) argued that 'The [Dublin] Guild was predominantly English in composition with a sprinkling of Welsh and Scotch and other foreigners'.[51] Thus the *DGMR* has often been seen as substantiating Henry II's initial charter in which he promised 'my city of Duuvelina' to the men of Bristol.[52]

There are, however, ways of approaching the *DGMR* other than relying entirely on the *de* + surnames and these can throw up rather different

48 F.W. Brooks, 'William de Wrotham and the office of the king's ports and galleys', *English Historical Review*, 40 (1925), 570–79. **49** Charles Plummer, 'Vie et miracles de St Laurent, archevêque de Dublin', *Analecta Bollandiana*, 33 (1914), 121–86, at 145–6. **50** John Bradley, 'Planned Anglo-Norman towns in Ireland' in H.B. Clarke and Anngret Simms (eds), *The comparative history of urban origins in Non-Roman Europe, 2 vols* (Oxford, 1985), ii, pp 411–67 at pp 420–2; Robin Frame, *Colonial Ireland 1169–1369*, 2nd ed. (Dublin, 2012), pp 104–5; Patricia Becker, 'An analysis of the Dublin Guild Merchant Roll *c.*1190–1265' (M.Phil, TCD, 1996). **51** John J. Webb, *The guilds of Dublin* (New York and London, 1929), p. 8. **52** Gilbert (ed.), *Hist. & mun. docs*, p. 1.

conclusions. For example, by far the most common occupational *sobriquet* in the earlier part of the roll (pre 1222–3 which is the first datable reference) are the forty-six examples of *palmer,* alongside thirty-one of *palmerus* (five in the genitive) and a further five as *palmerius* (the Latin equivalent to Middle English and Anglo-Norman *palmer*). This is a term originally used to describe those who had travelled to the Holy Land although it later developed in Middle English to refer to any pilgrim. This extremely high number contrasts with the frequency of other crafts and professions: the next most common occupational byname in frequency are the thirty-six examples of *pistor* or baker. In contrast, only one name was qualified by *crucesignatus*, the term used for those who had taken the cross in order to fight in the crusading armies. The most likely deduction, therefore, is that the many palmers named in the *DGMR* were probably more involved in the transport of the armies of the Third Crusade than in the actual fighting.[53] (The various accounts we have of Richard's crusading fleets stress their heterogeneous origins: a fleet of *Dani, Frisones, Angli et Flandrigenae* is said in the *Itinerarium* to have left Dartmouth in the early summer of 1189; in *Gesta regis Henrici*, in contrast, Richard is said to have appointed four justiciars of a fleet made up of men of England, Normandy, Poitou, and Brittany (*Britanniae*) and furthermore, the English contingent included Londoners.)[54]

Another approach to analysing the geographic origin of those listed in the *DGMR* is to examine the locational adjectives attached to certain merchants. Again, limiting the analysis to the pre 1222–3 section, this highlights the extent to which the members of Dublin's merchant guild belonged to almost the entire list of territories under Plantagenet control as well as to regions from outside their borders. The emphasis on the southwest of Britain remains, but this cohort is more focussed on coastal regions than on the Bristol channel (see table 1.1) The largest group are the thirty-two men identified as Cornish with a further five identified as being from Devon as well as seventeen from Wales. There are also eighteen Flemings and, of particular interest to this paper, seventeen 'Norensis' or 'Noreis'. These are Latinate and French forms of the Norse term *Norrœnir*, which the editor of *Tristrams saga ok Ísöndar* translated as Norwegians but which perhaps, in the context of the *DGMR*, may simply mean people originating in Norse-speaking communities. People from the western territories of modern France are also well represented, fourteen being simply identified as French in addition to a further five from Brittany and single instances of men described as Norman, Angevin, Poitevin and Gascon.

53 Catherine Swift, 'Palmers as ex-crusaders in Irish urban environments? The evidence of the Dublin guild merchant roll' in Edward Coleman, Paul Duffy and Tadhg O'Keeffe (eds), *Ireland and the Crusades* (Dublin, 2022), pp 70–5. 54 *Chronicles and memorials of the reign of Richard I*, ed. William Stubbs, 2 vols (Rolls Series, London, 1864) I, pp 64–5; *Gesta Regis Henrici Secundi Benedicti Abbatis*, ed. William Stubbs, 2 vols (Rolls Series, London, 1867),

Further afield, there are two men from Champagne, home to some of the most famous mercantile fairs in twelfth- and thirteenth-century Europe, two from Cologne and, surprisingly, two 'Suis' or Swiss. Obviously, this information does not negate the emphasis on the Severn Estuary indicated by the *de* + place-name identifiers but it does add another dimension and stresses the wider range of contacts enjoyed by early thirteenth-century Dublin merchants.

Table 1.1 Distribution of surnames pre 1222–3[55]

Cornubiensis 17	Corwalensis 8	Corwaleis 6	Cornwaleis 2		Total 33
Flandrensis 16	Flamang 1	Flemeng 1			Total 18
Walensis 13	Waleis 2	Wale 2			Total 17
Norensis 7	Norrensis 6	Noreis 3	Norreis 1		Total 17
Francigena 9	Franceis 4	Francus 1			Total 14
Deveneis 5					Total 5
Bretun 1	Britton1	Brittun 1	Britun 1	Brit 1	Total 5
Scot 5					Total 5
Burgensis 1	Burgeis2				Total 3
Anglicus 3					Total 3
Champanais 2					Total 2
Colonciensis 2					Total 2
Suis 2					Total 2
Peitivin 1					Total 1
Gascoin 1					Total 1
Normannus 1					Total 1
Angevin 1					Total 1
Sureis 1					Total 1
Ostmannus 1					Total 1
Hiberniensis 1					Total 1

Of course, what must be borne in mind in attempting to interpret this material is the nature of the *GDMR* itself. John T. Gilbert, the original editor, published it as a 'Dublin roll of names' and saw it as reflecting the civic community. In his 1982 article, John Bradley followed him in this and wrote that 'the majority of Dublin's earliest Anglo-Norman citizens came from the West Country, the Welsh Marches and the Severn estuary'.[56] In contrast,

ii, pp 110–16. **55** These figures are drawn from the online and searchable text available at https://databases.dublincity.ie/dmgr/freesearch_out.php (accessed 29 August 2022). Because the ordering of the folios on that site is different from that in the edition by Philomena Connolly and Geoffrey Martin, there are slight discrepancies with the published text but the general pattern remains the same. **56** Gilbert (ed.), *Hist. & mun. docs*, pp

Philomena Connolly and Geoffrey Martin pointed out that membership of the guild did not necessarily mean long-term residency.[57] In the nature of things, most merchants were travellers, and northern sailors in particular had to cope with weather conditions which made sailing a seasonal activity. The Anglo-Saxon Chronicle referred to the invading army of 871 as *mycil sumarliða* or a great fleet of 'summer sailors', the word which later became the personal name Somerled. Norse also has the term *farsumar* (literally 'summer travel') to denote the season for sailing and terms for overwintering: *vetr-seta* or winter-quarters and *vetr-seti/vetr-gestr*, a winter guest.[58] In *Heimskringla,* for example, a counsellor of King Harold's known as Guthormr 'had a place of retreat and winter quarters' at Dublin and was friendly with the mid-eleventh-century Dublin king, Echmarcach mac Ragnaill.[59] Should we then envisage the men whose names were inscribed on the *DGMR* as transitory inhabitants and perhaps only winter-residents in the city?

A hunt through the names of Dublin property owners and witnesses to Dublin land-grants in the contemporary Register of the hospital of St John the Baptist confirms the presence of men with names such as Radulfus Norreis (*c.*1190), Fulco Flandrensis (*c.*1200), Ricardus Wale (*c.*1220), Thomas Pictavensi (1232–3) and Willelmus Gascoin (1243–4). Furthermore, it seems reasonably likely that Radulfus Norreis is the same man listed in the early sections of the *DGMR* as Radulfus Norensis and at least conceivable that Ricardus Walensis may be the *DGMR*'s 'Ricardus de Cardif'. Early provosts of Dublin listed in the roll included Wido Cornubiensis and Thomas Pictavensis (from Cornwall and Poitou).[60] It appears, therefore, that at least some of these merchants, if not invariably resident in Dublin, certainly became Dublin property owners and active members of the urban community. Perhaps, this was simply a feature of increasing age: in the dialogue between the wise father and his son in the mid-thirteenth-century Norwegian *Konungs Skuggsjá*, the younger man begins 'I am now in my most vigorous years and have a desire to travel abroad'. His father advises him to keep his ship in good order and to carry the tools with which to repair it, and then adds:

> discontinue your own journeys at sea or as a trader in foreign fields as soon as your means have attained sufficient growth and you have studied foreign customs as much as you like … if you have much capital invested in trade … put one third into partnerships with men who are permanently located in market boroughs.[61]

vii–ix, xxx, 3–48; Bradley, 'Planned Anglo-Norman towns', p. 421. 57 *DGMR*, p. xiv. 58 Richard Cleasby, Gudbrand Vigfusson and William Craigie, *An Icelandic-English dictionary* (Oxford, 1957), pp 604, 144, 701. 59 Snorri Sturluson, *Heimskringla Vol III: Magnus Olafsson to Magnus Erlingsson,* eds Alison Finlay and Anthony Faulkes, Viking Society for Northern Research (London, 2015), p. 81. 60 *DGMR,* pp 49, 60. 61 *The King's mirror (Speculum Regalae): Konungs Skuggsjá*, trans. L.M. Larson (New York, 1917);

In her study of the prosopography of early Dublin as witnessed in the Register of the Hospital of St John the Baptist, Grace O'Keeffe makes the valuable point that, without corroboration, one cannot automatically conclude that occupational bynames in this period necessarily indicate that the person concerned practised such a profession. We simply do not know enough about the development of twelfth- and thirteenth-century nomenclature (particularly in urban contexts) to make such assumptions. O'Keeffe also demonstrates that the Dublin group of early Bristol settlers identifiable in the Register were rarely given names which indicate their origins and that it is only through analysis of Bristol documents and records as well as Dublin ones that one can see the same figures active on both sides of the Irish Sea.[62] Texts such as Henry III's letter of 1221 to the mayor and citizens of La Rochelle confirm the existence of a trade between that city and Dublin,[63] but the evidence of the *DGMR* itself confirms that the background of men who were known by locational adjectives was often more complex than at first appears. So, for example, of the large group of Cornishmen pre-1222–3, some are given *de* + placename identifiers in addition to the adjective *Cornubiensis*. These included Elyas Cornubiensis de Havreford (presumably Haverfordwest in Pembrokeshire), Johannes Cornubiensis de Glou' (Gloucester) and Stephanus Cornubiensis de Chilkenni (Kilkenny). Of those identified as Flemings, we find Arnoldus de Trum Flandrensis (presumably Trim in Meath); amongst the French is Walterus Francigena de Foure (Fore, Co. Westmeath) while the Welsh included David Walensis de Dundalc (Dundalk) and Hugo Walensis de Dunboin (Dunboyne). Of those described as Norensis or Noreis, the pre-1222–3 section of the *DGMR* lists merely Nicol filius Osberti Norensis de Bristollo and Radulfus Norrensis de Kilkenni.[64] While these men are identified as belonging to the group of Norse-speaking merchants, they had clearly established links in Britain and Ireland as well. Of course, that is not necessarily true of all the men identified as *Norreis* or *Norrensis* but it makes it impossible to substantiate the case for Scandinavian origins of these men any further.

The *DGMR* is largely, though not exclusively, written in Latin in this early pre-1222–3 section. The word 'skinner' is, therefore, not used as an occupational name in the early part of the roll although it does occur later on in the thirteenth century.[65] Instead, the text uses *pelliparius* of which there are a mere three examples. Of these, two are further qualified: Henricus Pelliparius de Lund' (i.e., London) and Thomas Pelliparius de Blakemor.[66] This last was

for discussion of the date, see Etchingham et al., *Norse-Gaelic contacts*, pp 95–105. **62** Grace O'Keeffe, 'The hospital of St John the Baptist, Dublin *c.*1188–1539: a historiographical and prosopographical analysis' (PhD, TCD, 2012) pp 9, 105–9. **63** Gilbert (ed.), *Hist. & mun. docs*, p. 77. **64** The easiest way to find this data is to use the online index at https://databases.dublincity.ie/dmgr/freesearch_out.php (accessed 29 August 2022). **65** See above, at n. 20. **66** *DGMR*, pp 8, 3, 11.

identified by Emma Williams as Blakemore in Yorkshire although the Domesday Book also lists a Blackmore in Somerset, close to the southern shore of the Severn Estuary,[67] while there are various Blackmoor, Blakemore and Blackmore place-names in Essex, Wiltshire, Worcestershire and Devon.[68]

It is tempting to argue that Dublin, as a newly established colony in which most available resources were seemingly invested in castle-building and military necessities, would simply not provide the requisite market conditions for large numbers of international fur-traders. In fact, the Dublin figures are similar to the situation in England in this era. In her study of the emergence of London skinners, Elspeth Veale has stated that 'even in the larger provincial centres specialized skinners were few, and they remained on the whole small groups'.[69] The two big centres of English fur-trading in the first half of the thirteenth century seem to have been Northampton and London and the royal Angevin household seems to have been their most important customer.

One particular set of accounts illustrates the price differential between imported and domestically produced furs in England at this date. Just as the mythical King Arthur gave new knights robes in Chrétien's depiction, King John was in the habit of providing his court with robes and other garments at Christmas time.[70] For Christmas at Windsor in 1207, Reginald of Cornhill (his purveyor in London) spent £296 7*s.* buying (among other things), nearly 300 fur-lined hoods. Eighty-nine were lined with rabbit fur costing 7*s.* 6*d.* each. Hoods lined with squirrel fur cost 13*s.* 4*d.* Hoods using deer fur (of which 182 were bought) cost 19*s.* or 20*s.* each. Eleven hoods were, however, lined with miniver (white fur such as ermine) and five were lined with sable. These hoods decorated with imported furs were almost three times as expensive as those with deer fur and cost roughly £2 13*s.* each. It is clear that these foreign furs were reserved for the highest echelons of John's court and this is confirmed by the fact that the queen, for the most part, dressed in miniver and sable. The fur used to line the king's own robes was more expensive again being the highest quality ermine which could only be found in the far north of Russia and some Scandinavian forests.[71] If the customer base for *pelliparii* or skinners (or at any rate those *pelliparii* working with imported furs) was limited to these very highest ranks in English society, it is not surprising that such merchants were not numerous in either England or Ireland in the early thirteenth century.

By the second half of that century, however, the western area around Christchurch Place in Dublin had already become known as *vicus pellepariorum*

67 https://opendomesday.org/place/ST2438/blackmore/ (accessed 24 August 2022). 68 https://www.surnamedb.com/Surname/Blakemore (accessed 24 August 2022). 69 Veale, 'Emergence of London skinners', pp 36–7. 70 Roger of Wendover, *Flores historiarum*, ed. H.G. Hewlett, 2 vols (Rolls Series, London, 1887), ii, pp 44, 97. 71 Henrietta Kaye, 'Serving the man that ruled: aspects of the domestic arrangements of the household of King John 1199–1216' (D.Phil., UAE, 2013), pp 202–5; the information on the hoods is drawn from *RLC*, i, p. 103b.

or Skinners Street.[72] The *DGMR* provides eleven names between 1222 and 1261 and among those with place-name identifiers were Walterus Pelliparius de Arclo (Arklow), Jordanus de Exonia (Exeter), Johannes de Hanne and Nicholaus de London. Under the spelling *pelleparius* (used seven times in this later section of the roll), there are men from Bordeaux, Carlisle, 'Templestrete' (probably Temple Street in Bristol), Ashley (there were at least a dozen towns and villages of the name in medieval England) and a William Pelleparius de Dublin. In addition, the Register of the Hospital of St John the Baptist refers to a family of *pelleparii* in Drogheda, including a widow who may have continued the trade after her husband's death and a son who owned a stone house facing the Boyne. In Dublin, the Register also mentions an heiress of the important de Lyvet family who owned land and buildings with stone storerooms on the *vicus pelliparium* and identifies these as assets which had originally been owned by a Thomas Cordwainer before coming into the family holdings.[73] These Register references make it clear that the *DGMR* is very unlikely to have included all the fur merchants operating in Dublin at a given time and reinforces the point that guild membership did not correlate precisely with citizenship of Dublin.

The existence of later *pelliparii* linked to Arklow and Drogheda draws attention to the wider dispersal of merchants throughout the colony as the thirteenth century progressed. This is also true of the members of the guild merchant described as *Norensis/Norrensis* in the post-1222 section of the roll and, in fact, this locational adjective is the best attested of the various ethnic adjectives attested in the roll in these later sections. Additional details attached to the various *Norensi* names in the *DGMR* link them to Exeter, Whitby, Bristol, Cardigan and Tanton in Britain and in Ireland to Antrim, Dundalk, Drogheda, Mullingar, Ratoath, Rindown and Trim.

It is possible that this widespread dispersal is due, in part, to the particularly open nature of the rights which had been granted to Dublin by its Plantagenet rulers. Their charters give Dublin all the liberties and free usages attached to Bristol and, in the case of Henry II's second Dublin charter, specify that they were to be quit of all charges covering travel throughout *terra mea Anglie, Normannie, Wallie et Hibernie*. This was unusually generous.[74] Mary Bateson drew attention to a municipal document from London which outlined the rights of Lotharingian merchants to sell wine freely (if not prevented by either the sheriff or the king's representative) although this must be by the tun rather than in smaller quantities. They should trade first with London merchants, before dealing with those from Oxford and Winchester and they could only stay forty days in London and the surrounding area. These rights are

72 Clarke, *Dublin, Pt 1* (IHTA), pp 9, 13. 73 O'Keeffe, 'The hospital of St John', pp 139–42. 74 Neil Middleton, 'Early medieval port customs, tolls and controls on foreign trade', *Early Medieval Europe*, 13 (2005), 313–58.

contrasted with those of Danish merchants (*Daneis*) who had the right to stay for a year and travel throughout England, while Norwegian merchants (*Noreis*), in contrast, were entitled to stay for a year but were not allowed to leave London. It is not clear exactly when these rules first came into being but they appear to have been in existence (if not necessarily enforced) during the reign of King John.[75]

The 1207 charter of Philip Augustus granted to the citizens of Rouen hints that the situation could be considerably more constrained for Dubliners in certain regions and, indeed, that the generosity of Henry II may have marked a new departure in the city's mercantile fortunes. Philip Augustus stressed that he was confirming rights which had been in operation in Rouen when Henry and Richard were kings in England and states that *nulla navis de tota Norm. praeterquam de Rothomogo poterit escipare ad Hiberniam excepta una sola, cui semel in anno de Cesarisburgo licitum erit eskipare* ('No ship from all Normandy was allowed embark for Ireland save from Rouen with the single exception of one each year from Cherbourg'). When ships from Ireland had passed Guernsey, they were only allowed to come to Rouen and if they did not have *tinbr martrinar* to pay to the city authorities, they were to pay ten pounds.[76]

The word *tinbr* otherwise *timber/tymber/timbre* was the word used in the fur trade to denote a unit of forty skins, also known by the Rus word *sorochok*. It is found in a list of tolls of David I of Scotland in the mid-twelfth century where it is used not just of imported sable but also of beaver, squirrel, marten and ferret which were all available locally from within Scotland.[77] According to the *Oxford English Dictionary*, the word remained in usage as a specialized term for forty pelts of fur up until the beginning of the twentieth century.[78] Part of the increased evidence for *pelleparii* throughout the Irish colony in the later thirteenth-century is presumably the ongoing development of an Irish export trade in local furs and it seems that this fed into an increasingly internationalized trade. The mid-thirteenth-century Norwegian *Konungs skuggsjá* stressed that French and Latin were the most useful foreign languages for Norwegian merchants to know and it is probably not a coincidence that the mid-thirteenth-century *pelliparii* in the *DGMR* included both Willelmus Franceis Pelleparius (1232–3) and Hugo Pelleparius of Bordeaux (1264–5).[79]

* * *

75 Mary Bateson, 'A London municipal collection of the reign of King John', *English Historical Review*, 17 (1902), 480–511, at 482, 495–502; this document is termed *Ley as Lorengs* and dated to the eleventh century by Middleton, 'Early medieval port customs', 334. 76 Duchesne, *Historiae Normannorum scriptores antiqui*, p. 1063. 77 Noonan and Kovalev, 'Furry forties', pp 653–62. 78 *Oxford English dictionary online*, s.v. 'timber', n. 2. 79 *DGMR*, pp 64, 109.

In the end, we cannot state unequivocally that Norwegians, Icelanders or other Scandinavians traded in early Dublin. It is clear from both references to *scingi* and from archaeological discoveries of walrus and of whalebone that northern goods arrived into Dublin during the pre-Anglo-Norman period. Various Norse sagas of thirteenth-century date indicate a literary acceptance of Dublin links to both Iceland and Norway and show a tendency to identify those links as occurring in the pre-Anglo-Norman past. The *DGMR*, which provides evidence for internationalized merchant activity in the city after it had been awarded charters by Henry II, indicates that merchants called *Norreis* and *Norrensis* (respectively, French and Latin terms for Norse-speakers) were resident on at least an intermittent basis in Dublin throughout the period covered by the roll. These formed part of a mercantile community that drew at least some members from all parts of the Plantagenet world while at the same time being clearly dominated, numerically, by neighbouring parts of Britain. The merchant city of Bergen, on the western Norwegian seaboard, may well have been in contact with Dublin given the amount of Irish detail in the Norse account of Tristan, produced for a western Norwegian king for whom Bergen was a key royal centre and whose biography stresses his links with the Irish Sea region. Indeed, Bergen may well have been the original hometown for some of the Irish *Noreis* who became members of Dublin's thirteenth-century merchant guild. Other traders, while still having identifiable Norse-speaking origins, seem to have already established links with English cities such as Bristol, Exeter and London before joining the Dublin guild.

Like Chrétien de Troyes, writing of Irish nobles at the fabled Arthurian court at Nantes, Norse saga-writers describing trading contacts with Ireland may simply have had their imaginations fired by the thought of intrepid travellers to far distant lands. On the other hand, though the hints of a Norse-speaking presence in Dublin are shadowy, they are also relatively numerous, deriving from a reasonably wide range of textual and archaeological sources ranging from the tenth to the later years of the thirteenth century. In attempting to reconstruct the international population which manned the medieval trading booths of Skinners Street, high on the ridge of the walled city overlooking the Liffey, fur-capped traders from Europe's far north must surely be allowed to play their part.

Before and after St John's hospital: evidence for a pre-Anglo-Norman cemetery on Thomas Street found on the shelves of Trinity College Dublin

JOSEPH HARBISON AND RENÉ GAPERT

INTRODUCTION

In 2011 the School of Medicine in Trinity College Dublin moved to a new building on Pearse Street – the Trinity Biomedical Sciences Institute. It had previously occupied buildings at the Lincoln Place end of the College, south of College Park, since 1824. Prior to that the school had occupied a building called the Anatomy House completed in 1711 at the far end of the Park in an area now occupied by the Ussher Library. A museum space was incorporated in the Anatomy House from the time of its construction and over the three centuries the School had collected a substantial collection of specimens and artefacts including illustrations, models, books and instruments but also preserved examples of zoological and human anatomy, most notably skeletal remains and bones. With the relocation of the School we entered an ongoing process to evaluate, preserve, record, and catalogue the collection.

Perhaps the most sizable component of the collection is an assemblage of over five hundred human skulls and crania which were predominantly collected in the nineteenth century. In the 1870s the School opened a Museum of Comparative Anatomy and around this time began actively to collect crania for the purpose of study. This later developed, in 1891, into the Anthropometric Laboratory, studying head and skull morphology to try to determine the origins of the Irish race. In the late nineteenth century the museum also became a regular recipient of human skulls found in the course of archaeological excavations or other building projects. When received, the circumstances of their collection were briefly recorded in a catalogue, often with the initial correspondence from the individual submitting them. In very few circumstances is there any substantial detail of the process or the exact location of their excavation or of any other artefacts collected with them. Details of acquisitions were recorded by hand in a bound catalogue kept in the Department. Part of the process of evaluation of the collection was to perform a reconciliation between the catalogue and the specimens stored in the museum and to confirm that all specimens were consistent with their acquisition number.

During the process of searching through the catalogue the following entries were encountered in respect of an assemblage of crania in the collection:

2.1 Gabriel Beranger's drawing of the tower of the hospital of St John the Baptist, 1780 (RIA MS 3.C.30, © Royal Irish Academy)

> 320. Cranium. Found at the foundation of St John's Castle Thomas Street Dublin April 1862. Nos. 320, 321, 322, 323, 324, 325, 326 were all obtained at Thomas St, and were deposited at TCD by the Science and Art Museum. Former Numbers 1=320, 2=321, 8=322, 3=323, 4= – , 5=324, 6=325, 7=326.
>
> 327. Cranium. "St John's Chapel" Thomas St.
>
> 328. Cranium. Foundation of "St John's Chapel" Thomas Street. Presented by Prof. A. McAlister.

The potential importance of these skulls was immediately apparent as 'St John's Castle', or St John's Tower as it is more accurately known, was the last part of the medieval hospital of St John the Baptist, which remained above ground until it was demolished in modern times: the Dutch artist and antiquarian Gabriel Berenger originally produced a watercolour drawing of it in 1780 but added the following note to a later copy that he made: 'NB it was taken down in 1800' (Harbison 1991, 96) (fig. 2.1). The modern Roman Catholic church of SS Augustine and John (commonly called John's Lane church), construction of which began in the early 1860s, stands on the site.

Given the link to the medieval hospital of St John the Baptist, it seemed reasonable to hypothesize that these crania could belong to individuals – patients or clergy – associated with it. We managed to identify the crania in the collection and thus began a long study to investigate and evaluate them and also to understand as much as we could about their discovery and the 'chain of custody' that resulted in their deposition in the Department, to allow us to determine the accuracy of their provenance and of resultant conclusions relating to their anthropological and osteoarchaeological evaluation.

THE HOSPITAL OF ST JOHN THE BAPTIST WITHOUT THE NEWGATE

Very full accounts of the history of St John's were previously published by Charles McNeill and also by Grace O'Keeffe both in an earlier volume in this series and in her subsequent doctoral thesis (McNeill 1925; O'Keeffe 2009, 2012). However, it is appropriate to give a brief account of the foundation, development and decline of the hospital here to give context to the later decline and demolition of the hospital and its buildings. St John's was founded at the behest of a Dublin citizen named Ailred (or Edred) having returned from a pilgrimage to the Holy Land. Ailred adopted the surname Palmer after his return, the palm being the symbol of the Jerusalem pilgrimage, and the hospital was sometimes referred to as Palmer's Hospital. The first certain date in the hospital's history is 1188 when it received a charter from Pope Clement III confirming Ailred's foundation and various grants of land to the new hospital, including one by the king, Henry II (*Reg. St John*, p. vi). It was both a hospital, catering for male and female, and a religious house, with male and female members, and both Ailred and his wife appear to have taken monastic vows. Their hospital, dedicated to St John the Baptist, was a house of Fratres cruciferi or 'crutched friars', a branch of canons regular of the Augustinians (McNeill 1925).

It is important to consider a medieval hospital in the context of its time. It operated very much as a poorhouse, orphanage, nursing home and hospice more so than the modern concept of a hospital (O'Keeffe 2012). There is no evidence that it had, for instance, a physician attached, patients being treated with nursing, nutrition and prayer although a surgeon may have visited. Its location was very suited to its purpose both in seeking alms and in separating the ill and destitute from the city proper. It was founded on what is currently Thomas Street but what seems to have been, in the twelfth century, a stretch of the Slige Mhór, the main road west from Dublin near its junction with the main route northwards, the Slige Midluachra, the junction possibly being formed by the famous Liffey ford of Áth Cliath which gave Dublin its Gaelic name. It was also built near the magnificent new royal foundation of St Thomas's abbey which began construction in 1177. All these factors made it a very good place for gathering alms from passing travellers and its royal patronage would have left it an attractive institution for members of the new Anglo-Norman citizenry to support philanthropically.

What, if anything, occupied the site prior to the hospital is unclear. If it was such a promising site for establishment of a religious foundation, it seems possible that there may have been a church on the site previously. There is a late reference to 'Saint Molloyes chappell' at or near the hospital site (*CARD*, iii, 56) and a couple of suggestions have been made as to who this saint might be. One is that this is a corruption of Mo Lua, an Irish saint of perhaps the sixth century, which might point to a very early ecclesiastical presence there (Clarke, *Dublin, Pt 1* (IHTA), p. 1); but while there are several Irish saints called Mo Lua, there is little to indicate a link to Dublin (Ó Riain 2011, 490–3). Another suggestion is that the saint in question is one widely venerated in Scotland, Mo Luóg of Lismore in Argyll (Bhreathnach 2020, 151); his cult in the Isle of Man might explain a Dublin church being dedicated it him, bearing in mind the strong Dublin–Manx links in the Viking Age. The problem with both suggestions, however, is that ecclesiastical records for medieval Dublin are relatively plentiful and it is therefore odd that no reference would be made to such a putative early church until as late as 1615.

There are further possibilities (Seán Duffy, pers. comm.). One is that 'Molloye' derives from 'Maudlin' (Berry 1903, 222). We know that there was a chapel dedicated to St Mary Magdalene attached to the hospital, mentioned in 1260 and rebuilt or repaired *c.*1308 by the well-known citizen of Dublin, John Le Decer (McNeill 1925, 62), but damaged again when the western suburb was fired on the approach of the Bruce army in 1317, annals reporting the burning of *ecclesia Sancti Johannis cum capella Beate Marie Magdalene* (*CStM*, ii, 353). St Mary Magdalene was often associated with leper hospitals (hence the reason they were called maudlin houses) found on the outskirts of towns. The Magdalen chapel in the grounds of St John's later operated as the chantry chapel of the barber-surgeons' guild of St Mary Magdalene (Berry 1903, 219–20; Guinness 1922, 147) and is probably what is erroneously called the 'chapel of St Margaret' listed among the hospital buildings in 1562 (Griffith (ed.), *Cal. inquisitions*, 154).

The latter record does, however, note the existence on the same site of another chapel, 'a house within the precincts which used to be the chapel of St

Eligius (*domus quae nuper fuit capella Sancti Eligii*)' (le Fanu 1930, 152). How one might get from Eligius's chapel to the 'Molloyes chappell' recorded in 1615 might seem at first sight improbable. But the Latin Eligius was St Éloi in French and St Loy in English. He is the patron saint of smiths and this building in the grounds of the hospital served as the chantry chapel of Dublin's guild of smiths. Their (re-)foundation charter from 1474 refers to the body as the 'fraternity or guild of St Eloi' and grants them 'a certain chantry of one chaplain or of more chaplains to celebrate divine service daily for ever in the chapel of Saint Eloi in the churchyard of St John the Baptist Without the New Gate'. When James II confirmed the guild's status in 1688, he referred to it as 'the guild or fraternity of Saint Loy' (*Guildae seu fraternitat Sanctae Loy*) (le Fanu 1930, 158). It might of course be the case that the chapel of 'St Loy' was a rededication of an earlier chapel of 'St Molloye' but it seems a bit convenient that they should sound so alike and, given that the mention of the latter is so late, and occurs only once, it might be safer to consider it an error.

Be that as it may, the hospital prospered until the early years of the fourteenth century. It had gained lands and granges in a number of areas of County Dublin and as far afield as Tipperary and Cork (Gwynn & Hadcock 1970, 212). The modern Palmerstown near Chapelizod and Palmerstown on the Dublin–Meath border near Ashbourne belonged to the hospital's founder, Ailred Palmer, and take their name from him (*Reg. St John*, p. vi). In its heyday in the late thirteenth and early fourteenth century it owned approximately 13,000 acres in various locations. It was also awarded fishing rights for a large length of the Liffey from which it could source food for its patients and provide further revenue. At its peak, it had places for 155 patients, which was considerable for a city of perhaps 8,000 inhabitants.

In the years following, however, a number of crises beset both the country and hospital. The country suffered a famine in 1308, followed by the Great European Famine that affected all of northern Europe from 1315 to 1317. Ireland also suffered the consequences of the Bruce invasion from 1315 to 1318 and the hospital was affected directly. As the Bruce's forces approached Dublin the suburbs were set on fire to deter the oncoming army: inadvertently, the hospital caught fire and was severely damaged. Then, in the 1320s, northern Europe, including Ireland, suffered a cattle murrain (Newfield 2009) that caused a severe economic depression. The consequences of all these events on an institution that depended to a large extent on patronage and alms are likely to have been severe. In 1334, the prior of the hospital complained of its impoverishment due to the attacks of the Scots and Irish and the burning of the suburbs and the hospital was forced to remit rents on some of its lands in Dublin in the 1330s and 1340s as their tenants were unable to pay. Later disasters such as the Black Death in the late 1340s obviously worsened matters.

There is very limited information on the impact of the plague on St John's specifically but clergy and nuns in the majority of Dublin's religious institutions were severely affected: the Franciscan monastery established just a few hundred metres away on the current Francis Street lost 23 friars, almost half their brethren (Gwynn 1935). One could assume the hospital and priory lost a substantial number of both brethren and sisters. In the late Middle Ages the hospital continued to deteriorate both financially and organizationally. In 1363 its prior was accused of misappropriating its assets to the detriment of the adults and orphans in his charge (see O'Keeffe in this volume, below), while in 1441 its reputation was further damaged by the trial of a later prior, 'a public fornicator who had begotten children' (Kelly 2003, 127, 129).

By the time of Henry VIII's Dissolution of the monasteries the hospital was really struggling. It had reduced to 50 beds and premises on the hospital site may already have been leased to merchants for other commercial and residential purposes prior to its actual abolition. In 1531 Archbishop Alen forced it to renounce all its remaining liberties and privileges. Between 1531 and 1539 the number of brothers reduced from six to three, suggesting that it was not very active and in 1540 the remaining assets of the hospital were sold for £54 7*s.* 7*d.*, about €40,000 in today's terms. Its church was immediately demolished and the building materials sold off to unnamed locals (Scott 2006, 223), leaving only the tower remaining: this is presumably the belfry listed separately from the church in accounts of the hospital's dissolution in 1540 (*Extents Ir. mon. possessions*, 56). This crenelated tower (fig. 2.1) later came to be known as 'St John's Tower' or 'St John's Castle' and is the structure referenced in the TCD museum catalogue.

St John's had, of course, an associated cemetery for burial of members of the order, as well as inmates and benefactors (*Reg. St John*, nos 65, 66, 370), and perhaps also occupants of the nearby streets. One of the earliest references to the chapel of St Mary Magdalene, dating from around 1260, states that it was located in the cemetery of the hospital (*Reg. St John*, no. 103). In 1540, at the Dissolution, St Mary Magdalene's (erroneously named St Margaret's, and described as 'now unoccupied for want of a tenant and of repairs') and the cemetery (described as containing about a half-acre and a building described as a revestry, where vestments would have been housed) were both valued as worthless (*Extents Ir. mon. possessions*, 55).

Unlike in London where St Bartholomew's and St Thomas's hospitals survived the Dissolution, all hospitals in Dublin, including St John's and St Stephen's, were closed. However, St John's seems to have continued in existence beyond this period in a very restricted form. In 1539 the site was leased to a surgeon, Edmund Redman, for twenty-one years although he may have held the lease before the Dissolution and was maintaining the hospital (Scott 2006, 222). Other parts of the site, including the kitchens, were occupied by a merchant, Thomas Stephens, which must have limited its capacity to function as a hospital. Yet over the course of the next century and a half the remaining buildings appear to have maintained some role as a hospital and poorhouse although it is initially difficult to find official recognition of its status as such. In 1561, it is described as being used for 'poor male residents', in 1562 there was 'a house there containing 50 beds (*grabat'*) (Griffith (ed.), *Cal. inquisitions*, 174), and funds were raised for its restoration in 1563. Later, in 1590, entry to it was restricted to all but 'decayed citizens' and when granted to Thomas Luttrell in 1609 it had accommodation for fifty sick persons.

It was still important or relevant enough to be recorded on Speed's map of 1610 as 'Iohn's House' (number 54 of 69 locations) where the tower is specifically indicated. In 1614, the city authorities, responding to a petition from one Dorby Lany, instructed that he be assigned a place in the hospital, but soon afterwards, in response to a complaint from the commons of the city, the same city fathers undertook an enquiry into abuses there. One of the complaints of the citizens was that, although the hospital was 'only supported and maintained by the devotion of the citizens', yet non-citizens were gaining preferment there at the expense of impoverished Dubliners. In 1626, work was ordered to the walls and roof of the hospital, while, three years later, the tower, called 'Saint Johns steeple, adjoyning to Saint Johns Hospitall in Saint Thomasstreete', was rented by the city authorities to be used as a house of correction; even then, though, it functioned as a refuge for the infirm as, in 1631, it was ordered that the former porter to the mayor be provided with lodgings for life there (*CARD*, iii, 87, 99, 195, 225, 256). There is a reference in 1666 to 'the late dissolved hospital of St John Baptist' (*Cal. S.P. Ire., 1666–9*, 245) though this may refer to the monastic institution as opposed to the house of correction and poorhouse whose existence seemed to drag on for generations. In the late seventeenth century the city and government authorities were increasingly concerned at the problems associated with the location of a poorhouse within the city boundaries, particularly the ease with which beggars could access the city centre, and St John's was certainly gone by the time of the establishment of a new workhouse at Mount Brown beyond St James's Gate in the opening years of the new century (Coakley 2018).

Therefore, the function of the site changed after 1700 or thereabouts. Although it is marked on both Charles Brooking's map of 1728 as 'St Johns Castle' and on John Rocque's map of 1756 likewise as 'Iohns Castle', there was still a religious dimension to the site. It has been stated that, around 1700, the Augustinians rented a stable on the western side of the tower to act as a chapel (Ossory Fitzpatrick 1907, 287) and a submission to the 1731 'Report on the state of popery' stated that 'one other mass house is in St Johns lane, belongs to the fryars Augustines and is supplyd by about eight Priests, four or five of which are resident in the s[ai]d parish' (anon. 1915, 138). The old chapel being ruinous, about 1740 it was taken down and replaced but, when additional ground was acquired in 1780, it was extended northwards towards John's Lane (Donnelly 1904, 37). It is possible that this structure can be seen to the right in Gabriel Berenger's drawing of the tower in 1780 (fig. 2.1). His painting of the rear of the tower also shows a number of pigs foraging and in 1800 the top of the tower was removed and the lower part used as a pig-sty. In 1862 the Augustinian order purchased houses surrounding the tower and the site began to be cleared for the new church of St Augustine and St John, known to most locals as John's Lane church, designed by Edward Pugin. It is in this process of clearing the site that the human remains were found.

PROVENANCE OF THE CRANIA

A question still remains as to the provenance of the crania in the TCD museum. How did they end up in the museum in Trinity College and how did they come to the Science and Art Museum in the first place? The record in the catalogue is that they were collected in April 1862 and this date is written directly on the side of one cranium:

> Found at the foundation of St John's Castle Thomas Street Dublin April 13, 1862. Deposited by Sci Art Museum.

The issue with this date, in terms of confirming the provenance or chain of custody of the assemblage, is that the Science and Art Museum was only established by Act of Parliament in 1877 (and evolved into the National Museum of Ireland in 1921). The date of excavation is therefore very specific but is some fifteen years before the museum was even founded. The museum was originally opened in collaboration with the Royal Dublin Society, which unfortunately has no record of the crania.

A likely reason for the crania coming into the possession of the Science and Art Museum is that, in establishing their earliest collections, they purchased a number of private collections from various sources, and that the crania were part of a collection thus acquired by the museum at its foundation. Even after the establishment of the National Museum, and indeed until the middle of the twentieth century, the curators occasionally sent human skeletal remains to the TCD Anatomy Department for examination and storage (and a number of these are being restored to the National Museum as part of the evaluation of the TCD collection). One of the crania is listed separately as having been donated by 'A. McAlister' and skulls and crania included in the catalogue on either side of the St John's collection were donated by the same person, Alexander Macalister, which suggests he may have been involved in the transfer. Although we do not have an acquisition date in the catalogue, Macalister's likely involvement narrows down the potential dates considerably.

Professor Alexander Macalister (1844–1919) was a polymath who entered the Royal College of Surgeons to study at the age of 14 and became an anatomy demonstrator aged 16. He graduated as a doctor (M.B.) from TCD in 1871 and was granted his doctorate in medicine in 1876 from the same institution. He was appointed professor of zoology in Trinity in 1869, aged 25, while still a medical undergraduate and in 1872 he became the professor of comparative anatomy. In 1877 he became professor of anatomy and chirurgery in Trinity and a consultant surgeon in Sir Patrick Dun's Hospital. In 1883 he left Dublin to become professor of anatomy in Cambridge University and went on to write the famous *Macalister's textbook of human anatomy*, late editions of which are still used today. It may be of particular relevance to this story that Macalister was also a keen antiquarian and historian and had an interest in anthropology. He wrote on Egyptology and his son was R.A.S. Macalister, the renowned archaeologist. In 1910 Macalister was part of a group that examined the remains of King Henry VI found in St George's Chapel at Windsor Castle.

It is our hypothesis that soon after the Science and Art Museum opened, and before Macalister's departure in 1883, the museum acquired a collection including the St John's Hospital crania and sent them to Macalister because of his interest in anthropology and history and they were then added to the TCD Anatomy Department's collection. Given his rather precocious student career, it is not impossible that he collected some of the skulls himself.

We know, however, that the discovery of the skeletal remains was known around antiquarian circles in Dublin. The writer and antiquarian Revd John O'Hanlon published quite a detailed report of his visit in 1862 to the site where the new John's Lane church was being built (O'Hanlon 1862):

> On May 23rd, whilst passing through Thomas-street, I dropped in to inspect the deep excavations at present making for the foundations of a new Augustinian church, which is about to be built on the site of the castle and priory formerly belonging to the Knights of St. John [sic]. Projecting from the sides of a deep trench, at and under the foundation walls of the castle, now in process of removal, I observed a large pile of skulls and human bones yet remaining in the earth, whilst other remains had been packed away in two large pine cases, or piled in a loose heap, awaiting a similar stowage for future re-interment.
>
> These remains were undoubtedly the result of a battle; not only from the evidences of their close and promiscuous position, but from the information afforded by one of the Augustinian fathers, engaged in superintending the operations of the workmen, who told me he had examined some of the skulls, and found not only perforations, seemingly

> caused by bullets, but even in one instance he found a leaden bullet lodged within some clay, with which the skull had been filled.
>
> I was also informed that several bog-oak coffins, with perfect skeletons lying at full length, had been discovered on the line of removed side-walls, forming the west boundary of John's-lane, and that there is reason to suppose further explorations would discover others, under the surface of the lane already mentioned. One of these skeletons had been accurately measured, and was found to be fully seven feet in length. The bones, as they now appear, are all quite blackish, and of various sizes.
>
> In cutting the foundations, which are very deep and wide, especially about the part whereon a new tower is to be built, the workmen came to a sewer, in which they found a perfect human skeleton. Some old persons were enabled to supply a traditionary and an explanatory account: that, about eighty years ago [*c.*1782], no less than eight prisoners escaped from an old prison in that vicinity, through the sewer; four are said to have come up alive, whilst the rest perished, probably on account of breathing foul air.
>
> In a part of the trenches now cutting a barrel was found, within it a human skeleton, with bones broken, and from all indications, it would seem that the person therein enclosed must have met some unnatural and violent death. A few coins have been discovered, and it is probable other matters of curious interest may come to light with the progress of these excavations.

O'Hanlon was a folklorist and a hagiographer who compiled the well-known *Lives of the Irish saints*, though his work is nowadays viewed as somewhat lacking in rigour. We might therefore query his conclusion that the exposed remains were the result of a battle, and take with a pinch of salt his assertion that one of the skeletons was seven feet long. He does, however, inform us from personal observation that 'a large pile of skulls and human bones' was visible 'at and under the foundation walls of the castle'. The latter is the tower of the medieval hospital of St John the Baptist, which presumably dated from the late Middle Ages if not from the hospital's heyday in the thirteenth century; and if a large pile of skulls and human bones was visible 'at and under' its 'foundation walls', they must antedate its construction.

O'Hanlon makes no mention of having kept any of the remains but notes that an Augustinian father was superintending the excavation. As part of our investigations, the archivist of the Augustinian order in Ireland was contacted but the order retains no record of the excavation or of any remains found and so it is unclear where they were reinterred.

Another antiquarian who visited the site was the O'Connellite activist Thomas Mathew Ray, who spent the period between 1856 and 1862 collecting

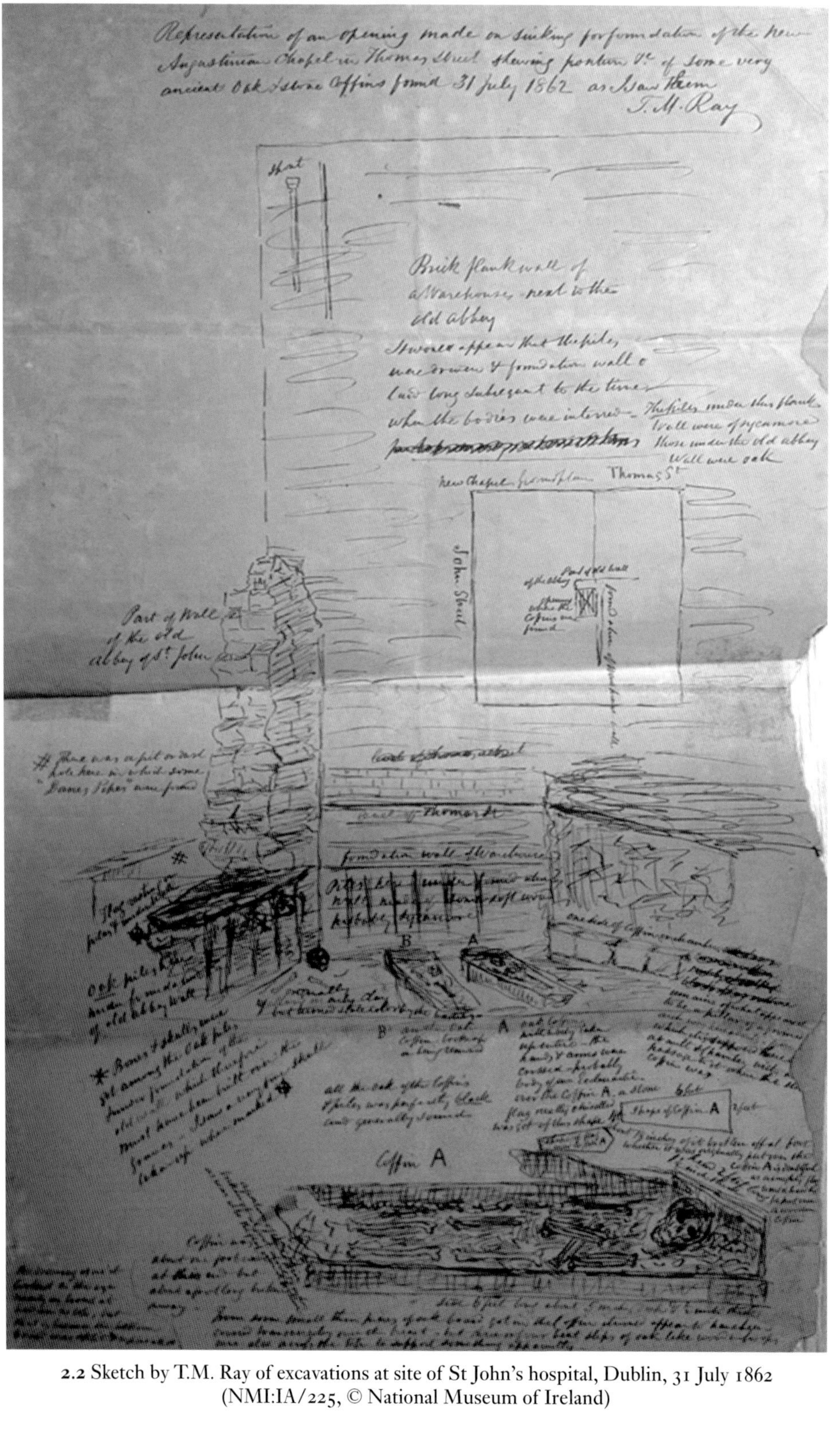

2.2 Sketch by T.M. Ray of excavations at site of St John's hospital, Dublin, 31 July 1862 (NMI:IA/225, © National Museum of Ireland)

objects found during the excavation of sewers and other sites around Dublin. He was certainly present at the excavation of St John's in 1862 as his account of the excavation and drawings of standing walls and coffins are preserved in an archive in the National Museum of Ireland, including one detailed sketch entitled 'Representation of an opening made on sinking for foundations of the new Augustinian chapel in Thomas Street shewing positions &c of some very ancient oak and stone coffins found 31 July 1862 as I saw them. T.M. Ray' (fig. 2.2). His illustration contains a sketch of 'part of wall of the old abbey [sic] of St John' to which he adds:

> Bones & skulls were got under the Oak piles under foundation of the old wall, which therefore must have been built over the graves – I saw a very fine skull taken up where marked,

and he indicates the spot. He also marks the site of two coffins, of one of which he states:

> Oak coffin with body taken up entire – the hands & arms were crossed – probably the body of an Ecclesiastic.

Much of Ray's superb collection of over 700 objects was given to the Science and Art Museum and he seems the most likely source of the crania. Certainly, we have been unable to identify a more likely source. Ultimately, whilst it is plausible and even likely that the crania held in the Anatomy Museum come from the St John's excavations, perhaps through Ray, we have been unable to establish conclusively this provenance.

FORENSIC ANTHROPOLOGICAL EVALUATION OF THE CRANIA

A detailed forensic anthropological evaluation was performed on the nine crania by Dr René Gapert who also took samples for Carbon 14 and stable isotope analysis. Many of the crania were partial with absent dentition, and no mandibles were available, so determination of age and sex was challenging and we present the most likely interpretation. Carbon 14 dating was performed in the Chrono Centre of Queen's University Belfast. Permission was obtained for the sampling from the National Museum of Ireland (Licence 5979). Results are tabulated below (table 2.1). Carbon date ranges are expressed using 1 sigma (68.3%) 2 sigma (95.4%) probability. Stable isotope data obtained from seven crania suggested some dietary protein content from freshwater fish and so some freshwater reservoir effect cannot be ruled out (Phillipsen 2013).

The crania were dated to a wide range of time periods from the eleventh to the seventeenth century. One cranium (327) clearly dated to before the

Table 2.1 Carbon 14 and stable isotope analysis from nine crania

Accession Number	Age (years)	Sex	Date range (1σ probability)	Date range (2σ probability)	Forensic findings
320	36–45	?M	**1045–1095** (0.578)	**1036–1191** (0.981)	8 small button osteomas (<2mm).
321	46+	?M	**1453–1513** (0.784)	**1446–1524** (0.649)	Groundwater level mark, post-mortem damage, likely excavation-related.
322	26–35	?M gracile	**1309–1361** (0.802)	**1297–1409** (1.0)	Groundwater level mark, post-mortem damage, likely excavation-related.
323	12–18	?F	**1152–1212** (0.704)	**1116–1220** (0.672)	Healed ante-mortem depression fracture to left forehead and ante-mortem fracture of right nasal bone. Cribria orbitalia, porotic hyperostosis in parts of both frontal and parietal bones. Enamel hypoplasia and dental calculus.
324	36–45	?F	**1043–1105** (0.612)	**1024–1190** (0.988)	Slight cribra orbitalia. Post-mortem damage to cranium
325	36–45	?M	**1348–1373** (0.393)	**1291–1399** (1.0)	Slight cribra orbitalia. Post-mortem damage to cranium
326	6–12	?	**1516–1596** (0.788)	**1479–1645** (1.0)	Groundwater level mark. Cribria orbitalia and porotic hyperostosis in lambda region and along saggital suture. Post-mortem damage.
327	46+	?M	**968–1016** (0.901)	**942–1021** (0.805)	Post-mortem damage
328	36–45	?M gracile	**1649–1671** (0.435) **1779–1799** (0.442)	**1644–1682** (0.392) **1761–1804** (0.433)	Infection of right maxilla alveolar from socket of right upper 2nd premolar. Possible minor arthritic changes to right temporomandibular joint.

foundation of the hospital and two others (320, 324) probably also antedated the hospital. Four crania dated to the era when the hospital was in operation (321, 322, 323, 325) and the remaining two (326, 328) probably date to after the Dissolution and the operation of the hospital as a poorhouse. Cranium 328 produced an alternate date in the period after the closure of the poorhouse. At this point the site was largely built over and whilst we have presented it for completeness, we feel that the earlier date is more likely.

Only one of the skulls showed evidence of healed pre-mortem trauma and likely dates to the early years of operation of the hospital. The presence of cribria orbitalia and porotic hyperostosis in some skills suggests some level of nutritional stress but it is noticeable that these findings occurred throughout the spectrum of calculated dates for the skulls – pre-hospital, during its operation and after closure.

We are aware of anecdotal reports of skeletal remains being detected in the area of John's Lane church over the last thirty years during construction of nearby apartment blocks; however available site reports for adjacent and nearby areas do not confirm these. This part of Dublin has been considerably redeveloped during the last three hundred years and most of what has been found is of post-medieval date.

A CEMETERY ANTEDATING THE HOSPITAL?

The finding in a relatively small assemblage of three crania that likely antedate the foundation of St John's hospital inevitably leads to questions as to what may have been on the site prior to its establishment. As previously mentioned, the site is very well placed since it is widely thought to have stood at the intersection of the two most important roads in the region. If that were the case, it would not be surprising if an earlier religious establishment had been founded at such a junction. And a site at a junction outside the town might also be suitable for a burial ground. But it is not possible to say much beyond this. As noted above, it has been suggested that the 'Saint Molloye's chapel' recorded in a very late source may refer to an early church dedicated Mo Lua or perhaps Mo Luóg but in fact this is more likely to be a corruption of the 'Maudlin' chapel or, more likekly perhaps, another chapel dedicated to St Loy we known to have part of the site in the Anglo-Norman period.

There is however one piece of evidence that may just be relevant. An object reported as being found in the area of St John's Castle was, in 1861, in the collection of the British antiquarian R.H. Brackstone, a collector of early Irish artefacts, and was acquired by the British Museum in 1868 (BM 1868,0709.52) (fig. 2.3). It is a cast bronze figurine, 18cm high by 4.3cm wide, depicting a bearded apostle or saint dressed in a bishop's robes decorated with fine scrolled spirals, and geometric patterns (https://www.britishmuseum.org/collection/object/H_1868-0709-52). It is pierced at the feet and breast in precisely the same way as the figurines on the well-known shrine of St Manchán (normally dated to *c.*1130) but has been described as 'of much finer workmanship and evidently earlier date' (Stokes 1894, 13). How this figurine

2.3 Cast bronze figurine, said to have been recovered from site of St John's hospital, Dublin in 1861 (BM 1868,0709.52, © Trustees of the British Museum)

got detached from the original piece to which it belonged we cannot know – and it may simply be lost loot from a monastic raid – but, given that it antedates the establishment of St John's hospital, it may just relate to an older church on the same site.

CONCLUSION

The rediscovery of these crania in our collection has allowed us an opportunity to revisit the decline of one of Dublin's earliest hospitals. The carbon dating and forensic anthropological analysis, added to the contemporary accounts from the early 1860s of the construction of John's Lane church, suggest the presence of a large, previously under-considered, cemetery in the area which may antedate the hospital and the Anglo-Norman invasion.

ACKNOWLEDGMENTS

The authors would sincerely like to thank the following for their helpful advice and assistance in our long process of investigation: Siobhan Ward, Michael Gill, Philomena McAteer, Martina Hennessy, the late Davis Coakley (School of Medicine, Trinity College Dublin), David Kelly and Fr Padraig Daly (Augustinians, Dublin), Nessa O'Connor (National Museum of Ireland) and Natasha Serne (Royal Dublin Society).

REFERENCES

Anon. 1915 'Report on the state of popery in Ireland, 1731'. *Archivium Hibernicum* 4, 131–77.

Berry, H.F. 1903 'The ancient corporation of barber-surgeons, or gild of St Mary Magdalene, Dublin'. *JRSAI* 33, 217–38.

Bhreathnach, E. 2020 'Saints' dedications and the ecclesiastical landscape of Hiberno-Norse Dublin: Irish, Scandinavian and others'. In S. Duffy (ed.), *Medieval Dublin XVIII*, 143–68. Dublin.

Coakley, D. and Coakley, M. 2018 *The history and heritage of St James's Hospital, Dublin*. Dublin.

Donnelly, N. 1904 *Roman Catholics. State and condition of R.C. chapels in Dublin, both secular and regular, AD 1749*. Dublin.

Guinness, H.S. 1922 'Dublin trade gilds'. *JRSAI* 52, 143–63.

Gwynn, A. 1935 'The Black Death in Ireland'. *Studies: An Irish Quarterly Review* 24, 25–42.

Gwynn, A. and Hadcock, R.N. 1970 *Medieval religious houses: Ireland*. Dublin.

Harbison, P. 1991 *Berenger's views of Ireland*. Royal Irish Academy. Dublin.

Kelly, M. 2003 *The great dying: the Black Death in Dublin*. Stroud.

le Fanu, T.P. 1930 'A note on two charters of the smiths' guild of Dublin'. *JRSAI* 60, 154–60.
McNeill, C. 1925 'Hospital of S. John without the New Gate Dublin'. *JRSAI* 55, 58–64.
Newfield, T.P. 2009 'A cattle panzootic in early fourteenth-century Europe'. *Agricultural History Review* 57 (2), 155–90.
O'Hanlon, J. 1862 Letter [re burials found on site for new Augustinian church, Thomas Street, Dublin]. *JRSAI* 7 [*Jn. Kilkenny & S.E. Ireland Arch. Soc.*, new ser., 4, no. 1], 148–9.
O'Keeffe, G. 2009 'The Hospital of St John the Baptist in medieval Dublin: functions and maintenance'. In S. Duffy (ed.), *Medieval Dublin IX*, 166–82. Dublin.
O'Keeffe, G. 2012 'The hospital of St John the Baptist, Dublin *c.*1188–1539: a historical and prosophographical analysis'. PhD, TCD.
Ó Riain, P. 2011 *A dictionary of Irish saints*. Dublin.
Ossory Fitzpatrick, S.A., 1907 *Dublin: a historical and topographical account of the city*. London.
Phillipsen B. 2013 'The freshwater reservoir effect in radiocarbon dating', *Heritage Science* 1, article no. 24.
Scott, B. 2006 'The religious houses of Tudor Dublin: their communities and resistance to the Dissolution, 1537-41'. In S. Duffy (ed.), *Medieval Dublin VII*, 214–32.
Stokes M., 1894 *Early Christian art in Ireland*. London.

Structures of import: St Peter's church, a unique sunken-floored structure and Dublin's southern suburb

PAUL DUFFY

INTRODUCTION

For over fifty years, the area of Dublin immediately south of the walled circuit of the medieval town has been the subject of particular archaeological study, debate and speculation. This is the neighbourhood of the *Dubhlinn* – the famous Black Pool at the confluence of the Liffey and the Poddle that is thought to have given its name to a pre-Viking ecclesiastical foundation, the first secure reference to which dates to AD 790.[1] It was likely the combination of this sheltered harbour and the presence of a pre-existing foundation that attracted the initial Viking activity identified by Linzi Simpson on the eastern edge of the pool and the emerging evidence for substantial Viking activity on its western side.[2] The location of this church/foundation therefore represents 'ground zero' for the establishment of Dublin and was crucial to the development of what would become the nation's capital.

Much work has been done in trying to identify the character and location of this foundation, and debate has centred upon two potential sites.[3] These are:

1. The large oval shape fossilized in the modern streetscape discernible in the alignment of Stephen Street Upper, Peter's Row and White Friars Street, which might possibly represent the location of a former enclosure, either secular or ecclesiastical (fig. 3.1).
2. The site of the church of St Michael le Pole on Ship Street Great in the vicinity of which a large number of pre-Anglo-Norman burials have been identified.

Successive excavations along Stephen Street and at Longford Street Little have failed to identify any material antedating the eleventh century.[4] Based on

1 Seán Duffy, 'The saint's tale' in Sparky Booker and Cherie Peters (eds), *Tales of medieval Dublin* (Dublin 2014), pp 7–17, at p. 7. 2 Linzi Simpson, 'Viking warrior burials in Dublin: Is this the *longphort*?' in Seán Duffy (ed.), *Medieval Dublin VI* (Dublin, 2005), pp 11–62; Alan Hayden, (forthcoming: see https://www.rte.ie/news/dublin/2020/0609/1146385-archaeological-dig/). 3 Clarke, *Dublin, Pt 1* (IHTA). 4 Tim Coughlan, 'Excavations at the medieval cemetery of St Peter's church, Dublin' in Seán Duffy (ed.), *Medieval Dublin IV* (Dublin, 2003), pp 11–39; John Ó Néill, 'Excavations at Longford Street Little, Dublin: an archaeological approach to Dubh Linn' in Seán Duffy (ed.), *Medieval Dublin V* (Dublin,

3.1 One of the locations proposed for the Dubhlinn foundation, after Clarke overlaid on Rocque's map of 1756

the lack of physical evidence, the purported Dubhlinn enclosure at Stephen Street has been called into question in recent years. By contrast, the only securely pre-Viking medieval dates from the city are clustered around the church of St Michael le Pole. In Phase 1 of Gowen's excavation at this site, a series of substantial postholes was found possibly associated with a hearth, the ash from which overlay a thick charcoal spread; the latter yielded a radiocarbon determination providing a date-range of AD 675–779 (1 sigma, 68% probability) or a wider date-range AD 663–872 (2 sigma, 95.4% probability).[5] Excavations *c.*70m to the southwest of the church identified five dispersed burials that returned dates within the eighth century/early ninth century, placing them before the establishment of the first permanent Viking settlement in AD 841.[6]

The following paper details the results of two archaeological excavations in this area that contribute to this discussion while also offering new insights into suburban, parochial and architectural developments in the Dublin of *c.*1050–1550.

THE EXCAVATIONS

The excavations were carried out at two separate sites within a year of each other, the first over nine months spanning the spring to autumn of 2018, at a large site extending from Stephen Street Upper southwards to Longford Street Great and east to Aungier Street (hereafter Aungier Street site),[7] and the second in 2019, *c.*50m to the northeast,[8] at the corner of South Great George's Street and Stephen Street Lower (hereafter George's Street site; fig. 3.2). The following paper frames the results of these excavations in the context of the archaeological and historical information for the immediate surrounds with particular focus on the putative Dubhlinn ecclesiastical enclosure, the medieval parish church dedicated to St Peter and the southern suburb of Dublin.

Given the constraints of space, this paper prioritizes discussion and contextualisation of the findings over the usual stratigraphic reports and specialist analyses, which are presented only in brief.[9] Both the Aungier Street and George's Street sites had important and complex phases postdating 1600 and, apart from brief explanatory notes as to where these later layers interfered with the medieval horizons, they will be reported upon elsewhere.[10] At the

2004), pp 73–90, at p. 89. **5** Margaret Gowen, 'Excavations at the site of the church and tower of St Michael le Pole, Dublin' in Seán Duffy (ed.), *Medieval Dublin II* (Dublin, 2001), pp 13–52. **6** Claire Walsh, 'Report on an archaeological excavation at Golden Lane/Chancery Lane, Dublin 8, Licence Ref. 04E0237' (unpublished report, 2005); Claire Walsh, 'An early medieval roadway at Chancery Lane: from Duibhlinn to Áth Cliath?' in Seán Duffy (ed.) *Medieval Dublin IX* (Dublin, 2009), pp 9–37; Mary McMahon, 'Early medieval settlement and burial outside the enclosed town: evidence from archaeological excavations at Bride Street, Dublin', *PRIA*, 102:4 (2002), 67–135. **7** 7–13 Stephen Street Upper; 7–19 Longford Street; and 71–75 Aungier Street. **8** 41–46 South Great George's Street; and 51–53 Lower Stephen Street. **9** For full stratigraphic reports and specialist analysis, see the final reports for both sites lodged with the National Monuments Service: Paul Duffy, 'Final report on excavations at 6–13 Stephen Street Upper, 7–19 Longford Street and 71–75 Aungier Street, excavation licence 17E0212, Dublin 2' (unpublished report, 2023); idem, 'Final report on excavations at 41–46 South Great George's Street and 51–53 Lower Stephen Street, Dublin 2, excavation licence 18E0661' (unpublished report, 2021). **10** E.g. Paul Duffy, 'Sinkings, flyings and other decorations: excavation at the Aungier Street Theatre, Dublin', *Irish Post-Medieval Archaeology Group Newsletter*, 2020/2021 (2022), 47–59.

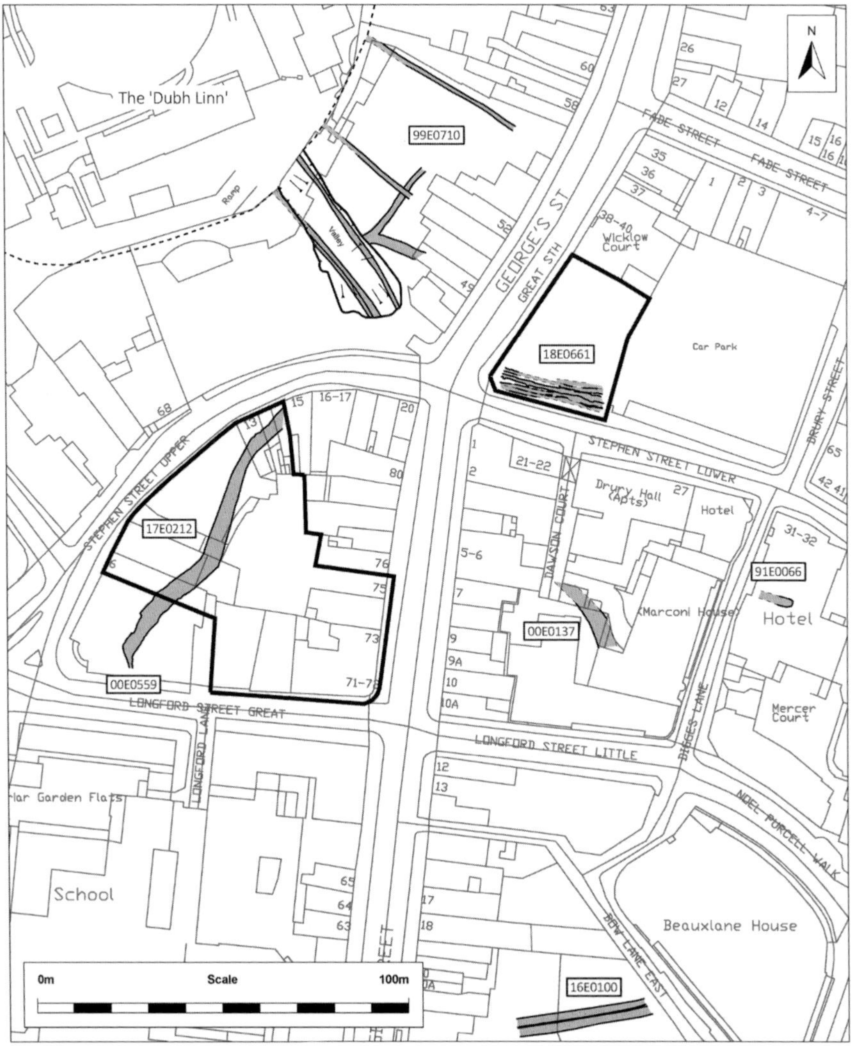

3.2 Location of sites showing all medieval ditches excavated in the area

Aungier Street site, the footprint of the Stephen Street façade, the Aungier Street façade and Longford Street façade had been lowered in the eighteenth century by up to 2m in places while the central area representing 45% percent of the overall site footprint had been lowered by up 1.5m during the construction of a dance hall in the 1950s. This extensive disturbance removed medieval levels across much of the site. At the George's Street site, a Victorian cellar along the western side of the site had removed an estimated 1.5m of medieval levels over *c.*70% of the site footprint.

AUNGIER STREET

The medieval elements encountered during the excavations included a large lime-kiln, a large, curving ditch offset from Stephen Street, two possible sunken pits/outbuildings, a sunken-floored structure (SFS), seven cesspits, two small plot boundary-ditches, the partial foundations of St Peter's church and a portion of its associated cemetery containing 224 burials. While stratigraphic relationships between the ditch, the cesspits and the church allow for clear phasing of these features, no such direct relationship existed between

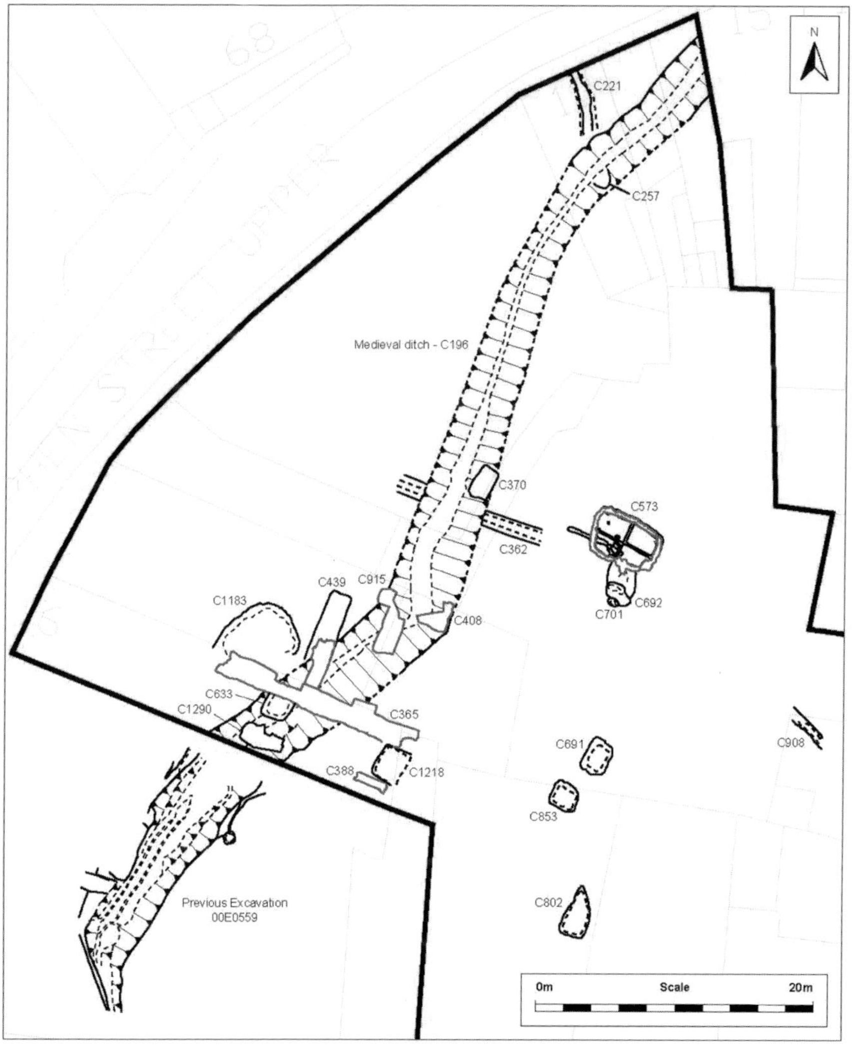

3.3 Plan of medieval features at the Aungier Street site

the other features and the SFS. Dating by Accelerated Mass Spectrography (AMS, i.e., radiocarbon dating), as well as analysis of the artefacts retrieved from the SFS, have allowed all of the medieval features to be phased relative to each other (fig. 3.3).

Aungier Street Phase I: 1050–1150

Lime-kiln

A very large, oval lime-kiln (C1183) was excavated close to the western extremity of the site. This feature measured 6m in length by 5.9m wide and was 1.38m deep. Residue from a final firing was encountered in the bottom of this feature, comprised of extensive solidified lime directly overlying a thick layer of charcoal representing the remains of the combustible fuel (fig. 3.4). A ring of oxidized subsoil fringed the feature and the final firing had been sealed by a deliberate backfilling event with layers of greenish brown silty clay. Due presumably to disturbance from later medieval activity along the western side of the feature, no stoke holes or flues were identified. No ceramic was retrieved from the primary fills of the kiln. An AMS (radiocarbon) date of 1028–1155 was returned from a sample of ash charcoal from the bottom of the kiln.[11]

Enclosure ditch

A large curving ditch (C196) traversed the northern portion of the site, generally mirroring the curve of Stephen Street, though set back from the street front (fig. 3.5). The ditch ran for a total length of 58m, generally northeast–southwest and exhibited a pronounced kink three quarters of the way along its length (see fig. 3.3). The average distance from the Stephen Street façade to the outer line of the ditch was 17m, although the ditch came significantly closer to the line of Stephen Street towards the northern limit of the site. The ditch continued beyond the northern limit of the site. To the southwest, the ditch exited the limit of the site, running southwards, corresponding to the large curving ditch excavated by Tim Coughlan in 2000.[12] Due to the intensive eighteenth-century cellaring along Stephen Street, only the bottom 0.4m of the ditch survived across the central portion of its run. The full height and width of the ditch survived outside of the cellared area to the northeast and southwest where the cut measured 4.6m wide and had a maximum depth of 2m. As with the ditch excavated by Coughlan, a drainage gully (C291) was evident running along the base of the ditch. This part of the ditch contained a silty clay fill (C285) likely to represent initial silting of the ditch. An AMS date of 1046–1253 was returned from a sample of blackthorn charcoal from the bottom of the drainage gully.[13]

11 2 sigma range quoted: Chronos UB 41109. 12 Coughlan, 'Excavations at St Peter's church', pp 12–14. 13 2 sigma range quoted: Chronos UB 41105.

3.4 Lime-kiln C1183 showing residue from firing, facing southwest

3.5 Photogrammetry model, ditch C196 running beneath seventeenth-century cellars fronting Stephen Street

3.6 (*above*) Section through ditch C196 showing find spot of curved roof-tile

3.7 Eleventh-century curved earthenware roof-tile

A fragment of a curved earthenware roof-tile was retrieved from this fill, just to the south of the cellared area (figs 3.6, 3.7). This represents the only artefact retrieved from the original fills of the ditch, although a later recut of the upper portion of the ditch (C232, discussed below) contained abundant ceramic. The ditch above this gully was filled with a range of bulk soils some of which contained animal bone and some shell and charcoal. These fills are likely to represent long-term silting and waste disposal within the feature over a period of disuse followed by deliberate backfilling. The seeds retrieved from the ditch fills chart an interesting progression. Blackberry, elderberry and raspberry seeds suggestive of marginal scrub were found in both the initial silting within the drainage gully and the later backfilled material within the ditch. The initial silting also contained weeds such as campions – usually plants of bare and grassy places – and common wind-dispersed seeds from plants of the daisy family, such as nipplewort and hawkbits. The later fills of the ditch, while containing a similar density of marginal scrub species, contained very few weeds from open, grassy places; instead, there were some seeds from water-loving plants such as water-cresses.[14]

The kink in the line of the ditch has the effect of redirecting the feature in a curving line to the south of the location of the lime-kiln (C1183). Although no direct stratigraphic relationship survived between the ditch and kiln, this kink suggests that the lime-kiln was in existence when the ditch was first set out.

Sunken-floored structure

A sunken-floored structure (SFS) was identified cut into the boulder clay towards the centre of the site (figs 3.8, 3.9). This area had been reduced by 1m–1.5m in the 1950s, resulting in the removal of any archaeological strata that may have survived above the boulder clay. This feature (C573), which represents the below-ground component of a house or workshop, survived as a large sub-rectangular cut with rounded corners and measured 5.4m long, 3.4m wide and 0.58m deep. This feature was only partially excavated in favour of preservation *in situ* and display to the public. The structure comprised several elements and had seen several phases of use. A sample of ash charcoal from a mid-floor level of the structure returned an AMS date of 1030–1150. The principal elements of the structure were as follows:

Stone-lining

The cut (C573) of the SFS was lined with cut blocks of local calp limestone (C571) set end on end with a slight inward batter and bonded with clay. The stone lining survived to a height of two courses though some collapsed stones indicated that there would have been at least three courses originally. A ring of

14 Penny Johnston, 'Organic plant remains report Aungier Street, Dublin 2' (unpublished report, 2021).

3.8 Sunken-floored structure (from photogrammetry model) in plan

3.9 View north along entrance passage from photogrammetry model of sunken-floored structure

heat-reddened boulder clay was evident surrounding the exterior of the stone lining, most evident in the northeast corner, and this corresponded to heat damage on the inner face of the stone in this area.

Floor level

Partial excavation of the feature in quadrants revealed a number of successive floor levels; the earliest comprised of a floor of charred timber and gritty sand/denuded mortar (C792) which directly overlay the subsoil. A carbonized wooden floor was also observed on the base of the passage (C782). The burning event which carbonized the floor was also responsible for the ring of oxidized clay around the exterior of the stone lining. Above the charred floor, several layers of imported clay, sandy clay and stony clay (C734, C572, C587, C588, C578, C715, C718, C719, C771) were laid down within the structure as successive floor surfaces. Several small pits and possible postholes were encountered within these floor fills. All were sealed by a sterile layer of redeposited clay (C572) which represented the latest floor level that has survived.

Entrance passage

A sloping entrance passage (C807) opened into the structure in the southern wall. This passage was truncated to the south by later pits and modern disturbance. It was 1m wide and 2.7m long. This passage was partially backfilled and slightly re-orientated toward the latter phases of the structure's life. A sample of willow charcoal from the original flooring of the passage returned an AMS date of AD 1046–1220.[15]

Doorway

The realignment of the entrance passage from northeast–southwest to north-northeastsouth-southwest was accompanied by the installation of a stone lintel flanked by two rectangular postholes/beam slots which would have carried a door (C742 and C808). The more substantial of the two postholes, and therefore the one from which the door is likely to have hung, measured 0.32m long and 0.1m wide and was excavated to a depth of 0.32m. Several iron items potentially relating to a door, including a key, a pivot and a latch, were found in the vicinity of the threshold (fig. 3.10a–c).

Cistern and gully

A stone-lined cistern (C604) measuring 1.6m long, 1.1m wide and 1.17m deep, cut through the final floor level. This feature was fed by a slate-lined gully (C608) which directed water into the cistern from outside of the structure. The gully channelled water from the west and measured 4.5m long with a maximum width of 0.36m and a maximum depth of 0.26m.

15 2 sigma range quoted: Chronos UB 41107.

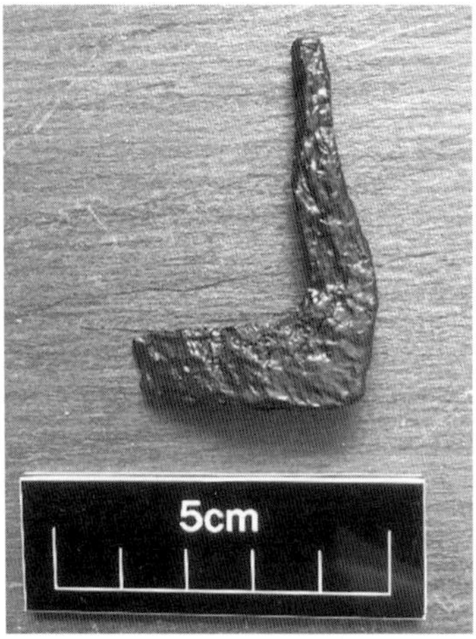

3.10a Iron hinge from sunken-floored structure

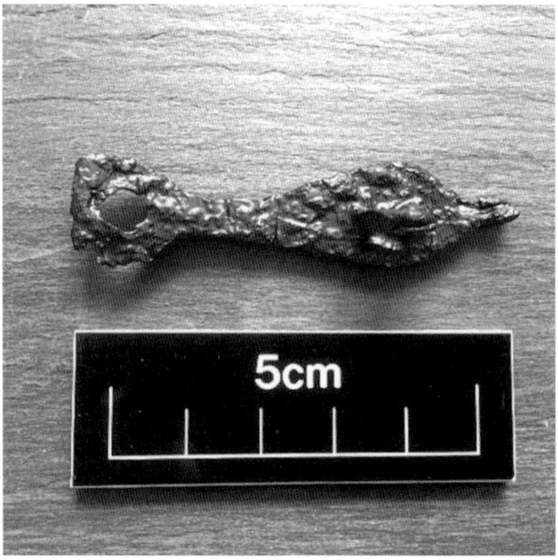

3.10c Iron latch from sunken-floored structure

3.10b Iron key from sunken-floored structure

Superstructure

The method of construction of the stone lining of the SFS was clearly not intended to support a superstructure. The building must therefore have been supported by posts or beams. Several possible postholes were identified at several of the levels. While these were not substantial features (C240, C286, C594, C655, C666, C679, C721, C742), it should be considered that the structure may have been supported by external posts, evidence of which has not survived due to the scarping of the boulder clay in the twentieth century.

Sunken pit features

Two further features that may belong to this phase were also excavated. These comprised of sub-rectangular pits of moderate size which contained clay-like fills and infrequent sherds of twelfth-/thirteenth-century ceramics. It is possible that these features represent storage pits/structures similar to the subterranean level of the SFS (C573) described above. Pit C340 was located 9m to the northwest of the SFS on a similar alignment and may represent a feature in the same property plot (see fig. 3.3). It measured 2.27m long, 1.45m wide and 0.5m deep abutting the ditch C196 on its southern side. On the southern side of the pit, a ledge had been cut into the underlying subsoil and this ledge was lined with flat, unworked limestone slabs (C418). The function of this feature would appear to be as an access step into the pit or as shelving for storage of items off the ground. Pit C257 measured 1.6m long, 1.2m wide and 0.6m deep and cut into the lower levels of the ditch C196 (Plate 16 and 17). It contained a light brown silty clay fill (C258) not consistent with cess or tanning functions. Towards the centre of this pit, an oval, stone-lined, socket was excavated. This socket, while reminiscent of the cistern feature (C604) discussed above, did not appear to be watertight and no gully was observed feeding into it. The socket (C240) measured 0.82m long, 0.62m wide and 0.36m deep. It would appear that this socket once supported a wooden post that may have carried a simple roof or awning over the pit.

Aungier Street Phase II: 1150–1300

Ditch recut

Following a period of silting up and subsequent backfilling, the ditch C196, which must have persisted to some extent as a shallow channel or visible depression/boundary marker, was recut (C232) in the late twelfth or thirteenth century to an average depth of 0.73m. This recut contained a number of fills along its length relating to numerous episodes of kitchen midden deposition (C229, C263, C762). These midden deposits primarily comprised cockle shell with oyster, clay and mussel shells also present in much smaller quantities. Lenses of charcoal (C256, C261, C1318, C723) were also noted dispersed between the kitchen midden deposits. Frequent sherds of locally-produced and imported medieval wares dating to the twelfth/thirteenth centuries were retrieved from the various fills of this recut.

Cesspits

A number of cesspits of medieval date were excavated across the site (see fig. 3.3). In two instances, these pits cut through ditch C196 and the later medieval recut C232. The cesspits were variably sub-rectangular (C691, C853), circular (C492, C633, C1290) or oval (C802) in form. Some of the pits were heavily truncated but, judging by their relative depths and locations, it is likely that they were all originally of similar size and depth. All pits were filled with layered material comprising black cess material, brown organic fills, greenish brown noxious-smelling fills and frequent charcoal, wooden fragments and animal bone. A sample from the cesspit (C752, S241) contained moderate to large quantities of fruit seeds such as blackberry/raspberry, figs, strawberries, cherries and plums. These are typical plant remains that tend to be recovered from medieval and later cess deposits. There were also inclusions of fly puparia, suggesting that conditions were fairly foul, with flies breeding in the pit. There were also many fragments from beetles, clay and straw inclusions and fish bones, as well as moss fragments (moss was frequently used as a medieval equivalent of toilet paper).[16] The plant macrofossil assemblage from pit C1289 comprised large quantities of fruit remains, particularly elder. There were also small quantities of seeds from other fruits, including blackberry/raspberry, strawberry and pear/apple pips. Other seeds in this sample were from plants that grew in the surrounding area and they indicate the presence of common weeds of waste ground such as nettles, goosefoots and knotgrasses. Moss fragments were also present in the samples from this cesspit. All pits contained fragments of ceramic of twelfth- to fourteenth-century date.[17]

Table 3.1 Dimensions of cesspits from Aungier Street

CONTEXT	L(m)	W(m)	D(m)
C492	2.46	1.4	0.42
C633	2.9	1.08	0.68
C691	2.45	1.8	1.30
C802	3.6	1.08	0.74
C853	1.64	2.02	0.94
C1290	1.5	0.9	0.68

Boundary ditches

Two stretches of narrow ditch were excavated. The first of these, C496, survived beneath the footprint of No. 13 Stephen Street and ran for 3m to the northwest before passing the site boundary. To the south it was truncated by a seventeenth-century cesspit. The ditch had a maximum width of 1.37m and was 0.33m deep. A second ditch (C221), of similar proportions to C496, was identified further south where it cut through the upper layers of the recut C232. This ditch ran southeast until it intersected with a concrete foundation. This feature was up to 1.4m wide and 0.5m deep. An additional section of this ditch was identified on the eastern side of the site suggesting a total length of *c.*30m (see fig. 3.3).

16 Johnston, 'Organic plant remains, Aungier Street'. 17 Siobhan Scully, 'Medieval and post-medieval pottery report, Aungier Street' (unpublished report, 2020).

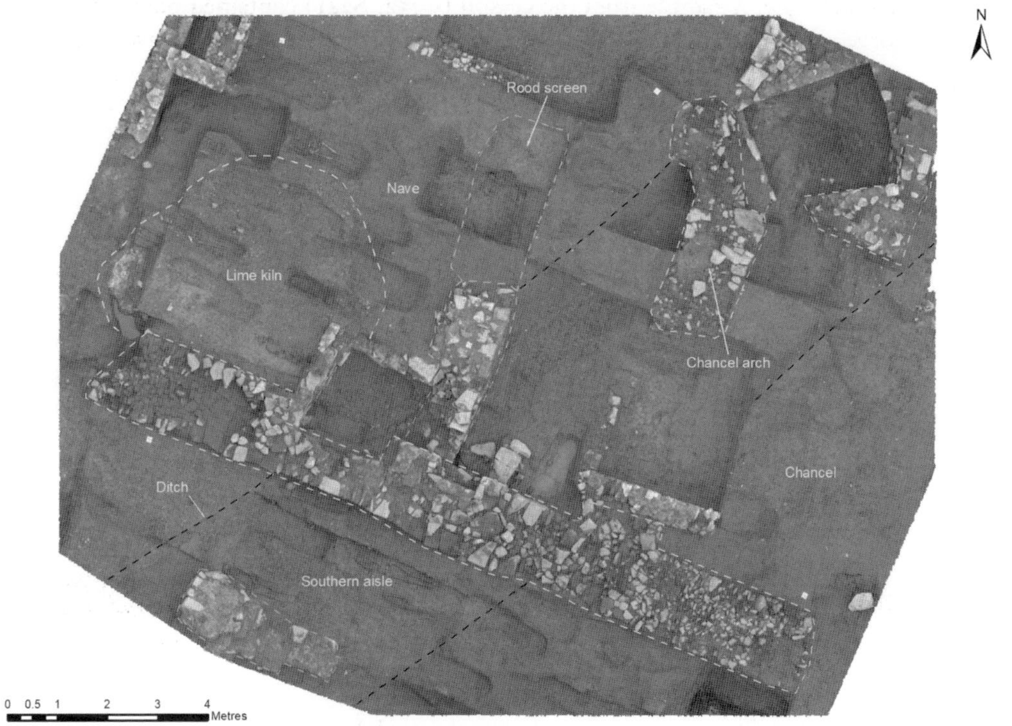

3.11 Geo-rectified orthophotograph showing St Peter's church

Aungier Street Phase III: 1300–1450

Excavation proved that the northwestern area of the site was the only area where medieval stratigraphy survived largely intact, although extensive intercutting and truncation by post-medieval features was evident.

St Peter's church

Several fragmentary medieval stone walls were identified in the northwestern corner of the site, immediately adjacent to the site excavated by Coughlan. The walls, though heavily disturbed in places by later cesspits and wells, are consistent with a large medieval building measuring 6.2m wide and surviving to a length of 13m (although the full extent was almost certainly longer). This structure is likely to represent the remains of a rebuild of St Peter's church, dating from the later fourteenth/fifteenth century and possibly relating to the impending repair recorded in 1370 (fig. 3.11).[18]

18 Clarke, *Dublin, Pt 1* (IHTA), p. 17; Nicholas Donnelly, *A short history of some Dublin parishes*, 4 vols (Dublin, 1905), ii, p. 135.

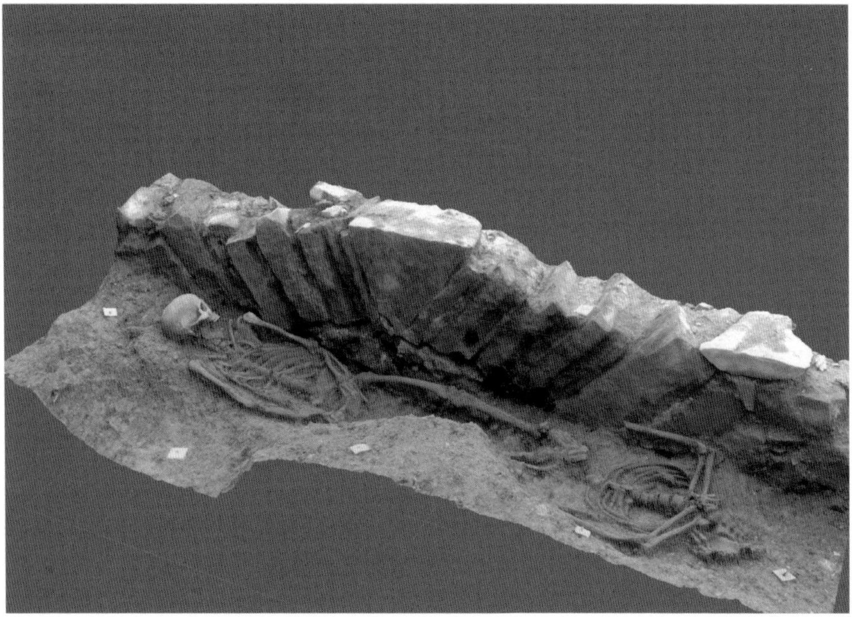

3.12 Photogrammetry model of structural arch in wall C365, *c.*fourteenth-century burial in foreground

This phase was dominated by a large east-southeast/west-southwest-running wall-foundation (C365). This structure (C365), which survived to a length of 13m and a maximum width of 1.8m, is likely to represent the southern church wall. The wall was cut away at its western end by a twentieth-century concrete basement which fronted onto Stephen Street. At its eastern end, the wall was truncated by a mid-twentieth-century ceramic sewer-pipe and associated manhole. The depth of the wall varied significantly from a single course of clay-bonded small- to medium-sized stones to a 1m deep section constructed with large limestone blocks bonded with a cream-coloured lime mortar. A structural arch survived towards the western end of the wall (fig. 3.12). This arch was found to span the soft fill of an earlier cesspit (C1290, described above) which in turn cut the backfilled ditch C196. The wall C365 was also found to cut the ditch C196 and the lime-kiln C1183. Where the wall intersected with these deep features, the wall coursing became deeper and extended to the natural subsoil.

Towards the eastern end of wall C365, a perpendicular, keyed-in wall was identified (C466). This section of wall was heavily truncated by several seventeenth-century cesspits. The central portion of the wall was robbed out to the depth of the lowest course and the cut had been infilled with rubble and broken mortar. The wall would have originally run for 6.2m before branching

3.13 Granite window-mullion with glazing groove and mason's mark

3.14 Sandstone base for freestanding column from internal furnishing such as a sedilia or tomb niche

3.15 Probable post-Reformation twin light, four-centred arch window head

3.16 Painted wall plaster fragments from the chancel area of St Peter's church

into a T-junction. A second structural arch had been constructed at the location of this junction to span a medieval cesspit; however, at this point a post-medieval tanning pit had largely cut through and destroyed the earlier features (see fig. 3.3). A later wall (C915), which ran parallel to C466, was considerably deeper at the southern end where it encountered the fills of the ditch C196. While this wall was medieval in date, it abutted the principal southern wall (C365), thereby post-dating it.

While no architectural fragments were recovered from the fabric of these walls, sixty-eight architectural fragments were recovered from seventeenth- to twentieth-century contexts. The majority of the fragments came from an eighteenth-century stone wall (C123) that overlay C365. These included several door jambs, mullions, fragments of window tracery, a column base, fragments with cusps and fragments of drip moulding surrounds. Stylistically, these fragments largely corresponded to a mid-Gothic style (cognate with the English 'decorated style') of *c.* fourteenth-/fifteenth-century date, although some were later, corresponding to 'perpendicular style' (figs 3.13–3.15).[19] All

19 For discussion of evolution of Gothic styles in Ireland and Dublin, see Tadhg O'Keeffe, *Medieval Irish buildings, 1100–1600* (Dublin, 2015), pp 37–50; Rachel Moss, 'Parish churches in Ireland 1350–1550' in P.S. Barnwell (ed.), *Places of worship in Britain and Ireland, 1350–1550* (Donnington, 2019), pp 180–1; Michael O'Neill, 'St Patrick's cathedral Dublin and its prebendal churches: Gothic architectural relationships' in Seán Duffy (ed.), *Medieval Dublin V* (Dublin, 2004), pp 243–76.

3.17 Selection of line-impressed and relief-decorated floor-tiles, vicinity of St Peter's church

masonry fragments from across the site were recovered from secondary, re-used contexts.

Further evidence for the former church included fragments of painted plaster which would have once adorned the interior of the church. Over sixty pieces of painted plaster were recovered from deposits within the footprint of the church building, including one fragment bearing a cross-crosslet (fig. 3.16). These red- and black-painted fragments find parallels from

3.18 Schematic plan of burials in Aungier St site and adjacent Stephen's St site relative to St Peter's church

fifteenth-century wall paintings at St Audoen's church in Dublin,[20] and at Kells priory, Co. Kilkenny.[21] In addition, multiple fragments of line-impressed floor-tile and medieval roof-tile were retrieved from deposits in and around the medieval walls (fig. 3.17).

20 Mary McMahon, *St Audoen's church, Cornmarket, Dublin: archaeology and architecture* (Dublin, 2006), p. 47. **21** Karena Morton, 'The wall painting fragments' in Tom Fanning and Miriam Clyne (eds), *Kells priory, Co. Kilkenny: archaeological excavations* (Dublin, 2007), pp 206–24.

3.19 Fourteenth-century burials showing level of preservation

Burials

A portion of the medieval graveyard of the parish of St Peter was found to survive in and around the footprint of the church. The burials surrounded the church walls and represent a continuation of the graveyard containing 150 burials excavated immediately to the west by Coughlan (fig. 3.18). A total of 224 burials were excavated and all were aligned west-northwest–east-southeast. Many of the skeletons were in a fragmentary condition due to truncation by later post-medieval structures or later burials; however the preservation levels were generally good (fig. 3.19). A large quantity of disarticulated human bone was retrieved during excavation (254 instances), reflective of the significant level of disturbance to the burial area. These deposits of *ex situ* bone appeared to have been frequently reinterred with some care within later graves, placed around the edges of the graves or upon the corpse. In excess of 200 iron coffin-nails were retrieved from graves and surrounding levels and in some instances, a coffin was inferred by the shape of the grave cut. No grave markers, or sockets that may have supported markers, were apparent. The uniform alignment of the burials, however, and the continual reuse of plots, in addition to the survival of thin ridges of relict topsoil and natural between rows of densely intercutting graves, indicates that the burials were consistently managed.

Nine burials were selected for dating and these showed a defined timeframe for the active life of the cemetery. Four of the burials returned dates clustered around the late thirteenth to late fourteenth century (*c.*1280–1380).[22] These dates correspond very closely to dates from two burials excavated immediately to the west by Coughlan.[23] Two burials dated from the early fourteenth to mid-fifteenth century,[24] while the remaining four burials dated from the mid-fifteenth to mid-seventeenth century.[25] All burials respected the principal walls of the church and all burials were interred following the orientation of the church wall C365. The density of burials within the footprint of the church, however, may suggest that the building was subjected to periods of inactivity during which time use of the cemetery intensified. The findings of Jennie Coughlan's osteological analysis regarding the burial tradition, the pathologies and demographic of the St Peter's population are published in this volume (below) but it may be worth remarking here on a number of burials of particular note:

Stone-lined graves

Two truncated lintelled graves (C501 and C554) were identified to the east of the church. Both of the graves had been heavily disturbed by construction in

22 UB 43078 2 sigma AD 1290–1399; UB 44296 2 sigma, AD 1283–1388; UB 44297 2 sigma AD 1297–1395; UB 44298 2 sigma, AD 1275–1380. **23** UB 44294 2 sigma, AD 1280–1388; UB 44295 2 sigma, AD 1280–1388. **24** UB 44303 2 sigma, AD 1310–1412; UB 44302 2 sigma, AD 1423–53. **25** UB 41145 2 sigma, AD 1440–1617; UB 44300 2 sigma, AD 1458–1634; UB

the 1950s. Both graves were constructed of flat limestone slabs, set end on end and bonded with white lime mortar. In both cases, a 'pillow' of stone and mortar had been constructed at the western end of the grave. One of the graves retained three large lintels (C501) but, upon excavation, modern repointing of the grave with cement mortar was observed on the interior face illustrating that the grave had been emptied, repaired and the bones reinterred *c.*1950. Two similar graves were identified on the adjacent plot by Coughlan.[26]

Violence: sharp force trauma?
A disarticulated skull (DSk 197), recorded immediately northwest of the church footprint in C1009, exhibited damage that is likely to derive from a blow from an edged weapon.

Aungier Street Phase IV: 1450–1600

Perpendicular-style gothic architecture
Several architectural fragments corresponding to this period were also retrieved from the site, namely, a twin light, four-centred arch window head, closely paralleling the style of doorway and stone type of St Audoen's and the cusped edge of an ogee-headed window and several hood fragments that are almost identical to a window of fifteenth-/sixteenth-century date from St Audoen's. A column base of geometric shape comparable to fifteenth- or sixteenth-century examples of freestanding columns either from cloisters, tomb recesses or a sedilia was also recovered (see fig. 3.14). A later building phase, most likely in the sixteenth century, was attested to by the presence of three fragments from door or window openings bearing casement moulding.[27] Danielle O'Donovan has pointed out that casement mouldings are rare in an Irish context,[28] and Rachel Moss writes that the rupture between the English and Irish traditions from the later fourteenth century meant that the repertoire of the perpendicular style Gothic was not adopted wholesale in Ireland.[29] However, the recent recovery of two fragments of casement moulding from excavations at the site of St Mary's abbey, Dublin,[30] suggests that perhaps the lost Dublin foundations were receptive to some of these motifs in the fifteenth and sixteenth centuries.

44301 2 sigma, AD 1487–1636. **26** Coughlan, 'Excavations at St Peter's church', pp 30–1. **27** Richard Morris, 'The development of later Gothic mouldings in England, *c.*1250–1400: Part I', *Architectural History*, 21 (1978), 18–57, at 39; and idem, 'An English glossary of medieval mouldings: with an introduction to mouldings *c.*1040–1240', *Architectural History*, 35 (1992), 1–17, at 12; Danielle O'Donovan, 'Building the Butler lordship, 1405–*c.*1552' (PhD, TCD, 2008), p. 173 for discussion of the perpendicular style in the Pale. **28** http://www.tara.tcd.ie/handle/2262/25950. **29** Moss, 'Parish churches', p. 181. **30** Work on this assemblage, excavated by Ed O'Donovan, is ongoing.

3.20 Armoured burial, conceivably a galloglass of Silken Thomas, 1534

Burials

As outlined above, burial within the graveyard of St Peter's church continued throughout this phase, up until the deconsecration of the ground in the later seventeenth century.

SK 128: Armoured skeleton?

To the immediate northwest of the church footprint, a burial was encountered with corroded ferrous accretions across the torso, shoulders and parts of the skull (SK 128). The skeleton was truncated above the pelvis by post-medieval activity, removing the forearms, hands, pelvis and lower limbs. The skeletal remains exposed on-site comprised a poorly preserved cranium, mandible, humeri, ribs and vertebrae (in section). While the accreted ferrous material was generally formless and in a very poor state of preservation, it was possible to ascertain several shapes, notably at the neck and shoulders. It is possible that the corroded metal across the torso represents the remains of a mail shirt or banded iron armour, while the objects at the neck and shoulders may represent components of a gorget and spaldrons respectively. It is notable that the corrosion suggested that the lower arms were not covered, a feature of galloglass mail (fig. 3.20). This burial was dated to 1440–1617.[31]

Southern aisle

A discontinuous stretch of heavily mortared wall survived along the southern limit of Yard 1. This feature (C388), like C365, represented the sub-foundation levels of a wall which was constructed deeper over underlying softer deposits. The wall survived as a narrower eastern portion and a more substantial western portion constructed of limestone blocks bonded with abundant cream-coloured lime mortar. These wall fragments correspond to areas where the wall traversed softer, underlying, fills. Both wall fragments were observed to cut burials as well as the graveyard soils, indicating that they are later than the initial burial phase.

GEORGE'S STREET

Despite extensive development of the site in the late nineteenth century including deep cellaring along South Great George's Street, some areas of dense, stratified archaeology survived, particularly in the southern portion of the site along Stephen Street. This southern limit was defined from the late eleventh/early twelfth century by substantial ditches which were maintained and slightly amended over the course of several centuries. It is likely that the earliest phase of these ditches paralleled a small ravine/inlet that emptied into the tidal pool of Dubhlinn and corresponds to pre-Anglo-Norman defences identified *c.*30m to the west by Linzi Simpson.[32] For a brief time in the later medieval period (*c.*1500), the majority of these ditches were backfilled and a structure built upon a foundation of driven stakes was erected. Soon after, this

31 2 sigma date quoted, Chronos UB 41145. 32 Linzi Simpson, 'John Rocque's map of Dublin (1756): a modern source for medieval property-boundaries' in Seán Duffy (ed.),

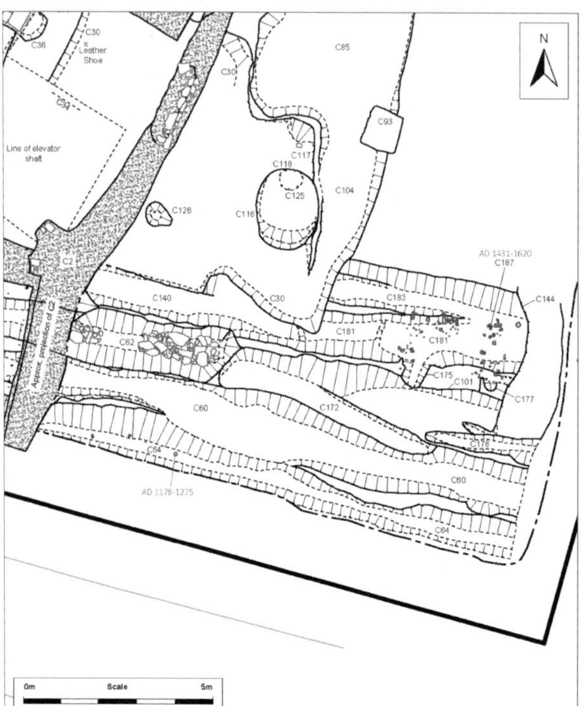

3.21 (*above*) George's Street site boundary ditches, facing east

3.22 Intercutting ditches and driven stakes in southern part of George's Street site

structure was cut away by a later ditch re-establishing the alignment of the earlier boundary. This boundary remained open into the seventeenth century.

Some disturbed sections of shallow north–south-running boundary ditches and two large pits dating broadly to the thirteenth century may indicate that plots were established on the site, running southwards from a street frontage somewhere to the north (Fade Street?), although this is not supported by the cartographic evidence. Alternatively, these pits could represent the beginning of a tanning enterprise on what was marginal ground outside of the city walls. Evidence for the continuation of this tanning activity from the sixteenth through to the eighteenth century was identified in the central area of the site.

George's Street Phase I: 1100–1250

Southern boundary ditches

A series of dense, parallel, intercutting east–west-running ditches and recuts characterized the southern area of the site (fig. 3.21). Potentially the earliest feature on the site was a large ditch (C64) that ran east–west along the extreme southern edge of the site, lying partially beneath Stephen Street. It was cut by the adjacent ditch C60. The remnants of a possible palisade in the base of the ditch were suggested by the presence of a row of four upright timbers with sharpened ends driven into the base of the cut (fig. 3.22). A sample from one of the timbers failed attempted dendrochronological dating but was subsequently dated using AMS to cal. AD 1178–1275.[33] An abundance of mostly locally-produced medieval ceramic with date-ranges spanning the late twelfth to fourteenth century were retrieved from several ditch fills. Two iron nails and an unidentified stone object, possibly a handle of a stone water-trough, were found in the ditch as well as a small amount of leather fragments, comprising one decorated and one undecorated leather strap (fig. 3.23), a possible shoe upper or vamp, and several fragments of two shoe soles. One of the soles has a pointed toe, narrow waist and rounded heel, comparable to late thirteenth-century shoes found at other excavations in Ireland.[34]

Specialist analysis showed that the ditch contained organic remains from common weeds of damp meadows (such as buttercups) as well as weeds of disturbed places (nettles, bramble and fat hen). Uncharred remains of goosefoots, sloe and thistles were identified as well. Charred remains included apple pips, legumes, grasses and cereals such as oat and wheat.[35] The ditch also contained a small amount of animal bone, with seven fragments determined to species. Cattle, pig and sheep/goat bone were identified, along with oyster, cockle, whelk and land snail shells.[36] The remains of two insects were found in

Medieval Dublin VII (Dublin, 2006), pp 113–51, at pp 125–7. 33 2 sigma date, Vilnius Laboratory ref.: FTMC-GB66-20. 34 Siobhan Scully, 'Leather artefacts and leatherworking report, 41–46 South Great Georges Street, Dublin' (unpublished report). 35 Penny Johnston, 'Organic and charred plant remains report, 41–46 George's Street, Dublin' (unpublished report). 36 Margaret McCarthy, 'Faunal remains report, 41–46

3.23 Decorated leather strap with castle motifs

fill C69, comprising a dung beetle and a 'rove beetle' species, as well as the larvae of a water flea species. This small assemblage might point to wet settlement material, possibly suggesting that slow-flowing water had been incorporated into the ditch.[37]

A short section of clay-filled, east–west-running ditch (C184), 5m north of and parallel to C64, was cut by ditch C181 and later tanning activity. This is the northernmost of the densely intercutting east–west-running ditches along the southern side of the site. Numbers C140, C165 and C181 all describe the same clay-filled, east–west-running boundary/drainage ditch, immediately south of and cutting C183. This ditch extended across the full width of the site, although it had been cut away by Victorian wall-foundations for a section of its length towards the west end of the site, and by sixteenth- and seventeenth-century tanning activity in the eastern part of the site. There was some evidence of silting and gradual backfill in the western side of the ditch but, at its eastern end, the ditch had been backfilled in a single event with

George's Street, Dublin' (unpublished report). 37 David Smith, 'The insect remains from 41–46 South Great St George's Street, Dublin' (unpublished report).

compacted clay. A timber pile structure (C187) was later constructed on this fill.

Medieval pottery, dating between the late twelfth to fourteenth century, was retrieved from several ditch fills. These were mostly locally produced wares, with three sherds representing English wares and one representing French ware.[38] A soil sample was taken from fill C147, and was found to contain no charred seeds, although uncharred seeds from brambles or raspberries were noted.[39] The same fill also contained a small amount of indeterminate animal bones, some of which probably originate from a medium-sized mammal such as a sheep, goat or pig.[40]

Plot boundaries

Former plot boundaries on the site were difficult to discern, but three heavily truncated narrow and shallow ditches are likely to represent the remains of former north–south-running plot boundaries. Ditch C178 was a shallow, narrow cut similar in dimensions to C21 and C175, occurring at the eastern limit of site and terminating close to the timber structure C187. This ditch was cut by both C60 and C155, and represents one of the earlier features in this area. The narrow ditch C21 was sealed by medieval garden soil C6, and contained a fill similar in composition (C22), although slightly darker and with higher occurrence of charcoal and marine shell fragments. The gully was heavily disturbed on its eastern side by the foundation cut associated with the Drury Lane carpark. Sherds of medieval and post-medieval ceramic, and an iron nail were retrieved from the fill of this feature. A short section of narrow, north–south-running gully (C175) followed a similar alignment to C21 further north. This feature was heavily truncated to the north and south by later ditches C181 and C155.

Cess/tanning pits

Two deep, oval pits were identified that had both been reused later (*c.*1600) for tanning activities but which had most likely originally functioned as cesspits in the rear plots of houses that occurred somewhere off site to the north. The deep oval pit (C33) was filled with black, odorous clays suggestive of tanning activity. The fills of this pit (C47–C49) contained a range of locally-produced ceramic ware dating from the late twelfth to fourteenth centuries. Several tile-fragments were found in fill C47 as well, one belonging to a medieval tile and five to possible post-medieval wall tiles. Eight bone fragments were retrieved from the same fill, representing cattle, sheep/goat and pig. The upper levels of the deep oval pit C118 were cut away by the large interlocking tanning pits C30/C117 of *c.*1600 date. In its size, shape and orientation it resembled pit

38 Scully, 'Ceramic finds, George's St'. 39 Johnston, 'Organic remains, George's St'. 40 McCarthy, 'Faunal Remains, George's St'.

C33. It was positioned at the same distance north (*c.*8m) of the Stephen Street façade. The fills (C119–C121) were similar in composition to those of C33. Fill C119 contained locally-produced pottery dating to the same period, from the late twelfth to the fourteenth century.

Table 3.2 Dimensions of cesspits George's Street

CONTEXT	L(m)	W(m)	D(m)
C33	2.4	2.2	1.72
C118	1.8	1.5	1.14

George's Street Phase II: 1250–1450

Numbers C62 and C122 describe the same clay-filled, east–west-running boundary/drainage ditch, immediately south of and cutting C140. This ditch extended across the full width of the site. It had been partially cut away by Victorian wall-foundations for a section of its length towards the centre of the site. There was some evidence of silting and gradual backfill at its western end, and a deposit of stones lined the base at its eastern end. It is unclear whether these stones were the initial action of a backfilling event or if they were intended to assist drainage. This ditch did not extend all the way to the eastern boundary of the site (as C140 and C183 had), but stopped at C172. The ditch fills contained a large amount of medieval pottery sherds and other medieval finds. The pottery dated between the late eleventh and fourteenth century, with a focus on the thirteenth century. Most of the ceramic was locally produced but some English and French wares were present. A copper alloy stick-pin of similar date to the pottery, a glazed medieval roof-tile, and a possible medieval iron nail were retrieved from fill C100. A sample was taken from C123, and contained uncharred plant remains of fruits, as well as weeds from the goosefoot, daisy and sedge families. Charred plant remains included a fragment from a cleaver, an indeterminate cereal grain, and an indeterminate nut kernel. Twenty-five bone fragments were retrieved from the fills of the ditch. The species identified are cattle, chicken and geese, as well as one adult male goat. The cattle bones show signs of butchery/processing, and the goat is represented by a complete chopped-off horn-core, likely associated with horn-working. The remaining fragments are indeterminate, with one calcined bone present.[41]

Feature C60 represents a large east–west-orientated ditch extending across the length of the site. It ran parallel to C62 and C64 immediately to the south, cutting both ditches. At its eastern end, the basal fills of C60 were cut by later medieval ditches C172 and C155, which followed the line of C62. A later recut

41 McCarthy, 'Faunal remains, George's St'.

of C60 (C101) cut the upper fills of C60, C172 and C155, refreshing the original line of C60. The ditch fills contained a range of ceramics with a combined date-range of the late twelfth to fourteenth century. The largest amount of medieval pottery was retrieved from fill C157. Most ceramic was locally produced, with only a few English and French wares noted. Three medieval tile-fragments were also found in C157, one belonging to a glazed floor-tile. Samples were taken from fill C61, C67, and C157. These contained both uncharred and charred plant remains. The uncharred remains included seeds from buttercups, nettles, goosefoots, raspberry/blackberry, elder, and nipplewort, with a woody thorn found in C157. Charred remains included a grain of naked wheat from C61, and two indeterminate grains from C67 and C157. The original ditch also contained a small amount of animal-bone fragments, most of which were indeterminate. The four diagnostic elements are all from cow, and show signs of marrow extraction. In addition to this, the ditch recut contained the largest animal-bone assemblage on-site, dominated by sheep/goat and cattle remains. These elements represent waste from butchery and possibly tannery activity. The cattle and sheep/goat were likely transported into Dublin and slaughtered locally. The recut also yielded the only identified horse-bone fragments on-site, as well as two bones from a whippet-sized dog.

George's Street Phase III: 1450–1600

The foundation level for a square/rectangular building partially survived in the southeast part of the site. This structure (C187) comprised clusters of sharpened squared-off stakes arranged in a broadly U-shaped plan (see fig. 3.22). The southern side of the structure was cut away by the later medieval ditch C101. The structure was also cut to the east by a post-medieval or modern ditch (C144). An outlier stake to the east of this cut suggests that the structure was once considerably larger. The stakes were driven into the compact clay fills of the ditches C181/C140 and C183. One piece of locally produced medieval pottery, dating to the late twelfth to fourteenth century, was retrieved from fill C173.

Analysis of the stakes identified eight native Irish tree/shrub taxa from young to semi-mature woodlands. The most common was oak, followed by birch, willow, ash, holly, hazel and oak/alder. This shows that the wood was selected from tall canopy oak and ash woodlands, as well as scrubland areas and wetland environments. Overall, the woodworking techniques used were standard methods evidenced in Ireland since prehistoric times. Posts and stakes were generally made from small- to medium-sized branch wood trimmed to shallow points. Most stakes were chisel pointed, followed by wedge and pencil pointed. Facets, when present, were generally large and flat, indicating the use of a large metal axe. Cutting angles were generally shallow, and the stakes were split in a variety of ways.[42] One of the timbers (T64) returned a 2 sigma calibrated radiocarbon date of AD 1431–1620,[43] dating this structure to the later medieval period.

DISCUSSION

St Peter's church: eleventh to fourteenth century

Before deciphering the excavated elements of St Peter's church, an entirely other, almost invisible building must be considered – that being the earlier structure that stood on-site in the eleventh century. Given its dimensions, the lime-kiln excavated on-site was undoubtedly used for the construction of something sizeable. The logic of locating lime-kilns as close as possible to the building project is self-evident and is a practice seen elsewhere in medieval Dublin and one that continued into the early modern period.[44] Substantial building work in stone in this period of Dublin's history was limited to the town defences – which did not extend as far as Stephen Street – and to churches and it appears almost certain that the lime produced in this kiln was destined to be mixed with aggregate and water to bond the stone walls of the original St Peter's church. The use of the word 'original' here is open to question, however: given that no artefacts or dates earlier than the eleventh century have been recovered from any of the excavations in the immediate vicinity of St Peter's, it seems unlikely that this stone church replaced an earlier wooden built structure.

The AMS date of the lime-kiln (AD 1028–1155) puts the construction of this earlier church at the cusp of a building boom which would result in Dublin transitioning rapidly from what appears in the sources, some might argue, as a town ambivalent to Christianization in the late tenth/early eleventh century into an ecclesiastical centre actively vying for primacy of the Irish church. Dublin by the 1130s boasted, by far, the densest concentration of churches on the island with the walled town and immediate suburbs served by more than twenty foundations.[45] In the immediate vicinity of St Peter's, there stood the church of St Michael le Pole (125m northwest), St Brigid's church (*c.*230m west-northwest), St Patrick's *ad insula* (*c.*330m southwest) and Christ Church cathedral (*c.*370m northwest). Other churches such as St Martin's, St

42 Ellen O'Carroll, 'Timber and woodworking report, 41–46 South Great George's Street' (unpublished report). 43 2 sigma date, Vilnius, FTMC-VG62-1. 44 See Seán Duffy and Linzi Simpson, 'The hermits of St Augustine in medieval Dublin: their history and archaeology' in Bradley et al. (eds), *Dublin in the medieval world*, pp 202–48, at pp 229–32; for an eighteenth-century example of this near Dublin, see Judith Carroll, 'Corduff Park Licence number: 05E0360': https://excavations.ie/report/2009/Dublin/0020637/ accessed 13 August 2021. 45 Clarke, *Dublin, Pt 1* (IHTA), map 1; Tomás Ó Carragáin, *Churches in early medieval Ireland: architecture, ritual, and memory* (New Haven, 2011), p. 236.

Werburgh's, St George's and St Paul's appeared within a radius of 250m of the site in the later eleventh or early twelfth century.

From the excavated evidence what, if anything, can be proposed of the form, layout and decorative features of this church? The question suffers at once from too little comparative evidence from within the Hiberno-Scandinavian towns and too much from the Dublin hinterland, Dublin having the densest concentration of pre-Romanesque stone mortared churches in the country.[46] The form of these churches is well known from sites such as Kill o' the Grange, Dalkey Island and Rathmichael, but do these conservative churches of Irish style represent the type of architecture that would have been adopted in Dublin itself? Ó Carragáin is of the opinion that churches within the port town would have employed forms more expressive of the degree of cultural separateness, something that might well have been diluted in the rural hinterland to the south given the intermixing with the native Irish.[47] Nessa Walsh has argued on the basis of AMS dates that these hinterland buildings date to the tenth century, predating the Dublin churches and belonging to a separate architectural tradition.[48] Tadhg O'Keeffe, among others, has identified Dublin as the likely landfall of Romanesque architecture in Ireland.[49] Several writers have also suggested that the building boom undertaken at Glendalough in the years around 1100 and the multiplicity of forms that appear (nave and chancel churches, arches, engaged round towers) arose as a direct response to innovative buildings that appeared in Dublin in the later eleventh century.[50]

The survival of decorated cross slabs across County Dublin is relevant here as very recognizable styles that correspond to defined areas of Dublin are apparent. The Rathdown slabs, as described by Healy, exist in relation to the architecturally conservative churches of south Co. Dublin.[51] They are without parallel in Ireland and are constrained to a small geographical area between the mountains and the sea of south Dublin/north Wicklow. Healy's 'Type A' slabs that occur primarily in the city itself display motifs that find parallels in the Isle of Man and in Wales. I have pointed to a slab from Fingal which bears stylistic comparison to the 'Type A' slabs but is much more ornate with close parallels at Begerin, near Wexford town and across the Isle of Man.[52] This is interesting considering that there are no pre-Romanesque mortared stone

46 Gill Boazman, 'Material culture and identity in the southern hinterland of Hiberno-Scandinavian Dublin' in Seán Duffy (ed.), *Medieval Dublin XVII* (Dublin, 2019), pp 15–62, at p. 28. 47 Ó Carragáin, *Churches*, pp 239–40. 48 For example, Kill o' the Grange, Dalkey Island, Tully, Killiney: see Nessa Walsh, 'Pre-Romanesque churches in County Dublin and its hinterland' in Seán Duffy (ed.), *Medieval Dublin VIII* (Dublin, 2008), pp 21–35, at p. 34. 49 O'Keeffe, *Medieval Irish buildings*, p. 27; Ó Carragáin, *Churches*, p. 236. 50 For a full discussion, see Ó Carragáin, *Churches*, pp 235–53. 51 Paddy Healy, *Pre-Norman grave-slabs and cross-inscribed stones of the Dublin area* (Dublin, 2009), pp 49–67. 52 Paul Duffy, 'The Balgriffin cross: Fingal's answer to the Rathdown slab', *Archaeology*

3.24 Architectural fragment with roll moulding (to left) built into late seventeenth-century wall

churches surviving in Fingal, but three churches with early and innovative Romanesque elements that might be significant not only in visualizing the form of Dublin's eleventh-century churches, but also to the story of the landfall of Romanesque architecture in Ireland. These are the church of Kilmacnessan on Ireland's Eye, St Patrick's church on St Patrick's Island off Skerries,[53] and St Doulagh's church, Kinsealy. All three churches have vaulted elements while the church of Kilmacnessan has a Romanesque door with an arch, inclined jambs with imposts and once had an engaged round tower, rising from the chancel vault.[54] St Patrick's church has two round-headed east windows within a vaulted chancel and St Doulagh's has a substantial and

Ireland, 32:2 (2018), 30–4. **53** Michael Ryan, Kevin Mooney, Frank Prendergast and Barry Masterson, 'Church Island: a description' in Ailbhe MacShamhráin (ed.), *The island of St Patrick: church and ruling dynasties in Fingal and Meath, 400–1148* (Dublin, 2004), pp 90–106. Evidence of a fourth such church at St Canice's, Finglas has recently been identified by the author: Paul Duffy, 'Architectural stone report, St Canice's church, Finglas' (unpublished report for Dublin City Council). **54** Robert Cochrane, 'Notes on the ecclesiastical antiquities in the parish of Howth, Co. Dublin', *JRSAI*, 3:4 (1893), 386–407; Clare Crowley, 'Cultural heritage study: Ireland's Eye North County Dublin' (2017,

notably steep barrel-vaulted and stone pitched roof.[55] Along with the chancel arches at Palmerstown and Killiney, this repertoire of elements are the best tools we have for visualizing what the late eleventh-/early twelfth-century St Peter's church may have looked like.

One unassuming architectural fragment retrieved from a late seventeenth-century wall built over the church comprised a roughly-shaped block of granite with a small angle roll on one corner (fig. 3.24). The angle roll is among the simplest and most widespread mouldings in Romanesque architecture. While not entirely diagnostic given that simple angle rolls persist in Gothic architecture, the character and crudeness of this piece is at variance with the crisp and highly ornamented mouldings of the rest of the assemblage. The roll itself is shallow, unlike the deeper Gothic mouldings, and has an almost waxen smoothness of a type encountered on tombs or doorways that have been subjected to centuries of compulsive human touch. This piece more than the other architectural fragments suggests itself as potentially contemporary with the eleventh-century lime-kiln. An angle roll of similar type is evident on the surviving west doorway at Sheepstown (Co. Kilkenny) with inclined jambs and impost mouldings. This door is very similar to Myshall (Co. Carlow), although the former does not have an angle roll and both doorways are closely paralleled in the Kilmacnessan west doorway on Ireland's Eye. Leask favoured a date in the eleventh century for both Sheepstown and Myshal.[56] Myshal is located *c.*50km inland from Wexford along the Slaney Valley and Sheepstown is *c.*30km inland from Waterford up the Nore Valley. It is conceivable, given their close similarities with Kilmacnessan, that these doorways represent a dissemination of Romanesque features inland from the Hiberno-Norse port towns of Waterford and Wexford.

Another equally slight, though potentially crucial, piece of evidence for this earlier church was found at the very bottom of the large ditch C196 close to the location of the later church. This was in the form of a curved earthenware roof-tile. The retrieval of this tile provides a tangible link to Ó Néill's ditch on the opposite side of Aungier Street, from which a similar curved earthenware tile was the only ceramic find in a presumed eleventh-century ditch that may constitute a continuation of C196.[57] The earliest accepted use of such tiles in Dublin dates to the 1020s and they have been linked to an early building phase at Christ Church.[58] This find, at the base of the near contemporary ditch that consciously kinks around the mid-to-late eleventh-century lime-kiln, may therefore indicate that the early St Peter's church was roofed in exotic, imported red earthenware tile.

unpublished report), pp 10–13. 55 Harold Leask, *Irish churches and monastic buildings* (Dundalk, 1955), i, p. 60; Rachel Moss, 'St Doulagh's church', *Irish Arts Review*, 20:2 (2002), 122–5. 56 Leask, *Irish churches*, i, p. 109. 57 Ó Néill, 'Excavations at Longford Street Little', p. 78. 58 Clare McCutcheon, *Medieval pottery from Wood Quay, Dublin: the 1974–6 waterfront excavations* (Dublin, 2006), p. 179; Mary McMahon, 'The architecture and archaeology of St Audoen's church, Cornmarket' (PhD, TCD, 2002), p. 98.

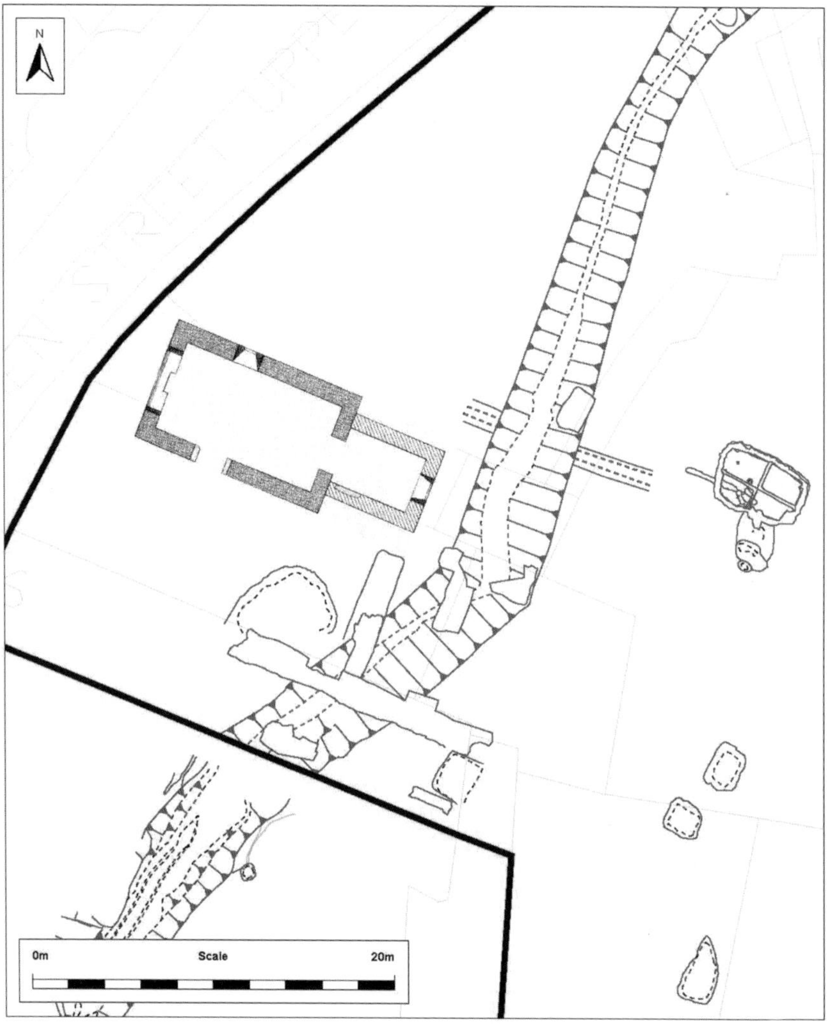

3.25 Plan of Palmerstown parish church (*c.*1100) overlain over possible location of eleventh-century St Peter's church

In estimating the possible dimensions/floorplan of this early church, there are three structures that can be drawn upon. Firstly, the fourteenth-century church (discussed below) which may have been added to the original church as an undifferentiated extension. Secondly, the church of St Michael le Pole located 125m to the north, where excavations have revealed the footprint of the church. And thirdly, Palmerstown, the closest example of a standing pre-Anglo-Norman church. As at St Peter's, evidence for lime-working was identified at St Michael le Pole. This was in the form of a large slaking pit located to the south of the associated graveyard and which returned an AMS 2 sigma date of AD 1022–1164, strikingly similar to that of St Peter's lime-kiln (AD 1028–1155). Edmond O'Donovan states that 'It is highly likely that the lime-production complex found in the Golden Lane excavation was used to build the stone church [St Michael le Pole's] at the site in the eleventh century'.[59] The location of the Michel le Pole lime-kiln relative to the church is also important as this seems to have been at the southern limit of the graveyard. There was no enclosing ditch or any discernible bank or palisade around St Michael le Pole's. Given that ditch C196 kinks around the St Peter's lime-kiln, it can be inferred that this also marked the southern extent of the St Peter's graveyard in the later eleventh century.[60] In situating the floorplan of Palmerstown in the area skirted by the ditch C196 and avoiding the lime-kiln, it is conceivable that the church sat within a space defined to the north by Stephen Street and to the south by the ditch C196 (fig. 3.25).

There was no evidence to indicate that this proposed eleventh-century church was replaced until the end of the fourteenth century. References to St Peter's church (sometimes St Peter's 'on the Hill') from 1179 and continuing through the thirteenth century suggest that this eleventh-century church, presumably with some modification, functioned as the church of the parish of St Peter until the later fourteenth century.[61] The use of pre-Anglo-Norman churches in Dublin is attested to at St Patrick's *ad insula* where the early church persisted and Michael O'Neill observes that 'the canons were apparently satisfied to use the pre-Anglo-Norman parish church of St Patrick's *ad insula* for more than thirty-five years'.[62] Antiquarian images of St Michael le Pole's make it clear that the eleventh-century church was used throughout the medieval period and likely retained some of its original form into the eighteenth century.[63] It is likely therefore that the architectural fragments recovered during the excavation, specifically those bearing thirteenth-century mouldings,[64]

59 Edmond O'Donovan, 'The Irish, the Vikings and the English: new archaeological evidence from excavations at Golden Lane, Dublin' in Seán Duffy (ed.), *Medieval Dublin VIII* (Dublin, 2008), pp 36–130, at p. 60. **60** The dating of the burials on-site shows a general trend for the earliest burials to be located north of the ditch, although none antedated the mid-thirteenth century. **61** When the parish was established remains a matter of some debate: see Adrian Empey, 'The formation and development of intramural churches and communities in medieval Dublin in a European context' in Bradley et al. (eds), *Dublin in the medieval world*, pp 249–76, at pp 251–3; Edel Bhreathnach, 'Saints' dedications and the ecclesiastical landscape of Hiberno-Norse Dublin: Irish, Scandinavian and others' in Seán Duffy (ed.), *Medieval Dublin XVIII* (Dublin, 2020), pp 143–68; Tomas Ó Carragáin, 'Church buildings and pastoral care in early medieval Ireland' in Elizabeth FitzPatrick and Raymond Gillespie (eds), *The parish in medieval and early modern Ireland: community, territory and building* (Dublin, 2006), pp 91–123. **62** O'Neill, 'St Patrick's cathedral', p. 249. **63** Gowen, 'Excavations at St Michael le Pole'. **64** Several finds parallel pieces from Christ Church which were identified by Moss as nave arcade voussoirs: Rachel Moss, 'Tales from the crypt: the medieval stonework of Christ Church cathedral, Dublin' in Seán Duffy (ed.), *Medieval Dublin III* (Dublin, 2002), pp 95–114, at pp 106–7.

represent phases of remodelling to the eleventh-century church.[65] Such remodelling of doorways and window opes is similar to that evident at St Audoen's church throughout the thirteenth century.

The Dubhlinn *'enclosure'/Dublin's southern and eastern suburbs*

As outlined at the beginning of this paper, the purported pre-Viking Dubhlinn ecclesiastical foundation has long been equated with a large pear-shaped entity fossilized in the streetscape around Aungier Street,[66] evident from at least the seventeenth century. Several excavations within this purported enclosure have identified substantial stretches of ditch and these findings have been used by subsequent writers to both support,[67] and refute,[68] the identification of this site with the eighth-century Dubhlinn foundation. Given its sharp turn to the east along Longford Street, Coughlan concluded that the stretch of ditch he excavated did not relate to a pear-shaped enclosure but rather, in conjunction with the stretch excavated by Ó Néill on the east side of Aungier Street, represented a smaller enclosure centred on St Peter's church, potentially sited in the northwest corner of the supposed large pear-shaped enclosure.[69] Duddy preferred the interpretation that the 'pear shape' was the result of streets developing around three separate enclosures, namely an enclosure around St Peter's church, one around St Stephen's church on the east side of Aungier Street and a southern enclosure surrounding the thirteenth-century Carmelite foundation of Whitefriars.[70]

The excavations at Aungier Street have shown with some certainty that the large ditch traversing the site (an extension of Coughlan's ditch) forms neither a part of a large pear-shaped enclosure, nor part of an enclosure centred upon St Peter's church. The ditch has been dated stratigraphically, artefactually, and through AMS dating (1046–1253) to the later eleventh/early twelfth century. While this puts the ditch in the same timeframe as the lime-kiln and presumed first phase of St Peter's church, the return of the ditch along Longford Street identified by Coughlan shows that the area enclosed by the ditch was to the south and east, and that the site of the original location of St Peter's church was consciously avoided and excluded from the circuit of the ditch.

65 Petrographic analysis confirmed that some fragments were of Dundry stone, a building material commonly employed at this time: Paul Duffy and Sara Pavia, 'Quarrying the past: petrographic analysis of Dublin's medieval building stone' (unpublished report submitted to the Royal Irish Academy). **66** Myles V. Ronan, 'Lazar houses of St Lawrence and St Stephen in mediaeval Dublin' in John Ryan (ed.), *Féil-sgríbhinn Eóin Mhic Néill: essays and studies presented to Professor Eoin MacNeill* (Dublin, 1940), pp 480–9, at p. 482. **67** Clarke, *Dublin, Pt 1* (IHTA); and idem, 'Christian cults and cult centres in Hiberno-Norse Dublin' in MacShamhráin (ed.), *The island of St Patrick*, pp 140–58, at p. 148. **68** Cathal Duddy, 'The role of St Thomas's abbey in the early development of Dublin's western suburb' in Seán Duffy (ed.), *Medieval Dublin IV* (Dublin, 2003), pp 79–97. **69** Coughlan, 'Excavations at St Peter's church', pp 12–14; Ó Néill, 'Excavations at Longford Street Little'. **70** Duddy, 'The role of St Thomas's abbey', pp 79–97.

Given that the sunken-floored structure (SFS) identified to the southeast of the church, squarely within the area enclosed by the ditch, is of comparable late eleventh-century date, it is likely that the ditch represents a feature that was intended to define and protect a secular space, probably a southern suburb of the pre-Anglo-Norman town. The identification of a long-standing boundary defined by a ditch and palisade along the southern side of the George's Street site is suggestive of settlement within a comparable eastern suburban enclosure at this time, indicating that settlement outside of the walled circuit of the town was considerably more extensive than previously thought.[71] The excavation of a terrace of eleventh- to thirteenth-century houses at Dean Street, *c.*550m to the southwest, the identification of a tenth-century structure fronting Thomas Street *c.*750m to the northwest and the presence of houses,[72] plots, ditches and streets north of the Liffey at this time, further illustrates the extent of suburban development.[73] Early dates retrieved from the graveyard of the abbey of St Thomas are a further indication of well-established communities outside of the walls, possibly along the early route known as Slige Mór.[74]

Defence was of crucial importance at this time as Dublin became a requisite possession for those with pretensions of high-kingship and several attacks on Dublin are recorded in the annals. It is tempting to associate the complete burning of the SFS with one of these events, particularly as several houses excavated by Hayden at Werburgh Street had been burned in the late tenth/eleventh century.[75] A drainage function was also clearly intended with the Aungier Street ditch and it is possible that, instead of curving around to the northeast to meet with the stretch of ditch excavated by Ó Néill, it drained into the natural inlet identified by Simpson,[76] as is almost certainly the case with the George's Street ditches.

By the time of the later medieval rebuild of the church in the later fourteenth century, it appears that much of the enclosed suburb had been subsumed into church land. The ditch had been backfilled in the thirteenth century and, following a relatively brief period of occupation during which several cesspits had been cut into the backfill, the late fourteenth-century church was built over it. At this time, the graveyard appears to have extended across the majority of the former suburb before being curtailed and enclosed by a graveyard wall immediately west of the church, probably in the sixteenth

71 For previous proposed extents of the suburbs, see H.B. Clarke, '*Urbs et suburbium*: beyond the walls of medieval Dublin' in Conleth Manning (ed.), *Dublin and beyond the Pale: studies in honour of Patrick Healy* (Dublin, 1998), pp 45–58. 72 Cathy Moore, pers. comm. 73 Aisling Collins, pers. comm. 74 Paul Duffy, 'Saints and skinners: excavations along the northern precinct of the abbey of St Thomas the Martyr, Dublin' in Seán Duffy (ed.), *Medieval Dublin XVIII* (Dublin, 2020), pp 194–242, at pp 235–8. 75 Alan Hayden, 'The excavation of pre-Norman houses and defences at Werburgh Street' in Seán Duffy (ed.), *Medieval Dublin III* (Dublin, 2002), pp 34–43, at p. 56. 76 Simpson, 'John Rocque's map

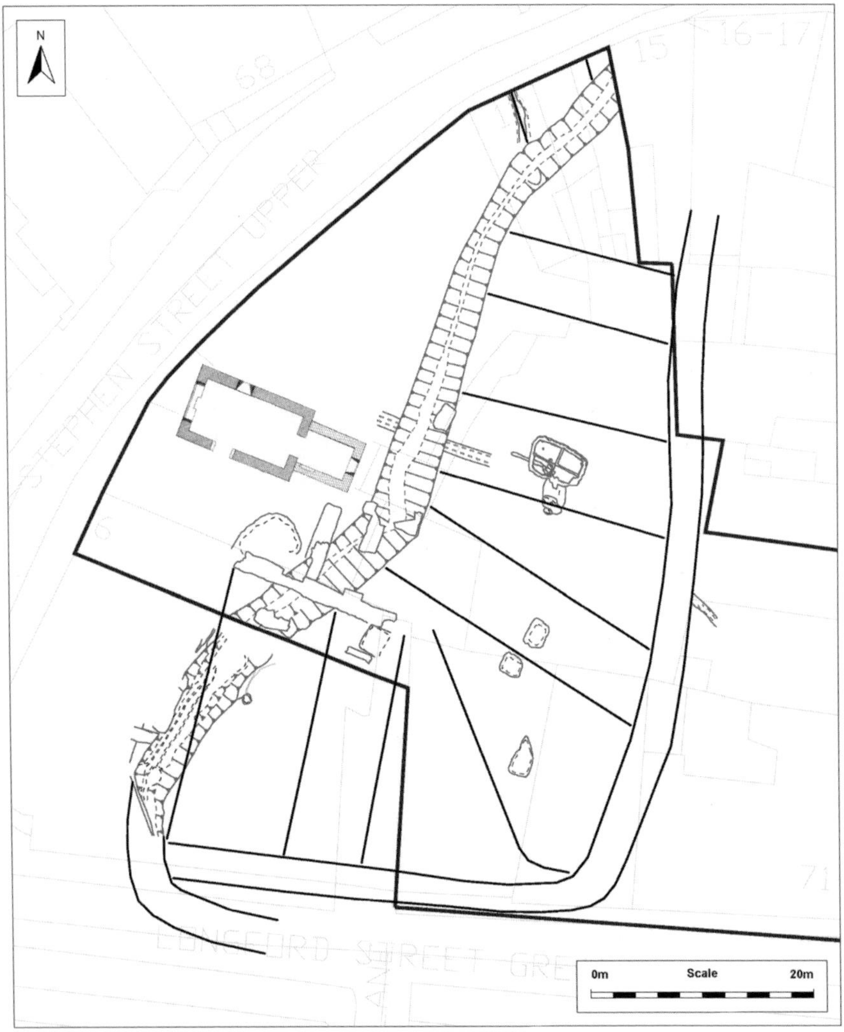

3.26 Conjectural plot boundaries within an enclosed suburb, based on location of cesspits

century.[77] The cesspits identified at Aungier Street compare well with those excavated on George's Street. Using as a model the excavated plots from Thomas Street (where cesspits were located to the rear of the toft areas) and incorporating the location of the cesspits, the SFS, and sunken pits from Aungier Street and George's Street, a tentative plot layout is here suggested for the proposed southern and eastern suburbs (fig. 3.26).

of Dublin', pp 125–7. 77 Coughlan, 'Excavations at St Peter's church', pp 26–30.

At George's Street, the eleventh-century ditches were also infilled, although the line of the boundary was cut and recut with successive ditches that also functioned as drainage. The continued importance of the George's Street boundary line was noted into the eighteenth century by Simpson.[78] The later medieval ditches and recuts appear to relate to the continued renewal of this boundary into the later medieval period. The stake-built structure (C187), which was constructed over several of the ditches (C140/C165/C181 and C183) and cut by subsequent ditches on the same line (C115 and C172), presents a brief interruption in the otherwise consistent pattern of this space representing a significant and longstanding boundary. The type of clustered stakes observed in C187 is consistent with pile foundations used beneath either sill-beamed or stone-built houses in Dublin where the underlying ground is soft. One of the stakes returned an AMS result of AD 1431–1620. It appears that the structure was not in use for long as it was cut away on its southern side by the re-establishment of the principal line of ditch C62. An explanation for this is suggested in the writings of Stanihurst, who, in 1577 recorded that the inhabitants of George's Lane 'being dailie and hourie molested and praied by their prolling mountain neighbours, were forced to suffer their buildings fall into decie and embraised themselves within the city walls'.[79]

The sunken-floored structure

The only indication as to the character of the buildings within this suburb come from the survival of an SFS near the centre of the site. The survival of this structure was due to the depth of its sunken floor which may originally have been up to 1.5m deep.[80] It is probable that significant ground reduction across the central part of the site in the 1950s, during construction of the 'Coffin' dancehall, removed contemporary structures which would have existed at ground level. The AMS dating of the original plank flooring returned a date of AD 1046–1220,[81] while an intermediary floor level dated to AD 1025–1154.[82] The last phase of activity in the structure, the cistern, contained ceramic that cannot be earlier than the mid-twelfth century but could be as late as the early thirteenth. This dating tallies with the date for the enclosing ditch C196 and a construction date in the last quarter of the eleventh century is proposed. Despite a catastrophic burning event *c.*1100 which would

78 Simpson, 'John Rocque's map of Dublin', pp 125–7. 79 *CARD*, ii, Appendix V. 80 Rebecca Boyd, 'Where are the longhouses? Reviewing Ireland's Viking-Age buildings' in H.B. Clarke and Ruth Johnson (eds), *The Vikings in Ireland and beyond: before and after the Battle of Clontarf* (Dublin, 2015), pp 325–45, at p. 330. 81 2 sigma date, Chronos UB 41107. 82 2 sigma date, Chronos UB 41106. 83 Patrick Wallace, *Viking Dublin: the Wood Quay excavations* (Dublin, 2016), pp 94–5; Helen Murray, *Viking and early medieval buildings in Dublin*. British Archaeological Reports 119 (Oxford, 1983), p. 15; Boyd, 'Where are the longhouses?', p. 330, and eadem, *Exploring Ireland's Viking-Age towns: houses and homes* (in preparation).

have consumed all but the stone-lined cellar, this structure may have continued in use into the early thirteenth century.

A complete reading of this structure was hampered by the fact that the original outside ground level did not survive, and the decision to preserve a portion of the internal clay floor surfaces as a potential repository for future research meant that some elements of the structure remained unexcavated. The presence of sunken-floored structures within the circuit of the town defences, while not quite common, has been documented on several sites. A unifying style is not evident in these earlier sunken-floored structures with some presenting as long and narrow in plan and others as small, wattle-built, and with rounded corners. In a Dublin context these buildings are termed 'Type 4' buildings and this label has been adopted for structures at Limerick and Waterford also.[83] Wallace has further divided 'Type 4' buildings into 'Type 4a' which are small (average 7.7 sq.m) ninth-century buildings *c.*0.6m in depth, and a 'Type 4b' which are eleventh-century buildings, larger (average 19.2 sq.m) and deeper (*c.*1.5m deep) and known from Peter's Street in Waterford and Limerick Castle. They are believed to represent below-ground storage cellars for two-storey dwellings. The SFS from the current excavation, with a surface area of *c.*17 sq.m conforms to certain criteria of the 'Type 4b' building, although its shape in plan is reminiscent of the 'Type 4a' buildings from Essex Street West.

The domestic/secular character of the activities carried out in the structure is inferred from the artefacts retrieved. These included iron artefacts possibly associated with a timber door, namely an iron key, an iron pivot and latch, as well as a small lead line weight and a large stone ball, potentially a fishing net weight,[84] a bone and a stone spindle whorl (both undecorated), an iron bucket-handle and three sherds of coil-built, imported ceramic from the latest phase of occupation.[85] The function of the gully-fed cistern within the floor of the structure, whether domestic or industrial, is not known, although similar features were found within the wattle-lined sunken structures at Essex Street West.[86] While an understanding of the various components and phases of the structure has been gained, a complete understanding of the structural arrangement was not possible. While several small postholes belonging to different phases of occupation suggest that the roof structure was supported by posts rising from within the structure, the reduction of the overall ground level in the 1950s by at least 0.4m and potentially as much as 1m would have removed any evidence for posts or wattling that may have risen from the external ground level. However, Murray notes that no associated ground-level structures are known from the structures she describes.[87]

84 Wallace, *Wood Quay*, p. 305. 85 Scully, 'Medieval and post medieval ceramic, Aungier Street'. 86 Linzi Simpson, 'Forty years a-digging: a preliminary synthesis of archaeological investigations in medieval Dublin city' in Seán Duffy (ed.), *Medieval Dublin I* (Dublin, 2000), pp 11–68, at pp 22–3. 87 Murray, *Viking and early medieval buildings*, pp 15–16.

3.27 Conjectural reconstruction of sunken-floored structure, *c.*1070 (by Matthew Ryan)

This ground reduction has also affected our understanding of the building's context, removing any other structures that may have survived in the immediate surroundings. The survival of the sunken pit features may suggest that denser settlement once occurred here. The two possible sunken-floored storage pits discussed above are likely to be contemporary with the SFS. Both features appeared to cut the earlier aceramic bulk fills of the ditch C196, but were subsequently cut by the later twelfth-/thirteenth-century recut of the ditch. The relative position of the SFS C573 and the sunken pit feature C340 recalls the arrangement of house, plot and outbuildings identified at the Viking levels at Fishamble Street.[88] Interestingly, in this sense, the plot associated with the SFS would have backed onto the line of the ditch C196 while fronting onto a street that would have run north–south to the rear of the current Aungier Street plots (see fig. 3.26).

A reconstruction drawing was drafted by the artist Matthew Ryan, showing the structure at its earliest phase, *c.*1070 (fig. 3.27). This image incorporates the inclined entrance passage, plank flooring, stone revetting as well as a bucket, pot, key and chain links for suspending a cauldron (all of which derive

88 Wallace, *Wood Quay*, p. 57.

from excavated evidence). However, to create the image, several significant unknowns had to be grappled with, namely, the nature of the superstructure, the function of the building and the presence of a hearth. Current thinking on the earlier SFSs in Dublin is that they did not have a floor at ground level and, due to the absence of hearths, that they were structures primarily used as workshops or storage spaces. The reading of the eleventh-century SFSs at Waterford and Limerick is that these had a primary floor at ground level, accessed by a ground-floor entrance while the undercroft/cellar was more of a storage area accessed by an external sloping passage.[89] Given the lack of evidence for a ground-level floor, it was preferred to represent the structure using the excavated evidence, with the primary activity in the structure taking place at the sunken-floor level. Some evidence for a hearth, in the form of oxidized clay, was uncovered towards the centre of the structure, although this may have originated in a later and lesser burning event.

Claire Walsh, in her study of the Waterford SFSs, points to parallels and possible origins for the Waterford structures in Lincoln, York, London and Chester. Chester in particular is significant given the strong medieval trading connections with Dublin and David Griffiths finds close parallels between rock-cut and timber-lined SFSs in Chester and those of Waterford. At least one of the Chester structures was accessed by a passage which opened into the side wall of the building,[90] like the Aungier Street example, but unlike the majority (possibly all) of the Irish examples which were accessed by passages opening into the gable end. The comparison with Chester is given more weight by John Bradley's claim that the nearby church of St Werburgh in Dublin could have been established around 1095 when relics of that saint were translated to St Werburgh's church in Chester.[91] It is interesting to note (though possibly circumstantial), that the stone-revetted structures at Waterford were in an area associated with a church dedicated to St Peter. The situation of the SFS excavated by Hayden at Werburgh Street in Dublin is perhaps less circumstantial given this link with Chester. What can be (and has been)[92] confidently stated is that the origin of the SFS in the Viking port towns lies in the (re?)importation in the eleventh century of the Germanic tradition of the *Grubenhaus*.

St Peter's church, c.*1370–1685*

That the large medieval structure excavated at the Aungier Street site represents the later medieval parish church of St Peter is borne out by the following evidence from the excavations:

89 Claire Walsh, 'Sunken buildings' in Maurice Hurley, Sara McCutcheon and Orla Scully (eds), *Medieval Waterford: excavations 1986–1992* (Waterford, 1997), pp 45–53, at p. 52. **90** David Griffiths, *Vikings of the Irish Sea* (Stroud, 2010), pp 131–3. **91** John Bradley, 'The topographical development of Scandinavian Dublin' in F.H.A. Aalen and Kevin Whelan (eds), *Dublin city and county: from prehistory to present* (Dublin, 1992), pp 43–56, at p. 49. **92** Claire

- the walls represent the remains of a large medieval structure, requiring substantial foundations of at least 13m length and 6.2m in width.
- the structure is surrounded by and contains medieval burials aligned to its exact orientation.
- the situation of the building on the highest point of the site with ground sloping away to the north and northeast corresponds to the church's designation in historic documents as 'St Peter's on the Hill'.
- a total of fifty-eight fragments of carved medieval masonry, consistent with ecclesiastical architecture, were recovered from the site: the majority of these were retrieved reused in walls of later structures built on top of the medieval structure.
- abundant fragments of line-impressed floor-tile and some relief-decorated floor-tile were retrieved from the graveyard soil and from the various grave fills, suggesting the presence of a tiled floor in the immediate vicinity.
- the retrieval of *c.*60 fragments of painted plaster from within the footprint of the building included a cross-crosslet design that may represent a consecration cross.[93]

The stratigraphic relationships discussed in the sections above show that this church cannot date to before the thirteenth century and is, in fact, much more likely to be a late fourteenth-century structure equating to the medieval parish church of St Peter that was deconsecrated and dismantled *c.*1685 during the development of the Aungier estate.[94] A reference in 1370 describing St Peter's church as 'in ruins, to be repaired,' with a papal indulgence granted of '1 year and 40 days to repair it',[95] presents a likely date for the church's reconstruction. Rachel Moss has challenged previous claims of stagnation in architectural projects in fourteenth-century Dublin listing many projects that were undertaken in the second half of the century. Arguing along similar lines, O'Neill has drawn attention to a master mason active in Dublin at this time named John More, suggesting that he may have worked at St Patrick's cathedral in and around the year 1370. This is of interest given that St Peter's may have been a property of St Patrick's at this time,[96] and may even have benefitted from the input of this John More.

Three main phases can be discerned in the fragmentary church foundations. The first phase consisted of an undifferentiated nave and chancel with the wall footing for the chancel arch integral to the southern and northern walls of the church. It is proposed that this structure dates to the last decades of the

Walsh, 'Sunken buildings', p. 52. **93** Karena Morton, pers. comm. See also Conleth Manning, 'Consecration crosses at Castlemartyr', *Archaeology Ireland*, 27.1 (2013), 40–42. **94** Desmond Moore, 'St Peter's church, Aungier Street', *Dublin Historical Record*, 14:2 (1956), 57–63, at 57. **95** Clarke, *Dublin, Pt 1* (IHTA), p. 17; Donnelly, *Dublin parishes*, ii, p. 135. **96** It was so by 1533: N.B. White (ed.), 'The Reportorium viride of John Alen, archbishop of Dublin, 1533', *Analecta Hibernica*, 10 (1941), 173–222, at 180 and 185.

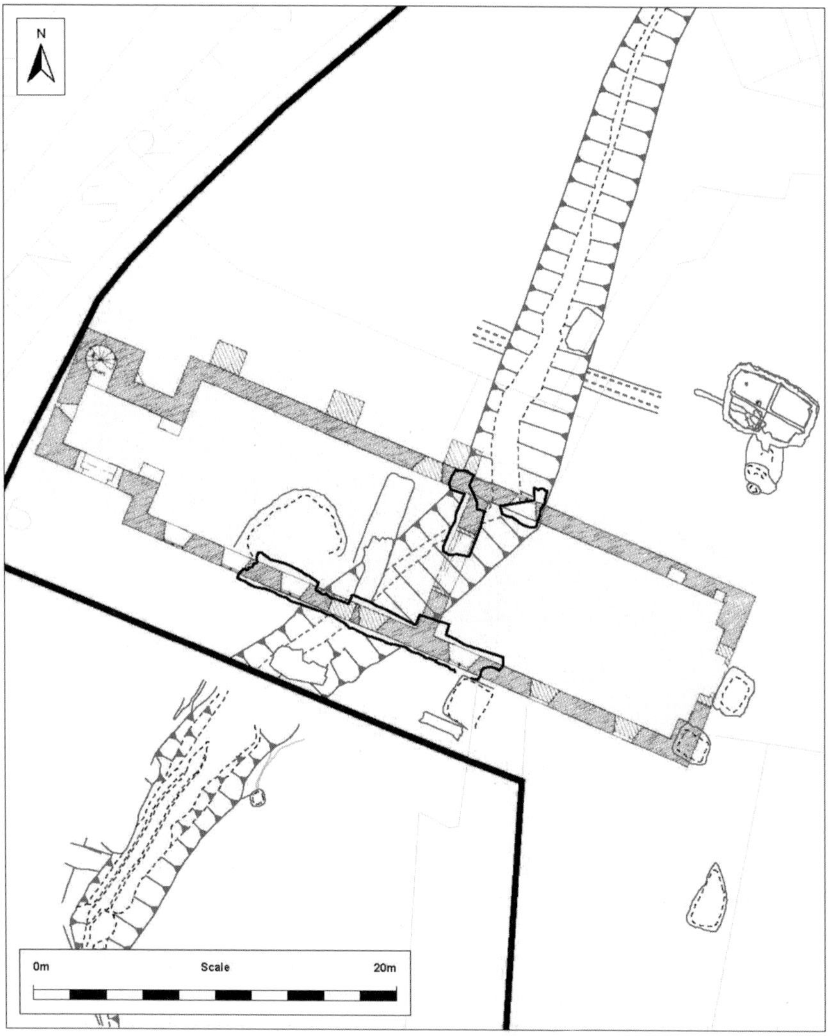

3.28 Plan of Newcastle Lyons parish church (prebendal church of St Patrick's cathedral), *c.*1400 superimposed over St Peter's

fourteenth century. In this form, the building compares very favourably with the parish church of Newcastle Lyons which has been dated to *c.*1400 (fig. 3.28). A second phase is visible in the insertion of a cross wall which abuts the southern and northern walls and runs parallel to the chancel arch. The distance between these two walls is only 2.9m. This inserted wall can be viewed as the foundation for a rood screen and, given it is of stone, it is possible that this footing, in conjunction with the chancel arch, was used as the supporting structure for a tower rising above the rood loft. Such arrangements survive at

3.29 Conjectural reconstruction of St Peter's parish church, *c.*1500 (by Matthew Ryan)

the fifteenth-century Ballindoon friary (Co. Sligo) and at the parish church of St Nicholas, Newtown Jerpoint (Co. Kilkenny). In a Dublin context, Ní Mharcaigh points to evidence for a rood screen and overarching belfry at the parish church of Kilmahuddrick,[97] and a rood loft is attested to at St Werburgh's church in the later fifteenth century.[98] At Werburgh's, the loft was accessed by a flight of stairs and may have resembled a similar arrangement, possibly with an overarching tower, as that proposed for St Peter's. The opening of a small doorway (attested to by flat lintel stones) in the southern wall of the nave might date to this phase.[99] A reconstruction drawing of this stage (*c.*1500) has been drafted by the artist Matthew Ryan (fig. 3.29) showing the structure as an undifferentiated nave and chancel church with a rood screen and central tower over a rood loft, contemporary bell-cote, a southern door with the top of the structural arch visible at ground level, internal painted plaster with sedilia and tiled floor visible in the cutaway. A third phase of

97 Máirín Ní Mharcaigh, 'The medieval parish churches of south-west county Dublin', *PRIA*, 97:5 (1997), 245–96, at 271. **98** Empey, 'Intramural churches', p. 272. **99** A similar insertion in the southern nave wall is evidenced at Palmerstown in the later medieval period: Ní Mharcaigh, 'Medieval parish churches', 257.

building and remodelling is suggested by the interrupted sections of stone foundation paralleling the southern nave wall at a distance of 3.5m to the south. This wall cut several burials of later date and is likely to represent a southern aisle that was added possibly in the first half of the sixteenth century. A similar southern aisle is recorded by Beranger at the medieval parish church of Clondalkin.[100]

These three phases are broadly mirrored in the motifs and mouldings encountered in the medieval architectural fragments retrieved from the vicinity of the church (described above). The presence of later forms, including the casement moulding and four-centred arch window light (see fig. 3.15),[101] illustrates that the church was possibly being renovated into the post-Reformation period and appears to have had a similar history in terms of the architectural fabric as nearby St Audoen's church. It is likely that, given its stated association with St Patrick's cathedral, possibly as a prebendal church, the (now largely replaced) late medieval decorative architecture of the cathedral served as inspiration for the later work.[102]

Cemetery

Over 150 skeletons were excavated by Coughlan during the course of the excavation immediately west of the Aungier Street site.[103] A further 224 *in situ* burials were excavated at the Aungier Street site and, taken together, this population represents the largest medieval cemetery excavated in Dublin.[104] The human skeletal remains from the combined excavations at Aungier Street and Stephen Street comprise a cross-section of the medieval population of St Peter's parish. Jennie Coughlan's paper dedicated to her osteological analysis is printed in this volume (below). As noted there, a range of AMS dates has been retrieved from burials across the cemetery and these were clustered within the hundred years between 1280 and 1380.[105]

Several later burials with date-ranges extending into the seventeenth century were also obtained. The presence of an armoured burial and the retrieval of a skull in an adjacent grave that had clear evidence of a life-ending wound created by an edged weapon suggests perhaps an episode of hasty burial of combatants in the church in the early sixteenth century. These burials could conceivably relate to the rebellion in 1534 of Lord Thomas fitzGerald (Silken Thomas). This statement is made on the following evidence: 1. Silken

100 Ní Mharcaigh, 'Medieval parish churches', 251. **101** This window finds close parallel in the post-Reformation eastern window of the parish church of St Mary's in Howth and in another post-Reformation, three-light window in the northern transept of Kells priory. **102** O'Neill, 'St Patrick's cathedral'. **103** Coughlan, 'Excavations at St Peter's church'. **104** Some comparative numbers of medieval burials excavated in the city: 272 at Golden Lane; 160 (142 plus 18) at the abbey of St Thomas the Martyr; 29 at the Hospital of St John the Baptist; five at the priory of All Hallows (Trinity College). **105** There remains the potential for earlier burials to survive on-site, associated with the eleventh-century church

Thomas famously fought with a guard of 140 galloglass and the short-armed mail shirt seemingly covering the armoured burial is characteristic of galloglass armour. 2. Given that a siege of Dublin Castle was a central element to this rebellion, St Peter's 'on the Hill', overlooking the castle, may well have been utilized as a base of attack or a withdrawal position following the failure of this operation and the ensuing rout. This scenario is perhaps more plausible in light of the fact that the rebels are known to have led an attack on the castle via Ship Street. St Peter's is located at the head of this street which slopes dramatically downward from the church towards the castle. Silken Thomas had similarly occupied the abbey of St Thomas the Martyr on the western side of the city when besieging Newgate and also took refuge in the Franciscan friary on Francis Street. The Ship Street attack was defeated by the use of 'wyldfyre' which has been described as a form of proto-flamethrower which used compressed air to force combustible liquid out of trumpet-like tubes.[106] The scorching and damage that such a weapon would have caused on an armoured body might well provide the explanation as to why, in the particular case of our armoured burial, the armour was not retrieved prior to interment.

CONCLUSIONS

It is suggested here that a church dedicated to St Peter was established on a rise in the landscape overlooking the 'black pool' of Dublin in the third quarter of the eleventh century; this followed the establishment of Christ Church (the cathedral church of the Holy Trinity), which provoked a building boom in churches that included St Michael le Pole's and St Werburgh's among others. It is also suggested that these churches employed innovative new motifs and forms that had been imported from England and the Continent, similar to the diversification of church forms that followed in Glendalough a decade or so later.

An extramural suburb was established/formalized soon after this by the excavation of a large enclosing ditch. This ditch avoided the graveyard associated with St Peter's church and does not form an element of the purported Dubhlinn enclosure, although there remains some potential for an earlier ditch to survive beneath the line of Stephen Street.[107] The

of St Peter. **106** Randolph Jones, '"Hys worthy seruice done in that vpror": Sir John Whyte and the defence of Dublin during Silken Thomas's rebellion 1534' in Seán Duffy (ed.), *Medieval Dublin XI* (Dublin, 2011), pp 275–97, at p. 286; Seán Duffy, 'Part 1: the medieval period' in Seán Duffy, John Montague, Kevin Mulligan and Michael O'Neill, *Dublin Castle: from fortress to palace, volume 1, Vikings to Victorians. A history of Dublin Castle to 1850*, ed. Ann Lynch and Conleth Manning (Dublin, 2022), pp 1–68, at pp 53–4. **107** This appears to have been the case further south along Peter's Row: see Ruth Elliot, 02E1779, http://excavations.ie/report/2004/Dublin/0011702/.

contemporary excavation of numerous ditches at the George's Street site further suggests that an eastern suburb was also in existence by the eleventh century. The sunken-floored structure was also built at this time, employing an older architectural form, attested to in Dublin from the ninth century. This form may have been employed as a deliberate manifestation of Scandinavian/Germanic influence at a time when Dublin's Scandinavian culture was perhaps being subsumed as its kings came more forcefully under the dominance of Ireland's provincial rulers.[108] The construction of both buildings, the secular and the sacred, were arguably undertaken in this spirit, which exhibited a willingness to import architectural ideas that would celebrate a past heritage. Ó Carragáin, writing of a sunken-floored structure in Waterford, is of the opinion that, 'This building, and many like it, reflects an openness to new architectural forms in the ports that was probably also reflected in ecclesiastical architecture.'[109]

The reconstruction of St Peter's church in the later fourteenth century is illustrative of another episode of importing architectural styles from abroad, this time by a different set of Dubliners. Examination of the surviving building materials from in and around the structure has allowed the reconstruction of some major events in the building's lifecycle to be proposed. Of particular interest is the retrieval of late gothic moulding, suggestive of continuing upkeep/patronage of the church into the seventeenth century. Rachel Moss writes that the rupture between the English and Irish traditions from the later fourteenth century meant that the repertoire of the 'perpendicular style Gothic' was not adopted wholesale in Ireland,[110] rather Insular styles developing or maintaining the earlier 'decorated style Gothic' motifs were common. The findings from St Peter's add to a growing corpus of material providing evidence of extensive adoption of 'perpendicular style Gothic' motifs in Dublin and the surrounding area.[111]

Drawing upon the ensemble of information presented above (along with some healthy speculation), the following timelines, phases and features can be proposed for the evolution of the two sites discussed and, by extension, some aspects of the wider setting:

- *c.*1060: St Peter's church is established within years of the construction of Christ Church and the stone church of St Michael le Pole. It is stone-built with imported red earthenware-tiled roof and conceivably comprising innovative Romanesque elements such as nave and chancel/west doorway with inclined jambs with angle rolls and imposts, round-headed arch and angle rolls.

108 This was also at a point when the church of Dublin tended to align more comfortably with Canterbury than with Ireland's chief church at Armagh. **109** Ó Carragáin, *Churches*, p. 238. **110** Moss, 'Parish churches', pp 180–1, though Moss does make a case for Dublin as a potential enclave for such motifs. **111** See O'Neill, 'St Patrick's cathedral', and

- *c.*1070: a large ditch defining a secular space immediately to the south of St Peter's church is installed to provide a physical boundary and defensive element for an emerging suburb. This suburb contains long, narrow plots, the width of a house's gable, fronting onto laneways and roads that have not survived. The sunken-floored structure is constructed as an ancillary building in one such plot. A large boundary ditch with internal palisade fence is constructed along the southern side of the George's Street site, draining into the natural inlet of the 'black pool'.
- *c.*1100: the sunken-floored structure is burned to the ground, potentially corresponding to the eleventh-century burning event observed at Hiberno-Norse houses on Werburgh Street.
- *c.*1170: the large ditch at Aungier Street is backfilled and replaced by a shallower ditch running along the same line. A similar process occurs at the large ditch on the George's Street site. A suburb is suggested by plot boundaries and cesspits.
- *c.*1200, the second phase ditch at Aungier Street is backfilled slowly with continuous deposits of kitchen midden material presumably from the suburb which remains active. A sequence of parallel ditches is dug, backfilled and recut over the following years at the George's Street site.
- *c.*1250, St Peter's church which has continued in use is upgraded with the installation of new sandstone and Dundry window surrounds. Cesspits are cut into the Aungier Street site ditch. Cesspits indicating possible plots are excavated at the George's Street site. Extensive burial around the church.
- 1370, St Peter's church 'in ruins, to be repaired'.[112] Boundary ditch at George's Street site alternately backfilled, recut and maintained.
- *c.*1371, St Peter's church rebuilt, partially over the former church site but extending southeast over the former line of the ditch. The church is possibly a possession of St Patrick's cathedral by this time. Elaborate painted plaster decorates the walls, incorporating several consecration crosses. A line-impressed tile floor is installed in the chancel and the church is roofed with locally-made roof-tiles with green and brown glazed crested ridge-tiles.
- *c.*1450, St Peter's church is remodelled, rood screen installed, forming a rood loft/tower over the chancel arch, sedilia with freestanding columns inserted into the north wall, doorway inserted into the south wall, large flat-headed window with hood moulding and four (?) trefoil cusped lights among other insertions.
- *c.*1500, the boundary ditches are infilled at George's Street site and a structure with driven stake foundations is constructed. A southern aisle is constructed at St Peter's church, possibly with a floor of relief-decorated

O'Keeffe, *Medieval Irish buildings*, pp 45–50. **112** Donnelly, *Dublin parishes*, ii, p. 135.

tiles, and the graveyard is made smaller with the construction of a rectangular walled space to the south of the church.

- 1534, following Silken Thomas's rebellion and siege of Dublin Castle, a galloglass warrior is buried hastily in full armour in the nave of the church before the rebels retreat.
- *c.*1550, some remodelling of the church with internal arcading or window reveals bearing 'casement moulding' and a twin-light window with four-centred arches. The structure at the George's Street site is removed and the boundary ditch is reopened.
- 1660s, the development of the planned Aungier estate commences. St Peter's church is deconsecrated and dismantled to make way for the construction of houses. The material is used as stone in the foundations of redbrick Dutch Billy-style houses.
- 1685, house plots along Aungier Street, Stephen Street, George's Street and Longford Street follow, effacing the previous large boundary ditches. The new St Peter's church is consecrated further south on Aungier Street.

Osteological analysis of the human skeletal remains from Aungier Street and Stephen Street, Dublin: a synopsis of the results

JENNIE COUGHLAN

INTRODUCTION

Excavations at 7–13 Stephen Street, 17–19 Longford Street and 71–75 Aungier Street (Licence Ref.: 17E0212), undertaken by Paul Duffy for IAC Archaeology, uncovered a range of archaeological features spanning the periods from the tenth/eleventh centuries through to the twentieth century (Duffy 2019). Within the area known as Yard 1, a series of stone walls was uncovered which have been interpreted as the probable remains of a fourteenth-century rebuild of St Peter's church (ibid.). Excavations within the area around the church uncovered the remains of a total of 224 discrete burials, a substantial number of which had been truncated by either later burials and/or building activity. The site was located immediately to the north of a previously excavated cemetery site at 1–5 Stephen Street (Licence Ref.: 00E0559ext.) (Coughlan 2003). Excavations at Stephen Street by Tim Coughlan of IAC Archaeology in 2001 and 2002 identified a total of 150 discrete burials. These burials represent the southern expansion of the cemetery recorded at Aungier Street. While excavations at Aungier Street did not identify either the boundary, or full extent, of the graveyard, the earlier excavations at Stephen Street did uncover a roughly north–south-orientated section of wall foundation which was interpreted as the partial remains of the perimeter wall (Coughlan 2003).

RADIOCARBON DATING

A total of nine skeletons from Aungier Street and two skeletons from Stephen Street were subject to radiocarbon dating. Results indicate that the cemetery was active from the late thirteenth century through to the mid-seventeenth century (see table 4.1).

BURIAL PRACTICES

Where identifiable, the majority of burials were aligned roughly west-northwest to east-southeast and were interred in a supine and extended position in

Table 4.1 Dating results from Aungier Street/Stephen Street

17E0212 Aungier Street		14C 2 Sigma Cal.
SK 32	Young middle adult male buried in rare southwest–northeast stone-lined grave	AD 1283–1388
SK 41	Possible armoured burial; middle adult of undetermined sex	AD 1297–1395
SK 52	Adult of undetermined sex; aligned west–east	AD 1275–1380
SK 103	Adult male located beneath line of church wall	AD 1458–1634
SK 109	Young middle adult male located near northwest extent of cemetery	AD 1487–1636
SK 116	Middle adult male located in north-western part of cemetery	AD 1423–1453
SK 118	Infant/young child located in north-western part of cemetery	AD 1310–1412
SK 128	Armoured burial; young middle adult of undetermined sex	AD 1440–1515; AD 1598–1617
SK 145	Young adult male at northwest limit of excavated cemetery	AD 1290–1399
00E0559 ext. Stephen Street		**14C 2 Sigma Cal.**
SK CVII	Old middle adult of undetermined sex; trapezoidal stone-lined grave	AD 1280–1388
SK LXXXIV	Young adult male; trapezoidal stone-lined grave	AD 1280–1388

accordance with typical Christian burial practices. Most burials were placed in simple earth-cut graves, although two heavily truncated lintelled graves were identified to the east of the church. These contained the remains of a young adult probable female (SK 26) and a young middle adult male (SK 32). Two additional stone-lined graves were recorded at Stephen Street (Coughlan 2003). These contained the remains of a young adult male (Burial LXXXIV) and an old middle adult male (Burial CVII) (Coughlan 2005). Significant levels of intercutting by later burials were recorded across the cemetery suggesting that grave markers, if used, were not maintained. There was, however, one identified area of the graveyard where the graves were respected. A series of twenty-one supine and extended inhumations was recorded along the western boundary wall at Stephen Street (Coughlan 2003). Although a number of these burials had been truncated by a post-medieval drain, they were not disturbed by later burials (ibid.). It has been suggested that there may have been markers on the wall above these burials which would have shown their position (ibid.). The individuals buried along the wall comprised males, females and juveniles (Coughlan 2005).

Only two instances of probable double burial were recorded at Aungier Street. The partially truncated remains of SK 19, an older child of approximately 11 years, were found over the lower half of SK 17, a young adult female. SK 17 was truncated, with the loss of the skull, upper torso and arms, but the lower half of the body was undisturbed. This possible double burial was located near the eastern extent of the known burials. The second double burial comprised SK 91, a probable female young adult, and SK 104, a young child of 3–5 years. In this instance the child was located over the left side of the adult burial with the head positioned in the crook of her left arm. This latter double burial was located in a cluster of burials near the southern extent of the Aungier Street section of the cemetery.

Only one adult burial deviated from the normative supine and extended body position. SK 160, an older adult male, was interred in a supine position with both legs partially flexed to the right. This individual suffered from chronic infection with extensive new bone formation recorded bilaterally on the tibiae and fibulae and, to a lesser extent, the femora. It is possible that the flexed position of the legs relates to factors associated with the identified lower limb infection rather than representing a deliberate modification of burial position. Although a second flexed burial was also recorded in this population, in this instance, the burial was of an infant of approximately 3–6 months at time of death (SK 7). This burial was highly fragmented but on-site photographs suggest that the infant was positioned slightly on their right side with legs gently flexed. This may have been considered a natural position for such a young individual. A number of sub-angular stones were recorded around the burial suggesting that the grave was stone-lined.

Armoured burials

At least one and possibly two of the burials from Aungier Street were buried in what has been interpreted as the probable remains of armour. SK 128 (see fig. 3.20 in Duffy, above) comprised the remains of a young adult of undetermined sex. This burial had been truncated by post-medieval activity with loss of the lower arms, hands, pelvis and lower limbs. During excavation corroded ferrous material was recorded on the torso, shoulders and parts of the skull (Duffy 2019). The presence of ferrous accretions over a significant portion of the surviving skeleton limited the information retrievable during osteological analysis and, with the exception of some unusual patterns of wear on the maxillary central incisors, there was very little information that could be gleaned. The second possible armoured burial recorded at Aungier Street was

SK 41, a middle adult of undetermined sex. Although most major skeletal elements were recovered with the burial, the bone was fragmented and the skeleton was incomplete. During excavations, areas of hardened iron panning were recorded in the grave, most notably over the area around the ribs and vertebrae. This impacted the survival of skeletal elements and the surface condition of most of the bones was found to be relatively poor with the vertebrae and ribs particularly poorly preserved. Given the identification of one individual who appears to have been buried in armour in the cemetery it is not inconceivable that this represents a second. There was no visible evidence for trauma or pathology on either of the skeletons with one notable exception. Small, roughly triangular notches were visible on the buccal surface of the maxillary central incisors of SK 128. These have been interpreted as probable deliberate modifications.

METHODOLOGY

The osteological analysis of human remains is undertaken to establish, where possible, demographic information (sex, age and stature) and to identify skeletal changes that can be linked to occupational, pathological or nutritional stresses. Estimation of age, sex and stature not only provides basic population data but can also aid in the identification of age-related skeletal changes, gender differences in diet and occupation and the frequency of disease through different population groups. All remains from Aungier Street were examined by the author and Maeve Tobin of IAC in accordance with standard osteological protocols. The skeletal remains from Stephen Street were previously analysed by the author (Coughlan 2005).

PRESERVATION

Variation in the preservation of skeletal material can impact heavily on the level of information retrieved during analysis. The skeletal remains from this site were assessed on two separate aspects of preservation, namely completeness, recorded as percentage of the skeleton present, and preservation, where consideration was given to the condition of the bone. The majority of skeletons scored higher for preservation than completeness which reflects the levels of truncation encountered across the site. In total, 121 (32.4%) skeletons from Aungier Street/Stephen Street were considered to display good or very good levels of completeness with 202 skeletons (54.0%) exhibiting good or very good levels of preservation (table 4.2).

Table 4.2 Completeness and preservation totals from Angier Street/ Stephen Street

Aungier Street/ Stephen Street	Very good (1)		Good (2)		Moderate (3)		Poor (4)		Very poor (5)	
	no.	%	no.	%	no.	%	no.	%	no.	%
Completeness	25	6.7	96	25.7	120	32.1	98	26.2	35	9.4
Preservation	24	6.4	178	47.6	157	41.9	13	3.5	2	0.5

RESULTS

Age at death

Analysis of the 224 individuals from Aungier Street identified 173 (77.2%) as adult with the remaining 51 (22.8%) recorded as juvenile. The Stephen Street skeletal population comprised 108 (72.0%) adults and 42 (28.0%) juveniles (Coughlan 2005). The combined number of adults from Aungier Street and Stephen Street was 281 (75.1%) with the remaining 93 individuals (24.9%) aged less than *c.*17 years at time of death. This gives a ratio of approximately 3:1 for adults to juveniles.

There was only one identified example of pregnancy recorded in this population. SK 43, a foetus of 32–6 gestational weeks, was found in the abdominal/pelvic region of SK 36, a young adult female. Although the neonatal remains were incomplete, on-site records suggest that the skull was low in the pelvic cavity which could indicate that the head was engaged at time of death. As this can occur anytime from approximately 34 to 36 weeks onwards there is no way of knowing whether death occurred during premature labour or if the mother and her unborn baby died as a result of non-pregnancy-related issues. Two perinatal burials were also recorded in the cemetery; SK 44 from Aungier Street and Burial CXXV from Stephen Street were both aged approximately 40 gestational weeks at time of death. As these two perinatal individuals were not found directly associated with an adult burial it appears that they died either during, or shortly after, birth.

Mortality in the juvenile population

A total of 90 non-neonatal/perinatal juveniles were identified during the analysis of the human skeletal remains from Aungier Street/Stephen Street and all juvenile age groups were represented in this population. Analysis of the age profile of the juveniles indicated that peak mortality occurred during childhood with a total of 71.1% (n=64/90) of individuals dying between the ages of *c.*1–12 years. Although older children appear to have been at the greatest risk of death, with 31.1% (n=28/90) of juveniles assigned to this age category, young children also comprised a significant proportion of the juvenile population. In the past, rates of mortality were commonly high for infants and young children and at Aungier Street/Stephen Street a minimum of 13.6% (n=30/221) of the total cemetery population, or 31.1% (n=26/90) of the juvenile population, were aged between *c.*1 month and 5 years at time of death. Of these, 26.7% (n=24/90) were young children aged 1–5 years. The remaining 4.4% (n=4/90) were infants of less than 1 year.

Although the number of infants recorded at Aungier Street/Stephen Street appears relatively low, it must be remembered that calculating infant mortality rates in past populations can be problematic and the recorded number of infants in a given cemetery population may not reflect the true rate of infant mortality. Aspects such as differential preservation and incomplete recovery of infant bones can result in infant deaths being under-recorded (Lewis and Gowland 2007). There may also have been cultural reasons for low infant numbers in a cemetery. Specific areas within a cemetery may have been set aside for infant burial or infants may have been interred in a designated area outside of the cemetery, a practice which appears relatively common in the archaeological record (Daniell 1997, 124). The osteological analysis of the skeletal remains from the ninth- to thirteenth-century cemetery at St Thomas's abbey in Dublin recorded a similarly low number of infants, with only one articulated infant identified (two further infants were identified in the disarticulated assemblage) (Tobin 2021). The low number of infants recorded stands in contrast to findings from the multi-phased medieval cemetery at Ranelagh, Co. Roscommon where 37.0% of juvenile deaths occurred in infancy (Murphy et al. 2019). It is suggested that the low number of infants recorded at Aungier Street/Stephen Street is more likely to reflect cultural or taphonomic factors rather than reflecting the true mortality rate of infants in this population.

Mortality in the adult population

Of the 281 adult individuals recorded in this cemetery, 91 (32.4% of adults) could only be assigned to the broad 'adult' age category due to incomplete survival and/or poor preservation. The remaining 190 adult individuals comprised 57 young adults (20.3% of adults), 43 young middle adults (15.3% of adults), 38 old middle adults (13.5% of adults) and 11 older adults (3.9% of adults). The remaining 41 individuals (14.6% of adults) were assigned the broader age category of middle adult (26–46 years) (table 4.3).

It was possible to estimate sex for a total of 202 of the 281 adult individuals in this population. Of these, 123 (43.8%) were assessed as male and 24 (8.5%) were assessed as probable male with 41 (14.6%) assessed as female and 14 (5.0%) assessed as probable female. This gives a ratio of males to females of 2.7:1. In a typical cemetery population it would be expected that males and

Table 4.3 Adult mortality rates by age and sex, Aungier Street and Stephen Street

	Male/ ?Male		Female/ ?Female		Undeter-mined		Total	
	no.	%	no.	%	no.	%	no.	%
Adult	24/281	*8.5*	5/281	*1.8*	62/281	*22.1*	91/281	32.4%
Young adult	37/281	*13.2*	13/281	*4.6*	7/281	*2.5*	57/281	20.3%
Young middle adult	28/281	*10.0*	11/281	*3.9*	4/281	*1.4*	43/281	14.6%
Old middle adult	22/281	*7.8*	13/281	*4.6*	3/281	*1.1*	38/281	15.3%
Middle adult	31/281	*11.0*	9/281	*3.2*	1/281	*0.4*	41/281	13.5%
Older adult	5/281	*1.8*	4/281	*1.4*	2/281	*0.7*	11/281	3.9%
Total adults	147/281	*52.3*	55/281	*19.6*	79/281	*28.1*	281	*100.0*

females would be roughly equally represented but at Aungier Street/Stephen Street almost three times as many males were recorded as females. While this finding suggests a strong bias in favour of males, it must be remembered that significant levels of disturbance were recorded across the site and biological sex was not determined for almost one third of the adult population. It is therefore possible that the identified ratio of males to females does not accurately reflect the demographic profile of this population.

Analysis suggests that adults were most vulnerable during the earlier years of adulthood with 20.3% of the adult population dying before *c.*25 years of age. A comparative analysis of age at death for males and females suggests that males were more vulnerable during this period than females, with 25.2% of males (n=37/147) assessed as young adult compared to only 9.1% (n=5/55) of females (table 4.3). While this would suggest that young males were subject to greater nutritional or pathological stresses than their female contemporaries, it again must be remembered that the excavated portion of the cemetery may not be representative of the entire population group. It is more commonly found in archaeological populations that there is a higher mortality rate in young adult females, thought to reflect a period of increased stress during early adulthood, perhaps related to complications during pregnancy and childbirth. From approximately 26–35 years of age the ratio of males to females appears roughly equal with 19.1% (n=28/147) of males and 20.0% (n=11/55) of females aged as young middle adult. A higher proportion of excavated females survived longer than males with 23.6% (n=13/55) of females aged as old middle adult and 7.3% (n=4/55) aged as older adult. This contrasts with the males of this population where 14.9% (n=22/147) were assessed as old middle adult and only 3.4% (n=5/147) survived into older adulthood.

Stature

A total of 49 male individuals and 19 female individuals survived with intact long bones allowing for stature estimation. Where possible, a combination of the femoral and tibial lengths were used as the preferred metric but, where this was not possible, preference was given to the tibia, followed by the femur, radius and, lastly, humerus. The average stature for males from Aungier Street was 171.3cm and 158.3cm for females. At Stephen Street the average stature for males was recorded as 168.3cm and females as 157.7cm (Coughlan 2005).

Indicators of physiological stress

Evidence for physiological stresses in archaeological populations largely derives from the identification of a small number of conditions affecting the skeleton and teeth. In this population physiological stress indicators were limited to cranial lesions associated with cribra orbitalia and porotic hyperostosis, and dental enamel hypoplastic defects. Although the aetiology of both cribra orbitalia and porotic hyperostosis is still not fully understood, it is generally accepted that they relate to a period of nutritional or pathological stress during childhood. A total of 60.0% (n=9/15) of juveniles with surviving orbits were affected by cribra orbitalia with 9.5% (n=2/21) of juveniles with crania affected by porotic hyperostosis. In the majority of examples, the lesions appeared non-active at time of death. Only four (26.7%) juveniles displayed active lesions associated with cribra orbitalia.

Analysis of the adult population identified orbital lesions indicative of cribra orbitalia on 13.6% (n=8/59) of individuals with surviving orbits and lesions indicative of porotic hyperostosis on 40.3% (n=27/67) of adults with recordable cranial vaults. A comparison with other pene-contemporary Irish populations indicates that prevalence rates of cribra orbitalia were generally lower at Aungier Street/Stephen Street but prevalence rates of porotic hyperostosis were higher. An exception to this was the population at St Thomas's abbey where only 3.3% of adults were affected by cribra orbitalia (Tobin 2021). At Ballyhanna, Co. Donegal, almost half (47.2%) of the adult population were affected by cribra orbitalia with 23.9% of adults affected by porotic hyperostosis (McKenzie and Murphy 2011) while at Ranelagh, Co. Roscommon, 40.6% of adults with orbits exhibited lesions associated with cribra orbitalia and 19.2% of adults had lesions indicative of porotic hyperostosis (Murphy et al. 2019). Enamel hypoplastic defects affected 14.7% of the adult population from Aungier Street/Stephen Street which appears roughly comparable to the findings from Ballyhanna where 17.7% of adult dentitions were affected (McKenzie and Murphy 2011). At St Thomas's abbey, 27.9% of individuals had hypoplastic defects (Tobin 2021) with 72.5% of adults from Ranelagh affected (Murphy et al. 2019). Three adolescents from Aungier Street/Stephen Street also had visible hypoplastic defects.

Another possible indication of physiological stress in archaeological populations is small stature. In this population five children appeared small for their age with dental development suggesting an older age than long-bone length. In at least two of these cases, short stature appears to have been linked to a genetic condition (see below) but in the remaining three there were no additional skeletal indicators of pathology. One of these individuals also exhibited hypoplastic defects indicative of physiological stress in early childhood.

Diet

There was little evidence to suggest that this population suffered from excessive dental pathology. Analysis of rates of caries and calculus can provide insight into diet with high levels of calculus combined with low levels of caries suggesting a high protein, low carbohydrate diet (Lillie 1996 in Murphy et al. 2013, 2550). At Aungier Street/Stephen Street, calculus deposits were recorded on 97.2% of adults with dentition with a total of 74.0% of adult teeth affected. Caries affected a total of 47.9% of adults and 6.1% of adult teeth.

A basic review of the isotope data from 11 individuals (10 adults and 1 infant) suggests a greater variation in dietary sources for some of these individuals than data from earlier Dublin populations. The nitrogen isotope signature recorded for the remains of an infant/young child of *c.*1 month to 2 years was relatively high, which most probably relates to breastfeeding. The adult population largely appears to have subsisted on a diet of vegetables, dairy and meat although four of the individuals who were found to have higher nitrogen levels most likely had a marine or fresh fish element to their diet. It is notable that between one third and almost half of the assessed individuals appear to have had a lower trophic diet. These included SK 41, a middle adult of undetermined sex, who may have been buried in some form of armour, SK 116, a middle adult male, and SK 103, an adult of undetermined sex. SK 41 dates to the fourteenth century while the latter two individuals have been dated to the fifteenth century. The armoured skeleton, SK 128, also exhibited lower values of $\delta^{13}C$ and $\delta^{15}N$ but in this instance the dating sample which provided the results derived from a molar and, as such, the recorded values represent a period of possible malnutrition during childhood.

Degenerative changes

Degenerative changes, although common throughout the adult population, were generally not considered severe. Although rates of joint disease increased with age, as would be expected, the identification of degenerative changes in young and young middle adults suggests that functional stresses also played a role in the development of joint disease in this population. Analysis indicates that males in this population were more commonly affected by degenerative changes than females, suggesting that there may have been some sex-based differentiation in tasks. Only one individual was affected by significant osteoarthritic changes. SK 229, an adult of undetermined sex, exhibited osteoarthritis through the right and left shoulders, elbows and hips. Although the degenerative changes in the hips were not severe, both the right and left forearms were slightly atrophied. The right radius and ulna also exhibited changes indicative of well-healed shaft fractures.

Trauma

A total of 45 (16.0%) individuals from Aungier Street/Stephen Street had suffered fractures, with almost twice as many males affected than females. All affected individuals were adult and most identified fractures were well-healed. Fractures of the lower limbs affected four individuals, all male. Examples of these include SK 167, a young adult male, who exhibited changes to the femoral neck which suggested a possible well-healed femoral neck fracture. It is possible that this occurred in adolescence although this could not be confirmed. In young individuals, fractures to the neck of the femur are most commonly caused by high-energy injuries such as a fall from height. One old middle adult male (SK 15) exhibited bilateral angular deformity of the proximal fibular shafts which may represent Maisonneuve fractures that can occur as a result of rolling or twisting the ankles. Both fibulae appeared robust with marked muscle attachments at the attachment of the *soleus* muscle which acts to plantar flex the foot and would be active in actions such as running, jumping and walking on tip toes. The right calcaneus also exhibited marked muscle attachments and it may be that the deformity visible of the fibular shafts relates to muscle action rather than traumatic fracture.

There was a single proximal left humeral shaft fracture which affected SK 150, a young adult male. In this example the fracture was well-healed but there was medial displacement of the proximal third of the shaft. Although healed, there was some thickening of the shaft around the fracture site which was indicative of callus formation. Extensive callus formation can indicate malposition, imperfect immobilization, infection or a comminuted fracture. In this instance there is a large cloacha present immediately inferior to the greater tubercle indicating the presence of infection in the form of osteomyelitis. Although this was not active at the time of death, when the infection was active there would have been a visible skin fistula on the arm. The identification of osteomyelitis in association with the fracture suggests that it may have been a compound fracture which would have left the wound and fracture site open to infection. Humeral shaft fractures can be caused by a direct blow or by a fall. There was no atrophy of the left arm bones indicating that, once healed, the arm was fully functional.

As discussed above, SK 229, an older adult of undetermined sex, displayed evidence for healed mid-shaft fractures of the right radius and ulna. The fractures were misaligned leading to angular deformity of the forearm. Both the right and left radii and ulnae were atrophied and there was severe osteoarthritis recorded in the right and left shoulder. SK 16, an old middle adult female, had suffered a fracture to the distal left radial shaft. In this example the fracture was well-healed with very little displacement noted. This type of fracture is known as a Colles fracture and can occur as the result of a fall on outstretched hands. SK 67, an old middle adult male, exhibited changes to the mid-third of the left ulnar shaft indicative of a partially healed fracture. In this example, although there was some bone formation around the site of the fracture, healing was not complete and the weakened bone had broken post-mortem. The left radial tuberosity appeared irregular and it is probable that there was some muscle damage associated with this injury.

Vertebral compression fractures can occur secondary to conditions such as osteoporosis or as a direct result of high-energy trauma such as a fall from a height. A total of five of the Aungier Street individuals had suffered vertebral compression fractures with an additional seven of the Stephen Street population similarly affected. All affected individuals were male.

Spondylolysis is the term given to a stress or fatigue fracture which results in partial or complete non-union of the vertebral body and the neural arch (Ortner 2003, 147). This fracture is most commonly observed at the fifth lumbar vertebra. At Aungier Street spondylolysis affected two individuals, SK 161 and SK 208, both young adult males.

Soft tissue trauma

Some activities can result in damage to the soft-tissues (muscles, ligaments and tendons). In most cases these injuries will simply result in pain, bruising or swelling but in some instances the damage is severe enough to prompt a bony reaction. At Aungier Street a small number of visible bony reactions to soft-tissue trauma were identified. Examples of this included SK 1, an old middle adult male, who had a calcaneal spur on the right calcaneus (heel). This bony outgrowth results from a build-up of calcium deposits on the underside of the heel which can occur as the result of strains or repeated damage to the foot muscles and/or ligaments (webmd.com). Heel spurs, while not necessarily painful in themselves, may occur in association with a condition known as plantar fasciitis, a painful inflammation of the plantar fascia of the foot. Modern studies suggest that heel spurs most commonly occur in individuals who partake in activities such as running and jumping (ibid.). SK 1 was also affected by bilateral degenerative changes at the calcaneal-talar joint and right talar-navicular joint. SK 170, a young adult male, had a small bony spur on the

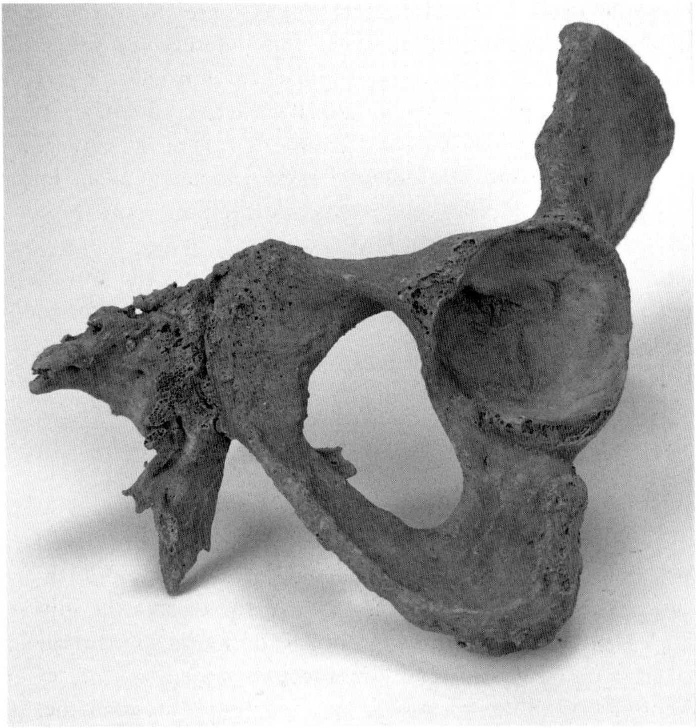

4.1 SK 138; probable myositis ossificans with bone formation at the right pubis

distal right fibular shaft. The location of the spur suggests that it may relate to the talofibular ligament which can be damaged when the ankle is rolled. SK 179, an adult of undetermined sex, had a large bony spur on the anterior margin of the distal fibular shaft with no visible fracture line. This again may represent the site of muscle or tendon damage. SK 207, an adult of undetermined sex, had a bony spur on the proximal right tibia which may represent damage to the tibial collateral ligament or *vastus medialis*. Both the ligament and muscle act to support and stabilize the knee (physio-pedia.com).

The most extreme example of soft-tissue trauma in this population affected SK 138, an old middle adult male who exhibited extensive osseous formation in the pelvic region with a notably large osseous growth extending horizontally from the pubis (fig. 4.1). It is suggested that this may represent an example of myositis ossificans at the site of trauma to the adductor muscles which act to adduct (move outwards from the body) and laterally rotate the thigh at the hip joint. Myositis ossificans describes a form of heterotopic ossification resulting from either direct trauma or intramuscular hematoma with bony tissue forming inside the muscle or other soft-tissue after injury. On the dorsal surface of the left pubic bone there was a second area of osseous formation which may represent the site of trauma at the insertion of *obturator internus* which also acts to laterally rotate the thigh at the hip joint. The pelvis was fused at the pubic symphysis with the dorsal surface of the pubic symphyseal joint obliterated by a ridge of bone which appears part of the same ossification process. There were also robust muscle markings throughout the lower limbs with additional marked muscle attachments of the left humerus.

Os acromiale

Os acromiale describes a condition whereby the acromial epiphysis fails to fuse to the acromion process of the scapula. Although individuals may be genetically predisposed to this condition, it generally occurs when stresses are placed on the rotator cuff muscles during adolescence. Os acromiale affected five individuals in this population, all of whom were male. At Stephen Street two individuals, both male, were similarly affected.

Interpersonal trauma

Only four examples of interpersonal violence were identified in the Aungier Street/Stephen Street population. In three of these cases the injuries were sustained in, or around, the time of death. The only example of healed trauma affected Burial CVIII, an old middle adult of undetermined sex. In this instance there was evidence for healed blunt-force trauma on the left parietal and right mastoid. The blow to the mastoid had displaced the inferior portion of the mastoid process which had subsequently healed at a 90-degree angle.

Peri-mortem trauma was identified on three individuals. SK 68, a young adult male, suffered significant peri-mortem violence. A single blade wound was identified extending across the posterior skull, curving from the medio-posterior aspect of the left parietal in a superior and lateral direction through the medio-posterior half of the right parietal. The wound measured 106.0mm in length and, in places, penetrated through the cranial vault. The force of the blow resulted in a number of radiating fractures extending from both ends of the wound. A second area of probable trauma was identified on the left parietal, with a roughly elongated depression visible immediately superior to the squamosal suture at the posterior-lateral aspect of the parietal. The depression, which did not penetrate the cranial vault, measured 17.2mm x 8.0mm and has been interpreted as probable blunt-force trauma. A small radiating fracture extended from the anterio-inferior border of the depression. The ribs and vertebrae of this individual were highly fragmented but there is some evidence to suggest that this individual was subject to additional violence in the form of blows to the body. The most compelling examples of this are a small number of probable peri-mortem vertebral fractures visible in the mid-thoracic region of the spine with the left transverse processes of T5–T8 separated from the neural arch. The location of these probable fractures suggests that this individual suffered peri-mortem blunt-force trauma across the mid-back region although, given the levels of fragmentation through the thoracic region, it is difficult to ascertain with certainty whether these fractures occurred peri- or post-mortem. Unfortunately, the ribs were also highly fragmented and, although the colouration at the edges of the fragments suggests that they may have been fractured around the time of death, this could not be confirmed. On-site photos also show a small triangular perforation near the inferior angle of the right scapula. This bone was damaged during excavation and there was no evidence of a perforation identified during analysis but the photographic evidence suggests that this may represent the site of a penetrating injury to the shoulder. In addition to the trauma described above, this individual was also decapitated. A single blade wound from behind cut through the second cervical vertebra resulting in removal of the superior aspect of the spinous process and exposing the underlying trabecular bone. The blade wound extended anteriorly, cutting through both the right and left superior articular facets and the dens. The force of the blow caused flakes of bone to be lifted from the posterio-lateral aspect of the dens. There is no evidence for trauma through the mandible or C1.

SK 97 comprised the fragmented and incomplete remains of a young middle adult male. The cranial vault was highly fragmented with only the incomplete left parietal, the left temporal, a fragment of left occipital and the fragmented and incomplete remains of the frontal bone recovered. Two sharp-force wounds were visible on the skull. The first was located approximately mid-way on the left parietal and extended medio-laterally. The second wound was near the top of the head extending medio-laterally across the mid-frontal region. Neither wound showed evidence of healing, indicating that they occurred in or around the time of death.

A large blade wound was visible extending through the left inferior parietal of Burial LXXXVII, a young middle adult male. This wound did not penetrate the cranial vault. A second blade wound, visible on the left temporal, removed a section of cortical bone from the temporal/mastoid suggesting that the blow came from above, or behind, hitting the side of the head behind the ear. A third blade wound was identified cutting through the left neural arch of the second cervical vertebra. Although this may suggest that there was an attempt to decapitate this individual, the blow does not appear to have come directly from behind and it may simply represent a blow to the side of the neck during an attack. Again, none of these wounds showed any signs of healing and would have occurred around the time of death.

Genetic malformation

A small number of individuals exhibited unusual forms of spinal malformation which may relate to a congenital syndrome. Klippel-Feil syndrome (KFS) describes a congenital condition resulting in fusion of two or more cervical vertebrae (Ortner and Putschar 1981, 355). Affected individuals commonly have a short neck, a low posterior hairline and limitation of neck movements (rarediseases.org). People affected by this syndrome may experience headaches, muscle or nerve pain and other neurological problems (ibid.). SK 224, a young adult female, exhibited fusion between C2 and C3 with the centrum, apophyseal joints and neural arch all involved. There was no evidence for degenerative changes and it is suggested that this fusion had a congenital origin. Although the skull was not recovered with this burial, there was a small section of additional bone fused to the anterior aspect of the left superior articular facet of C1 which suggests that there was also partial fusion between C1 and the occipital condyle of the skull. The posterior aspect of the articular facet was unaffected. It is impossible to ascertain whether this individual suffered from KFS or was affected by a simpler form of congenital fusion.

Two individuals were affected by an unusual form of spinal malformation. The term 'butterfly vertebrae' describes a sagittal defect in the vertebral body which occurs during embryogenesis and results in non-fusion of the lateral halves of the centrum (Katsuura and Kim 2019). The presence of multiple butterfly vertebrae affecting a single individual may suggest that this developmental defect exists as part of a syndrome (ibid.). Conditions which can be associated with butterfly vertebrae include Klippel-Feil syndrome and spondylocostal dysplasia. Spondylocostal dysplasia describes a rare genetic disorder which is characterized by defects of the spine and abnormalities of the ribs. These can include butterfly vertebrae, vertebral fusion and fused, misaligned, broadened, split or forked ribs (rarediseases.org). The affected individual may have short stature, a small thoracic cavity and a shortened neck and are likely to experience limited mobility, lung problems, scoliosis and back pain (ibid.).

SK 20, an older child of 7–12 years, was affected by a range of skeletal malformations through the spine and ribs (fig. 4.2). It should be noted that the vertebrae were fragmented, making identification of all potential malformations difficult. Identified vertebral deformities included fusion between the first cervical vertebrae and skull (atlanto-occipital fusion) which may have decreased the diameter of the occipital foramen and caused neurological complications. There was also non-fusion of both the neural arch and dens articulation of C1 and, although there is some post-mortem damage around the dens articulation, the bone appears relatively small and underdeveloped. The corresponding dens on C2 also appears small and

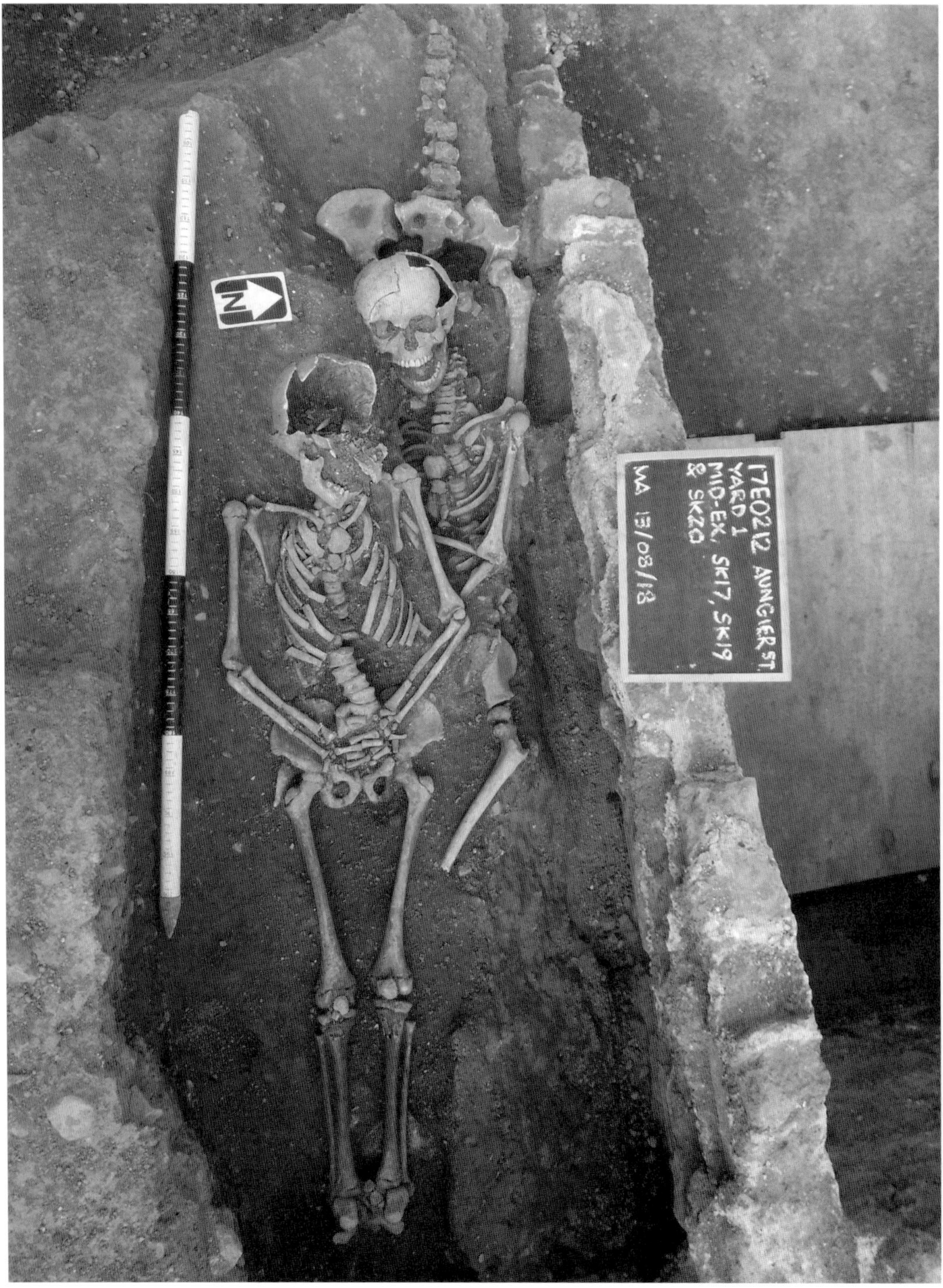

4.2 SK 20 in situ showing rib and lumbar abnormalities

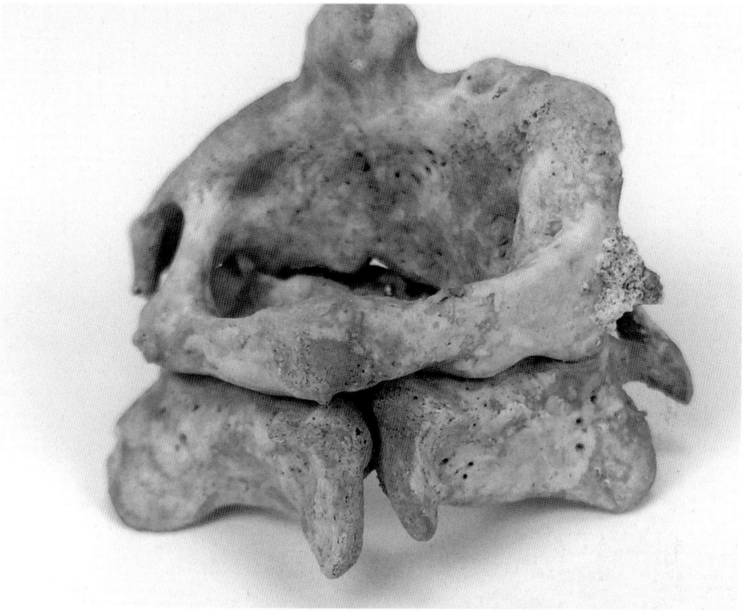

4.3 SK 20; C2 and C3 posterior view

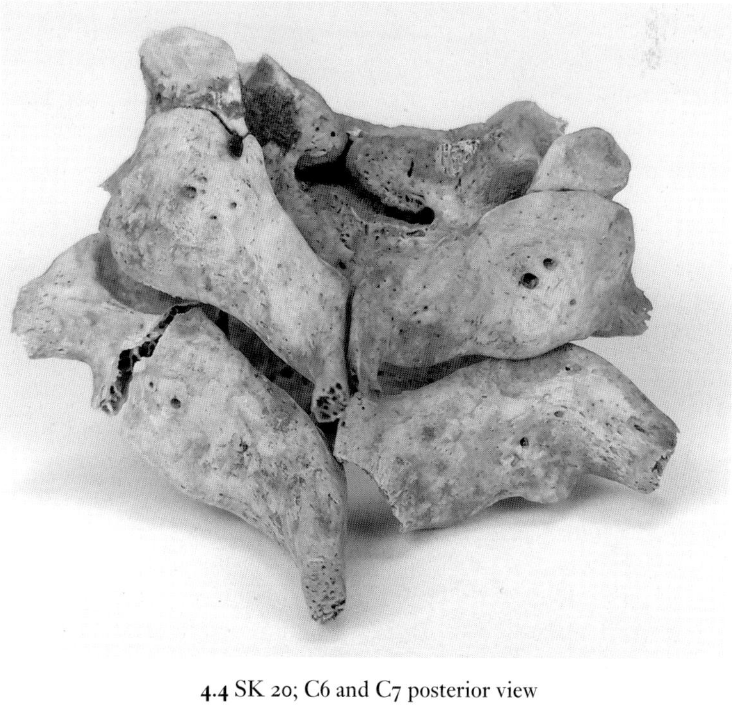

4.4 SK 20; C6 and C7 posterior view

4.5 SK 20; T1 to T3 anterior view

slightly malformed with a very slight rightwards tilt to the bone (fig. 4.3). The pedicles of C2 were malformed and extended downwards rather than horizontally, with both of the superior articular facets convex in appearance. The right pedicle was visibly more robust than the left with the right half of the centrum also larger than the left. C2 and C3 and C5 and C6 were fused and there was also non-fusion of the posterior arches of C3 to T1 (fig. 4.4). Butterfly vertebrae were identified at T2 and there was fusion between the right hemi-vertebra of T2 and T3 (fig. 4.5). The rest of the thoracic vertebrae were fragmented and incomplete but no significant malformations were noted. In the lumbar region of the spine the right side of the neural arches were smaller than the left. Unfortunately, levels of fragmentation meant that the spine could not be assessed for scoliosis but, given the underdevelopment of the right neural arches and articular facets through the lumbar region, combined with other vertebral malformations, it is suggested that it is probable this individual did suffer curvature of the spine. Although the majority of ribs were normal in appearance, there was fusion of the first three right ribs and the left first and second ribs. On the right side, fusion occurred at the rib head while the left first and second ribs were fused through the body of the rib. Also worth noting is that the right humerus was slightly more robust than the left. The right humerus also had a small cortical bone excavation at the insertion of *latissimus dorsi/teres major*. These muscles act to extend, adduct and medially rotate the arm. Although it is difficult to know why this slight discrepancy in humeral robusticity occurred, it is tempting to relate it to the vertebral defects observed and it may be that this child used a crutch.

There was a discrepancy in the age assessment of this individual based on dental development/eruption sequences versus long-bone length. Long bone length suggested an age of *c.*7–8 years with dental development aging this individual as 8–12 years. As dental development is considered more reliable in aging juveniles, the discrepancy suggests that this individual was relatively small for their age. Short stature is a known feature of spondylocostal dysplasia (ibid.). The multiple deformities through the spine and rib suggest that this child was born with a congenital condition such as KFS or spondylocostal dysplasia. Although it is not always the case, conditions such as KFS can be accompanied by other more life-limiting abnormalities such as heart or lung problems while a reduction in the size of the thorax associated with spondylocostal dysplasia can result in breathing difficulties (rarediseases.org). This individual also had multiple dental enamel hypoplasias indicating periods of illness or nutritional stress during early childhood.

A second child, SK 214, who was aged 5–8 years at time of death, was also affected by developmental changes through the lower spine with butterfly vertebrae recorded at L4 and L5 and fusion between the neural arch of L4 and L5. Although no defects were noted through the rest of the vertebrae or ribs, it is interesting to note that there was, again, a discrepancy in age estimation based on the dentition versus long-bone length. In this example, long-bone length suggested an age of 4–5 years while dental development gave an age range of 5–8 years.

Enlarged fontanelle

SK 7 comprised the moderately preserved remains of an infant of *c.*3–9 months. The right humerus was missing and there was some fragmentation of the long bones, most notably through the lower limbs. No hand or foot bones were recovered and the vertebrae and ribs were fragmented and incomplete. The frontal bones of the skull survived complete but the parietals and occipital were incomplete. Reconstruction of the skull allowed for the identification of a large opening at the anterior aspect of the parietals. This has been interpreted as a probable enlarged anterior fontanelle although differential diagnosis includes a dermoid or epidermoid cyst. While enlarged fontanelles can occur in association with conditions such as achondroplasia, hypothyroidism, Down syndrome and rickets, or can occur as the result of increased intracranial pressure (aafp.org), they may also simply represent normal variation (ibid.). This infant exhibited areas of very slightly raised porous bone along the superio-lateral quadrant of both orbits. The cause of the enlarged fontanelle could not be ascertained in this instance.

Cranial synostosis

Cranial synostosis describes a condition where one of more of the sutures of the skull fuses prematurely. Untreated, cranial synostosis can cause head and facial deformity and, in cases where the skull does not grow enough to make room for the developing brain, it may result in developmental delays, cognitive impairment, seizures and blindness (mayoclinic.org). SK 69, a young adult female, had an elongated and narrow cranial vault indicative of premature fusion of the sagittal suture (termed scaphocephaly). The sagittal suture was completely obliterated and both the coronal and lambdoidal sutures were barely discernible. In this example, the cranial vault, while elongated, appears in all other ways to be of normal size and it is unlikely that this condition adversely affected this individual.

CONCLUSION

The analysis of the human skeletal remains from the medieval cemetery at Aungier Street/Stephen Street has added significantly to our knowledge of the population of St Peter's parish in Dublin from the late twelfth to the mid-seventeenth centuries. Although the demographic profile of the population suggested that both infants and adult females were under-represented in this cemetery, it must be remembered that the full extent of the cemetery was not identified during excavations. Significant levels of truncation and disturbance were also recorded across the burial area which resulted in poor preservation in some instances. It is therefore important to remember that the excavated portion of the cemetery may not be representative of the population as a whole.

There was little evidence to suggest that this population was subject to excessive nutritional, pathological or physical stresses. There was some evidence for interpersonal violence but the numbers of individuals affected was small. There was, however, a small number of individuals affected by changes through the vertebrae and ribs which may represent evidence for a relatively rare genetic condition known as Klippel-Feil syndrome. The skeletal malformations may have been associated with a range of life-limiting symptoms not visible in skeletal remains.

BIBLIOGRAPHY

Bass, W.M. 1987 *Human osteology: a laboratory and field manual.* Missouri Archaeological Society, Missouri.

Brooks, S.T. and Suchey, J.M. 1990 'Skeletal age determination based on the os pubis: a comparison of the Acsadi-NemeSKeri and Suchey-Brooks methods'. *Human Evolution* 5, 227–38.

Brothwell, D.R. 1981 *Digging up bones*. 3rd ed. British Museum (Natural History), London.

Buikstra, J.E. and Ubelaker, D.H. (eds) 1994 *Standards for data collection from human skeletal remains*. Arkansas Archaeological Survey Research Series, no. 44. Fayetteville, Arkansas.

Coughlan, Jennie 2005 'Report on the inhumations from Stephen Street, Dublin'. Unpublished specialist report for IAC Ltd.

Coughlan, Tim 2003 'Excavations at the medieval cemetery of St Peter's church, Dublin'. In Seán Duffy (ed.), *Medieval Dublin IV*, 11–39. Dublin.

Cox, Margaret and Mays, Simon (eds) 2000 *Human osteology in archaeology and forensic science*. London.

Daniell, Christopher 1997 *Death and burial in medieval England*. London.

Duffy, Paul 2019 'Preliminary Excavation Report for 6–13 Stephen Street Upper, 7–19 Longford Street & 71–75 Aungier Street, Dublin 2'. Unpublished report.

Katsuura, Yoshihiro and Kim, H.J. 2019 'Butterfly vertebrae: a systematic review of the literature and analysis'. *Global Spine Journal* 2019; 9(6):666–79.

Lewis, M.E. and Gowland, Rebecca 2007 'Brief and precarious lives: infant mortality in contrasting sites from medieval and post-medieval England (AD 850–1859)'. *American Journal of Physical Anthropology* 134.1, 117–29.

Lillie, M.C., 1996 'Mesolithic and Neolithic populations of Ukraine: indications of diet from dental pathology'. *Current Anthropology* 37, 135e142.

McKenzie, C.J., & Murphy, Eileen 2011 'Health in medieval Ireland: the evidence from Ballyhanna, Co. Donegal'. In Sheelagh Conran et al. (eds), *Past times, changing fortunes: proceedings of a public seminar on archaeological discoveries on national road schemes, August 2010*, 131–43. Dublin.

Miles, A.E.W. 1962 'Assessment of the ages of a population of Anglo-Saxons from their dentitions'. *Proceedings of the Royal Society of Medicine* 55, 881–6.

Murphy, Eileen et al. 2019 'Osteoarchaeological analysis of the human remains from Ranelagh, Co. Roscommon'. Unpublished specialist report.

Murphy, Eileen et al. 2013 'Iron Age pastoral nomadism and agriculture in the Eastern Eurasian steppe: Implications from dental palaeopathology and stable carbon and nitrogen isotopes'. *Journal of Archaeological Science* 40, 2547–60.

Ortner, D.J. and Putschar, W.G.J. 1981 *Identification of pathological conditions in human skeletal remains.* Washington DC and London.

Roberts, Charlotte and Cox, Margaret 2003 *Health and disease in Britain: from prehistory to the present day*. Stroud.

Roberts, Charlotte and Manchester, Keith 1995 *The archaeology of disease.* 2nd ed. Stroud.

Scheuer, J.L., Musgrave, J.H. and Evans, S.P. 1980 'The estimation of late fetal and perinatal age from limb bone length by linear and logarithmic regression'. *Annals of Human Biology* 7, 257–65.

Smith, B.H. 1991 'Standards of human tooth formation and dental age assessment'. In M.A. Kelley C.S. Larsen (eds), *Advances in dental anthropology*, 143–68. New York.

Suchey, J.M., Wisely, D.V., Katz, D. 1986. 'Evaluation of the Todd and McKern-Stewart methods for ageing the male os pubis'. In K.J Reichs, (ed.) *Forensic osteology: advances in the identification of human remains*, 33–67. Springfield, MA.

Tobin, Maeve 2021. 'Osteological analysis of human remains retrieved from St Thomas's abbey, Thomas Street, Dublin 8 (Licence 16E0054)'. Unpublished specialist report prepared for IAC Ltd.

Ubelaker, D.H. 1989 *Human skeletal remains: excavation, analysis, interpretation*. 2nd ed., Washington, DC.

Williams, P.L. and Warwick, Roger (eds) 1980 *Gray's Anatomy.* 36th ed., Edinburgh.

DIGITAL REFERENCES

https://rarediseases.info.nih.gov/diseases/10280/klippel-feil-syndrome (accessed 25 April 2021)

https://www.mayoclinic.org/diseases-conditions/craniosynostosis/symptoms-causes/syc-20354513 (accessed 3 April 2021)

https://www.webmd.com/pain-management/heel-spurs-pain-causes-symptoms-treatments (accessed 15 April 2021)

https://www.physio-pedia.com/Medial_Collateral_Ligament_of_the_Knee (accessed 15 April 2021)

https://www.aafp.org/afp/2003/0615/p2547.html (accessed 1 June 2021)

From Norse gods to Norman knights: preliminary analysis of an incised slate from The Coombe, Dublin 8

RUTH JOHNSON

INTRODUCTION

This paper considers the find context, form, and imagery, lettering and potential function, of an incised stone that was recovered from a twelfth-century domestic plot during excavations in The Coombe in Dublin. It documents the process used in its recording, describes the object in detail, where it was found both topographically and in an archaeological context as well as giving its likely date. It considers some parallels both for the slate's function and for the incised letters and pictographs on it and reflects on what the object tells us about the nature of Dublin's southern suburb, outside the walled town in the late twelfth century.

DESCRIPTION (fig. 5.1)

The 'slate' is a flat stone, dark grey in colour with green mottling. It measures 176mm in length, 130mm across, and 6mm in maximum thickness. The slate is covered on both sides with fine cut-marks (that resemble the knife marks on a breadboard) and has graffiti on both faces. Some of the background lines are arcs and these may have been drawn with the aid of a template or compass. The inscribed stone was one of two pieces of similar-looking stone found during the excavations from the same level, the second piece of which is not inscribed. Although the stone is described here as a slate, the exact stone type and origin have yet to be confirmed scientifically and it is best considered to be mudstone. In trying to determine the origin of the stone, George Sevastopulo,† a geologist at Trinity College Dublin, was consulted. He carried out a visual examination of it and commenced work on a non-destructive scientific examination and analysis (fig. 5.2). A fragment of the non-inscribed slate was also prepared for analysis using destructive techniques under an 'alteration licence' from the National Museum of Ireland. The results of these investigations are pending as the geological analysis was not completed before Prof. Sevastopulo's death.

For this paper, Side A is considered to be the obverse and Side B to be the reverse, although it is debateable whether the medieval artist or artists

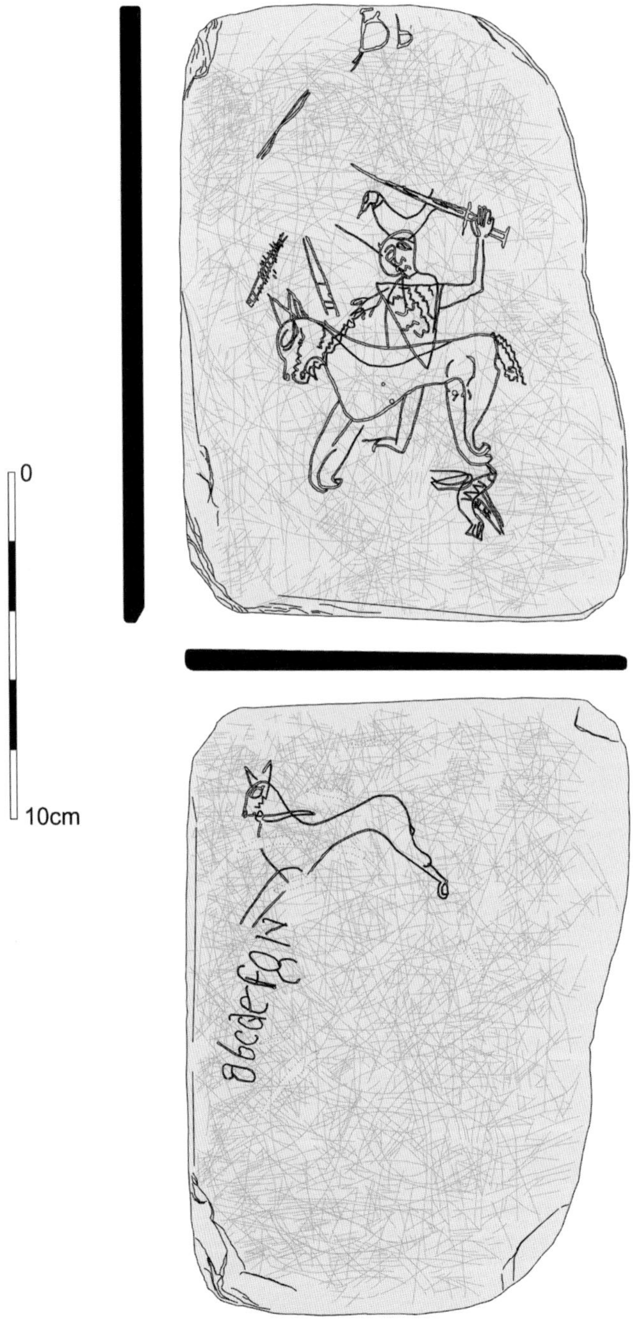

5.1 Scale drawing of slate (Johnny Ryan): Side A (*top*) and Side B (*bottom*)

5.2 George Sevastopulo BA, MA (Cantab), PhD(Dubl), FTCD Emeritus (1941–2021), geologist and palaeontologist

themselves saw it that way. The most compelling argument for this interpretation is that the image on Side A is central to the slate with lettering placed directly above it, lending coherence to the layout of the marks on this side. Side B in contrast has lettering and an animal drawn in the upper left hand quadrant, which appear to have been incised from different angles and are more like doodles.

Side A (fig. 5.3)

On the obverse, Side A, is a central composition of a human-like figure, apparently mounted on a large quadruped. While it is possible that the figure is intended to be female, for the purposes of this description, the pronoun 'he/him' is used rather than 'she/her' or 'they/them'. This figure is brandishing a sword in his left hand and carries a small triangular-shaped shield in his right hand. The person's face is bisected diagonally by a straight line from the left and a large bird is perched on his head, in the style of a crested helmet. This bird has a long pointed beak, an oval eye and a neck or collar detail, and is facing in the same direction as the animal. A second bird,

5.3 Photograph of slate Side A with scale bar (Kevin Weldon)

which was thought initially to be a fish, is positioned below the hind feet of the quadruped and is rotated ninety degrees clockwise.

The two birds, although similar in form, do display some differences (fig. 5.4a). The bird on the person's head is simply drawn, and its wings are not shown, the main details being its large eye and a collar around its neck. The bird below the animal's hind leg is far more detailed (fig. 5.4b). It has its wings outstretched as though in flight, sports a curved beak, a broad feathered tail and has zigzag lines indicating body feathers. Above the main composition are two ladder marks (fig. 5.5), fanning out around the head of the quadruped. Above the central composition, in a title position at the top centre of the slate, are two inscribed letters, which could be read either as 'Bb' or as 'Db'. These letters are discussed in more detail below.

The quadruped (fig. 5.6) is drawn in profile with its head towards the left. It has a rounded forehead, large triangular upward-pointed ears, and a big oval eye, which is underlined. It has a small straight muzzle, on which is a zigzag line, either depicting teeth, or the cheek piece of a bridle. Having said that, there is no headstall, brow band, nose band, throatlatch, nor any obvious bridle hardware depicted. Lightly-incised wavy lines running from the animal's mouth to the rider's hand indicate reins. The animal's body is robust, with a deep chest from which the barrel of the body narrows from front to back. A

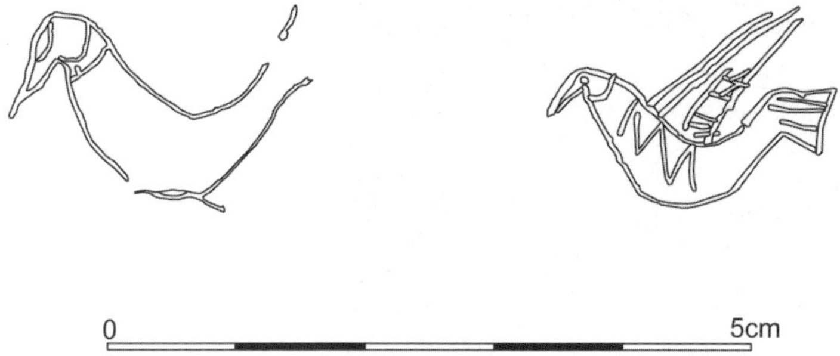

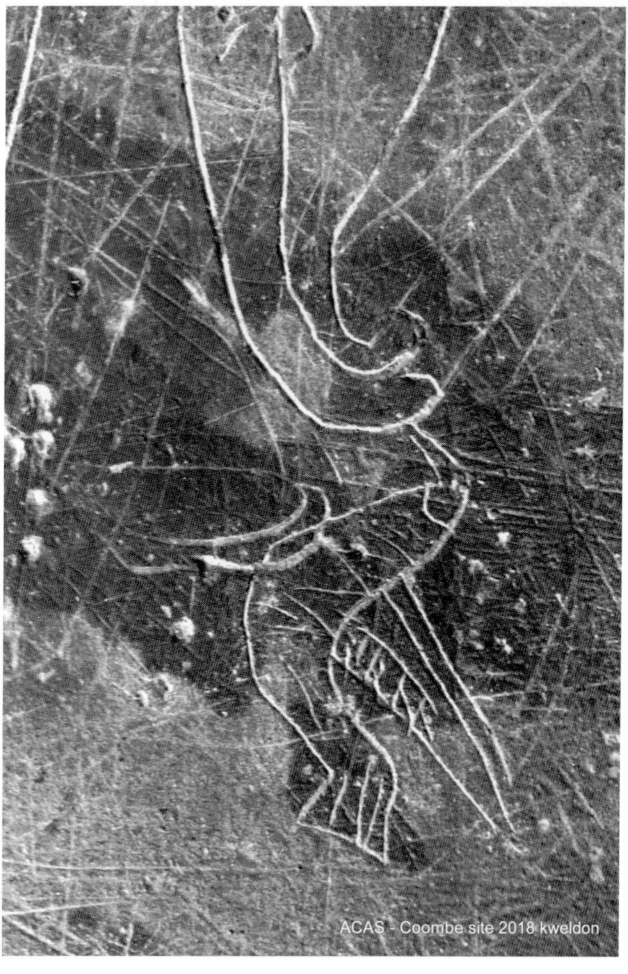

5.4a (*above*) Scale drawing of two birds side by side for comparison (Johnny Ryan)

5.4b Photograph of detail of Side A showing bird 2 and rear hooves (Kevin Weldon)

5.5 Photograph of detail of Side A showing horse's head, arcs and ladder marks (Kevin Weldon, for ACAS)

faint line beneath its upper back indicates that the body originally started out more slender in form and was modified to give the animal a larger and stronger appearance. The four legs of the animal are arranged in pairs with the feet turned backwards in a stylized way that is suggestive of movement. Both the fore and hind hips are depicted and the tail is made up of faint wavy lines, similar to the reins.

The humanoid figure (fig. 5.7) is shown partly in profile with the upper body turned slightly towards the viewer. He appears to be riding the quadruped but only one of his legs is visible so it is also possible, though less likely, that he is standing behind it. The foot of the human figure is angled slightly forward and his toe is turned upwards with the heel down below the toe, in a classic riding position. The foot has a long pointed shoe, with its toe drooping downwards, resembling footwear with pointed toe extensions found in mid-to-late twelfth-century contexts from Waterford. Riding without stirrups would be difficult to achieve while a brandishing weapon, so the absence of any saddle is more likely to reflect the naivety of the sketch rather

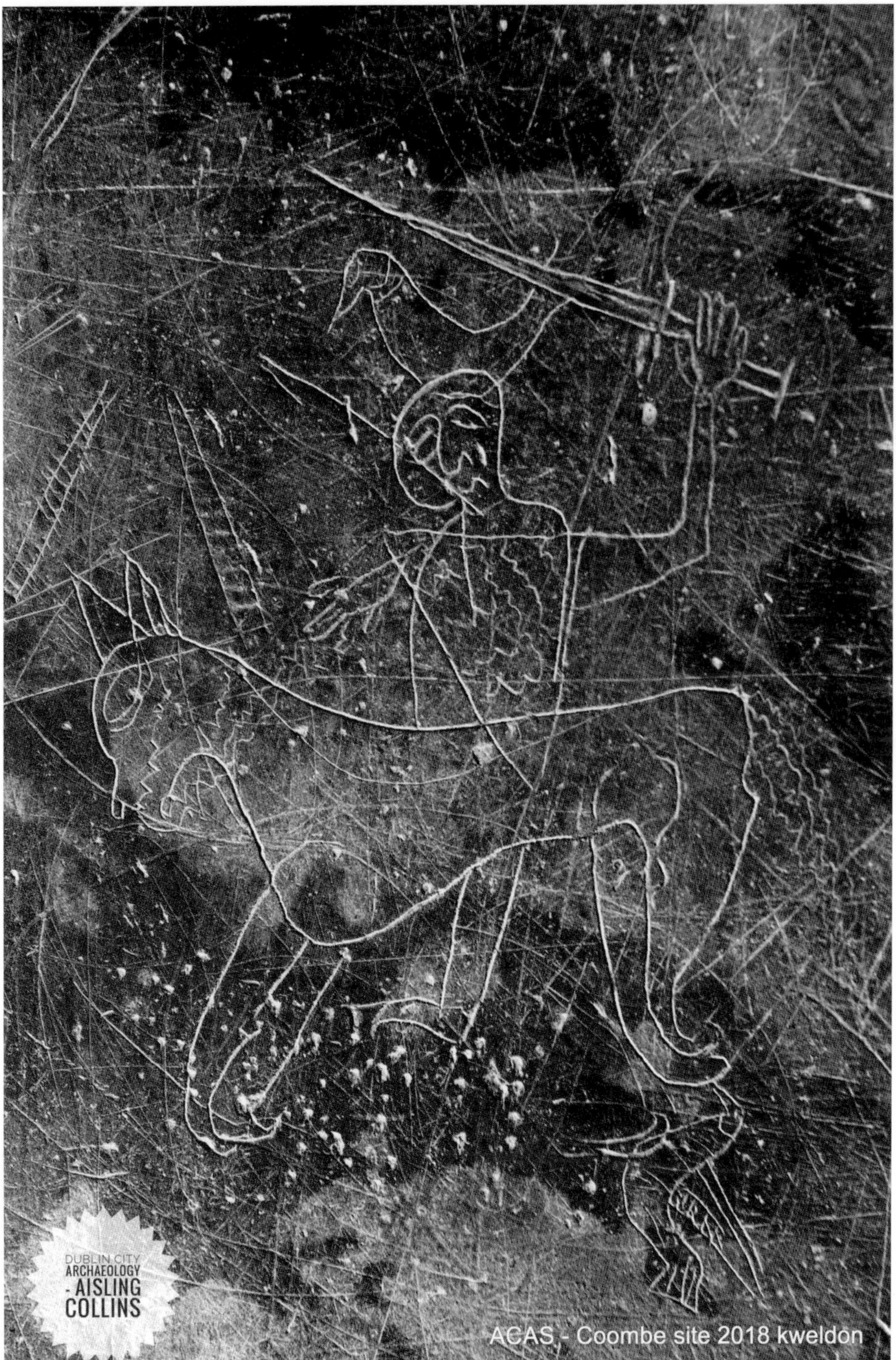

5.6 Photograph of detail of Side A of horse and rider (Kevin Weldon, for ACAS)

5.7 Photograph of slate Side A (Kevin Weldon)

than historical reality. There is no sign of a saddle or stirrup and this, combined with the figure's leg position, gives the impression that he is riding bareback.

The figure's head is rounded, and there is no obvious sign of a helmet, coif, head covering or hair, giving the rider a bald appearance. His face is asymmetrical, and drawn in such a way as to suggest that he is facing in the direction that the animal is moving, while at the same time gazing out towards the viewer. The figure's eyes are large pointed ovals with arcs above them for eyebrows, and the downward angles of the eyes and brows give him a solemn look. A deep indentation on the figure's left cheek looks like a tear, which adds to the sad impression but this dent may be post-deposition damage to the

5.8 Photograph detail of Side A showing man's head, bird, hand and sword (Kevin Weldon)

stone rather than a deliberate feature. His nose is hooked and bulbous, formed by a continuous line drawn from the forehead and right eye. The left cheek is accented with an uptick of the line, suggestive of a nasolabial fold. The small mouth is also downturned, completing the unhappy visage.

A line, resembling an arrow, lance or spear shaft, runs through the figure's face, close to his right eye but it is questionable whether this line relates to the primary composition, or represents a weapon of assault such as an arrow or lance. As previously noted, two ladder-like marks are located in the space above the animal's head, fanning out like the rays of a sun and the line cutting through the man's face could be another one of these that is unfinished. It is unclear whether these laddered lines belong to the main composition but they do respect it and are likely to have been drawn after the animal and human. There is also a faintly incised shape formed of two arcs that vaguely resembles a bow.

The figure's lower left arm is horizontal and his upper arm is raised vertically at a forty-five-degree angle, brandishing a sword over his head (fig. 5.8). The palm of the left hand, which in reality should be gripping the hilt, is spread out facing towards the viewer with all five digits extended and fully visible. The right hand is also depicted, apparently holding the reins. This

5.9 Photograph of slate Side B (Kevin Weldon)

hand is not well-drawn by comparison and seems foreshortened, though this is probably a result of the naïve drawing style.

Side B (fig. 5.9)

When flipped over on its bottom axis, the 'reverse' of the slate or Side B has an incomplete incised quadruped shown in profile in the upper left quadrant. It also bears several letters of the Latin alphabet in this area, mostly in the lower case, which read either as *abcdefg* or *abcdefghik*. If the latter, the end characters are superimposed on the animal's leg. Though unfinished, the animal on Side B of the slate is relatively-speaking more accomplished and more confidently drawn than the one on Side A. It has a deep chest and its slender body is graceful in appearance and confident in its execution (fig. 5.10). Two legs, one front and one back, are depicted, though the fore leg is unfinished. The hind leg stretches out behind the body, giving the impression that the animal is moving. The rear hoof-hock and fetlock are drawn with some detail but the tail is virtually non-existent. The animal has a small face, with a short nose, a lentoid eye, and large triangular ears, pricked at different angles giving the animal an alert look. There is a zigzag detail that suggests the mouth or a bridle cheek piece and a firmly drawn lappet, rein or collar stretches backwards across its neck. This horizontal lappet is composed of two parallel lines and is noticeably different from the reins on Side A, which are formed of wriggly lines. Despite the differences in execution, when the animals from each side of the slate are compared side by side and/or overlaid, they can be seen to have the same general form and thus belong to the same 'stable' but may be the work of different hands, perhaps a master and an apprentice (fig. 5.11).

RECORDING

Various methods have been employed to record the slate and its graffiti since it was discovered. It was photographed on discovery and before and after conservation by Kevin Weldon. Composite images were then captured by the Discovery Programme. These invaluable images were generated using a technique known as Reflectance Transformation Imaging (RTI). Following recording, the data was transcribed by the Discovery Programme and supporting background images were supplied in Adobe Illustrator. These interpretation drawings proposed 'primary' engravings shown in dark black, and fainter 'secondary' ones shown in light grey (fig. 5.12).

Following scanning, Dublin City Council commissioned an illustration of the slate by the archaeologist Johnny Ryan. From first-hand examination of the slate using a magnifying glass under natural and artificial light, and with the

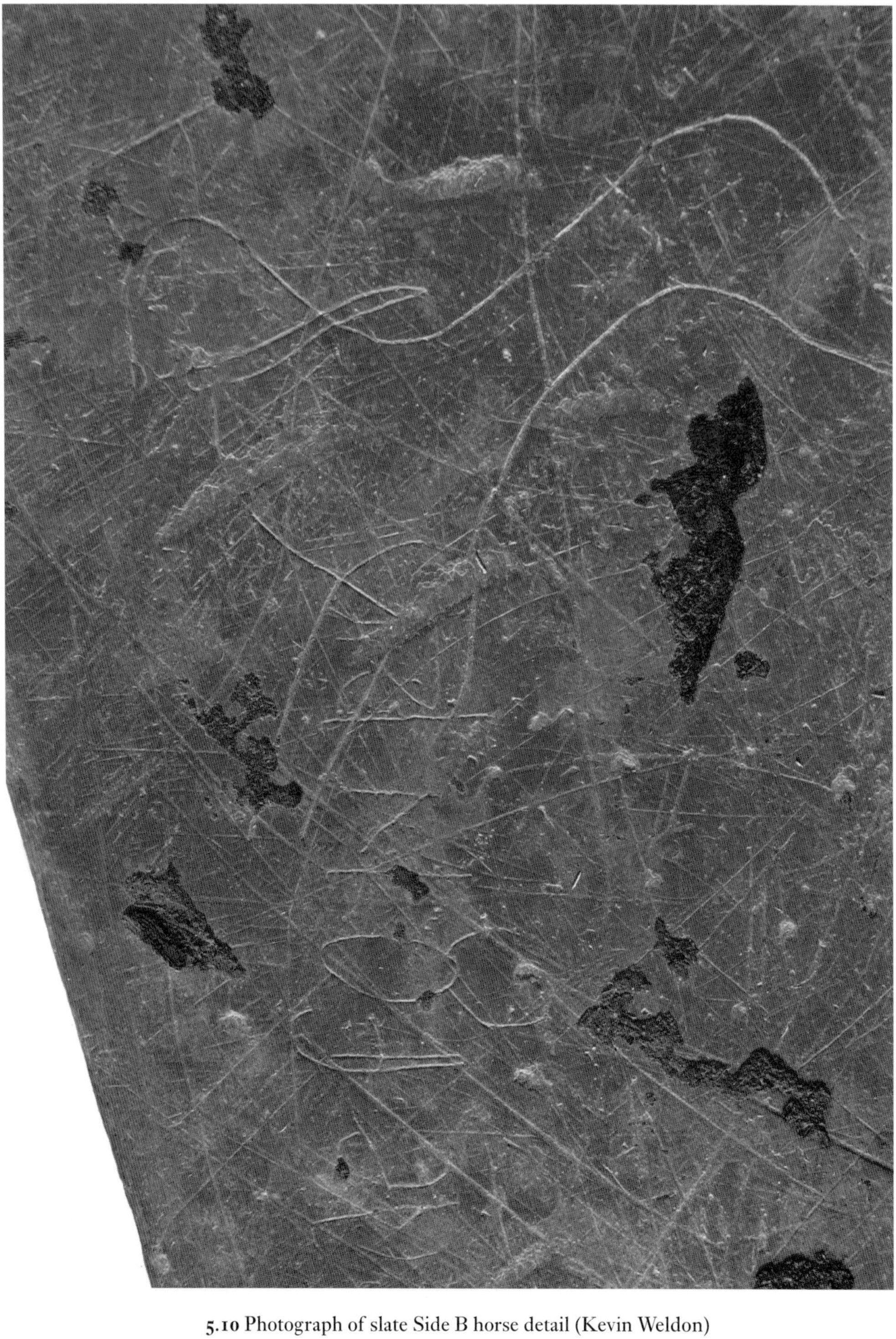

5.10 Photograph of slate Side B horse detail (Kevin Weldon)

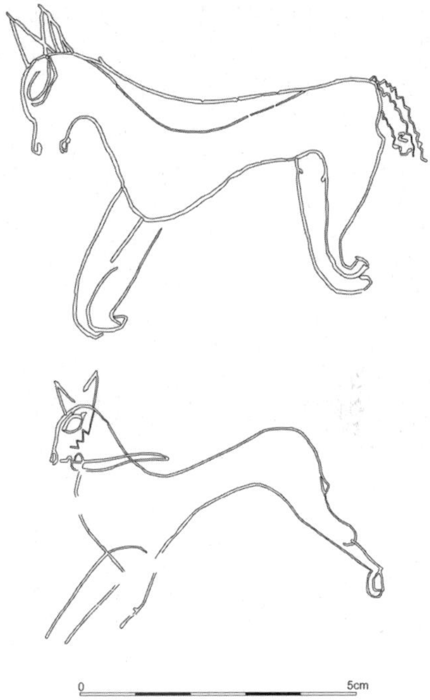

5.11 Scale drawing of the two horses for comparison (Johnny Ryan)

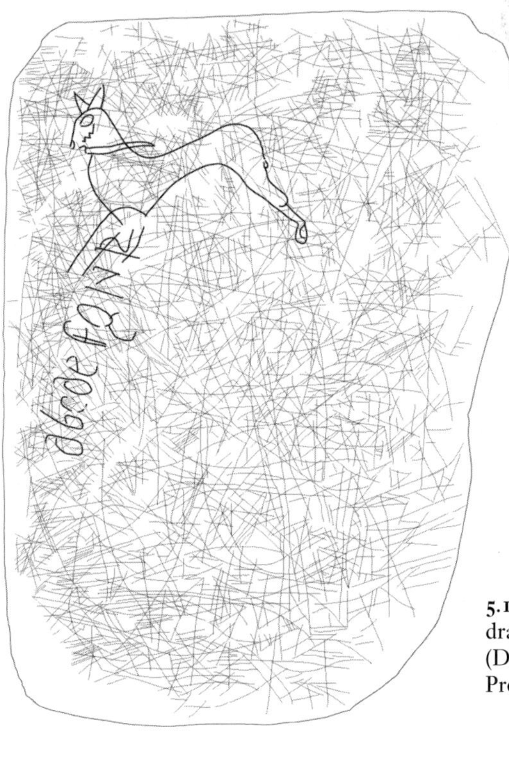

5.12 Interpretation drawing of Side B (Discovery Programme)

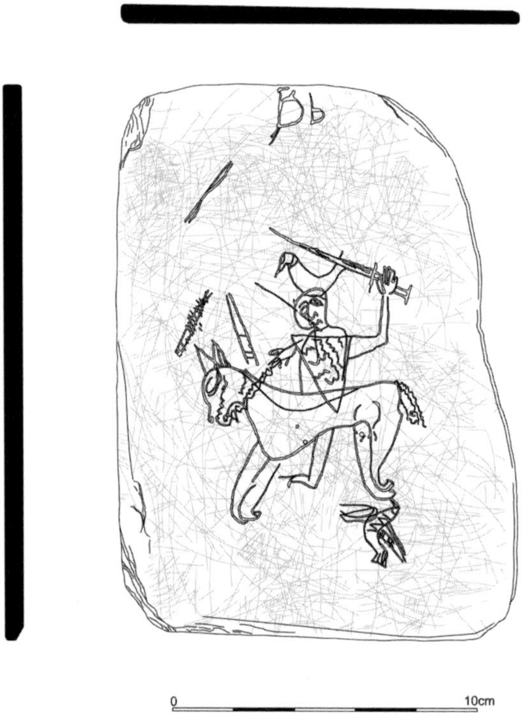

5.13a Interpretation drawing of the slate Side A (Johnny Ryan)

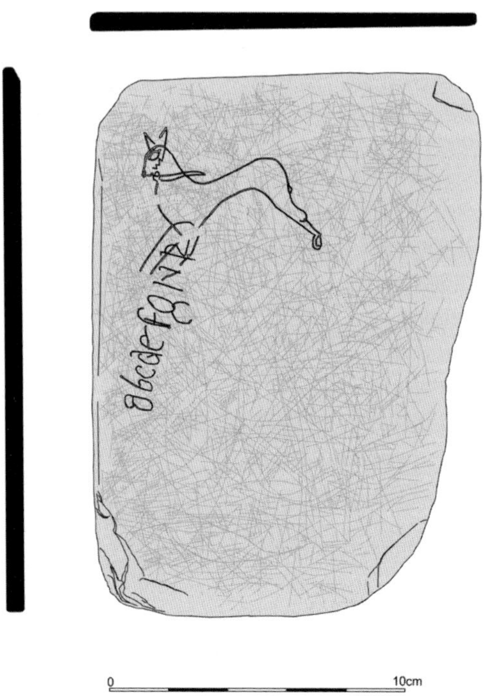

5.13b Interpretation drawing of the slate Side B (Johnny Ryan)

photographs and the RTI scans for reference, the writer and illustrator collaborated to produce a digital interpretation drawing of the main subjects (figs 5.13a–b). The process was greatly aided by the RTI derived images, which allowed for a close inspection of marks to determine the order of cutting. The illustration was undertaken using Computer Aided Design (CAD) following consideration of various options. The traditional method of pen and ink on drafting paper was discounted in favour of a digital illustration/interpretation, because of the amount of 'background noise' caused by the many cut-marks on the slate. Digitizing began with the lines clearly belonging to the main composition on the obverse of the slate, namely the animal and humanoid figure. Ryan identified the order in which the different elements of the main composition were incised. First to be drawn was the animal, the back of which had been redrawn to widen the body. Then came the animal's tail, the rider's head and body, followed by his arms, the bridle, the sword and finally the bird on the human figure's head. He posited that the medieval artist may have been right-handed because the lines were drawn to the right rather than to the left. A short report by Johnny Ryan is included in the final excavation report.

CONTEXT AND DATE

The incised slate was discovered during excavations at 124–8 The Coombe, Dublin 8 (fig. 5.14). The Coombe lies within a zone of archaeological potential for the historic city of Dublin, which is a Recorded Monument (DU018-020). The site at 124–8 The Coombe is bounded to the north by The Coombe, to the east and to the south by New Row South, with Fallon's Bar on the corner. This site was excavated over the winter of 2016–17 finishing in March 2018, as a requirement of planning permission, prior to its redevelopment as a Hyatt Centric Hotel by the Hodson Bay Hotel Group. The excavation was directed on behalf of the developer by Aisling Collins Archaeological Services (ACAS), under archaeological licence.[1] In a development management capacity, Dublin City Council's archaeologists and planners visited the site on a frequent basis during the excavations. The information in this section of the paper draws from the final archaeological excavation report by the site director Aisling Collins and supervisor Kevin Weldon.[2]

The adjacent site to the west at 118–23 The Coombe had been previously excavated by Claire Walsh in 2008–9.[3] Walsh found evidence there of a Hiberno-Norse community living outside the walled city on a street that was

1 Licence reference number 16E0080. 2 Aisling Collins and Kevin Weldon, '124–28 The Coombe Dublin 8: on behalf of Hodson Bay hotel group. Planning decision order no. PO554, decision date 16 February 2017, application no. 4337/16. Archaeological excavation licence 16EOO80. Archaeological excavation report' (unpublished report, ACAS, August 2019). 3 https://excavations.ie/report/2008/Dublin/0019411/, accessed 27 February 2022.

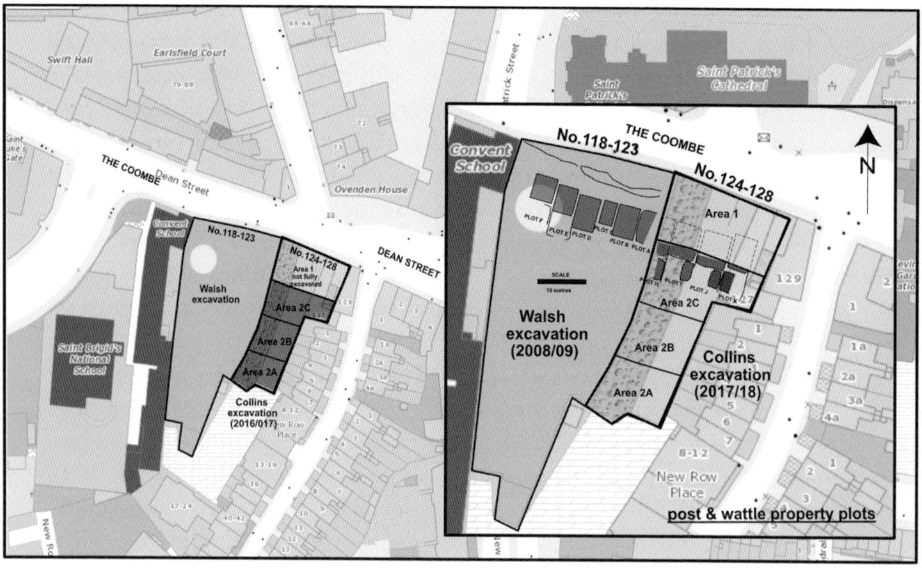

5.14 Site location map (ACAS)

aligned east–west along the Coombe watercourse. At the lowest levels, above the natural subsoil, she found an early roadway and an associated ditch. Over this was a terrace of post-and-wattle houses, labelled A–G from west to east. These houses were of Wallace's Type 1, being of sub-rectangular form with their narrow ends addressing the street frontage,[4] set in long fenced plots of approximately 5m in width. This phase of occupation was radiocarbon dated to the eleventh and twelfth centuries.[5] C14 dating of the fence on the earliest roadway indicates a date in the second half of the eleventh century for the continued use of the roadway and a date from the doorjamb of a large post-and-wattle house structure (F182 level 1, plot B) gives a late eleventh- to early twelfth-century date for the initial layout of plots. Pottery, mainly Dublin coarse-ware, was present in very small quantities in the occupation horizons of the second or third level of houses, while the underlying levels were characterized by the absence of pottery. The site provided important new archaeological evidence for the expansion of the late Hiberno-Norse town beyond the walls and for the formation of a southern suburb, presumably under municipal authority in the late eleventh to early twelfth century. The dearth of material goods from the occupation levels led Walsh to conclude that the occupants of the street were quite low down the social scale.

4 P.F. Wallace, *The Viking age buildings of Dublin*, Medieval Dublin Excavations 1962–81 Ser. A, 1 (Dublin, 1992). 5 Claire Walsh, 'The excavation of an early roadway and Hiberno-Norse houses at the Coombe' in Seán Duffy (ed.), *Medieval Dublin XI* (Dublin, 2013) pp 113–37.

124–8 The Coombe was excavated by Collins and her team in two main parts for logistical reasons. Area 1 to the north was only partially excavated and the lower levels are now preserved *in situ* beneath the hotel foyer. Area 2 to the south was subdivided into three smaller areas (A, B and C) all of which were fully-excavated down to the natural subsoil. The organic preservation at the northern end of the site was exceptional because of waterlogging caused by the Coombe stream. At its deepest point, towards the road, the archaeology was found to extend 3m below present ground level. The overall excavation recorded multiple phases of activity dating from the eleventh century down to the nineteenth century. A reconstruction drawing of the various building levels identified here from AD 1100 to 2019 was produced by the archaeological illustrator Conor Mc Hale for the Hudson Bay Group and is reproduced here with their kind permission (figs 5.15a–b).

The excavations revealed that the watercourse silted up in the mid-to-late twelfth century, after which the area to the south was levelled and the property plots were laid out. There were a total of four plots, each containing a post-and-wattle house and an outbuilding. These plots were labelled H–K to align with Walsh's recording system for the early street (fig. 5.16a). The main buildings, the fronts of which are now preserved *in situ*, would have addressed the street frontage. These were large Hiberno-Norse Dublin Type 1 houses, with three building levels in evidence.

The slate (F222) came from phase 1 of building level 3 in plot I of area 2C (fig. 5.16b), located to the immediate rear of the first house built on the plot (F226). Plot I was the widest of the four plots uncovered by Collins, measuring 6m across. The main structure in Plot I had double wattle walls and multiple phases of occupation were represented by at least three clay floors within it. In the yard behind the house was a central stone path (F221) measuring 7m long north–south. To the rear of the house to the east of the path was also a smaller sub-rectangular outbuilding (F227) measuring 4.2m long by 2m wide. This structure was constructed of single post-and-wattle walls and the deposits in it indicate that it was an unroofed animal pen. The slate was found on the ground surface (F262) just outside the back door of the house, close to a series of three small refuse pits (F173, F176 and F215). According to the finder, the archaeologist José Luis Silesy, it was lying face down, having been lain down with smaller stones to make up a gravelly surface over the boggy ground.

There is no radiocarbon date for this building level, but it overlies a fenced ditch which was the earliest feature found on the site. C14 dating of the fence returned a date in the second half of the eleventh century. A date from the doorjamb of an early house structure gave a late eleventh- to early twelfth-century date for the layout of these plots, providing a *terminus post quem* for building level 3 and the first Hiberno-Norse houses. A late twelfth-century C14 date for the slate's context is similarly supported by associated pottery and finds from the floor levels. Sherds of green-glazed pottery from this level have

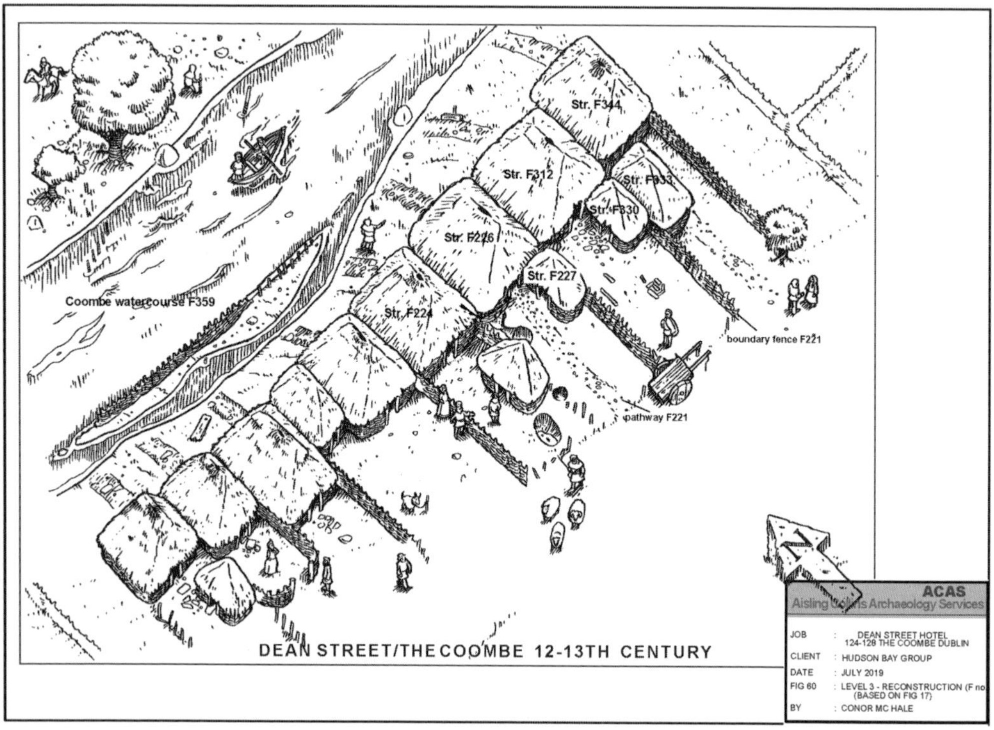

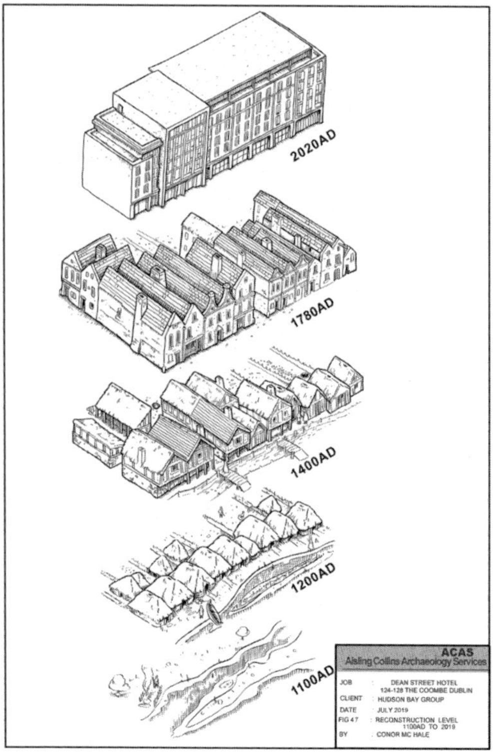

5.15a (*above*) Reconstruction of the site, twelfth to thirteenth century (Conor McHale for ACAS)

5.15b Reconstruction of building levels, AD 1100 to 2020 (Conor McHale for ACAS)

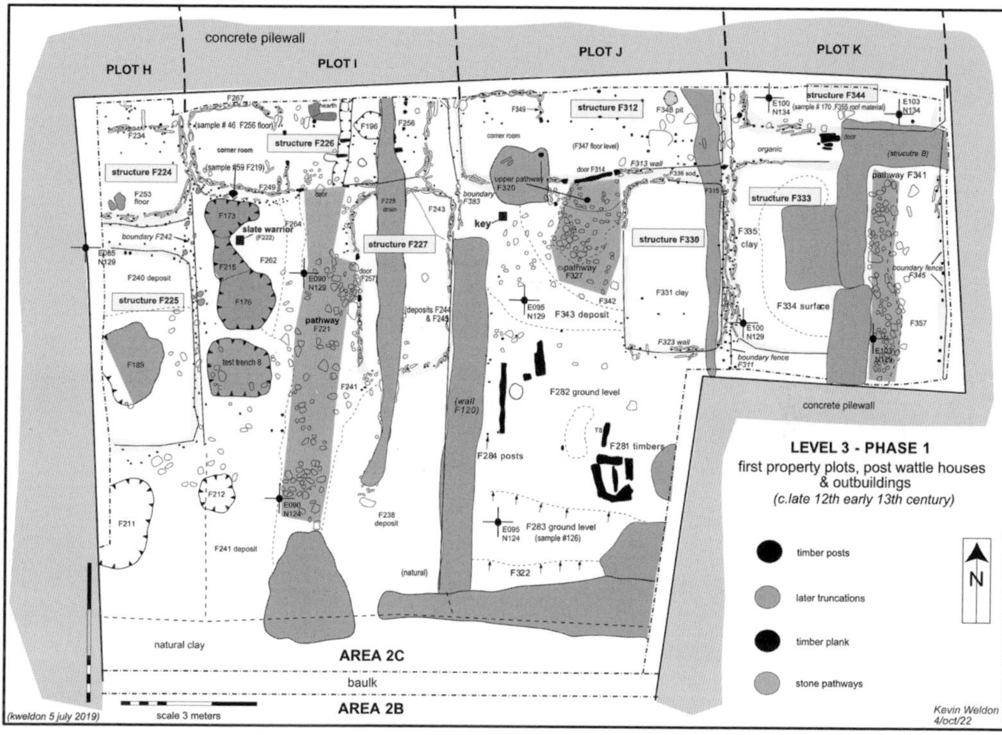

5.16a (*above*) Plan of level 3, phase 1 showing the first property plots, post-and-wattle houses and outbuildings (ACAS) **5.16b** Photograph of find spot during excavation

5.17 Photograph of key from Plot J (Kevin Weldon for ACAS)

been analysed by the pottery specialist Clare McCutcheon, who observed that mica in the clay is typical of late twelfth-century Dublin-type coarse-ware. Other finds from building level 3 plot I include an uninscribed slate, two stick pins, a horseshoe fragment, a clench bolt, a yew wood spoon, two leather shoes, a boot, some leather scraps, and a bone cylinder. A unique well-made and repaired copper alloy key, similar to examples from tenth- and eleventh-century contexts in Anglo-Saxon and Anglo-Scandinavian contexts, was found behind the house next door in plot J, phase 1, building level 3 (fig. 5.17).[6] Other noteworthy finds came from phase 3 of building level 3, where a distinctive Scandinavian-style wooden bench-end was found that was reused in a drain in the yard of plot I. There was also found in neighbouring plot J a socketed arrowhead of Halpin's Type 4.[7] This type of arrowhead is found in both pre-Anglo-Norman and Anglo-Norman Dublin, and a military function is considered to be more likely here than hunting.[8] The range of finds from Collins's site appears to challenge Walsh's interpretation that the Hiberno-Norse street was low in status.

6 Aisling Collins and Kevin Weldon, '124–28 The Coombe Dublin 8' (unpublished archaeological excavation report, 2019), p. 95. 7 Andrew Halpin, *Weapons and warfare in Viking and medieval Dublin: National Museum of Ireland medieval Dublin excavations 1962–81* (Dublin, 2008), Ser. B, vol. 9. 8 Collins and Weldon, '124–28 The Coombe' (unpubl.

DISCUSSION

The slate was deposited in a street of domestic buildings spanning the late twelfth to the early thirteenth century that belonged to a phase of suburban habitation approximately 650m outside the walled town. It lay possibly at the intersection of two of the great roads of early Ireland, Slige Dála and Slige Chualann,[9] the street being situated on the south bank of the Coombe stream, a tributary of the River Poddle, on course to meet the diverted Poddle at 'Cross Poddle' (fig. 5.18). Known in later sources as the 'Commons Water', this stream would have been a vital source of fresh water and power for the Hiberno-Norse inhabitants of the suburb.[10]

The discovery of pre-Anglo-Norman houses outside the town walls on The Coombe and elsewhere at Stephen Street,[11] Chancery Lane,[12] and to the north of the Liffey at Church Street,[13] suggests that the Hiberno-Norse town already had fully established suburbs in these locations prior to the Anglo-Norman invasion. The work of the archaeologist Paul Duffy (pers. comm.), and the historian Edel Bhreathnach,[14] on the pre-Anglo-Norman church foundations in Dublin further suggests that the suburbs were developing into settled parishes before the English takeover. Contrary to the usual narrative, by the late twelfth century, it is conceivable that all the main roads into and out of the town were lined with the houses of craftsmen. Differential preservation of organic materials in wet and dry conditions may well have led to the loss of the archaeological evidence, with post-and-wattle houses and plot fences surviving only in areas of localized flooding closest to the Liffey, Poddle and Coombe watercourses. Variable *in situ* preservation of this type has been demonstrated in Ribe, Denmark by Sindbaek and others.[15] It is suggested here that the decayed habitation deposits in unsaturated areas beyond the town walls may have been identified as 'garden soil' by excavators heretofore.[16] Speed's map of Dublin from 1610 shows the Coombe watercourse with a row of houses to the south of the stream and a bridge, and it is possible that this early modern map reflects the mid-to late twelfth-century scenario.

rept), p. 104. 9 See H.B. Clarke, 'Christian cults and cult centres in Hiberno-Norse Dublin and its hinterland' in Ailbhe MacShamhráin (ed.), *The island of St Patrick: church and ruling dynasties in Fingal and Meath, 400–1148* (Dublin, 2004), p. 141, fig. 9.1. 10 Clarke, Dublin, Pt 1 (IHTA), p. 7. 11 https://heritagemaps.ie/documents/Therefore_ArchaeologyReports/17E0212_1.pdf, accessed 4 September 2022. 12 Excavation licence 18E00250. 13 https://heritage maps.ie/documents/Therefore_ArchaeologyReports/09E0517.pdf, accessed 4 September 2022; this excavation is currently unreported (see www.excavations.ie for a summary). 14 Edel Breathnach, 'Saints' dedications and the ecclesiastical landscape of Hiberno-Norse Dublin: Irish Scandinavian and others' in Seán Duffy (ed.), *Medieval Dublin XVIII* (Dublin, 2020), pp 143–68. 15 Søren M. Sindbaek and Anna K.E. Tjellden, 'The emporium's *in situ* preservation conditions' in Søren M. Sindbaek, *Northern emporium, Vol. 1: the making of Viking Age Ribe* (Højbjerg, 2022), pp 315–27. 16 See Sindbaek, *Northern emporium, Vol. 1*.

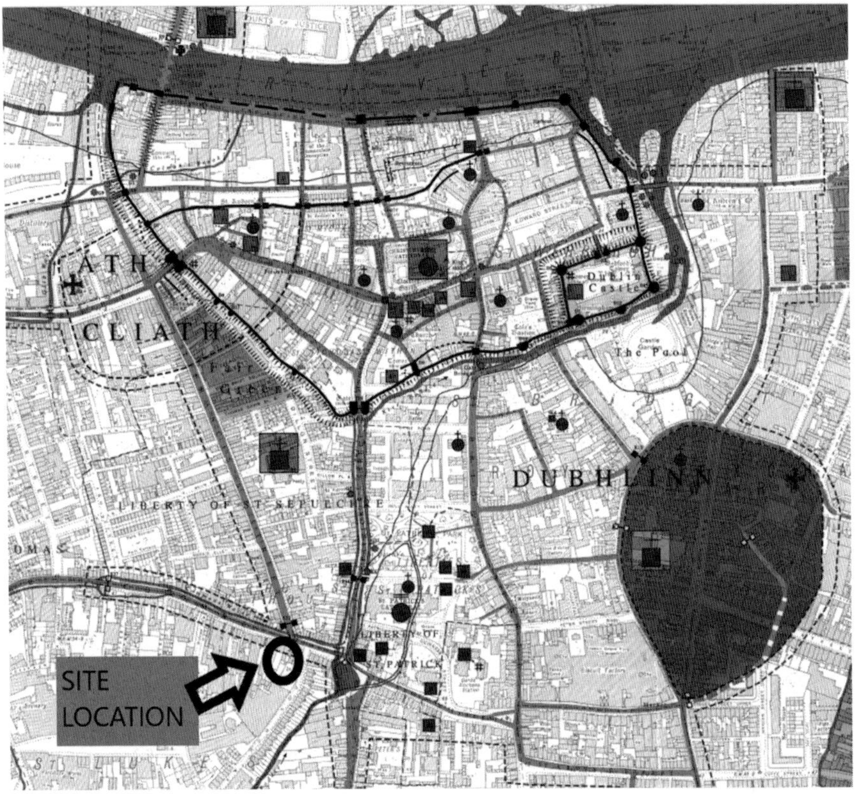

5.18 Site location on Coombe stream and possible adjacent long-distant routes (after Clarke, *Dublin, Pt 1* (IHTA), map 4)

In 1170, Dublin was taken by the Anglo-Normans and in 1172 Henry II granted it to his 'men of Bristol'.[17] By the late twelfth and early thirteenth century, there are documentary references to development along the Coombe. The Coombe was in the parish of St Patrick, which was often linked with Donore, a liberty granted to St Thomas's abbey on its foundation in the late twelfth century. Áine Foley notes that the hospital of St John the Baptist, located outside the Newgate, was granted certain properties along The Coombe in the thirteenth century.[18] The artisans granting and holding the lands there were recorded in the hospital's surviving register.[19] Dyers, weavers, carpenters and others are represented in the register, indicating that the street was occupied by a range of craftsmen practising complementary trades,

17 Seán Duffy, 'Town and crown: the kings of England and their city of Dublin' in Michael Prestwich, Richard Britnell, and Robin Frame (eds), *Thirteenth Century England X. Proceedings of the Durham Conference 2003* (Woodbridge, 2005), pp 95–117. 18 See Áine Foley, in Collins and Weldon, '124–28 The Coombe' (unpubl. rept). 19 *Reg. St John.*

utilizing the water course for their respective industries. For example, between 1259 and 1260, Richard the Tanner's wife granted lands in Donore to the hospital, with 'edifices' formerly held by Quintin the Dyer, close to the tail-race of a mill belonging to St Thomas's abbey. Other names include Hugh the Carpenter and Dodeman the Weaver (*textor*). The plot sizes are recorded as ranging from 16ft in front and 50ft in width in the centre, to 20ft in front, and it is likely that this was also the plot size in the twelfth century. Collins's excavation found that the street underwent a major phase of redevelopment in the thirteenth century, at which time the post-and-wattle plots were dismantled and the ground was levelled and consolidated with a 600mm layer of imported clay, sealing the wet organic levels below. The Hiberno-Norse property plots that had been laid out in the twelfth century were found to have been maintained in the subsequent phase of stone buildings and show extraordinary continuity over each of the successive building levels down to the nineteenth century.

The connection between The Coombe and St Patrick's church may also be early. Claire Walsh identified a lease map dated 1838 showing that the site in question was owned by the vicars' choral, having been granted land on the south side of the Coombe/Kevin Street route, *c.*1506.[20] In *c.*1270 a grant records that Simon the chaplain gave John, son of Geoffrey the miller, lands with edifices beside the Coombe, formerly held by John White, a dyer.[21] The lands of the 'community of canons of St Patrick' are furthermore cited as the western boundary in a grant of 1270, indicating that the cathedral held lands here in the late thirteenth century.[22]

The late twelfth-century context for the slate puts it on the cusp of the late Hiberno-Norse and the early Anglo-Norman period. This was a time of immense political and cultural upheaval during which Dublin transformed from an international trading centre with a mixed Hiberno-Norse population into an Anglo-Norman colonial town. The transitional date presents a particular challenge when interpreting the object and its graffiti in cultural terms. Should one look to Insular, Viking, Anglo-Norman or other sources for artistic comparisons? What was the function of the object and how best can it be classified? Is the figure a portrait of a known mythological, religious or historical character and would their identity have been recognizable to a contemporary onlooker? What does the combination of literacy and artistry tell us about the nature of the domestic suburb in which the slate was found and what might we infer about the ethnicity and occupation of its inhabitants?

20 See Áine Foley, in Collins and Weldon, '124–28 The Coombe' (unpubl. rept). **21** *Reg. St John*, no. 173. **22** Ibid.

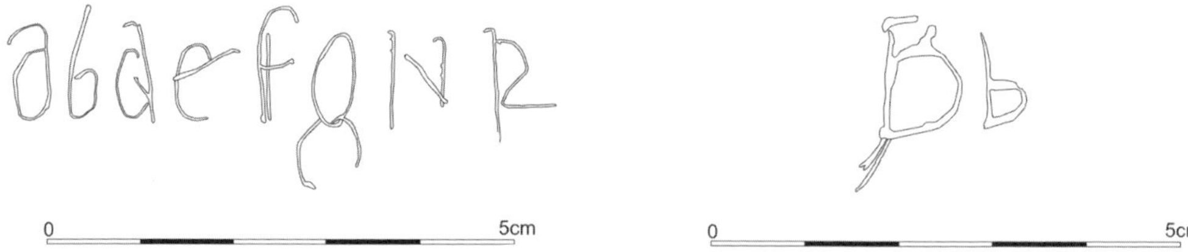

5.19a Scale drawing of the letters on both sides (Johnny Ryan)

5.19b Photograph of letters on Side A (Kevin Weldon for ACAS)

5.19c Photograph of letters on Side B (Kevin Weldon for ACAS)

Script (figs 5.19a–c)

The slate has been examined for the purposes of this paper by some specialists in medieval script. The calligrapher and medieval historian Dr Timothy O'Neill (pers. comm.) inspected the slate first-hand and compared the lettering on the slate with graffiti in the main passage tomb at Knowth, Co. Meath, where the letters relate to Irish scripts of the ninth and tenth centuries.[23] He considered the scribing tools and materials in the execution of the letters on the slate to be similar to Knowth, the forms of which remained current in the scribal tradition through to the sixteenth century and beyond. However, he observed that the lower case *a*, *d* and particularly the *g* on the reverse of the slate show little or no resemblance to the letter forms on the corbels at Knowth.[24] He concluded that the script is not of Gaelic origin, nor is it rendered in an Irish-language hand. He observed that

> Considering historical styles it has some vague elements that might relate to chancery-italic styles of the later sixteenth century. The *d* and *e* for example, or what might be a double *f*, feature in handwriting manuals of the period. The odd *g* would likewise relate more to this style, as would the *a* and *b*, than to the more cursive copperplate that became widespread in the seventeenth century. [The] same applies to the two *B*'s on the other side.[25]

In summary, O'Neill's reading of the inscription is that the capital letter in title position on the obverse is a *B* (not a *D*), that the hand is not Gaelic in style, and that it is comparable with later medieval writing.

Correspondence via email with Michelle Brown (of the British Library)[26] led her to say that the graffiti are

> a little reminiscent of some of the Tintagel drawings … The style of lettering doesn't get us too far … save to say that the *f* may be double contoured (what we call a skeletal form) and the *g* is double bowed like an 8, both of which suggest Norman, rather than Gaelic, influence. I think the *Db* is right and that the other inscription is just an abecedarium (a trial of the alphabet), *abcdefghik* (the *H* is written as a capital with a downwards sloping cross-stroke, like an N, the I is in ligature with the K and there's a horizontal stroke above that forms a pair with another above it and is probably not part of the abcedarium inscription. The drawings

23 F.J. Byrne, et al., *Excavations at Knowth Vol. 4: historical Knowth and its hinterland*, Royal Irish Academy (Dublin, 2008), iv, p. 92, p. 94. 24 O'Neill noted that the deformation of scribal letters caused by the materials makes interpretation difficult; the script thus requires further analysis and comparison with Hiberno-Norse samples of lettering. 25 Tim O'Neill, pers. comm. 26 With reference to the RTI images and interpretation drawings.

of the horse and of the rider with bird-crested helm appear to be by the same hand. A 12th-cent date seems to fit.

Brown's reading of the *Db* differs from O'Neill's but like him she considers the hand to be Norman rather than Gaelic in style and also observed the use of capitals in the abecedarium (or abecedary) on Side B.[27] Brown's reading of the drawings and letters as the work of a single hand and her suggestion that the bird above the rider is a bird-crested helm will be discussed further below.[28]

Bernard Meehan, former Head of Research Collections in Trinity College Dublin, also inspected the lettering on the slate in person, noting by email that 'It must be a pen trial. I just wonder if it's all the same phase or does another hand take over at "*f*"?' He also remarked that the last three letters in the abecedarium may be capitals. In summary, the three experts consulted all agreed that the lettering is in Norman rather than Irish script and that the letters from the alphabet *a-g* (or *a-k*) inscribed on Side B can be interpreted as an abecedarium. It is hoped that these and/or other experts will develop the preliminary work on the script, leading to a greater understanding of the piece.

The meaning and 'title' position of the letters *Bb* (or *Db*) inscribed at the top of Side A above the main composition are tantalizing but likely unknowable. It is tempting to speculate that they are the initial of a famous character, for example, Brian Bóraime (d. 1014), Diarmait Mac Murchada (d. 1171), or perhaps of a saint. It is more likely of course to be the initial of the artist or simply the practice of upper and lower cases. Whatever their meaning, the letters must have been learned by copying from a manuscript, a motif-piece, coin, a seal, a writing tablet or other written source known to the maker.

Classification

A key question for interpreting the slate is object classification, that is, whether the slate is best described as a piece of graffiti, as a craftperson's motif-piece or as a writing tablet associated with scribal learning.

Motif-piece?

The term motif-piece was devised by Uaininn O'Meadhra to replace the traditional term trial piece for 'small portable odd-pieces or scraps of material (usually bone or stone, sometimes wood or even leather) with carved or incised positive patterns discretely and sporadically positioned over their surfaces'.[29]

27 Abecedaria (abecedaries) list the letters of the alphabet in order and are the practice exercises of a literate or semi-literate individual. **28** Picking up on the bird crested-helm idea, Howard Clarke (pers. comm.) remarks that the out of scale bird may be intentional since a scaled version would be too small to be read as a crested helm. **29** Uaininn O'Meadhra, *Early Christian, Viking and Romanesque art: motif pieces from Ireland*, 2 vols

According to O'Meadhra's motif-piece criteria, patterns are supported by the piece rather than serving as decoration, do not follow any fixed plan, can be superimposed on one another, lie randomly and can, though not always, be unfinished or incompetently worked, often with mistakes and repetitions and are always positive.[30] The slate from The Coombe displays all the key characteristics of motif-pieces as described. Motif-pieces functioned as leisure activities, learning attempts, modelli or exempla, moulds or dies and in some cases as talismans. They are predominantly Insular in their distribution, with a small number from the Irish Sea littoral and the colonial Viking world, and they date to the early medieval period. Approximately 250 or so motif-pieces have been recovered from excavations in Dublin, where they are associated with craft-working, especially fine metalworking, exhibiting stylistic traits of Insular and Scandinavian-derived art. In this regard, a particularly fine slate motif-piece, measuring 11.5 x 9.0 x 0.8 cm, with expertly worked intricate knot work, zoomorphic and foliate patterns carved on both faces, was found during excavations of Hiberno-Norse building levels at Christchurch Place in Dublin. Another slate motif-piece, possibly a reused whetstone, was found at Winetavern Street. Several slate motif-pieces came from excavations of early medieval Irish sites such as at Lissue, Co. Antrim, and Nendrum and Gransha, Co. Down but none of these examples have lettering on them.[31] The classification of the slate from The Coombe as a motif-piece in the Insular Celtic tradition falters mainly because of the combination of Latin inscriptions and artwork, which is not at all typical of the Irish motif-piece corpus.

Writing tablet or scholar's slate?

This leads to the question of whether the slate would classify as a writing tablet. Writing tablets of slate and other materials, with graphic symbols scratched directly on the surface or into wax recessed into the surface are well known from Antiquity. The carrier material in which the sacrificial wax layer is applied usually consists of wood but medieval writing tablets were also made of ivory, silver, horn or slate and served as 'vehicles for informal composition, learning exercises, note taking, correspondence, document production and accounting'. Tablets were widely used as learning tools in the schoolroom. A cultural import from the post-Roman world, such tablets were used for literacy and learning during the first millennium in Ireland. First drafts and writing exercises were done on wax tablets because they were practical, cheap and easily available. Wax tablets differed in size depending on their function. Based on a statistical analysis of Continental post-Antique examples, Élisabeth Lalou proposed the following format sizes for tablets; small (10 × 5cm), medium (20 × 10cm) and large (35 × 25cm). At 17.6 x 13cm, The Coombe slate roughly

(Stockholm, 1979). **30** O'Meadhra, *Motif pieces from Ireland*, i, p. 13. **31** Ibid., pp 41, 67, 99–100.

approximates to Lalou's 'medium' format.[32] The earliest known example of a writing tablet from Ireland is a set of six wooden wax tablets dating to the late sixth century discovered by a turf cutter in Springmount Bog, Co. Antrim in 1913. These tablets are the earliest surviving example of Irish writing in the Latin script. They form a booklet of texts from the Book of Psalms and are considered to be the work of a monk or a scholar at a monastic scriptorium.

The slate from The Coombe was deposited on a secular site rather than a monastic scriptorium, but it may nevertheless be associated with a nearby school. In a late twelfth-century context in that general location, the most likely place for teaching Latin literacy was St Patrick's collegiate church, established by Archbishop John Cumin in 1192 to educate the clergy, which was later upgraded to cathedral status in *c.*1220. The abecedarium on the reverse of the slate helps to classify the Coombe slate as a scribal learning tool. Slates or tablets bearing evidence for literacy and learning have been found elsewhere in the Irish Sea region. Early medieval inscribed slates are known from monasteries such as at Nendrum and Downpatrick, Co. Down,[33] and from later medieval churches such as at Smarmore, Co. Louth. Incised slate fragments came from other early medieval sites such as Cahermacnaghten, Co. Clare,[34] while a slate bearing ship graffito came from Kilclief, Co. Down.[35] They have been found on medieval defensive sites such as at Tintagel Castle in Cornwall,[36] Nevern Castle in Wales and late medieval inscribed slates bearing musical notation were found during excavations at Swords Castle, Co. Dublin.[37] In Dublin city, a stone bearing an incised griffin was found in the city ditch.[38]

The most significant insular early medieval inscribed slate collection comes from the monastic island of Inchmarnock in the Firth of Clyde, Scotland.[39]

32 Elisabeth Lalou, 'Inventaire des tablettes médiévales et présentation genérale' in eadem (ed.), *Les tablettes à écrire de l'antiquité à l'epoque modern: actes du colloque international du Centre National de la Recherche Scientifique, Paris, Institut de France, 10–11 octobre 1990* (Brepols, 1992), pp 233–88; see also Thomas Wozniak, 'Stand und perspektiven der erforschung ausgewählter schriftträger: wachstafeln' ['Status and prospects of research on selected writing medium: wax tablets'] in Irmgard Fees and Aanrea Stieldorf (eds), *Archiv für diplomatik schriftgeschichte siegel- und wappenkunde* (Cologne, 2021), pp 345–86. **33** https://www.qub.ac.uk/sites/communityarchaeology/OurProjects/Communityexcavations/Downpatrick/#:~:text=In%20August%202018%20and%20August,by%20the%20PEACE%20IV%20programme, accessed 23 August 2022. **34** Excavation licence reference 08E435:064. See https://excavations.ie/report/2008/Clare/0019126/, accessed 23 August 2022. **35** Finbar McCormick and Ole Kastholm, 'A Viking ship graffito from Kilclief, Co. Down, Ireland', *International Journal of Nautical Archaeology*, 46:1 (2017). https:// pureadmin.qub.ac.uk/ws/portalfiles/portal/122453674/Kilclief_ship_Final_1_.pdf, accessed 23 August 2022. **36** https://www.english-heritage.org.uk/about-us/search-news/tintagkilel-archaeology, accessed 29 June 2022. **37** See fig. 11. Slate Fragments E4619:106:74 and E4619:112:19 in the excavation report by Christine Baker https://heritagemaps.ie/documents/Therefore_ArchaeologyReports/E004619_1.pdf, accessed 27 September 2022. **38** Antoine Giacometti, Archaeology Plan (pers. comm.) **39** Excavations to the north of St Marnock's church at Inchmarnock revealed the remains of

Literacy is attested to here by fragments of slate with practice writing and text in Gaelic, Latin and ogham script. Those that are not gaming pieces have been classified as motif-pieces. The most famous of the Inchmarnock slates has been dubbed the 'hostage stone' because it bears a sketch appearing to show an individual being led in chains towards a Viking ship.[40] Another slate from Inchmarnock bears a hunting scene and one has horses. Provisionally dated to the eighth or ninth century, the Inchmarnock group contains abstract designs and graffiti, as well as practice pieces for the creation of designs in other media. Many were found associated with debris from metalworking and may have been produced as pattern books. Significantly, the Inchmarnock excavations identified a schoolhouse juxtaposed with the craft workshops. For this reason, the slates from Inchmarnock have been interpreted as evidence of instruction and training in design between a master and pupil(s), and possibly for fosterage in a monastic context.[41] Incised stones were recovered from the early medieval Irish monastery of Nendrum, Mahee Island in Strangford Lough, Co. Down where the excavator also located a monastic schoolhouse.[42] This monastery was founded in the fifth century and came to an end at some time between 974 and 1178, though its church served a parish until the site was abandoned in the fifteenth century. The building yielded about thirty slate tablets bearing designs along with a bell and a stone with an inscription in runes.

A stone inscribed with Latin text, Greek letters and Christian symbols was excavated at Tintagel Castle in 2017. This stone appears to have been used for writing practice and is dated to the seventh century. The letter style, language and use of Christian symbols together provide evidence of Mediterranean influence and contact with Cornwall in the post-Roman period, at which time Tintagel was both an important trading port, and a settlement of high status, and possibly even a royal seat. Another stone discovered at Tintagel in 1998 bears several inscribed words including the Celtic name 'Artognou'.[43] Incised slates were also discovered embedded into a southern entrance during

an early monastic enclosure, together with a number of workshops yielding approximately one hundred incised slates. Among them, fourteen are text-inscribed, some are gaming boards. Several are non-text-inscribed slates, some bearing figurative scenes and geometric motifs. See Christopher Lowe, *Inchmarnock: an early historic island monastery and its archaeological landscape* (Edinburgh, 2008), pp 114–74. **40** See https://www.researchgate.net/figure/The-Hostage-Stone-from-Inchmarnock-Scotland-The-image-appears-to-show-an-individual_fig3_309586148, accessed 23 August 2022; Christopher Lowe, 'Image and imagination: the Inchmarnock "hostage stone"' in Beverley Ballin Smith, Simon Taylor and Gareth Williams (eds), *West over sea: studies in Scandinavian sea-borne expansion and settlement before 1300: a festschrift in honour of Dr Barbara E. Crawford*. The northern world 31 (Leiden, 2007), pp 53–67, at p. 53; https://brill.com/view/book/edcoll/9789047421214/Bej.9789004158931.i-614_005.xml?language=en, accessed 23 August 2022. **41** Lowe, *Inchmarnock*, pp 114–74. **42** H.C. Lawlor, *The monastery of Saint Mochaoi of Nendrum* (Belfast, 1925). **43** See https://www.english-heritage.org.uk/about-us/search-news/tintagel-archaeology, accessed 29 June 2022.

excavations at Nevern Castle in Wales. The slates had been bedded on their edges, so that the designs could not be seen by the people passing through and were in all probability incised by the workmen building the gateway. The feature was constructed in the final quarter of the twelfth century, *c.*1170–91.[44] Thirteen of the slates had designs inscribed into one or both faces. Some of the doodles are of warrior and weapons. Their location at the threshold and the nature of the designs on them suggest that they were deliberately-placed apotropaic symbols.[45]

Fifty-one medieval inscribed slates were recovered from the site of Smarmore, Co. Louth.[46] The majority of the written inscriptions on the Smarmore slates relate to plant-based medical recipes, for healing of wounds and include treatments for injuries to horses. Some of the texts are ecclesiastical in content and four of them are inscribed with polyphony or musical notation.[47] Preliminary results of recent scientific analysis to the Smarmore group found no wax but detected that a thin layer of a complex pigmented substance or 'paint' had been applied to the surfaces enabling the lightly incised inscriptions to stand out (1961:8 and 1961:12).[48] Future XRF examination of the slate from The Coombe is recommended to see whether any wax or paint had been applied to it, as this would help to confirm or discount its proposed classification as a writing tablet.

Graffiti?

Another question with regard to classification is whether the term graffiti is a suitable term to describe the combination of letters and drawings incised on the slate. Graffiti in the medieval context are often found on the walls of places of worship, pilgrimage, defence, or incarceration and provide a 'window into the medieval world and the minds who created it'. Graffiti are quite common in the Middle Ages and early modern period but research into graffiti is still in its infancy, and they have often been dismissed as irrelevant doodlings by children. A major study is now underway by Thomas Wozniak whose survey of medieval graffiti representing knights, riders, horsemen and men-at-arms finds that depictions of horsemen and knights, battles, tournaments and duels are a popular subject for graffiti all over Europe throughout the Middle Ages.[49]

44 Chris Caple, 'The apotropaic symbolled threshold to Nevern Castle–Castell Nanhyfer', *Archaeological Journal*, 169:1 (2014), 422–52. 45 See https://neverncastle.wales/neverns-apotropaic-slates/, accessed 1 June 2022. 46 A.J. Bliss, 'The inscribed slates at Smarmore', *PRIA*, 64C (1965/66), 33–60; slates 1960: 1–51. 47 Derek Britton and A.J. Fletcher, 'Medieval Hiberno-English inscriptions on the inscribed slates of Smarmore: some reconsiderations and additions', *Irish University Review*, 20:1 (1990), 55–72, at 59–60. 48 See https://www.researchgate. net/publication/340647983_Archaeometric_Analysis_of_Late_Medieval_Inscribed_Slates_from_Smarmore_Co_Louth and https://soundcloud.com/the-royal-irish-academy/a-clean-slate-the-science-of-writing-on-slate-in-late-medieval-ireland?in=the-royal-irish-academy/sets/seminar-revealing-the-past accessed 13 March 2022. 49 Thomas Wozniak, 'Ritter, reiter und bewaffnete im kontext mittlealterlicher graffiti' in

Ritter, Reiter und Bewaffnete 137

A01 10. Jh. Libušín (Bez. Kladno), Pläner, 31 x 20,5 cm (Zeichnung T. Wozniak nach Militký 2000, 165 Abb. 07.02.07)

A02 10./11. Jh. Pfalz Werla, Heißluft-Auslaßsteinfragment 17 x 38–40 x 20 cm, (Zeichnung T. Wozniak nach Ring 2001, 19 Abb. II. 3)

A03 11./12. Jh. Schlettstadt, Fideskirche, Portal, 90 x 80 cm (Zeichnung T. Wozniak nach Forrer 1912/13, 240 Abb. 4)

A04 11./12. Jh. Quedlinburg, Krypta St. Marien, 35 x 16 cm, 69 cm (Zeichnung T. Wozniak)

A05 12. Jh. Moings, Pfarrkirche Saint-Martin (Zeichnung T. Wozniak)

A06 12. Jh. Moings, Pfarrkirche Saint-Martin (Zeichnung T. Wozniak)

A07 12. Jh. Moings, Pfarrkirche Saint-Martin (Zeichnung T. Wozniak)

A08 12. Jh. Moings, Pfarrkirche Saint-Martin (Zeichnung T. Wozniak)

A09 12. Jh. Moings, Pfarrkirche Saint-Martin (Zeichnung T. Wozniak)

5.20 Twelfth-century horsemen from Moings, France (from Wozniak, 'Ritter, reiter und bewaffnete', 137–8, A05–A11)

Determining the date of graffiti is generally difficult, but details such as weaponry, armour and costume provide clues, as do writing forms. Half of the graffiti in Wozniak's catalogue were mounted. He interprets these figure variously, for instance, the standing men-at-arms can be seen as watchmen or guards, mounted men with weapons in churches could be interpreted as armed pilgrims, the participants of tournaments or as hunters. Interpretation depends on the date, content and context, for example, whether the graffiti are in a Syrian crusader chapel, a Norwegian stave church or a fifteenth-century English castle. In St-Martin's church at Moings in France, thirty-seven figures are depicted on the north wall, which can be dated to the twelfth century. Nine of these are on horseback (fig. 5.20). A number of these horsemen (A05–A11) are identified on the basis of the shape of the nasal helmet as dating between 1120 and 1150. When compared with the examples in Wozniak's study, which are quite simple and naïve, the main image of horse and rider on the slate seems to compare quite well in both subject and execution with other graffiti of the same period, albeit on a portable object rather than the wall of a church or castle. It may be that the graffiti in this case are secondary to the main function of the object as a writing tablet.

ART-HISTORICAL DISCUSSION

Discussion of the slate's classification leads to other questions such as whether the pictures on it are drawn in the Insular, Scandinavian, or Continental idiom, what artistic parallels there may be, who the main subject is, and whether the warrior scene is a copy or a creation by the artist.[50]

Many people who have seen the slate and/or pictures of it have remarked on the wolfish appearance of the quadruped on Side A. This is primarily because of the zigzag mouth detail that resembles sharp teeth. Wolves feature widely in Norse mythology and it has been suggested that the animal on Side A might be a depiction of a pagan Norse character. Fenrir (Old Norse, meaning fen-dweller) is perhaps the most famous wolf in Norse mythology. He features in thirteenth-century Icelandic texts by Snorri Sturluson (1179–1241), including the *Poetic Edda*, the *Prose Edda* and *Heimskringla*.[51] According to the myths, the gods restrained Fenrir having learned through a prophecy that he would kill Odin at Ragnarok. The question arises whether the composition depicts this battle between Fenrir and Odin. Wolves also feature elsewhere in Norse mythology, for example, in Snorri Sturluson's *Gylfaginning*, the giantess Hyrrokkin rides to Baldr's funeral on a great wolf with snakes for reins. One of the image stones that formed part of the now

Polly Lohmann, *Historische graffiti als quellen. methoden und perspektiven eines jungen forschungsbereichs* (Stuttgart, 2018), pp 111–42. **50** Uaininn O'Meadhra, 'Copies or creations? Some shared elements in Hiberno-Norse and Scandinavian artwork' in H.B. Clarke and Ruth Johnson (eds), *The Vikings in Ireland and beyond* (Dublin, 2015), pp 373–402. **51** See, e.g., Jackson Crawford, *The Poetic Edda: stories of the norse gods and heroes*

destroyed Hunnestadt 3 (DR 284) monument in Sweden showed an animal ridden by a human figure holding two snakes, which is generally considered to be a depiction of Hyrrokkin.[52] Other wolves feature on the Tullstorp Runestone (DR 271) and the Lund 1 Runestone (DR 314).[53] Tom Birkett was consulted about the Odin identification stating by email 'I'd expect Odin to be depicted with a spear rather than a sword, and most likely with one of the eyes scratched out … I've not seen a shield of that sort associated with Odin either. The two birds are intriguing though, and would definitely be one of the defining features of the god'. He also considered it late for any Scandinavian to be representing the old gods.

While it may be tempting to interpret the quadruped as a wolf from Norse mythology, there are more convincing parallels for the warrior and beast in the Insular, Scandinavian and Continental artistic repertoire. The zigzag mouth detail of the quadruped on Side A may represent a horse's bit, rather than a wolf's teeth, and the presence of reins suggests that the animal is wearing a bridle or halter.[54] The leg position of the human figure suggests that he is mounted astride the animal. The horse is 'the most characteristic animal of the Middle Ages … a symbol of social status, closely bound to aristocratic, knightly and chivalric culture, and a potent weapon on the battlefield'.[55] Riding figures, warriors and hunters on horseback are found widely across contemporary Viking, Insular and Continental art. There are numerous depictions of warriors on horseback in Germanic art of the first millennium, one of the most famous being a mounted warrior shown in combat with a serpent on the helmet from a seventh-century Vendel grave in Sweden.[56] Like the figure on the slate, the warrior is shown holding a spear and shield and is accompanied by two birds. This pre-Viking horseman is commonly identified as the god Odin who is often depicted on horseback. According to the legends, Odin's mount was Sleipnir, a flying, eight-legged horse, as depicted on the Tjängvide stone in Gotland, Sweden, *c.*AD 700-800.[57] In the *Prose Edda* by Snorri, Odin's ravens Huginn ('thought') and Muninn ('memory' or 'mind') flew around the world gathering information and reporting it back to him. The Vendel animal, like the quadruped on the slate, has four legs not eight. The figure on the slate has two eyes rather than Odin's one, but despite this, there are two birds in the image, which hints at the possibility of it being him.

(Indianapolis, 2015). **52** I am grateful to Dr Declan Taggart for the reference to Hyrrokkin. **53** See https://app.raa.se/open/runor/search, accessed 23 August 2022. **54** John Clark *The medieval horse and its equipment* (Woodbridge, 2011), pp 43–8. I am grateful to Eleanor Wilkinson-Keys for this reference and information on the *The Warhorse Project* (at Exeter University and the University of East Anglia), seeking to understand more about the warhorse *c.*800–1600 across a wide variety of disciplines. **55** https://medievalwarhorse.exeter.ac.uk/about/, accessed 25 June 2022. **56** Seventh century depiction of Odin on a Vendel helmet plate, found in Upplan – Medievalists.net, accessed 11 September 2022. **57** http://www.worldtree project.org/document/121, accessed 24 September 2022.

However, as the context date for the deposition of the slate is the late twelfth century, by which time the population of Dublin had long since been Christian and was now under Anglo-Norman rule, subjects such as Odin or Fenrir from Old Norse mythology seem unlikely and other parallels and symbolism for the drawing must be sought.

Ravens aside, birds and their positioning in medieval art may serve as a device to confer religious or military validity to an individual. Birds serve as Christian symbols on Irish high crosses of the early medieval period. On Muiredach's Cross, Co. Louth, there is a bird, perhaps a phoenix symbolizing the Resurrection, on the head of Christ and a dove is perched on David's harp representing the Holy Spirit.[58] A large bird shown frontally with outspread wings sits atop the head of Christ in the crucifixion on a high cross at Durrow, Co. Offaly. Although the birds on the slate have a dove- or corvid-like appearance, are large in size, with strong bills, an alternative interpretation is that they are supposed to be birds of prey. Michelle Brown has suggested that the bird on the man's head may represent a bird-crested helm. A spectacular Iron Age chieftain's helmet of this type with a bird of prey crest-attachment was discovered in a warrior burial at the Celtic settlement and La Tène cemetery at Ciumeşti (Satu Mare) in Transylvania, Romania, dated 280/277–175 BC.[59] The Aquila ('eagle' in Latin) was also the standard of a Roman legion and eagles are found on crested helms of late Antique and post-Roman type. Raptors, and particularly falcons, are also commonly found accompanying riders in contemporary medieval hunting scenes, such as on the Bayeux Tapestry. There are 217 birds on the tapestry, found in the borders and elsewhere in naturalistic and fantastic scenes. Hawks are shown on the wrists of Harold, William, and Guy count of Ponthieu, in scenes within the main register, but the two birds on the slate are quite different from the Bayeux raptors and the horseman is thus more likely to be a warrior than a hunter.

Returning to the horse and rider, in early medieval Irish art, the typical representation of a horseman is quite distinctive and has a great longevity of use. Susanne McNab has traced the Irish rider motif,[60] which survived in a 'particular mannered form' from the Iron Age throughout the early medieval period in manuscripts, metalwork and the art of the stone high crosses, exemplified by the riders on folios 89r and 255v of the Book of Kells.[61] Typical details are 'a horse with a downwards slanting eye, a heavy fringe of mane, a long luxuriant tail and a well-collected stance with head down, hind quarters under, and fore leg stepping forward. The rider is seated low on the horse's

58 Peter Harbison, *The high crosses of Ireland* (Bonn, 1992). **59** https://balkancelts.wordpress.com/tag/ciumesti-burial, accessed 27 September 2022. **60** Susanne McNab, 'Celtic antecedents to the treatment of the human figure in early Irish art' in Colum Hourihane (ed.), *From Ireland coming: Irish art from the early Christian to the late Gothic period and its European context* (Princeton, 2001), pp 161–83. **61** https://digital collections.tcd.ie/concern/works/hm50tr726?locale=en&page=5, accessed 24 September 2022.

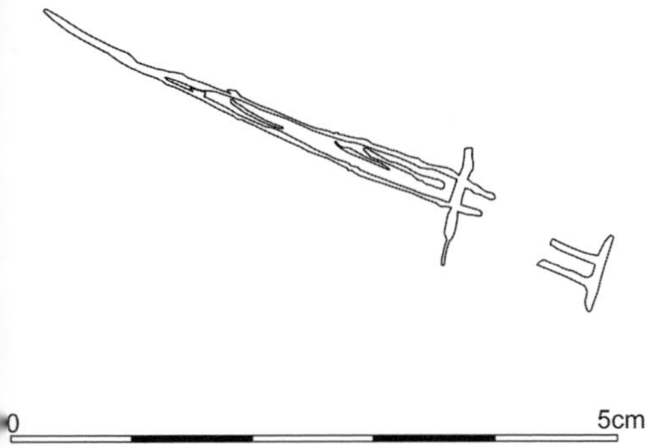

5.21 Side A sword detail drawing (Johnny Ryan)

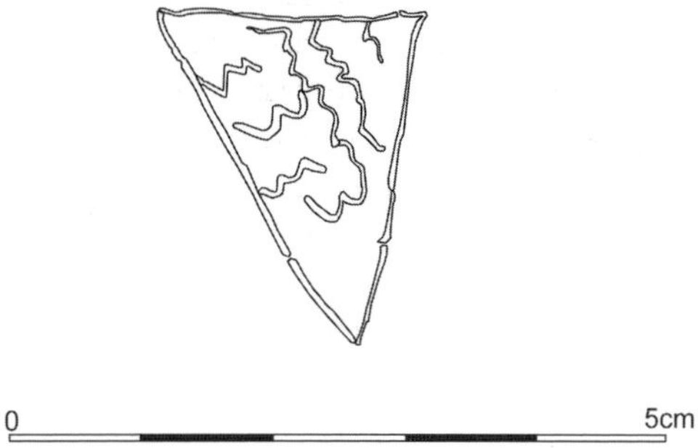

5.22 Side A shield detail drawing (Johnny Ryan)

back with his legs swinging forward over the horse's shoulder and his hands low or concealed inside a cloak, and he has a Kells profile'. The horse and rider on the slate do not closely resemble in detail the early medieval horseman described by McNab. The horse on it has no mane, a short tail and its stance is markedly different to the Kells riders. The medieval art historian Roger Stalley (pers. comm.) has observed the peculiar leg position of the horse on the slate, with the front and rear feet together and curling backwards and under; it brings to mind the enigmatic beast found on some Pictish symbol stones, but this may just be coincidental rather than a stylistic indication of connections with Scotland.[62] While there are some similarities between the rider's body position and that of the typical early medieval horseman, it is notable that the human face on the slate does not have the 'Kells profile', typified by a 'beaky nose profile, with its large frontal eye, elongated jawline and curling tail of hair',[63] that was used in Ireland up to and throughout the Romanesque period. Nevertheless, the nose, mouth and eye treatment of the face do bear comparison with the merman in the book of Kells and thus can be seen to sit comfortably in the early medieval Irish art repertoire.[64] The nose and eye are linked in a manner that resembles the treatment of the five personified senses on the ninth-century Anglo-Saxon Trewhiddle-style Fuller brooch,[65] and are found elsewhere in the Insular artistic milieu.

The sword held aloft by the figure is of a type that would sit equally well in a late-Viking or Anglo-Norman context, having a central fuller, a straight pommel and straight lower hilt guard (fig. 5.21). The illustrator Johnny Ryan

62 https://ima.princeton.edu/2017/07/31/pictish-stones-iconography-and-interpretation, accessed 27 September, 2022. **63** McNab, 'Celtic antecedents', p. 163. **64** See 'Luke; Genealogy of Jesus', in *The Book of Kells,* TCD MS 58: f. 201r; https://digital collections.tcd.ie/concern/folios/8p58pd15t?locale=en, accessed 23 August 2022. **65** https://www.british museum.org/collection/object/H_1952-0404-1, accessed 24 September 2022.

5.23 Silver equestrian seal of Robert FitzWalter, Stamford (Lincolnshire), *c.*1213–19 (British Museum)

noted that the sword had been lengthened by a single stroke, but whether this was deliberate or a tool slip is uncertain. The shield is triangular in form and has a device of six wavy diagonally opposed lines in two pairs of three (fig. 5.22). It is interpreted as a heater shield and the squiggles on it may be a heraldic device, as heraldic display was a common secondary shield function. Smaller than the kite-shaped shield, such heater shields could be used either mounted or on foot.[66] This form developed in Europe during the late twelfth century, a date that fits well with the context of the slate. It is the shield form depicted on the great seals of King Richard I,[67] and King John,[68] or the

66 The term was coined by antiquarians based on the resemblance in form to a Victorian clothes iron. **67** See the seal impression cast in the British Museum taken from the reverse of the second seal of Richard I showing the king riding a horse, the first such appearance of the royal arms of England: see https://www.britishmuseum.org/collection/object/H_2000-0103-6, accessed 25 May 2022. **68** See the impression of the magnificent contemporary seal-matrix of John's baronial opponent Robert FitzWalter (fig. 5.23).

Henry Yallup, keeper of edged weapons and armour at the Royal Armouries UK, was consulted by email about the sword, shield and possible bird helmet. He suggested that given the period the sword could be a rendering of a 'Viking' type such as Petersen type 'M', dated to the first part of the tenth century by Blindheim.[69] These have the capital I-shaped hilt with cross longer than upper hilt bar and no pommel cap. He felt that the triangle-shaped object is the wrong shield shape for the period and suggested that it may instead be clothing or that the squiggles may be the texturing of a stylized sleeveless mail shirt. In the absence of any evidence of a helmet he suggested that the bird might be allegorical rather than a crest like the much earlier 'Celtic' raven-helmet of Ciumestri Maramures in Romania. Keith Dowen of the Royal Armouries observed by email the similarities between the horseman and mid-to-late twelfth-century seal matrices, in particular the characteristic manner in which the sword is held over the head. He noted that flat-top kite-shields are known from the mid-twelfth century and that the first depictions of the traditional triangular knightly 'heater' shields appear towards the end of the century.

The most famous Anglo-Norman artwork of the period is the Bayeux Tapestry, an embroidery that depicts the events leading up to the Norman Conquest of England. The tapestry was made in the eleventh century *c.*1075,[70] and tells the story from the point of view of the conquering Normans. Numerous riders and mounted warriors are depicted on the Tapestry, making it a useful reference for the main composition on the slate. There are obvious similarities between the body position of the Bayeux riders and the slate man but there are also notable differences. The Bayeux soldiers are equipped with long kite-shaped shields, wear body armour, have pointed helmets and their horses are saddled. As noted above, the line that cuts through the face of the figure on the slate could be interpreted as an arrow which raises the question of whether the character on the slate may be Harold Godwinson. According to William of Malmesbury and Henry Huntingdon, writing in the twelfth century, Harold died by an arrow wound at Hastings in 1066. In Harold's death scene on the Bayeux Tapestry, the arrow however is not original, having been added during repairs in France in the nineteenth century, following a later literary tradition.[71] Nevertheless, arrow shots to the head would have been a very real part of warfare in twelfth-century Ireland. Contemporary Irish

reverse of the Great Seal of King John at https://www.bl.uk/collection-items/great-seal-of-king-john, accessed 25 May 2022. **69** Fedir Androshchuk, *Viking swords: swords and social aspects of weaponry in Viking Age societies* (Stockholm, 2014), p. 69. **70** For this dating, see H.B. Clarke, 'The identity of the designer of the Bayeux Tapestry', *Anglo-Norman studies*, 35 (2013). **71** https://www.historytoday.com/shot-through-eye-and-who%E2%80%99s-blame, accessed 25 September 2022.

depictions of mounted Hiberno-Norman knights are harder to find for comparison. The thirteenth-century copy of Gerald of Wales's *Expugnatio Hibernica* in the National Library of Ireland has riders in the margins as well as portraits of noble figures, such as Raymond ('le Gros') fitz William (*c.*1140–*c.*1190), a Cambro-Norman military commander during the invasion of Ireland.[72] In it, Raymond is shown on foot. He is unarmoured and about to draw a long sword from its sheath. Facially, the portrait of le Gros offers a good parallel for the Coombe figure, and as previously noted this face type is found in Irish and Insular art from as early as the eighth century.

Twelfth-century parallels for the pictogram on the slate may alternatively be sought in the corpus of medieval European equestrian seals and seal matrices.[73] Equestrian seals were used in the high Middle Ages and are characterized by the depiction of the owner as a mounted knight, generally in full armour. Such seals were used by the nobility to convey authority and legitimacy when authenticating documents. Equestrian seals originated in the later eleventh to early twelfth century, the oldest example being that of William I of England, *c.*1067.[74] Seals from the 1170s to 1190s serve as a useful reference for the sword and shield depicted on the slate.[75] Many seals of this period show heraldic devices on the shields, bringing to mind the squiggles on the shield on the slate. If the image on the slate is interpreted as a copy of an equestrian seal, the artist that inscribed the slate must have actually seen a late twelfth-century seal or matrix first hand, in which case the drawing could be deemed a copy rather than a creation. Whose seal it could have been and in what capacity the artist had seen it is unknown.

Henry II, the English king at the time of the Anglo-Norman invasion in 1169, had an equestrian seal. It is thus highly likely that such seals were known and even used in Dublin in the twelfth century but there are no contemporary examples surviving from Ireland. Armstrong recorded fourteen medieval equestrian seals in his 1913 study.[76] Raghnall Ó Floínn has recently shown that while the number of known medieval Irish seals has doubled since Armstrong's survey, none of the more recently identified ones are equestrian or heraldic seals.[77] The National Museum of Ireland has a number of equestrian seal matrices in its image database, all of which are later in date than the slate. The closest parallels are a silver seal matrix of Macon Mac Conmara (MacNamara),

72 Holdings: Topographia Hibernica: (nli.ie), accessed 22 May 2022. 73 Matrices were used for making impressions on wax seals. 74 J.F. Nieus, 'Early aristocratic seals: an Anglo-Norman success story', *Anglo-Norman Studies*, 37 (2016), p. 101. 75 The equestrian seals from this period show the transition in shield form from the long kite-shaped shield of the eleventh century to the smaller triangular heater shape of the late twelfth and thirteenth century depicted on the slate. The helmets become more rounded and the horseman becomes stylized as a knight. 76 E.C.R. Armstrong, *Irish seal-matrices and seals* (Dublin, 1913). 77 *Personal seals in medieval Ireland* by Raghnall Ó Floínn https://www.youtube.com/watch?v=Jcxhi54iMFo, accessed 24 September 2022.

lord of Clann Chuiléin in East Clare, and a silver seal matrix of Domhnall Mac Carthaigh (MacCarthy), king of Desmond (*c.*1302–6).[78] The earliest known equestrian seal likely to have been used in Ireland is that of Strongbow, the earl of Pembroke, a key figure in the Anglo-Norman invasion of Ireland. If the picture on the slate is a copy of an equestrian seal, and if the artist were Irish, copying an Irish seal, it might just suggest the Irish adoption of heraldic symbols preceding the invasion of 1169.

Another potential subject for the rider on the slate is a Christian warrior saint, or a crusading knight. Anne Pedersen and Sigmund Oehrl recently identified two unusual brooches from late Viking-Age Denmark (*c.*AD 1050–1100) that feature a horseman killing an Urnes-style serpent with a spear.[79] These two brooches may be the earliest representations of St George and the dragon in Scandinavia, the iconography being directly influenced by Byzantine models following the first crusades of the eleventh century.[80] Another less likely possibility for the main subject on the slate is Samson killing the lion, a Christian motif popular in Romanesque art in which Samson often appears to be astride the lion in the battle. This scene is famously found in a late twelfth-century carving at Arles in Provence, *c.*1152–90.[81] Christian saints and biblical subjects would certainly have been in the popular consciousness whilst crusading knights may have been a familiar sight in Dublin after the conquest of Ireland given that the headquarters of the Knights Hospitaller were located just west of the town in Kilmainham.

The leading expert on motif-pieces art historian Uaininn O'Meadhra was consulted by email and she noted that the slate has been used many times over. She was open to the possibility that it might be a motif-piece originally but is unconvinced. She also discounted it as a scholar's work, given that the lettering, the details of the horse, and the hands of the rider are so erratic. She suggested that this latest phase is graffiti by a creative Anglo-Norman occupant of the city, not necessarily a craftsman even though the face is typical for a manuscript. O'Meadhra also observed the (possibly compass-drawn) arcs and pointed angles suggesting pentagrams and marigolds, which would usually indicate superimposed ship-drawings. There is no trace of any clear pattern of arcs and perpendiculars typical of architectural drawings of the period but she suggested these marks might be abstracted in future careful study. She suggested that the script of the alphabet on Side B (the *abcdefg* and possibly

78 I am grateful to Maeve Sikora, keeper of Irish antiquities in the National Museum of Ireland, for supplying these references. 79 Anne Pedersen and Sigmund Oerhl, 'Late Viking-Age dragon-slayers – two unusual Urnes-style brooches from Sjælland, Denmark', *Medieval Archaeology*, 65:2 (2021), 322–67. 80 https://www.tandfonline.com/doi/abs/10.1080/00766097.2021.2000250, accessed 25 September, 2022; Pedersen and Oehrl, 'Late Viking-Age dragon-slayers'. 81 https://quod.lib.umich.edu/a/aict/xrq074/RQ074?lastkey=aict_ti;lastpage=browse;lastvalue=s;size=50;start=1;subview=detail;view=entry, accessed 29 September, 2022.

hik under the hoofs) was Anglo-Norman, eleventh- to thirteenth-century, noting the open upper arc of the *a*, and fig-of-eight-shaped *g* and Continental-curled *d*. Her initial interpretation of the rider was a soldier in chainmail 'in classic poise with pointed shoe and raised sword and triangular shield', and suggested that the bird above him could be his falcon. She noted the possible arrow through his eye and references King Harold at Hastings. She questioned whether the bird/fish/creature at the feet of the horse belongs but that it might depict some fable.

CONCLUSIONS

In conclusion, the inscribed stone is considered most likely to be either a writing tablet bearing scholar's pen-trials or a motif-piece in the Insular tradition. It belongs to a group of graffiti- and text-inscribed stones known from early medieval Insular monastic sites such as Inchmarnock in Scotland and contemporary medieval defensive sites such as Nevern Castle in Wales. The context suggests that the slate was created in a secular milieu associated with the parish of St Patrick's located in a Hiberno-Norman suburb of Dublin around the time of the Anglo-Norman invasion. The Coombe is close to St Patrick's collegiate church, established by Archbishop John Cumin in 1192, and to the boundary between what would become the medieval liberty of St Sepulchre and the liberty of St Thomas. This southern suburb of Dublin had grown up outside the town walls in the Hiberno-Norse period prior to the taking of Dublin in 1170.

The main subject, a warrior on horseback, has numerous forbears in Germanic and Insular art. The image is indeed steeped in many Insular, Norse and Continental artistic and cultural influences familiar to the inhabitants of the international port town and trading centre. One possibility is that it may be a copy of an equestrian seal of a type presumed (though not proven) to be in circulation in Dublin in the late twelfth century. Such seals were used by knights such as Strongbow who were active in Dublin in the immediate aftermath of the Anglo-Norman invasion. It seems likely, in this suburban context, that the artist or artists were ordinary Hiberno-Norse Dubliners rather than elite Anglo-Norman incomers. The slate came from a building type normally considered to be culturally Hiberno-Norse but whether the subject is a Norse god, an Irish noble, a Norman knight, a crusader or a saint remains unknown. Having said that, it is most likely in this date and location to be an example of Christian iconography, or the portrait of a contemporary noble, than a depiction of a pagan hero.

The piece displays differential skill and artistry and the crude main composition on Side A may be the work of a different hand from the letters and the horse on Side B, perhaps, respectively, the work of a craftsperson and apprentice or a teacher and student. The writing on it suggests that the slate was used by a scholar or religious novice, perhaps associated with a school at nearby St Patrick's collegiate church or one of the many ecclesiastical foundations nearby, such as St Thomas's abbey, which was established by Henry II in the late twelfth century just 900m from the site. The Coombe site is only 900m, a stone's throw (pardon the pun), from Dublin Castle the English royal centre, which was completed *c.*1230, but which is presumed to have been the seat of royal power in the Hiberno-Norse town prior to the Anglo-Norman invasion.[82] Warriors and armed noblemen on horseback would have been a common sight in both Hiberno-Norse and Anglo-Norman Dublin. We might even conjecture that the artist was recording their own personal memory of a key historical event such as the siege of Dublin. Whatever the identity of the subject and the meaning behind the scene, whether it is a copy or creation, one thing we can say for certain is that whoever incised the letters and made the drawings on it was well-informed culturally and politically, educated and playful, just like so many Dubliners today.

EPILOGUE

When the slate was in my care, I was able to show it under supervision to my family, friends and colleagues, in some cases videoing their reactions as they deciphered the marks on it. I have never seen an artefact generate such excitement in people of different ages and backgrounds. Each person showed such delight as they discovered the pictures and letters and there was lively deliberation over identification of the images as a horse, wolf, lion, fish or bird. I received many emails about the identity of the main subject, the god Odin being a particular favourite of many, most especially that of archaeologist Eóin Ó Duinn. Each suggestion sent me seeking out new references and was followed up for this paper. A version of this paper was presented for feedback at the 19th Viking Congress, and I look forward to hearing from others as a result of its publication in *Medieval Dublin*.

ACKNOWLEDGMENTS

I am particularly grateful to the site director Aisling Collins, and the site supervisor Kevin Weldon, for inviting me to research the slate and for providing photographs, plans and reports; to the other members of the site

82 See Seán Duffy, 'Part 1: the medieval period' in Seán Duffy, John Montague, Kevin Mulligan and Michael O'Neill, *Dublin Castle: from fortress to palace, volume 1, Vikings to Victorians. A history of Dublin Castle to 1850*, ed. Ann Lynch and Conleth Manning (Dublin, 2022), pp 1–68.

excavation team: Conor McHale, Peter Dodd, Rory Blount, Brendan Fagan, Mark Kelly, José Luis Silesy (who found the slate), Christina Hughes, Maggie Kobik, Ian Dunne, Jack McIlroy and Ingela Waas; to Jackie MacDermott, the finds specialist, for sharing information on the other finds; to Linzi Simpson and Áine Foley, archaeological advisor and historical consultant to ACAS, for sharing their research. Excavation of the site was undertaken for John and Johnny O'Sullivan in advance of construction of the Hyatt Centric Hotel, who funded it and embraced the history of the site incorporating it into the ethos and brand of the Hyatt Centric Hotel on The Coombe. Part of the medieval street frontage is preserved *in situ* under the new hotel and will be available for future generations.

The paper would have been impossible without financial support from Dublin City Council towards the cost of the illustrations and by affording me time to coordinate preparation of the drawing and scan. The Council CEO Owen Keegan approves funding the publication of the *Medieval Dublin* volumes on an annual basis, understanding that this series represents a fundamental contribution to the city's archaeological heritage; thanks also to my colleagues Níall Garahy and Niall Colfer in the Archaeology, Conservation and Heritage Section. Scans were undertaken as a commercial exercise by Anthony Corns and Gary Devlin with Rob Shaw of the Discovery Programme for ACAS and I am extremely grateful to them and to former CEO Edel Breathnach for enabling this work; the idea of RTI scanning came from Elizabeth FitzPatrick, who kindly shared an advance copy of her paper on the Smarmore slates; the images were prepared by Johnny Ryan, many of whose observations on the graffiti are incorporated in this paper (full account available in the final excavation report).

I am grateful to Philip Bromwell, who filmed a news piece for RTÉ, which is still available on their website; the video and accompanying article continue to attract attention worldwide (e.g., when Thomas Wozniac saw the piece he contacted me to let me know of his extensive research into the corpus of medieval European graffiti); Tim O'Neill, Bernard Meehan and Michelle Brown for comments on the script and hands; Uaininn O'Meadhra, Caroline Paterson, Roger Stalley and Raghnall Ó Floinn for art-historical insights; the latter two supported the 'seal theory' above, as did Brigitte Miriam Bedos-Rezak and Keith Dowen in correspondence; Declan Taggart and Tom Birkett for insights into Viking mythology; Henry Yallup and colleagues at Royal Armouries, for their help via email; Howard Clarke for reading a draft; and delegates of the 19th Viking Congress for feedback. This paper is dedicated to the memory of George Sevastopulo.

Anglo-Norman elite, pilgrims and the Hiberno-Norse in the medieval cemetery of St Thomas the Martyr, Dublin: osteoarchaeological evidence

MAEVE TOBIN

INTRODUCTION

Archaeological excavations undertaken at the rear of 30 and 32–36 Thomas Street by Paul Duffy of IAC Archaeology revealed extensive archaeological remains representing part of the precinct for the abbey of St Thomas the Martyr (Duffy 2021). Approximately 124 discrete graves and 75 deposits of disarticulated human remains were recorded at this time within the northern portion of the medieval cemetery associated with the abbey. The human skeletal remains retrieved from the burial ground were subject to osteological analysis by the author, and the results of this assessment provide a greater understanding of the community who chose to be, or were afforded the honour of being, laid to rest at this prestigious site with its royal affiliations. Significantly, a programme of radiocarbon dating has indicated that while this part of the cemetery was primarily active during the first one hundred years of the abbey foundation, the burial ground had pre-Anglo-Norman roots.

ARCHAEOLOGICAL AND HISTORICAL CONTEXT

Much research has been published on the abbey, informed by historical records and archaeological investigations (e.g., Walsh 2000; Foley 2017; Duffy 2021), and therefore only a brief discussion is included here for context. The initial dedication to St Thomas the Martyr was associated with a chapel enclosed by a precinct in 1172–4 (Duffy 2021). It was consolidated as a priory in 1177 by Henry II and was subsequently elevated to abbey status, making it perhaps the only royal abbey in Ireland at this time.

Significantly, radiocarbon dating has identified burial activity that antedated the Anglo-Norman foundation, and this was likely associated with a church (Duffy 2021, 236; table 6.1). This previously undocumented foundation must have had sufficient status to have been deliberately selected as the site of the later Anglo-Norman dedication. Adapting an established setting had practical and financial benefits for the royal administration. There are other examples of earlier burial at Anglo-Norman religious houses, but in the case of the Augustinian friary in the eastern suburbs these are thought to be unrelated (Ó Donnabháin and Hallgrimsson 2001, 72).

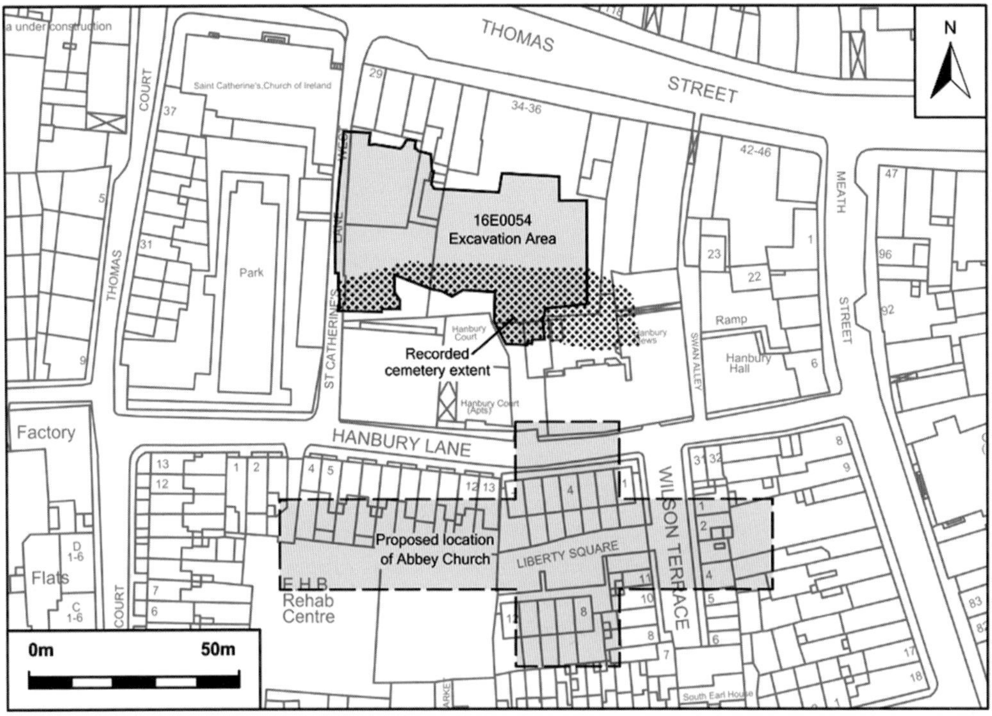

6.1 Site location showing extent of cemetery identified to date

The wealthy abbey of St Thomas underwent several phases of building and expansion in the thirteenth and fourteenth centuries (Foley 2017, 35; Duffy 2021, 242), involving craftsmanship and imported materials from southern England and France. The extent of the abbey precinct, bounded by a ditch and later wall, and the location of the church, have been approximated through archaeological investigations (Paul Duffy pers. comm.; fig. 6.1). The abbey is considered to have had significant influence on the development of the western suburb of Dublin and it was a highly desirable resting spot for the Anglo-Norman elite, including affluent merchants of ultimate Bristol extraction (Leigh Fry 1999, 180; Foley 2017, 50). A lay family's burial within a monastic precinct was an assertion of social identity and religious piety (Mays 2006, 181) and to this end many grants of land were made by the new nobility and higher echelons of society seeking to form a link with the new royal establishment.

The canons regular of St Thomas were of the order of St Augustine (Victorine rule), and their vows of chastity, poverty, and obedience were complemented by promoting care of the sick and hospitality for pilgrims

Table 6.1 Radiocarbon dates and isotope data (¹⁴Chrono Lab dataset intcal13.14c)

Sk	Description	Element	Lab Number	^{14}C Result BP	2 Sigma Calibration	^{13}C	^{15}N	C:N Ratio	Collagen Yield %
20	MA ?M stone-lined	Femur	UB 40201	1037 ± 40	AD 894–1146	-19.0	10.3	3.14	2.30
93	Ado. near wall	Rib	UB 41788	961 ± 26	AD 1020–1154	-19.3	11.1	3.10	2.30
73	MA M	Humerus	UB 41786	941 ± 25	AD 1029–1155	-19.5	10.0	3.12	1.90
72	OA F	Scapula	UB 41785	925 ± 23	AD 1034–1160	-18.7	11.5	3.12	1.70
29	MA F plague pit?	Humerus	UB 40202	895 ± 31	AD 1040–1214	-18.8	11.5	3.14	2.30
16	MA ?F stone in mouth	Fibula	UB 41783	877 ± 23	AD 1047–1220				
53	MA F	Rib	UB 40733	863 ± 28	AD 1049–1252	-19.1	12.1	3.12	5.90
32	A ? under Sk20	Fibula	UB 41784	877 ± 26	AD 1045–1222	-19.5	11.0	3.13	1.20
19	MA M under Sk20	Rib	UB 40730	865 ± 26	AD 1049–1247	-18.5	-11.1	3.12	1.90
		Tooth	UB 40200	796 ± 28	AD 1191–1275	-18.8	10.1	3.15	6.90
142	OC	Rib	UB 40205	842 ± 29	AD 1059–1263	-20.2	9.1	3.17	1.90
108	OMA M pilgrim	Rib	UB 40204	845 ± 22	AD 1161–1249	-18.8	11.7	3.15	4.10
46	MA M stone in mouth	Rib	UB 40732	824 ± 26	AD 1168–1261	-19.4	11.5	3.15	3.00
1	YC stone-lined	Tibia	UB 40199	812 ± 26	AD 1170–1267	-19.0	13.3	3.19	1.10
98	OMA M pilgrim	Tooth	UB 40203	809 ± 22	AD 1190–1267	-19.3	10.4	3.14	12.10

(Key: M: male; ?M: possible male; F: female; ?F: possible female; YC: young child; OC: older child; Ado: adolescent; A: adult; MA: middle adult; OMA: older middle adult; OA: older adult)

(Foley 2017, 40). The historical records note at least one high-born woman, Strongbow's sister Basilia de Clare, served at St Thomas's as a nun (Duffy 2021, 239). The abbey was also responsible for establishing and maintaining the slightly later nearby parish churches of St Catherine and St James (Clarke, *Dublin, Pt 1* (IHTA), 18). The latter site is likely to have been the Irish starting point for people attempting the pilgrimage to Santiago de Compostela in Spain (discussed further below). Over time the relationship between the religious and lay communities became fractious due to clashes for power and control of resources, and this led to the precinct being attacked by the citizens of Dublin. The abbey gradually declined after the fourteenth century until the lands were ultimately surrendered to the crown at the time of Dissolution in 1539 (Foley 2017).

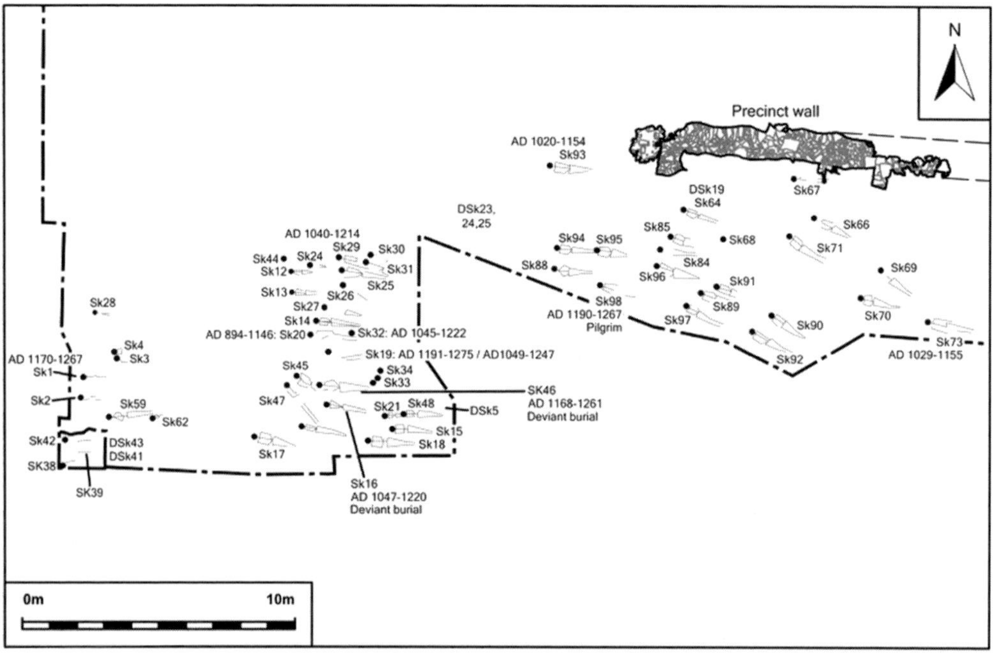

6.2a Western portion of investigated cemetery

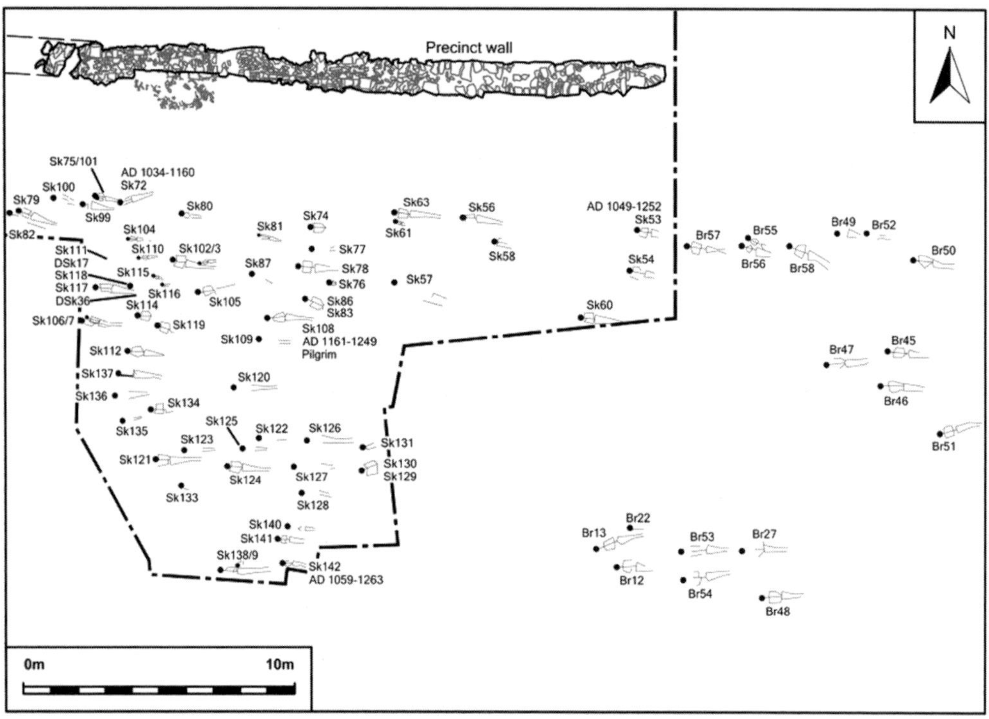

6.2b Eastern portion of investigated cemetery

BURIAL PRACTICES

The recorded extent of the cemetery (shown in fig. 6.1 as a hatched area) was confined to the north by an east–west-aligned ditch and later precinct wall. Between 2016 and 2018, 124 graves were excavated, that appear to have been roughly ordered in rows (figs 6.2a, 6.2b). Previous archaeological investigations to the immediate southeast revealed multiple graves, of which eighteen were excavated in 1998 (Walsh 2000), bringing the total number of recorded burials to 142. Analysis (Buckley 2003) of the eighteen skeletons identified the remains of fourteen adults and four children (identified as Br12–58 on fig. 6.2b) and the osteological findings for these individuals have been integrated with the current data, where possible, for a holistic discussion of the site. Buckley (ibid.) hypothesized that the low level of nutritional or physical stress observed in these remains reflected their status as more affluent members of society.

Burial at religious houses was permitted in any consecrated area, including the most desired areas within the church and cloisters, although access was rigidly determined by status, position and identity (Collins 2021, 352). The investigated burials at St Thomas's are all extramural within the northern limit of the graveyard (north of the church), likely forming the 'public' section. Urban monasteries appear to have had greater social permeability with the local community (Gilchrist and Sloane 2005, 65) but it is likely that poorer individuals were buried in the cemeteries attached to parish churches. The relative contemporaneity of the foundation for St Thomas's and the adjacent parish church of St Catherine may indicate that they shared a burial ground; no boundary was identified during excavation (Duffy 2021) though this does not preclude its existence. Burial to the north of a church was regarded as a position of honour in earlier times; however, by the later medieval period it was considered to be undesirable, reserved for 'unfortunates' or those who died without the grace of God (Leigh Fry 1999, 163). It may have been the case that the canons and patrons of St Thomas's followed a similar predefined spatial hierarchy on their adoption of this site.

There was a clear distinction of land use in the medieval period, with intensive successive tanning and domestic activity to the north of the precinct boundary, and burial to the south. Burials generally respected each other during the lifecycle of the cemetery and the low incidence of intercutting may indicate that above-ground markers had been used. By the seventeenth century, however, the tanning and waste pits had extended into the disused cemetery, truncating and disturbing many of the graves. Where observable the grave-cuts survived as simple shallow pits, with the exception of three unusual stone-lined examples (Sk1, Sk20 and Sk46). Two graves had possible evidence for ear-muff stones by the head, that of a young adult male (Sk45) and an adolescent (Sk112); and a third grave (adult Sk34) contained a possible pillow stone. No evidence for coffins was inferred from grave form or body position, although their use was not common at this time (ibid., 128). The graves were generally aligned west–east although slight deviations were noted. A central group of at least fifteen burials was distinct in terms of their more organized nature and similar northwest–southeast alignment, perhaps reflecting contemporaneous use within a defined period. All of the bodies had been placed in an extended supine position, and where observable the majority had their arms laid in one of three positions: extended with hands over the pelvis (forty-four), crossed on the chest (thirty-four), or extended by the side (nine) – the most commonly recorded postures of the time (Daniell 1997, 118). Although no specific pattern of burial positioning was identified, which may have reflected a temporal shift in practice, there was slightly less variety within the females who had a higher tendency to be buried with arms crossing the chest. Interestingly two individuals, young child Sk1 and adult male Sk134, were buried with their right hand flexed under the chin and left hand extended on the chest.

The graves at St Thomas's were mostly recorded as a single stratigraphic layer although the density increased slightly towards the south, and at one particular cluster in the west. The singularity of the latter group suggests a deliberate desire to be buried close to a specific person and this is discussed further below. Disturbed and disarticulated bone was frequently placed overlying or alongside later interments. In one instance a large charnel pit (DSk 1), containing multiple skulls and long-bones, was recorded adjacent to the cluster of graves in the west. To the immediate north of this pit at least four adults (Sk25–27, 29) appear to have been covered by a lime deposit. The excavator believed this was laid down to combat the spread of infection and may represent plague burials (Duffy 2021, 206), and if this is the case it is interesting that they were nonetheless buried within the precinct.

Infants and children are frequently under-represented in monastic cemeteries (Daniel 2005, 115) but no age-related segregation was evident in this portion of the cemetery at least. The grave-cuts were hard to discern during excavation; however, in at least three instances the proximity of skeletons suggests coincident burial of non-adult individuals (young children Sk3 and Sk4; adolescent Sk30 and older child Sk31; adult male Sk102 and young child Sk103). In a further instance it appears that the grave of an older child (Sk115) may have been deliberately targeted for the later adjacent burial of a young child (Sk116). Graves containing coterminous double burials are often recorded in early medieval and medieval cemeteries (Gilchrist and Soames 2005, 157), frequently containing at least one juvenile individual (Ó Donnabháin 2000, 106). Reasons for group burial include contemporary death events and practical efficiency, familial links, and periods of high stress associated with specific epidemics (Murphy and Donnelly 2018).

METHODOLOGY

Osteological analysis was undertaken to enhance the archaeological record by identifying the demographic composition (age and sex) and health status (affected by occupational, pathological or nutritional stresses) of this medieval community. Following excavation all human remains (Sk1–142 and DSk 1–75) were cleaned and boxed according to best practice. Several of the site designations were reassigned as disarticulated deposits, bringing the total number of discrete graves recorded at this time to 124. Soil samples taken from the graves were sieved to maximize retrieval of small bone fragments or artefacts. Osteological analysis followed standard protocols set out by several authors, including but not limited to those outlined in Buikstra and Ubelaker (1994), Brickley and McKinley (2004), Scheuer and Black (2004), Hillson (1996) and Whittaker (2000). A summary of the findings for each individual is tabulated in Appendix 6.1 (see below, p. 208). Age and sex were estimated using a number of standard morphological and metrical methods, although sex identification was only attempted for later adolescents or adults. Broad age categories were assigned where possible (the ranges for which are detailed in Table 6.2), and five categories of sex estimation were designated (female, possible female, male, possible male, and undetermined). Osteological data from several other medieval populations has been used to draw comparisons and distinctions, specifically those established or active in the thirteenth century at nearby St Peter's church (Coughlan 2021) and in the Augustinian friary in what is now Temple Bar (Ó Donnabháin and Cosgrave 1994), and the rural communities at Tintern abbey, Co. Wexford (Ó Donnabháin 2000) and Ballyhanna, Co. Donegal (McKenzie and Murphy 2018).

Table 6.2 Age profile at St Thomas's (incl. Buckley 2003)

<table>
<tr><th>Age category</th><th>Age-range (years)</th><th colspan="2">2016–2018 excavation</th><th>1998 excavation</th><th colspan="2">Number identified and % of total</th></tr>
<tr><td>'Unaged' adult</td><td>17+</td><td>19 (15%)</td><td rowspan="6">81 adults (64.3%)</td><td>1</td><td>20 (13.9%)</td><td rowspan="6">95 adults (66%)</td></tr>
<tr><td>Older adult</td><td>45+</td><td>6 (4.7%)</td><td>3</td><td>9 (6.3%)</td></tr>
<tr><td>Older middle adult</td><td>35–45</td><td>11 (8.7%)</td><td></td><td>11 (7.6%)</td></tr>
<tr><td>Middle adult</td><td>25–45</td><td>13 (10.3%)</td><td>9</td><td>22 (15.3%)</td></tr>
<tr><td>Young middle adult</td><td>25–35</td><td>16 (12.6%)</td><td></td><td>16 (11.1%)</td></tr>
<tr><td>Young adult</td><td>17–25</td><td>16 (12.6%)</td><td>1</td><td>17 (11.8%)</td></tr>
<tr><td>Adolescent</td><td>12–17</td><td>6 (4.7%)</td><td rowspan="4">45 juveniles (35.7%)</td><td></td><td>6 (4.2%)</td><td rowspan="4">49 juveniles (34%)</td></tr>
<tr><td>Older child</td><td>6–12</td><td>12 (9.5%)</td><td>2</td><td>14 (9.7%)</td></tr>
<tr><td>Young child</td><td>1–6</td><td>22 (17.5%)</td><td>2</td><td>24 (16.7%)</td></tr>
<tr><td>Infant</td><td><1</td><td>5 (4%)</td><td></td><td>5 (3.5%)</td></tr>
</table>

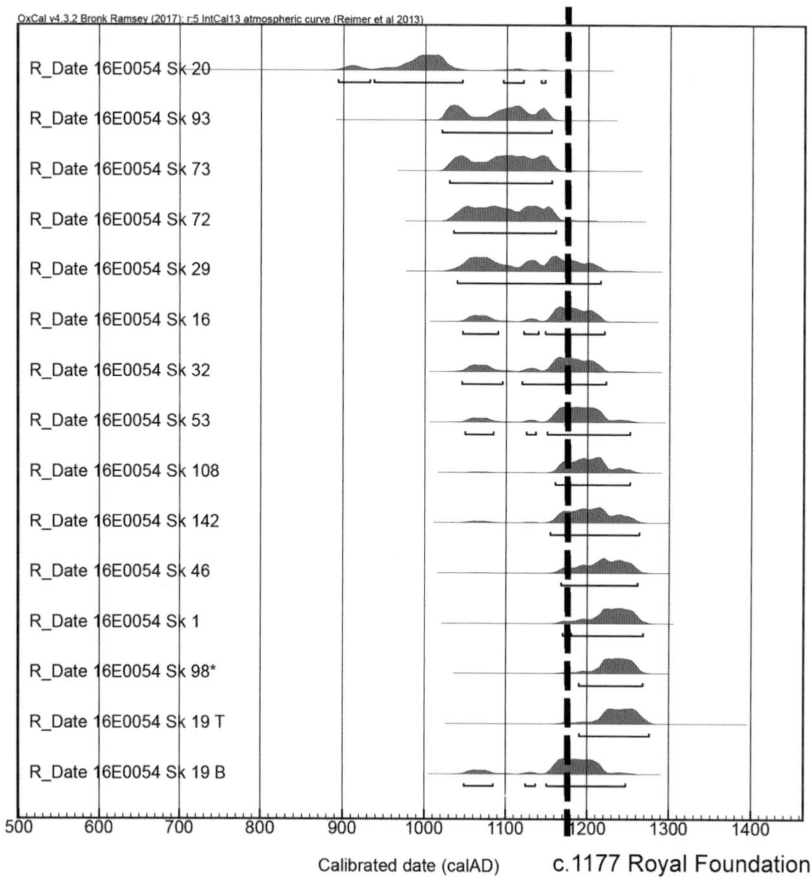

6.3 Calibration chart (OxCal v4.3.2) of referenced radiocarbon determinations

Skeletal condition

Preservation and completeness of the skeletal remains was assessed using a grading system of four categories: good, moderate, poor, and very poor. Condition can be affected by multiple factors, including age and sex of the individual, size and robusticity of the bone, burial environment (acidity of soil/protection of grave), and post-depositional disturbance. Over one third of the graves (38%) recorded between 2016 and 2018 survived in very poor or poor completeness, with the remainder recorded as moderate (42%) or good (20%). Many of the skeletons (such as Sk70 and Sk75) in the eastern half of site were stained dark brown by leaching of tanning and cess fluids; with a smaller number displaying accretions of mortar-like material. Despite this, the general level of preservation was recorded as good (37%) or moderate (44%), and there was no variability evident due to location, age or sex.

Dating

Samples of bone and tooth root were selected by the author from fourteen individuals for the purpose of radiocarbon dating at the ^{14}Chrono Centre. The programme of dating aimed to investigate the temporal development of the cemetery and several notable customs. The dated burial activity spans a period of approximately 300 years (table 6.1 and fig. 6.3). Significantly the 2 sigma calibrated date-ranges of at least four individuals straddle the mid-eleventh and early twelfth century, indicating a previously unknown cemetery (and possible church) in the western suburb of the Hiberno-Norse town. The remaining dated skeletons indicate that this segment of the cemetery was predominantly used during the first 100 years of the abbey establishment, with little or no dated burial here following the fire that destroyed part of the abbey in 1289 (Foley 2017, 86). It is likely that burial activity moved to a more desirous part of the cemetery at the time of the rebuild, or that the place fell out of favour with the later generations of the Anglo-Irish community. As a by-product of the dating process, carbon ($\delta^{13}C$) and nitrogen ($\delta^{15}N$) isotope data were generated. This was plotted by the author and compared with data from a thirteenth-century cemetery at St Peter's church (1km to the east) in an attempt to draw basic inferences about diet.

CEMETERY POPULATION

The primary focus of the analysis was to collate demographic data, although it is acknowledged that these skeletal remains represent a) only a portion of the cemetery and b) two culturally distinct groups. With the exception of the dated individuals, it is not possible to accurately separate the earlier Hiberno-Norse from the later Anglo-Norman burials and therefore they are discussed together. The investigated graves reflect a cross-section of the community, with individuals of all ages and both sexes represented (table 6.2).

Sex estimation

It was possible to estimate sex for 82 of the 95 adults (table 6.3). A slightly higher ratio of males to females (1.6:1) was noted which may reflect the male-dominated elite patronage of the abbey. Cemeteries attached to important abbeys would be expected to have special areas reserved for burial of members of the monastic orders and the preponderance of males in these areas would be much higher than that recorded at St Thomas's (Gilchrist and Sloane 2005, 204). The conventional area for these burials is to the southeast of the church or intramurally and, although not absolute, archaeological investigations of religious houses in England have identified a much higher percentage of men in these areas (Mays 2006, 181). Exceptions to this rule are known, however, with segregated religious burial to the north and northeast of the church being identified in some cases (Gilchrist and Sloane 2005, 60). There is often little difference in the manner of burial to distinguish members of the religious orders from the lay population, and in the absence of osteological analysis it is difficult to identify an exclusive burial area for the canons. The distribution of both sexes at St Thomas's appears to be evenly spread across the investigated burial area dispelling the idea of segregated burial in this area. This is perhaps unsurprising given the location of the excavation, to the north and outside of the estimated church site.

Table 6.3 Distribution of adult age-at-death by sex (incl. Buckley 2003)

Age category	Male and probable male	Female and probable female	Undetermined sex	Total
'Unaged' adult	11.7% (6/51)	9.7% (3/31)	84.6% (11/13)	21.1% (20/95)
Young adult	17.6% (9/51)	25.8% (8/31)	0% (0/13)	17.9% (17/95)
Young middle adult	21.6% (11/51)	9.7% (3/31)	15.4% (2/13)	16.8% (16/95)
Middle adult	23.5% (12/51)	32.3% (10/31)	0% (0/13)	23.2% (22/95)
Older middle adult	15.7% (8/51)	9.7% (3/31)	0% (0/13)	11.6% (11/95)
Older adult	9.8% (5/51)	12.9% (4/31)	0% (0/13)	9.5% (9/95)
All adults	53.7% (51/95)	32.6% (31/95)	13.7% (13/95)	

Age-at-death profile for non-adults

A third of the investigated St Thomas's population (49 people) had failed to reach adulthood. Rates of mortality were high for infants and children in the past, with an expected range between 30% and 50% of a medieval cemetery population (Gilchrist and Sloane 2005, 204; Buckley 2003). The profile at St Thomas's is comparable with that identified in the medieval communities at Ardreigh in Kildare and Ballyhanna in Donegal (McKenzie and Murphy 2018, 98). The non-adult individuals at St Thomas's ranged in age from full-term baby to late adolescent (table 6.2), including two infant skeletons that were retrieved from disarticulated deposits (DSk3 and DSk17). Approximately 59% of the non-adult population succumbed to death before the age of six, reflecting a peak in mortality at this particularly vulnerable time in childhood. The first year of life is known to have the highest risk of death in the past; however, the post-weaning period is also a particularly precarious time for children – exposing them to parasitic bacteria, malnutrition, life-threatening health issues, all combined with a high risk of misadventure. Stable isotope studies have indicated that weaning was undertaken between the ages of two and three in medieval rural Ireland (Geber 2010), and data from St Thomas's suggests a similar timeline for this community (discussed further below). Five infants are recorded, two of whom died near to or at the time of birth (aged approximately 40–4 weeks' gestation). This number likely falls far below the true rate of infant death in this community; however, the vulnerability of these remains often reduces their survivability in archaeological contexts and the phenomenon of separate burial of babies may have been practised (Donnelly and Murphy 2008).

Children in this community had a greater chance of surviving into adulthood once they reached older childhood, and higher again once they entered puberty. Six adolescent individuals (Sk30, Sk64, Sk68, Sk74, Sk93 and Sk112) were recorded; with four aged between 12 and 15 at time of death and the remaining two on the cusp of adulthood. Only one of the adolescents (Sk93) was subject to radiocarbon dating and this indicated that their burial was carried out at least twenty years prior to the foundation of the abbey. The children and adolescents buried here during the abbey lifetime most likely represent scions of wealthy lay benefactors, although they may have been servants or novices in the monastic house (Mays 2006, 181). Children of similar ages have been recorded in the cemeteries of contemporary religious houses, e.g., Tintern abbey and St Catherine's nunnery (Ó Donnabháin 2000, 108, 124; Collins 2021, 361).

Age-at-death profile for adults

It was possible to estimate age-at-death for 75 adult individuals at St Thomas's abbey (table 6.2). The remaining 20 mature skeletons were too incomplete to determine age-range and are only recorded as 'adult'. Approximately one third of all adults at St Thomas's died before reaching the age of 35, with the average surviving adult lifespan in this group calculated at 28. At the other end of the scale only 10% of this group survived into older adulthood, with no difference in the sexes evident (table 6.3). The latter number is lower than the recorded average in contemporary British monastic cemeteries (Gilchrist and Soames 2005, 204) but similar to the profile identified at the Dominican friary in Drogheda (Halpin and Buckley 1995). Males (40%) were slightly more vulnerable during early adulthood than females (35.5%) at St Thomas's. While this may reflect poorer childhood experience, more arduous work life or greater exposure to infectious agents, this disparity may simply reflect the higher proportion of men in this section of the cemetery. This bias in young adult death contrasts with other known cemeteries where the opposite is identified, often attributed to the greater perils of death for women of child-bearing age. The fact that this is not evident here may highlight the higher standard of life that these women experienced, perhaps with access to health practitioners.

Stature

Although stature has been commonly taken as an indicator of general health and wellness in past populations, genetic potential must be considered in addition to childhood nutrition. At St Thomas's, data was only available for 39 men (76%) and 19 women (61 %) due to the fragmentary nature of the remains. The average height for males was estimated at 171.9cm (5ft 6in) and for females as 158.2cm (5ft 2in). This group compares favourably with their contemporaries in other urban or monastic settings (table 6.4), although both sexes at St Thomas's are distinctly taller than their counterpart in the rural medieval Gaelic community at Ballyhanna. The shortened stature in this latter population was interpreted as the result of poor nutrition and health in childhood and adolescence (McKenzie and Murphy 2018, 171), suggesting that better conditions prevailed for the St Thomas's cohort in an urban setting.

Table 6.4 Comparative stature estimates (cm) for medieval populations

Site	Period century	Male		Female		Source
		n	Mean	n	Mean	
Ballyhanna, Donegal	8th–17th c.	188	167.1	209	154.8	McKenzie and Murphy 2018
Ardreigh, Kildare	11th–15h c.	321	170.1	351	159	
St Thomas abbey, Dublin	11th–13th c.	8	171	6	156	Buckley 2003
St Thomas abbey, Dublin	**11th–13th c.**	**31**	**172.9**	**13**	**160.3**	
Stephen/Aungier St, Dublin	13th–17th c.	73	169.8	25	158	Coughlan 2021
Dominican priory, Cork	13th–16th c.	17	170	6	157	Power 1995
Temple Lane, Dublin	13th–16th c.	19	169	?	159.2	Ó Donnabháin and Cosgrove 1994
Tintern abbey, Wexford	13th–15th c.	38	171.1	16	159.8	O'Donnabháin 2000

Non-metric variation

Non-metric traits are additional features which occur in a minority of skeletons; and while most of these have genetic origins, some are related to mechanical stress or environment (Finnegan 1978; Brothwell and Zakrzewski 2004; Berry and Berry 1967). A selection of eight cranial and eleven post-cranial traits were examined bilaterally in this assemblage, recorded as present, absent or unobservable (Appendix 6.2 below, p. 221). Only four of the cranial traits were present, with relatively low prevalence, including two adults (Sk79 and Sk86) displaying retention of the metopic suture. While traits examined on a population level may be tentatively taken to reflect shared ancestry (Ó Donnabháin and Hallgrimsson 2001), individual relatedness would require DNA analysis to confirm.

Disarticulated remains

Seventy-five deposits of disarticulated bone were recovered during the excavation comprising 2,533 fragments. While all regions of the skeleton were evident, over one third of the recorded elements derived from the skull. Only one example of a charnel pit (containing DSk1) was identified at this time, although another was noted to the east (Walsh 2001). DSk1 accounted for the largest single deposit of disarticulated bone in the cemetery and analysis of intact crania indicated a minimum number of eight individuals (seven adults and one young child) are represented. A single infant femur was also recorded in DSk1.

DENTAL ANALYSIS

Dental remains were recorded per tooth/socket and individual to determine patterns of frequency and severity of disease affecting the community. The dentition of 33 non-adults and 43 adults were recovered during the course of the current excavation and these individuals are discussed below. Eighteen young children, 10 older children and 5 adolescents were recorded with surviving dentition, although only 3 (Sk13, Sk21 and Sk110) had complete arcades. 221 deciduous and 156 permanent teeth were observed in occlusion in the sub-adult dentition. Partially formed crowns and unerupted teeth were recorded present but not included in the analysis. The adult remains relate to 56% (14) of the females and 62% (27) of the males; with two individuals of indeterminate sex associated with four loose teeth. These individuals produced 813 sockets and 837 teeth. Thirteen (1.5%) of the teeth survived as roots reducing the number of observable crowns to 824. All adult age groups are represented, although no complete dental arcades survived. The earlier data (Buckley 2003) relating to 3 juveniles and 11 adults has been amalgamated with the current results in Appendix 6.3 (below, p. 222) to compare the overall prevalence of pathologies at St Thomas's with contemporary populations.

Attrition

Dental attrition is generally related to the consistency of food in the diet, although age is also a factor. Some extra-masticatory use of teeth, such as occupational practice, can also impact tooth wear. Unsurprisingly the non-adult dentition displayed mild or moderate levels of attrition, with only 1% of deciduous teeth scored as severe. Although the adult remains predominantly (80% of teeth) displayed mild or moderate attrition, with little difference

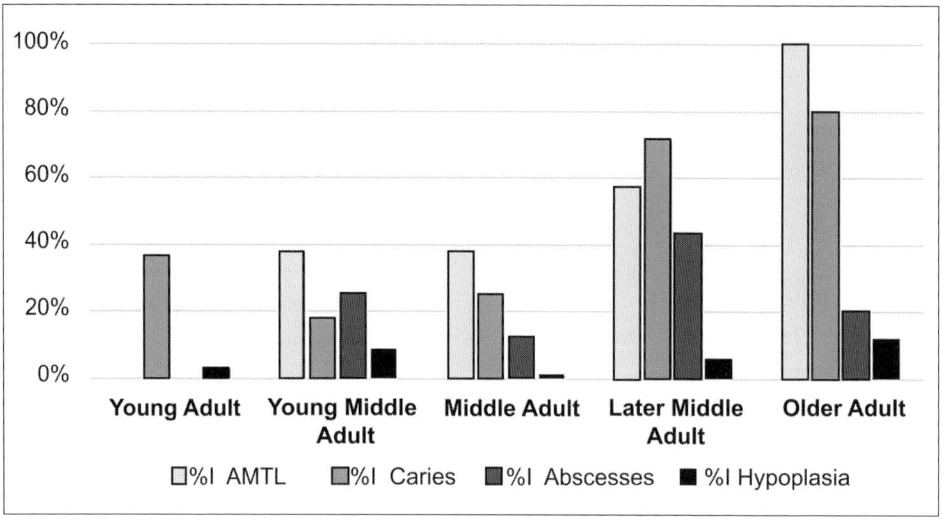

6.4 Percentage of individuals affected (%I) by dental disease by age

between the sexes, males over 35 years of age were more likely to be affected by severe wear than their female counterparts. This disparity is largely accounted for by three older men (Sk38, Sk121 and Sk129) who displayed high frequencies of heavy wear reducing multiple teeth to polished roots and causing *in vivo* loss of others. The posterior teeth displayed the highest frequency of heavier wear, which contrasts with the pattern identified at the Dominican priories at Drogheda and Carlingford where heavier wear on the anterior teeth was predominant (Buckley 2003, 101). This distinct pattern of anterior wear was recorded in the dentition of eight adults at St Thomas's, possibly reflecting higher meat consumption for these individuals (ibid.).

Ante-mortem tooth loss

Loss of teeth during life has multiple causative factors including nutritional deficiencies, trauma, dental diseases, and inadequate oral hygiene; and prevalence in archaeological populations is found to increase with age. Ante-mortem tooth loss (AMTL) had occurred in 39% (15) of the adults with surviving sockets, with a loss of 4.6% (37) of teeth. While men were more susceptible to AMTL than their female counterparts, on average females lost more teeth per individual (mean is 3) than males (mean is 2.3). As expected, the age profile for AMTL at St Thomas's shows a greater prevalence in the more mature individuals, with 60% (9) of the people affected estimated to be over 35 at their time of death (fig. 6.4). All of the 5 older adults with surviving dental remains were affected by AMTL. For both sexes the most affected tooth positions are the first molar (19.5%) and second molar (7%); with the latter

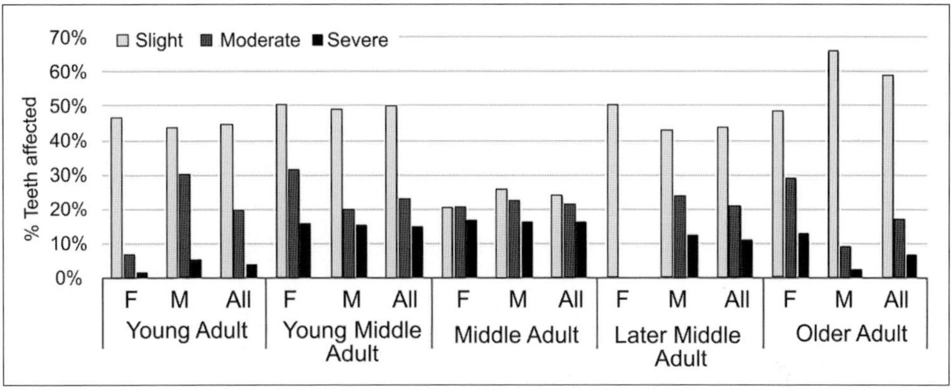

6.5 Severity of adult calculus by age and sex (% of teeth affected)

are also affected by the highest prevalence of caries and abscesses in this population. Interestingly six (55%) of the adults excavated in 1998 had lost 48 teeth during life (Buckley 2003, 101), although two individuals accounted for the majority (41 teeth) of this loss. Combining both datasets, the prevalence of AMTL at St Thomas's increases to 42% of adults and 7.9% of teeth affected. This is lower than nearby St Peter's cemetery where over half of the adults were affected (Appendix 6.3, below p. 222), although the prevalence of affected tooth positions is roughly comparable (Coughlan 2021). Therefore, while fewer people were affected at St Thomas's than St Peter's the severity of the individual loss was greater, perhaps suggesting that the former cohort continued to live longer with the effects of dental disease. Changes in diet and increased pathogen load in later medieval urban settings are likely factors in this generational difference. Conversely, only a third of adults were affected by AMTL in the medieval Gaelic population at Ballyhanna; however, this was likely related to the higher mortality of younger adults (McKenzie and Murphy 2018, 155).

Calculus

All of the recorded juveniles displayed mild deposits of calculus, with severity increasing by age (fig. 6.5). Heavy deposits of calculus were only recorded on the dentition of one non-adult individual; ten (47%) teeth of older child Sk104 displayed varying levels of plaque. Calculus deposits were recorded on 95.4% (forty-one) of the adult dentitions, affecting 72.9% of teeth. The majority (43%) of teeth were affected by slight deposits, with less than 10% associated with severe levels of calculus. This is a similar to the earlier findings (Buckley 2003, 102) with a combined prevalence of 90% (Appendix 6.3, below p. 222). Calculus generally affected both sexes similarly although young males and older females were more likely to be associated with heavier deposits than their counterparts. This may reflect poorer dental health or variation in diet for these cohorts.

Caries

Caries develop at points of weakness where demineralization of the crown or root occurs, most frequently where calculus accumulates (Hillson 1996, 269). Multifactorial causes are known, including diet, abrasive food texture, consumption patterns, oral acidity, age, genetics, sex, enamel composition and the nature and flow of saliva (Larson 1997, 65). Only one juvenile, young child Sk4, at St Thomas's was affected by caries, and in only one tooth (0.4% of all deciduous teeth). Approximately 39% (17) of the adults with observable dental remains had caries, with 5.2% of teeth affected. Frequency increased with age (fig. 6.4), but there was no significant difference in the prevalence or severity of caries between males (40.7%) and females (42.9%) who appear to have been affected similarly. The slightly higher number of the latter group is accounted for in the older adult cohort where all females were affected compared with only two thirds of their male counterparts. Older adult females also exhibited the highest frequency of affected teeth (25.8%), although this deceptively high number only reflects two individuals with multiple tooth loss and widespread decay. No difference was evident in the prevalence of caries in the upper (4.9%) and lower (4.5%) dental arcades. The most frequently affected tooth is the second molar (12.5%), with the recorded locations including roots (27.9%), occlusal surface (25.6%), distal surface (20.9%), mesial surface (18.6%), buccal surface (4.7%), or obscured (2.3%). The combined datasets indicate that 5.5% of teeth and 40.7% of individuals were affected by caries. This is comparable with other medieval populations in Dublin and Drogheda but lower than identified at Tintern abbey (Appendix 6.3, below p. 222), possibly reflecting variation in diet (more meat than carbohydrates?) between the urban lay and rural religious communities.

Dental abscesses

The presence of a visible buccal or lingual sinus in the bone is evidence that, at some time, there was a painful abscess, which eventually drained and became chronic (Ogden 2008, 52). Inflammation of the pulp cavity, exposed due to caries or severe attrition, spreads to the root and a painful accumulation of pus is only relieved by the formation of a drain (Hillson 1996, 284). Approximately 0.9% of observable tooth positions and 17.9% (seven) of adults were associated with an abscess. The affected individuals were almost exclusively men, with the exception of female Sk16 who had distinctly poor dental health (discussed below). Unlike other dental pathologies the prevalence of abscess formation does not increase with age, although a slight peak in the older middle adult cohort (42.9%) was noted (fig. 6.4). The maxillary teeth were more likely to be affected than the mandibular arcade, with over half (57%) of the affected tooth positions in this population recorded in the upper arcade. Abscesses were most commonly associated with the maxillary second molar (6.8%), coincident with the highest frequency of caries. Combining the dataset from the two excavations at St Thomas's, the prevalence of affected individuals rises slightly to 20%; however, this rate is nearly 50% lower than that identified in nearby St Peter's and in the Augustinian friary (Appendix 6.3, below p. 222).

Periodontal disease

Periodontitis is a chronic slowly-progressive inflammatory process affecting the gingiva, periodontal ligaments, cementum, and alveolar bone (Aufderheide and Rodríguez-Martin 1998, 401). In archaeological populations it is identifiable as resorption of the bone, generalized horizontal erosion, or localized vertical erosion; and can lead to infection, abscess and ultimately loss of teeth. There are multi-causal factors in prevalence, including age, diet and health. Widespread low-level periodontal disease was recorded in the dentition of 78% (50) adults affecting 45.9% of tooth positions (Appendix 6.3, below p. 222). The incidence of periodontal disease increased with age, and all adults aged over 35 were affected in at least one tooth socket. The most severe expression was recorded in the dentition of 12 adults, comprising 9 males and 3 females who were aged 25 and older. Seven of these adults had associated ante-mortem tooth loss, with highest individual loss (three positions) recorded in the dentition of middle adult male Sk73.

Enamel hypoplasia

Hypoplastic defects, such as furrows and pits, or breaks in normal enamel formation, represent periods of stress experienced in early childhood when the teeth are forming (Hillson 1996, 165). At St Thomas's these were associated with 21.8% of the individuals with surviving dentition, comprising 27.9% of adults (12) and 17.1% of non-adults (6). The majority of defects appeared to occur between the ages of 3 and 5. The affected juveniles ranged in age from young child (1), older child (4) and adolescent (1). Older child Sk142 was the only child with more than one tooth affected, with defects visible on 50% (4) of their teeth. The isotope data for this child shows a particularly poor diet was consumed (see below) and perhaps this is associated with the chronic periods of stress evident in the teeth. Adolescent Sk74, aged around 14 at time of death, had observable defects on two teeth although no other stress markers were identified. Adding the data from the earlier excavation the overall prevalence rises to 33% (18) of all adults or 35% (26) of all individuals with dentition; and 6.4% of teeth affected. These figures are much higher than those identified in the populations at nearby St Peter's and Tintern abbey (Appendix 6.3, below p. 222). The latter site was more comparable but no evidence for sex-based difference in the prevalence of hypoplasia was identified at St Thomas's, with 28.6% of females and 29.6% of males affected. The prevalence per tooth at St Thomas's is almost three times that identified at later St Peter's where low incidence was taken to suggest that periods of stress must not have lasted long enough (either through recovery or death) to affect the growth patterns of the teeth in the population (Coughlan 2021). By this rationale childhood immunity in the earlier population appears to have been more robust, to survive (at least in the short term) periods of stress. Unfortunately for some, these may have had a reductive impact, lessening the immune response for subsequent illness or episodes of malnutrition.

Anomalies

Smooth shallow grooves or notches were identified in the upper incisors of five adults (11%) of both sexes at St Thomas, reflecting repetitive use of the teeth for non-masticatory purposes. Congenital absence or non-eruption of the third permanent molar was recorded in the dentition of at least ten individuals (23%) equally represented in males and females. The most commonly observed pattern was bilateral absence of the mandibular third molars and unilateral absence of the lower right third molar; and one person displayed absence of all four third molars. One upper incisor had failed to erupt in the dentition of an older female (Sk14), although it was visible in the crypt, with the roots observed extending in the sinus cavity. There is no evidence for infection in the sinus. Two young adult males (Sk17 and Sk45) displayed bilateral widened interdental spaces, and overcrowding was observed for at least three adults.

PATHOLOGY

Infection

Infectious disease was a primary cause of death in the past with many factors determining a person's vulnerability, including age, sex, immune status, population density, and malnutrition status (Roberts and Manchester 2005, 174). While some studies (ibid., 173) have indicated similar morbidity in elite and non-elite groups, the nature of monastic life, slightly removed from the lay community with access to better sanitation and nutrition, meant that members of the religious orders likely lived healthier lives (Mays 2006, 186; Gilchrist 2020, 74). A relatively low prevalence of disease and trauma was evident at St Thomas's and this is thought to reflect the above-average living standards of its wealthy patrons, and perhaps indicates access to some form of medical practitioner. Peaks of morbidity have been linked with urban expansion and population influx, and this is likely reflected in the higher prevalence of disease identified in the later St Peter's population (Coughlan 2021). Interestingly, the osteological paradox means that the individuals with evidence for infection in fact represent the healthier cohort of the community as their immune response allowed them to live through their bout of chronic illness rather than succumbing to death in the acute phase (Ortner 2003, 113).

At least 43% (24) of adults at St Thomas's were affected by a period of resolved or chronic non-specific infection, evidenced by the presence of periosteal new bone formation on the lower limb long-bones. The majority of lesions were rated as mild or moderate in severity, and largely healed by the time of death. The anterior tibia was the most affected location, a common indicator of systematic infection, although it may also be associated with localized infection due to repeated microtrauma (such as shin splints) caused by excessive activity (Waldron 2009, 116). In a smaller number of cases (six adults) the infection appears to have spread to the bone cortex (known as osteitis), identified as localized thickening of the femoral and tibial diaphysis. These individuals also displayed evidence for muscular stress in the thighs, knees and ankles, perhaps indicating traumatic causation for the infection. Two people, an adolescent (Sk30) and an adult male (Sk117), displayed bilateral periosteal new bone growth on the external surface of the anterior ribs, likely indicative of a resolved localized trauma. Only one individual in the current study displayed evidence for a specific infection, young child Sk13 having bilateral expression of chronic outer ear infection which had healed by the time of death. This inflammation commonly occurs in children who are repeatedly exposed to water (such as swimming), and causes pain and some degree of hearing loss.

Metabolic disorders

A metabolic disorder occurs when the metabolism process fails and causes the body to have either too much or too little of the essential substances, such as iron, needed to stay healthy. They may be inherited or acquired due to poor diet and illness (Stuart-Macadam 1992). While there is some debate as to the actual relationship with iron deficiency anaemia, there is consensus that lesions in the orbital roof (*cribra orbitalia*) and cranial vault (*porotic hyperostosis*) reflect periods of physiological stress in childhood. Approximately 16.3% of the population (49) with observable orbit remains were affected by *cribra orbitalia* (table 6.5). All but one of these individuals (young adult female Sk15) died in childhood at periods of peak growth and development likely associated with weaning stresses (Ó Donnabháin 2000, 118). Combining the data from the earlier excavation the prevalence raises slightly to 16.9%; however, this is much lower than that identified at contemporary Francis Street (25%; Buckley 2003, 103), St Peter's (22%; Coughlan 2021) and over half of the prevalence identified at Tintern abbey (38.7%; Ó Donnabháin 2000, 119). As noted at the latter site, the disease was most severe and had a higher frequency in the older child age-range, suggesting a long-standing period of stress post-weaning. No sex-based assessment could be carried out for prevalence as only one adult female and one adult male were recorded with observable lesions. Although cranial vaults were observable for 63 individuals, no expression of porotic hyperostosis were recorded. This lack of observance is unusual and it is thought to reflect the post-mortem wear and disturbance in this cemetery.

Table 6.5 Distribution of *cribra orbitalia* at St Thomas's abbey

Age group	NI	Degree of severity			%I *Cribra Orbitalia*
		Mild	Moderate	Severe	
>1 year	1	-	-	-	0% (0/1)
1–6 years	11	3	-	1	36.4% (4/11)
6–12 years	5	2	1	-	60% (3/5)
12–18 years	2	-	-	-	0% (0/2)
18–25 years	8	-	1	-	12.5% (1/8)
25+ years	22	-	-	-	0% (0/22)
All Individuals	49	5	2	1	16.3% (8/49)

Degenerative joint disease

Degeneration of joint surfaces is one of the most commonly recorded conditions in archaeological populations. Both incidence and prevalence increase with age but genetics, race, obesity, trauma and movement are important factors (Waldron 2009, 34). Osteoarthritis and vertebral osteophytosis are discrete conditions with distinctly different lesions; however, the severity and distribution of both are reflective of lifestyle and occupation. The identification of osteoarthritis in archaeological populations requires the presence of eburnation or two or more lesions (ibid.), otherwise it was scored as normal degeneration. Specific causation is hard to determine but it is primarily taken to represent daily wear and tear of the joints. Secondary osteoarthritis, however, refers to cases where degeneration is precipitated by trauma earlier in life or congenital abnormality (Ortner 2003, 547). Overall, 50% of the adult population were affected by some form of joint disease, with a distinct preponderance of males (28) representing 65.1% of this cohort, in contrast with 48% of females.

Vertebral osteoarthritis: Twenty-one (34.4%) adults with at least one pre-sacral vertebra present were affected by degenerative lesions on 2.6% of the recorded intervertebral articular facets (table 6.6). These had become arthritic in 8 adults (4 males and 4 females). This prevalence is lower than expected and all lesions were recorded as mild or moderate. Most affected individuals were aged over 35 at time of death, and the lesions were most frequently recorded in the lower cervical and upper thoracic vertebrae. Among the men degenerative changes were evenly spread throughout the spine in relatively low frequencies (max. 7.2% for T4). The female population was marked by a distinct absence or low occurrence (0.9%) in the neck (C1–7) when compared with their male counterparts (4%). Although the numbers are quite low, this profile contrasts with that identified at Tintern abbey where twice as many neck vertebrae were affected in females (20%) than males (9.9%), leading to the suggestion that they had habitually carried loads on their heads (Ó Donnabháin 2000, 115). The most extensive single array of lesions, albeit mild or moderate in severity, was recorded throughout the entire spinal column of older middle adult male Sk70, who was also affected by Schmorl's nodes in five lower vertebrae. The prevalence identified at St Thomas's is comparable with other known medieval populations, but lower than that recorded at St Peter's (Coughlan 2021).

Table 6.6 Percentage of individuals (%I) affected by osteoarthritis

	%I affected by spinal osteoarthritis				%I affected by extraspinal osteoarthritis		
	Female	Male	Undet.	All adults	Female	Male	All adults
Young adult	16.7% (1/6)	11.1% (1/9)	–	13.3% (2/15)	0% (0/7)	0% (0/9)	0% (0/16)
Young middle adult	33.3% (1/3)	11.1% (1/9)	0% (0/2)	14.3% (2/14)	0% (0/3)	9.1% (1/11)	6.3% (1/16)
Middle adult	60% (3/5)	50% (3/6)	–	54.5% (6/11)	16.6% (1/6)	28.6% (2/7)	23.1% (3/13)
Older middle adult	0% (0/2)	75% (6/8)	–	60% (6/10)	0% (0/3)	25% (2/8)	18.2% (2/11)
Older adult	100% (3/3)	66.7% (2/3)	–	83.3% (5/6)	33.3% (1/3)	66.6% (2/3)	50% (3/6)
Unaged 'adult'	0% (0/2)	0% (0/0)	0% (0/3)	0% (0/5)	0% (0/3)	20% (1/5)	5.3% (1/19)
All adults	38.1% (8/21)	37.1% (13/35)	0% (0/5)	34.4% (21/61)	8% (2/25)	18.6% (8/43)	12.3% (10/81)

Vertebral osteophytosis: New bone deposits (osteophytes) are laid down around the margins of vertebral bodies to compensate for the degeneration of intervertebral discs. This is a relatively common condition in archaeological populations and has been identified in 42.6% of adults (table 6.7). More men (51.4%) than females (33.3%) were affected, mirroring the pattern of

Schmorl's nodes; however, the frequency of the disease was roughly comparable in both sexes (5.4% in females and 5.8% in males). A peak in prevalence was noted in the middle and older middle adult cohort (7.2% and 14.1% respectively) but severity was generally mild or moderate.

Schmorl's nodes: Depressions form in the vertebral bodies when the intervertebral disc herniates due to severe strain and compression. It is thought that manual labour such as excessive heavy lifting can be a factor, especially if experienced during the adolescent period. Twenty-six (42.6%) adults with at least one or more pre-sacral vertebral body were affected by Schmorl's nodes (table 6.7), although this is reduced to 32% once the data from the earlier excavation is combined. The recorded prevalence per hemivertebra is 7.4%, which is significantly lower than that identified (23.1%) in the nearby Augustinian friary (Ó Donnabháin and Cosgrave 1994, 19). This suggests that occupants of St Thomas's were subject to less weight-bearing tasks in formative years than their counterparts in the lower social orders. Males were twice as likely to be affected as females, and they also exhibited a higher frequency, over three times (10.6%) that encountered in females (3.1%). The stark contrast between the sexes is more evident in the young adult category where 55.6% of males were affected by Schmorl's nodes, but none of the females. This indicates that boys were more likely to be engaged with physically challenging tasks from a young age. The trend for increased prevalence with age identified elsewhere in medieval Dublin (Coughlan 2021) was not mirrored at St Thomas's. The vertebral segments most affected by Schmorl's nodes are in the lower thoracic and upper lumbar region, including T11 (13.4%), T12 (20%), L1 (17.8%) and L2 (13.8%).

Table 6.7 Percentage of individuals (%I) affected by Schmorl's nodes and osteophytes

	%I affected by Schmorl's nodes			%I affected by osteophytes		
	Female	Male	All adults	Female	Male	All adults
Young adult	0% (0/6)	55.6% (5/9)	33.5% (5/15)	0% (0/6)	33.3% (3/9)	20% (3/15)
Young middle adult	33.3% (1/3)	44.4% (4/9)	42.9% (6/14)	100% (3/3)	22.2% (2/9)	35.7% (5/14)
Middle adult	40% (2/5)	66.7% (4/6)	54.5% (6/11)	20% (1/5)	66.7% (4/6)	45.5% (5/11)
Older middle adult	0% (0/2)	50% (4/8)	40% (4/10)	50% (1/2)	75% (6/8)	70% (7/10)
Older adult	33.3% (1/3)	33.3% (1/3)	33.3% (2/6)	66.6% (2/3)	100% (3/3)	83.3% (5/6)
Unaged 'adult'	0% (0/2)	0% (0/0)	20% (1/5)	0% (0/2)	0% (0/0)	20% (1/5)
All adults	19% (4/21)	51.4% (18/35)	39.3% (19/61)	33.3% (7/21)	51.4% (18/35)	42.6% (26/61)

Extra-spinal osteoarthritis: Nineteen adults (23.5%) were affected by extra-spinal joint degeneration at one or more locations, which had become arthritic in at least 8 locations in 10 individuals (12.3%) (table 6.6). Where observed, severity was mild or moderate, and prevalence increased with age. In general, males (32.6%; 14) were slightly more prone to degenerative changes than their female (20%; 5) counterparts, and the only individuals to be affected at three or more locations were males aged over 35 years at time of death. Where osteoarthritis was confirmed, possible evidence for sex-based difference was indicated, with the females affected in the hips and knees, and males affected in the jaw, shoulder, elbow, wrist, hip and foot (table 6.8). This highlights that men were subject to a wider range of mechanical and environmental stress in their daily occupations. The shoulder joint exhibited the highest level of degeneration, with almost a fifth of individuals affected.

Much higher prevalence for spinal and extra-spinal osteoarthritis, osteophytosis and Schmorl's nodes was identified at the nearby St Peter's (Coughlan 2021), the Augustinian friary (Ó Donnabháin and Cosgrave 1994, 17) and in Tintern abbey (Ó Donnabháin 2000, 117), reflecting the more laborious occupational activities of the lower status inhabitants of Dublin and the rural religious community respectively. We can infer that the men and women buried in St Thomas's experienced better conditions during adolescence and early adulthood than their contemporaries.

Table 6.8 Distribution of extra-spinal joints affected by osteoarthritis

Joint	Left	Right	Bilateral
Jaw	0% (0/43)	2.5% (1/40)	0% (0/37)
Shoulder			
Acromioclavicular	2.8% (1/36)	2.8% (1/36)	3.3% (1/30)
Sternoclavicular	2% (1/50)	2.4% (1/42)	2.7% (1/37)
Elbow	2% (1/50)	1.7% (1/58)	0% (0/44)
Wrist	2.1% (1/47)	0% (0/44)	0% (0/37)
Hip	5.7% (3/53)	1.6% (1/60)	1.9% (1/51)
Knee	1.8% (1/57)	1.7% (1/58)	1.8% (1/56)
Foot	2.6% (1/39)	0% (0/39)	2.6% (1/39)

TRAUMA

Fractures are the most commonly recorded form of trauma in archaeological populations, and well-aligned bones are rare osteological evidence for medical intervention in the past (Gilchrist 2020, 80). The most frequently affected bones are the ribs, radius, ulna, hand, fibula, and tibia (Waldron 2009, 149). Causation can vary, including accidents, repetitive stress, interpersonal violence, or as a result of pathological stresses (ibid.). The incidence of recorded trauma was relatively low at St Thomas's with 13.5% (11) adults displaying definitive evidence for traumatic injuries. No evidence for trauma was identified in the non-adult remains although this may reflect their fragmented nature. While the sample was small it was clear that more males (18%; 9) than females (6%; 2) were affected, and that the type and location of the injuries appear to reflect a sex-based difference in causation. Injuries generally associated with accidental trauma more often affected females (distal radius and fibula) whereas those most likely to be related to interpersonal violence affected males (rib, distal ulna, hand, blunt-force trauma of skull, anterior tibia). Two females (Sk15 and Sk53) displayed well-healed fractures of the distal right radius (forearm) which were well-healed by the time of death. This location is commonly known as a 'colles' fracture and usually is the result of accidental fall or trauma. The younger female (Sk15) had also sustained a fracture to the right distal fibula, a location generally affected by direct insult to the bone by falling on an object, or receiving a kick from an animal, although violent action cannot be ruled out.

Two men displayed evidence for fractures in the right hand, affecting the fifth metacarpal of Sk126 and the finger phalanges of Sk138. The latter individual, a middle adult male, displayed traumatic fusion of the fourth proximal and intermediate hand phalanges in his right hand. The original fracture location is not observable due to the level of remodelling, which resulted in the two bones fusing in a slightly flexed position (45-degree angle). A similarly-aged man identified at nearby St Peter's with the same healed trauma of the left hand also appeared to suffer blunt-force trauma to the skull (Coughlan 2021), further associating such an injury with interpersonal violence.

The older male Sk114 provided the best accumulative evidence for injury sustained due to interpersonal violence as a younger man. His burial was located in the centre of the excavation area, to the immediate west of pilgrim Sk108; however, later intercutting removed the lower half of his skeleton. An unidentifiable corroded iron object (measuring 12mm by 14mm) was accreted to the cranium, between the left mastoid process and occipital condyle but it appears to have been lodged post-deposition during later disturbance. Well-healed oblique fractures were observed affecting the posterior portion of four consecutive right ribs and the distal right ulna, while the right elbow was affected by osteochondritis dissecans. In addition, his neck and upper torso exhibited spinal osteoarthritis and Schmorl's nodes were noted in six vertebral bodies. The trauma to the ulna is known as a 'parry' fracture as it is frequently received as a defensive wound; also evidenced in the remains of two other men (Sk19 and Sk63) at St Thomas's. The location of the fractured ribs is suggestive of a kick or punch when a victim is prone on the ground (Waldron 2009, 151). Osteochondritis dissecans can be caused by direct insult or repetitive microtrauma due to excessive normal compressive strain, and the

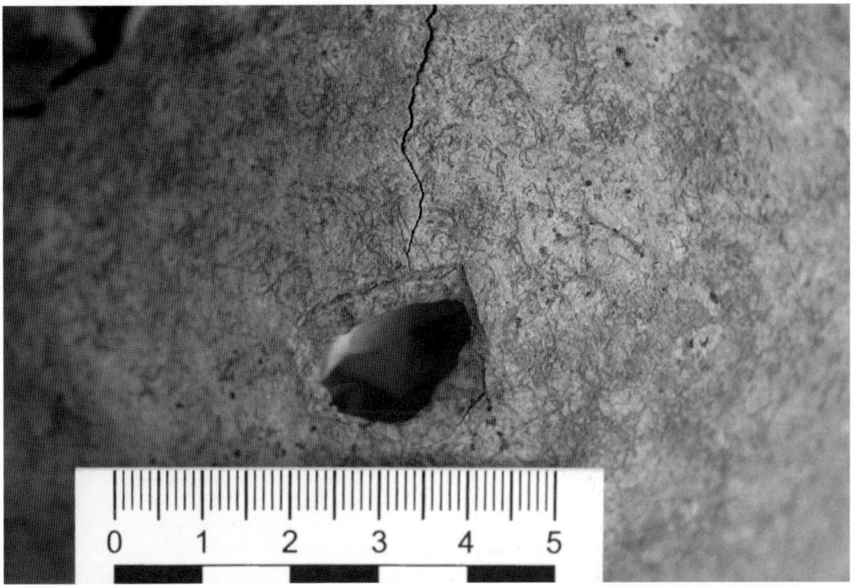

6.6 Evidence for peri-mortem blunt force trauma in the skull of adult male Sk73

humeral capitulum is the second most commonly recorded location in archaeological populations (ibid., 153). The shear force required to cause such a repetitive trauma in the elbow may be consistent with wielding a heavy object (such as a medieval broadsword or similar weapon) in a downward motion, although this does not preclude other occupational actions. Although the timeline for each of the injuries is not known, they had clearly occurred well before death. The location and frequency of the wounds tentatively suggests that this man may have been hurt in combat, or during repetitive practice training in his later adolescence or early adult years.

There was no evidence for sharp-weapon trauma at St Thomas's; however, a single case of peri-mortem injury was recorded. The older middle adult male Sk73 displayed a sub-rectangular perforation (measuring *c*.21mm by 17mm externally) in the superior posterior right parietal, indicative of blunt-force trauma to the back of his head (fig. 6.6). As the force of the injury caused radiating fractures, the shape of the multi-faceted object could not be ascertained, although it is likely to have had three straight sides. There is very slight remodelling of the exposed bone, suggesting that this man may have lingered for a short while before succumbing to death. An accidental cause, such as falling from a height onto an object, cannot be ruled out; however, most interpersonal violence represented in the archaeological record focuses on the head and torso (Larson 1997, 157). Accepting that the majority of people are right-handed, if this injury was sustained due to deliberate force, its location suggests he received a blow from someone approaching from behind, and slightly higher than him (Roberts and Manchester 2005, 109).

In addition to the above, seven vertebrae in six individuals were affected by spondylolysis, a stress fracture resulting in partial or complete separation of the body and neural arch (Ortner 2003, 147). This equates to 12% of all adults with observable lumbar remains, or 11% when the data from the earlier excavation is combined. All the recorded examples were expressed bilaterally with non-union of the separated bone, and all affected individuals were male. In four cases the fifth lumbar vertebra was affected, in one case the fourth lumbar vertebra, and in one case both the fourth and fifth. The recorded prevalence is higher than that identified in rural medieval Ireland (McKenzie and Murphy 2018, 303; Ó Donnabháin 2000, 121) and the expected range (5%) for archaeological populations (Waldron 2009, 153). Multiple causative factors are known, including genetic predisposition, repetitive strain (rotation or hyperextension) and trauma; therefore, it is difficult to determine why this population appears to be an outlier.

DIET

Documentary sources indicate that the medieval diet was relatively healthy and well-balanced, primarily based on cereal and dairy products (Lyons 2015, 132). The former were consumed through a wide variety of pot-based dishes, ale and bread, supplemented by vegetables, herbs, fruit, fish and meat (Collins 2021, 339). Irish diet was dominated by 'C_3' plants (wheat, barley, oats and other root staples) and osteological analysis of tooth wear patterns has indicated that food was quite abrasive at this time due to the level of grit retained in ground cereal (Ó Donnabháin 2000, 113). Grain-based meals made up 70% of the daily calories for the average thirteenth- and fourteenth-century Dublin resident, although meat and fish consumption increased as living standards improved (Murphy and Potterton 2005, 238–9). The Augustinian monastic orders are thought to be fairly generous in terms of diet, although items such as meat were still subject to strict regulations (Mays 2006, 183). More fish was consumed in the religious communities than lay populations (Gilchrist 2020, 81). The perishability of fresh fish made it the preserve of the elite and it was often gifted by the aristocracy (Collins 2021, 339).

Broad patterns in food consumption can be inferred on an individual level through analyses of multi-isotope data taken from human bone and teeth. As bone remodels at a variable rate the isotope signature taken from a sample of collagen reflects the latter years of life, whereas data from dentine reflect the period in childhood when a tooth was forming (Lee-Thorp 2008; Beamount and Montgomery 2016). Variability in isotope values can indicate difference between marine and terrestrial food resources, and between plant and animal

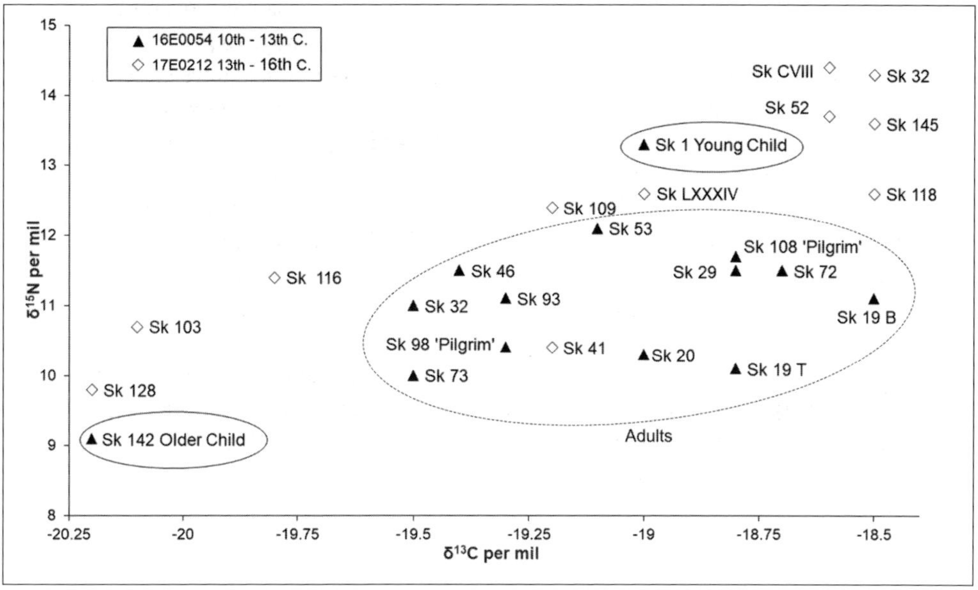

6.7 Comparative isotope data for radiocarbon dated individuals from two medieval urban Dublin populations (St Thomas's indicated by triangle)

products. Terrestrial plants have a lower carbon value than aquatic plants; and nitrogen values vary as one ascends the food chain, being elevated in freshwater fish and mammals (Mays 2006, 187). Investigation of the medieval Gaelic diet experienced at Ballyhanna revealed that there was no apparent difference in the quantity or type (terrestrial *vs* marine) of dietary protein evident between the sexes or ages; once beyond the infant weaning period (McKenzie et al. 2020). This study also revealed a correlation between increased prevalence of caries (per individual and per tooth affected) for the later medieval populations and the greater availability of plant-based carbohydrates (ibid.).

The isotope data for thirteen of the dated individuals (table 6.1; fig. 6.7) at St Thomas's indicate $\delta^{13}C$ values range from -18.5‰ to -20.2‰ (mean – 19.05‰) and $\delta^{15}N$ values range from 9.1‰ to 13.3‰ (mean 11.1‰). The investigated sample represents less than 10% of the excavated population; however, all but two (children Sk1 and Sk142) appear to have subsisted on a relatively similar, balanced diet. The three female adults have a slightly higher nitrogen value, suggesting minor difference in food consumption between the sexes; however, the small sample size (6 men and 3 women) hinders true interpretation. The isotope signatures for the two samples (tooth and bone) taken from young adult male Sk19 reflect slight differences in diet over his lifetime. A higher species richness value was indicated by the bone sample (*B) for the latter years of life when compared with the childhood period represented by the tooth data (*T). Similarly, the results from the two 'pilgrims' reflect the less varied diet in early life of Sk98 (tooth root), and the higher meat or fish component in the latter life of Sk108 (bone). This apparent improvement in diet with age may reflect a normal variation in diet between juveniles and adults at this time; or it could represent elevation of status as these adults progressed through life.

Analysis of individuals from Viking-era ninth- to twelfth-century Dublin indicated homogeneity of diet, and while terrestrial protein sources formed the greater portion of food, marine protein was also evident (Knudson et al. 2012). Notably, the St Thomas's individuals had comparatively less marine component (pers. comm. Paula Reimer), (^{14}Chrono) in their diet than the previous inhabitants of Dublin. This is particularly surprising given the proximity to the coast, suggesting that it was a conscious decision. The values do not however preclude the presence of freshwater fish in the diet, which may have been stocked in ponds by the wealthy lay and religious houses (Foley 2017, 46). In monastic York, studies have shown that the religious brethren consumed more marine produce than the layfolk and this was associated with a lower rate of dental caries (Mays 2006, 183). Interestingly, an opposite scenario is reflected by the religious community at Tintern abbey which has almost twice the prevalence of caries as the lay community at St Thomas's. This stark difference is likely the result of many factors, and to truly investigate this dataset we would need to investigate the remains of the religious community at St Thomas's. The data was compared with values for eleven recently dated individuals recorded in the thirteenth-century cemetery (DU018-378) associated with St Peter's church located approximately 1km to the east (Coughlan 2021). Several of these adults (incl. Sk32 and SkCVIII) had much higher nitrogen values than the St Thomas's adult population, indicating a higher species richness in their diet (fig. 6.7). This is likely linked with their elevated status, as indicated by elaborate stone coffins, and improved living conditions of the fourteenth century (Murphy and Potterton 2005).

The two investigated children are outliers in the data, reflecting differing life circumstances. The older child Sk142, aged approximately 8 years at time of death, was likely buried in the late twelfth century with pillow stones framing their head. Very low nitrogen and carbon isotope values for this child confirm the osteological findings (*cribra orbitalia* and hypoplastic defects of at least four teeth) that they were experiencing physiological stress for some time prior to death. They appear to have subsisted on a very low trophic value diet in their last months or years, with little or no meat or fish protein evident. At least two of their teeth were affected by caries, which may indicate that they subsisted on soft sticky foods (McKenzie and Murphy 2018, 144). Malnutrition is a lack of adequate nutrition that can be caused by not having enough to eat, not eating sufficient quantities of certain foods, or being unable to utilize the food that is being consumed due to illness. The link between

6.8 Young child Sk1 in partially stone-lined grave

malnutrition and increased risk of infection is well established (Ortner 2003, 114) but it cannot be determined whether illness caused the poor uptake of nutrition or vice versa, contributing to the early demise of Sk142. The nitrogen value for the young child Sk1, who was buried in a stone-lined grave (fig. 6.8), is relatively high when compared with the general population at St Thomas's. Breast-milk has a distinct isotopic signature resulting in elevated ^{15}N values: nursing infants, therefore, have higher values than their mothers (Beamount and Montgomery 2016). Isotope values highlighted that weaning occurred by the second or third year of life in medieval Gaelic Ireland (Geber 2010, 182). While no evidence for physiological stress was observed for Sk1 using standard osteological methods, the isotope data, combined with this person's age, suggest that they were in the process of being weaned. A peak in mortality between the ages of one and six was identified at St Thomas's, likely reflecting the precarious post-weaning period when children were introduced to new food sources exposing them to bacterial infection (McKenzie et al. 2015, 165) while greater mobility put them at higher risk of misadventure.

UNUSUAL GRAVES

Elaborate burials

Three graves situated in the western limit of the site deviated from the norm in that they had been lined with stones (Sk1, Sk 20 and Sk 46). There is variability with recorded grave linings in the mid-twelfth and thirteenth century, with the definition ranging between intermittent stone linings and finely-finished shaped structures with head-niches (Gilchrist and Soame 2005, 134), the latter being identified at nearby St Peter's (Coughlan 2021). The most complete grave was associated with the young child Sk1 (described above). Given the young age of the occupant, the increased attention and effort afforded for this child's burial may reflect the high status of their family, although it is not unknown for infants to be afforded this rite (Gilchrist and Soame 2005, 136). The partial remains of cobble-stone lining were recorded in the grave for adult Sk46 (fig. 6.9), an individual who may have been singled out, though for an unknown reason (discussed further below).

The most elaborate stone-lined grave was associated with the young adult male Sk20 (fig. 6.10). Unfortunately, this grave was largely truncated by later burials, removing the skull and right side of the skeleton. The remains represent a young adult male who likely died in his late twenties. His living stature was estimated at 170cm, comparing favourably with his contemporary counterparts (table 6.4). The post-mortem loss of cranial remains restricted osteological analysis but it was clear that this young man had suffered from a chronic infection that remained active in the latter years of his life. Inflammation of both leg bones and surrounding tissues may have resulted from localized muscle trauma; however, infections such as these may also have travelled in the bloodstream from another locus. He may have experienced daily pain or restricted movement as a result of this long-standing illness, and it likely to have contributed to his premature death. The distinctly laborious mode of this man's burial belies his relatively young age, suggesting that he was an important figure in the community. His resting spot appears to have become a focus for later interments (Duffy 2020, 205) and this desire by others to be buried in his vicinity may also point to his enduring status, or perhaps represent a family plot. Radiocarbon dating indicated quite a long date-range for Sk20 (table 6.1); however, calibration of the combined site data (fig. 6.3) and its stratigraphic relationship with underlying Sk32 indicates a high probability that this man died in the eleventh century. Considering this timeline, the manner of his burial raises significant questions about his identity

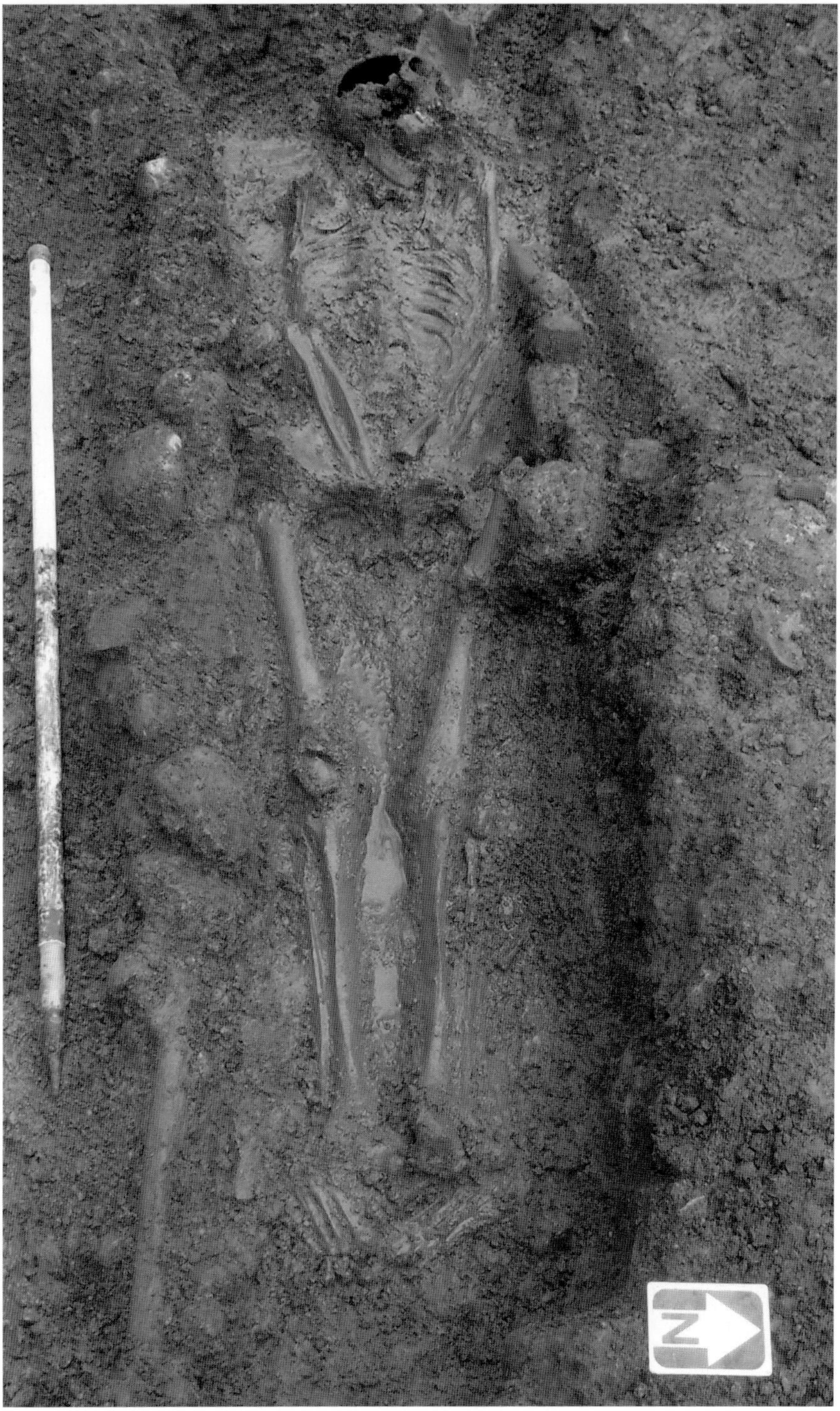

6.9 Adult male Sk46 in partially stone-lined grave; stone placed in his mouth

6.10 Middle adult male Sk20 in stone-lined grave (Sk32 feet at northeast corner)

in Hiberno-Norse Dublin. It is particularly interesting given the sea-change occurring within the nearby city walls regarding the official recognition of Christianity by its elite residents (Clarke 2015, 263).

Silencing the dead or evidence for penitence?

Two adults, a male (Sk46) and a possible female (Sk16), buried side by side in the western portion of site were found with large stones wedged in their hyperextended mouths. The excavator has interpreted this as a deliberate action in the funerary rite but post-depositional factors cannot be ruled out. Both individuals had died in their late twenties or thirties and their adjacent burial may suggest their death was coincident; likely occurring sometime in the early years after the abbey's foundation (table 6.1). The woman (Sk16) has an earlier calibrated date-range, extending into the eleventh century; however, on balance it is more likely to relate to the Anglo-Norman phase of burial. Partial remains of a cobble-stone lining had survived in the man's grave (fig. 6.9); which differed in style to the two other lined graves discussed above. Several individuals have been recorded in the archaeological record in Ireland with stones deliberately placed in their mouths but, where dated, this has been identified as an early medieval practice (Whitty 2012; Read 2010, 48). The phenomenon of placing items in the mouth has been identified as a minority burial rite at both parish churches and religious houses in England, with stones, tallow plugs, coins and ash recorded; however, causation is debatable (Gilchrist and Sloane 2005, 78). Perhaps most significantly, in light of the presence of pilgrims at St Thomas's (discussed below), is a young man buried in a prestigious grave at the Cluniac priory of St Ethernan in Fife during the fourteenth century. His mouth had been wedged open by an animal bone to accommodate the placement of a scallop shell (ibid., 79). The medieval psyche was overwhelmingly concerned with the notion that those who had a 'bad death' may refuse to pass on, and return to haunt or disturb the living (Daniells 2005, 97; Collins 2021, 351). Suggested reasons for placing items in the mouth at the time of burial include atonement for some form of spoken heresy, or to prevent the dead from speaking; however, it is open to interpretation (Gilchrist and Sloane 2005, 79).

Osteological analysis identified that the woman suffered from very poor dental health and a chronic infection that was active at the time of her death. Extensive deposits of new bone observed on all surfaces of the lower limb long-bones and slight expansion of both tibiae can likely be attributed to osteomyelitis, an infection that had spread to the bone (Ortner 2003, 55). The exact cause or source of the infection is unknown in this instance; bacteria may enter the body locally at an open wound or travel through the blood from injury elsewhere in the body. This woman also suffered from chronic infection of the gums, associated with the *in vivo* loss of at least two posterior teeth and severe decay and infection of two others. The most severe infection was associated with an abscess that was actively draining into the mouth at the time of her death. Given that there was no effective treatment for such an infection in the medieval period, it is possible that the chronic infection was complicated by osteomyelitis. Daily tasks, including eating, may have been limited or hindered by the pain this woman experienced; and it is possible that her long-term illness may have set her apart in some way from the community. Interestingly she was one of only five adults to display evidence (smooth shallow grooves on the mesio-buccal surface of the upper first incisors) of extra-masticatory use of her teeth, perhaps related to her occupation.

The man (Sk46) buried in the adjacent grave also displayed similar levels of periodontitis associated with severe dental attrition of the posterior teeth although no evidence for further infection was observed. We cannot know why (or if) the stones became a deliberate part of the funerary rite. The visibility of such an action to the general mourners is debateable, depending on the timeline for the insertion of the stone and whether the body had been shrouded, and perhaps reflects private penitence. It is curious that while they were distinguished in this fashion, they were still afforded burial in this sought-after consecrated ground. The inclusion of a decapitated individual in the contemporary Augustinian friary in the eastern suburbs suggests that there was some leniency in the regulations for who could be buried at these important sites.

Prevention of contagion?

At least four adults (Sk25–27 and Sk29) appear to have been covered by a lime deposit at the time of burial, which the excavator believed may have been laid down to combat the spread of infection (Duffy 2021, 206). There were no discernible grave-cuts between the skeletons, and while this was a common issue during excavation, in this instance it likely means that these adults were buried together in one large pit. Their coincident burial points to contemporary death, and possible shared cause; however, acute infection leading to death has no osteological manifestation. The radiocarbon date-range for this burial event straddles the pre- and post-abbey period, reflecting a 170-year timeframe. While this antedates the arrival of the well-documented Black Death, episodes of other fast killing 'plagues' are recorded in the annals throughout the medieval period. Analysis identified these remains as representing two males (Sk25 and Sk27) and one female (Sk29) who appeared to die at a similar age, in their early thirties. It was not possible to estimate sex or an accurate age-range for the fourth adult (Sk26) due to the level of incompleteness. Likewise, the poor preservation of this latter individual hindered observation of any possible pathological lesions or trauma. The other three adults did however display evidence for chronic non-specific infection, which was most severe in one of the men (Sk25). His infection had spread further, causing inflammation of the femora which was active at the time of death. A variety of causes can be attributed to osteitis; in this case bacteria may have entered the blood stream at the point of traumatic injury to the left knee and surrounding muscles. Mild expression of periosteal new bone growth is present on the tibiae of the other two adults reflecting resolved periods of illness. While these conditions are not the cause of death, they likely had a reductive impact on the immune system so that, when the next infection was contracted, these adults were less able to survive.

PILGRIMS

Pilgrimage was a core part of medieval life, and functioned at local, regional and international levels to fulfil the differing social and religious needs of the community. It was carried out as an act of devotion, penance or thanksgiving, and by those seeking a cure for an ailment or to reduce their time in purgatory (Cunningham 2018, 17). Places such as Rome, Jerusalem, Canterbury and Santiago de Compostela were visited by Irish pilgrims, with the latter site gaining particular popularity with the Anglo-Norman community in the twelfth century (ibid., 95; Ó Riain-Raedel 1998, 19). The abbey of St Thomas itself was likely a place of pilgrimage, a possible shrine of Thomas Beckett having been identified during the 2017 excavation (Duffy and O'Keeffe 2017). The journey to Santiago was long and arduous, crossing difficult terrain with limited access to clean water, fresh food or shelter, increasing exposure to disease and other hazards such as robbery. As such, many pilgrims died abroad and this was accepted as a likely outcome from commencement. Pilgrims returning from Santiago carried a souvenir of their achievement, a scallop shell, and this symbol is still synonymous with the journey today. The shells were hung around the body or attached to clothing or a satchel in a prominent location to mark the person's pilgrim status, an important identifier when reliant on the kindness of strangers during travel (Cunningham 2018, 84). The souvenir was considered to have such importance, believed to help save the pilgrim on judgment day, that it was sometimes buried with the owner (ibid.; Fitzpatrick 2010, 17), although recorded archaeological cases are relatively few (Gilchrist and Sloane 2005, 96).

Two middle-aged men (Sk98 and Sk108) buried at St Thomas's in the late twelfth or early thirteenth centuries were accompanied by large perforated scallop shells, indicating that they had likely completed the journey to Santiago. These individuals are the earliest radiocarbon-dated burials in Ireland to have distinct emblems of this pilgrimage, their chronological range in Britain generally falling between the thirteenth and fourteenth centuries

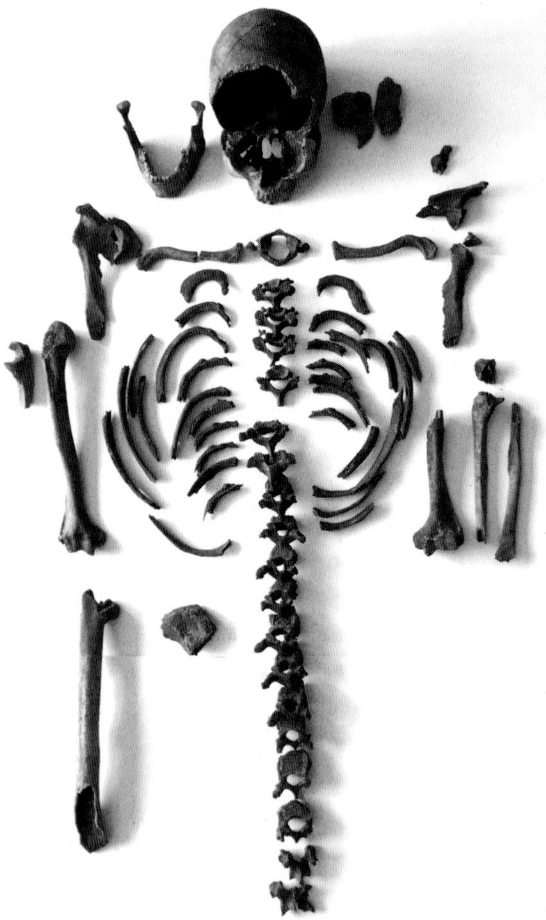

6.11 Skeletal remains of middle adult possible male Sk98 who was buried with pilgrimage souvenir

(ibid., 98). A starting point for the Irish traveller is St James's church in the nearby parish and a pilgrim's hostel was founded in 1216 (Clarke, *Dublin, Pt 1* (IHTA), 7). The religious community at the abbey likely also provided hospitality to returning pilgrims, so it is not surprising that some of these people were subsequently afforded burial in the grounds. A seventeenth-century account suggests that the adjacent St Catherine's cemetery was used for the burial of strangers to the parish; however, archaeological investigation did not identify a boundary between the two cemeteries (Duffy 2021, 239). The opportunity to undertake an international pilgrimage would have been limited to those members of society who had access to time, money, and the worldview to enable such an endeavour and the first recorded pilgrims travelling from Ireland to Santiago were Anglo-Norman officials and senior ecclesiastics (Cunningham 2018, 95). The men identified at St Thomas's likely

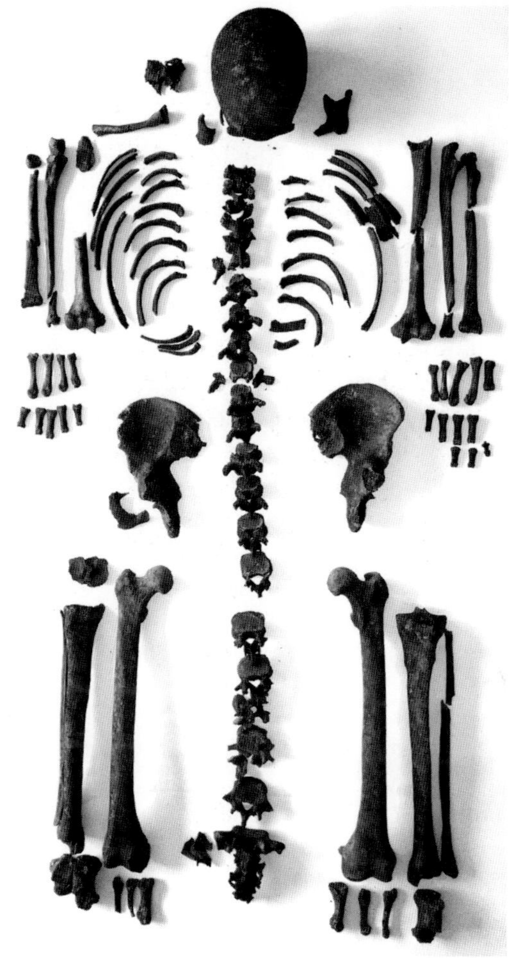

6.12 Skeletal remains of middle adult male Sk108 who was buried with a pilgrimage souvenir

had links with nobility or gentry, the religious orders, or the mercantile class. Similar shells have been identified in burials across the country at Ballyhanna in Donegal, St Mary's cathedral Tuam, Claregalway friary in Galway, the Augustinian priory of St Mary's in Mullingar, the priory of the Holy Cross in Tralee and Ardreigh in Kildare (ibid., 86); however, radiocarbon dates are not available. These individuals have been identified as a middle-aged female at Ballyhanna (McKenzie and Murphy 2018, 45), a middle-aged male at Tuam (Clyne 1990, 22), an adult male at Ardreigh (Moloney et al. 2016), and two individuals at Mullingar (Ó Riain-Raedel 1998, 17) for which the author has no demographic data.

While the radiocarbon dating suggests relative contemporaneity for the two men at St Thomas's, the slightly staggered calibrated date-ranges could be interpreted as representing different generations. Both of the men died in their fourth or fifth decade of life; however, it is not possible to determine at what age they may have undertaken the pilgrimage; or indeed if they repeated the journey. People travelled at various points in their lives, some travelling as young adults whereas others undertook the journey at the end of their lives (Cunningham 2018, 100). One of the graves (Sk98) had been heavily truncated by later activity, with resultant loss of the lower limbs (fig. 6.11), restricting assessment. The shell was identified over the right upper arm, similar to the person identified at Mullingar (ibid., 19), suggesting that it had either been hung around the neck or stitched onto the sleeve of his clothing. This man suffered from poor dental health, associated with very heavy attrition levels indicative of a highly abrasive diet. This pattern contrasts with that identified for the general population, suggesting distinct variance in this individual's consumption which may reflect living under different, somewhat reduced, circumstances for a long period (such as pilgrimage).

The second grave (Sk108) was more complete (fig. 6.12) than Sk98 and as such provided more information on this man's health; however, his teeth and facial bones had been lost post-mortem. In this instance the shell was identified overlying the lower torso, suggesting that it had been hung around the neck or waist. This man suffered from a prolonged period of physiological stress evident as chronic infection in the lower limbs and osteoarthritis of the spinal column (affecting multiple vertebrae C6, T8–11); which was most severe in the neck region. Both of these conditions would have caused the sufferer daily pain and stiffness. There are multiple causes of osteoarthritis, including advanced age, occupational wear and tear, infection and trauma. While a specific cause cannot be determined, the inflammation of the legs may be due to excessive micro-trauma associated with a relative increase in the frequency or intensity of strenuous exercise over a prolonged period. Undertaking a pilgrimage would certainly have put the body under strain due to months of travel on foot or horseback subsisting on a restricted diet and exposed to disease; and the long-lasting result of such a journey is likely reflected in the skeleton of this man. Published osteological evidence for the physical effects of pilgrimage on the body is limited. The woman buried at Ballyhanna was affected by vertebral spondylolysis, a relatively common stress fracture likely caused by a repetitive strain (McKenzie and Murphy 2018, 45). While it is possible that she personally undertook the pilgrimage, it was suggested that perhaps she had been given the shell souvenir by a loved one who returned from the continent (ibid.). The man buried in Tuam suffered from age-related spinal degeneration and osteoarthritis of the hips and shoulders (Clyne 1990, 22). While these conditions may be the result of regular occupational stresses, they would have been exacerbated by the rigours of pilgrimage.

CONCLUSION

The osteological analysis of this population, which straddled a period of intense social and political upheaval, reflects a relatively healthy, well-fed community, albeit from the elite strata of Dublin society. It has confirmed many of Laureen Buckley's earlier findings while presenting a more complete reflection of the community. The northern portion of the abbey cemetery was populated during the first hundred years of its foundation, with a shift in the focus of burial likely following the late thirteenth-century rebuilding programme. While this cemetery was a highly desirous location for the upper echelons of society, no obvious restrictions, in terms of age or sex, were identified in the investigated portion of the burial ground. A slightly higher ratio of males to females was noted, which may relate to the male-dominated religious community or the high-status abbey patrons. No conclusive evidence of a segregated burial area for the religious brethren was identified, although this is likely to have existed nearer to the church and intramurally.

The skeletal remains exhibited low prevalence of disease and trauma when compared with the contemporary occupants of the Augustinian friary in the eastern suburbs, or indeed subsequent generations buried in St Peter's parish churchyard. Resolved periods of chronic non-specific infection were evident in almost half of the adult population; however, it is important to note that these are the individuals who survived the acute phase of illness, and that others likely succumbed to death before skeletal manifestations could occur. Where trauma was observed, there appeared to be a difference in causation, albeit statistically unviable, with females more prone to 'accidental' events and males affected by direct insult or interpersonal violence. Only one case of distinct peri-mortem injury was observed, that of a middle-aged man with evidence for blunt-force trauma on the back of the head.

The adult population appeared to subsist on a varied diet, albeit with limited marine intake. This is somewhat surprising given the proximity to the coast and the 'elite' status of this lay cohort; however, the data does not preclude the consumption of freshwater fish. This community consumed a notably less marine component than the previous Viking-era population, and had a less varied species-richness than the later medieval population at St Peter's. Prevalence of dental pathologies was equivalent or lower than other known medieval populations, likely reflecting variation in diet between the urban lay community and the rural religious community. Twice as many individuals at St Thomas's appear to have survived periods of physiological or nutritional stress in childhood than nearby St Peter's, and the numbers were higher again at the Augustinian friary. While this may suggest that better childhood conditions prevailed from the fourteenth century, it is also possible that the affected individuals in the later population succumbed to death before any osteological manifestation developed. As expected for the medieval period, peaks in mortality were evident between the ages of one and six, and in early adulthood, the former likely reflecting the sensitive post-weaning period.

At least one child had been afforded a more elaborate stone-lined grave, a rare practice within the investigated sample of the cemetery. A seemingly important young male from the earlier phase of cemetery use was also given the prestige of a more formal grave, and this appears to have become a focus for later burials. Interestingly, two of the middle-aged men buried at the abbey were accompanied by souvenirs of pilgrimage to Santiago de Compostela, representing the earliest radiocarbon dated archaeological evidence for pilgrims returning to Ireland. The inclusion of the scallop shell highlights the importance of this journey for those who could afford the financial and physical hardships of pilgrimage in the twelfth and thirteenth centuries. Months of travel on foot and restricted diet would have taken their physical toll and this seems to be evident in the skeletal remains.

Most importantly, perhaps, there is now evidence for a pre-existing eleventh-century Hiberno-Norse cemetery (and probable church) at this location prior to its identification in the 1170s as the site of Henry II's great abbey dedicated to St Thomas the Martyr. That this site was chosen for this purpose, the only royal abbey in Ireland, speaks perhaps to the importance of the previous establishment and future research is needed to investigate the genetic ancestry and longevity of its community.

ACKNOWLEDGMENTS

My thanks are due to several people who contributed to this chapter. Site context was shared by Paul Duffy; figs 6.1 and 6.22 were produced by Robert Burns; and David McIlreavy provided comment on early drafts. Barra Ó Donnabháin and Jennie Coughlan shared their unpublished specialist reports for Temple Lane and Aungier Street, and Paula Reimer gave some insight on the isotope data.

APPENDIX 6.1. INVENTORY OF BURIALS

(Key: I: infant; YC: young child; OC: older child; Ado: adolescent; A: adult; YA: young adult; YMA: young middle adult; MA: middle adult; OMA: older middle adult; OA: older adult; ES: extended supine; MSM: musculo-skeletal markers; OA: osteoarthritis; DJD: degenerative joint disease; FX: fracture; AMTL: Ante-mortem tooth loss; SN: schmorl's nodes). (*data from Buckley 2003)

ID	Estimated Sex	Estimated Age Category	Estimated Age Range (years)	Estimated Stature in cm (bone)	Preservation	Completeness	Burial Position	Grave Anomalies	Orientation	Dental Pathology	Pathology & Trauma	Developmental Anomaly
Sk1	?	YC	2–4		Moderate	Good	ES, R hand under chin, L hand on chest	stone-lined grave	W–E			
Sk2	?	YC	1–2		Poor	Poor	ES, arms extended at side		W–E			
Sk3	?	YC	1–2		Moderate	Moderate	ES, arms crossed over chest		W–E			
Sk4	?	YC	3–5		Good	Moderate	ES, arms crossed over chest		W–E			
Sk12	?	YC	3–5		Poor	Moderate	ES, hands crossed over pelvis		W–E		Non-specific infection	
Sk13	?	YC	3–6		Moderate	Moderate	ES, hands crossed over pelvis		W–E		Bilateral *otitis externa*	
Sk14	F	OA	40–50		Moderate	Moderate	ES, 1 hand over pelvis, 1 hand over torso		W–E	6/10 sockets AMTL, 5/14 teeth caries, 1/14 teeth hypoplastic defect, periodontitis and calculus; non-eruption of upper L canine	Moderate DJD C5/6, T4-8, T10-11	Bilateral deviation of distal MT5
Sk15	F	YA	17–25	150.7 (Fe)	Moderate	Good	ES, arms crossed over chest		W–E	Periodontitis and calculus	Resolved period systematic infection, bilateral cribra orbitalia; healed FX R mid-shaft radius and R dist. fibula	
Sk16	?F	YMA	25–35	165.4 (Ra)	Moderate	Good	ES, hands crossed over pelvis	Stone in mouth	WNW–ESE	Calculus, periodontitis, 2/22 sockets AMTL, 1/27 teeth caries, 1/22 sockets periapical abscess	Chronic active infection, osteomyelitis; MSM upper arm	

ID	Estimated Sex	Estimated Age Category	Estimated Age Range (years)	Estimated Stature in cm (bone)	Preservation	Completeness	Burial Position	Grave Anomalies	Orientation	Dental Pathology	Pathology & Trauma	Developmental Anomaly
Sk17	M	YA	20–25	175.6 (Fe)	Good	Good	ES, arms crossed over chest		W–E	Bilateral medial rotation canine, widened interdental space	SN T7–9	Spina bifida occulta; bilateral bony spur T12
Sk18	?F	MA	30–40	170.7 (Fe)	Good	Good	ES, arms crossed over chest		W–E	Moderate periodontitis and calculus		
Sk19	M	YMA	25–34	174.6 (Hu)	Good	Good	ES, hands crossed over pelvis		W–E		Active non-specific infection; DJD dist. L MT1; SN T6–12; healed FX R dist. ulna; bilateral spondylolysis L4	
Sk20	?M	YMA	25–30	170.1 (Fi)	Moderate	Moderate	ES, arms extended at side	Slab-lined grave	W–E		Chronic systematic infection, tibial osteitis?	
Sk21	?	YC	2–4		Poor	Moderate	ES, arms crossed over chest		W–E			
Sk24	?	YC	1–3		Poor	Very Poor	ES		W–E			
Sk25	M	YMA	30–34	181.8 (Fe)	Moderate	Moderate	ES, hands crossed over pelvis	plague pit?	W–E		Non-specific infection - femoral osteitis, robust MSM upper and lower limbs	
Sk26	?	A			Poor	Poor	ES	plague pit?	W–E			
Sk27	M	YMA	30–34	176.4 (Fe)	Good	Poor	ES, arms extended at side	plague pit?	W–E		Non-specific infection	
Sk28	?	I	0–1 month		Poor	Moderate	ES, hands crossed over pelvis		W–E			
Sk29	F	YMA	30–34		Moderate	Moderate	ES, hands crossed over pelvis	plague pit?	W–E		Non-specific infection	

ID	Estimated Sex	Estimated Age Category	Estimated Age Range (years)	Estimated Stature in cm (bone)	Preservation	Completeness	Burial Position	Grave Anomalies	Orientation	Dental Pathology	Pathology & Trauma	Developmental Anomaly
Sk30	?F	Ado	15–18	162.5 (Ra)	Moderate	Poor	ES, hands crossed over pelvis		WNW–ESE		Infection - localized torso?	
Sk31	?	OC	7–10		Poor	Poor	ES, hands crossed over pelvis		WNW–ESE			
Sk32	?	A	20+		Moderate	Very Poor	ES		NW–SE		Non-specific infection	
Sk33	?	OC	5–8		Good	Very Poor	ES		S–N?			
Sk34	?M	YMA	25–35		Moderate	Poor	ES	pillow stone?	W–E	2/22 sockets AMTL		
Sk35	?	A	20+		Moderate	Poor	ES?		W–E			
Sk38	M	OA	45+		Poor	Poor	ES		W–E	Periodontitis and calculus, 3/21 sockets AMTL, 3/26 teeth caries, 1/21 sockets periapical abscess and cyst	DJD C2-7, T1-6	
Sk39	?	YC	3–4		Moderate	Very Poor	ES		W–E			
Sk42	?F	OMA	40–44		Moderate	Poor	ES		W–E		Chronic non-specific infection	
Sk44	?	I	6-12 months		Poor	Poor	ES?		W–E			
Sk45	M	YA	20–25	173.9 (Ra)	Moderate	Moderate	ES, hands crossed over pelvis	Ear Muff?	W–E	Calculus, 2/31 teeth caries		
Sk46	M	MA	30–40	175.4 (Fe)	Moderate	Good	ES, hands crossed over pelvis	Stone in mouth, grave lined cobbles	W–E	Periodontitis and calculus	DJD C2 and T8	Flattened spinous process T4-6
Sk47	F	YA	17–25	162.2 (Fi)	Moderate	Moderate	ES, arms crossed over chest		NW–SE			
Sk48	F	OMA	35–45	151.9 (Fe)	Moderate	Good	ES, arms crossed over chest		W–E	4/21 teeth caries, calculus and periodontitis	Bilateral DJD gleno-humeral joint	

ID	Estimated Sex	Estimated Age Category	Estimated Age Range (years)	Estimated Stature in cm (bone)	Preservation	Completeness	Burial Position	Grave Anomalies	Orientation	Dental Pathology	Pathology & Trauma	Developmental Anomaly
Sk53	F	YMA	30–35	157.3 (Ra)	Good	Moderate	ES, arms crossed over chest		W–E	Calculus and periodontitis;	MSM R forearm, DJD radio-carpal surface and T6-11, SN T9-10; healed FX R dist. radius	
Sk54	F	MA	30–40	160.3 (Fe)	Moderate	Moderate	ES, arms crossed over chest		W–E	2/4 sockets AMTL	SN 7-11, L1-2	
Sk56	F	YA	20–25	159.1 (Fe)	Good	Moderate	ES, arms crossed over chest		W–E	2/26 tooth caries, 2/26 teeth hypoplastic defect, calculus and periodontitis	DJD T1-2, T6.	
Sk57	?F	YA	20–25	156.8 (Hu)	Good	Very Poor	ES, hands crossed over pelvis		NW–SE			Bilateral hip dysplasia
Sk58	?M	MA	25–45		Moderate	Moderate	ES, arms extended at side		W–E	Calculus and periodontitis, 3/26 sockets AMTL, 5/26 teeth caries, 1/26 sockets abscess	DJD T7-9	
Sk59	M	YMA	30–35	167.6 (Fe)	Good	Good	ES, arms flexed, hands over upper torso		W–E	Moderate calculus and periodontitis, 1/7 sockets AMTL, 5/12 teeth hypoplastic defect.	Active non-specific infection; resolved period of nutritional stress; mild OA T7-12, SN T7-9, T11, L11	Spina bifida occulta S1
Sk60	M	YA	20–25	172.1 (Fe)	Good	Good	ES, arms crossed over chest		W–E	Calculus and periodontitis	Chronic infection; MSM upper and lower limbs; Bilateral spondylolysis L5; Microtrauma shin splints assoc. bacterial infection?	Spina bifida occulta S3-5
Sk61	?	YC	1–2		Good	Moderate	ES, arms crossed over chest		W–E			

ID	Estimated Sex	Estimated Age Category	Estimated Age Range (years)	Estimated Stature in cm (bone)	Preservation	Completeness	Burial Position	Grave Anomalies	Orientation	Dental Pathology	Pathology & Trauma	Developmental Anomaly
Sk62	?	YC	3–5		Poor	Poor	ES, arms flexed, hands over upper torso		W–E			
Sk63	M	OMA	35–45	168 (Fe)	Good	Good	ES, arms crossed over chest		W–E	2/23 sockets AMTL, periodontitis	MSM upper limb; active non-specific infection; DJD T8-12; healed oblique FX dist. L lateral ulna; bilateral spondylolysis L5	Abnormal shape incisors
Sk64	?	Ado	11–13		Good	Moderate	ES, arms crossed over chest		NW–SE	Calculus		Spina bifida occulta S1 and S3
Sk65	?M	MA	30–40	162.4 (Fi)	Moderate	Very Poor	ES		W–E			
Sk66	M	YA	17–25	161.4 (Fe)	Good	Moderate	ES, arms extended, 1 hand over pelvis		W–E		SN T9, 11-12, L1	
Sk67	?	A	17+		Good	Poor	ES		W–E		Non-specific infection	
Sk68	?	Ado	15–18		Poor	Poor	ES, hands crossed over pelvis		W–E			
Sk69	?F	MA	25–45		Moderate	Poor	ES, hands crossed over pelvis		W–E		Chronic non-specific infection?	
Sk70	M	OMA	35–45	163 (Fe)	Good	Good	ES, arms crossed over chest		WNW–ESE	Calculus and periodontitis, 2/32 sockets AMTL	OA C2-7 T2-12, L1-4, R knee, sterno-clavicular joint; MSM upper limb	Spina bifida occulta S1
Sk71	M	MA	30–40		Moderate	Moderate	ES, hands crossed over pelvis	blue stain on leg bones	NW–SE		MSM upper and lower limbs, femoral and tibial osteitis; DJD R elbow, T4, 8-11, L sternoclavicular joint.	
Sk72	F	OA	45+		Poor	Moderate	ES, hands crossed over pelvis		W–E		Bilateral OA knee joints, active chronic infection – radial, tibial and fibular osteitis DJD C7/T1, T4/T5, SN T7, L1-3	

ID	Estimated Sex	Estimated Age Category	Estimated Age Range (years)	Estimated Stature in cm (bone)	Preservation	Completeness	Burial Position	Grave Anomalies	Orientation	Dental Pathology	Pathology & Trauma	Developmental Anomaly
Sk73	M	OMA	35–40	168.8 (Fe)	Good	Good	ES, arms extended at side		WNW–ESE	Calculus and periodontitis, 3/22 sockets AMTL, 3/19 teeth hypoplastic defects, 4/19 teeth caries, 1/22 sockets periapical abscess	MSM upper and lower limbs, DJD T6-12, L1-5, SN T11-12, L1-2, S1, healed non-specific infection; high impact blunt force trauma to the sup. post. R cranium with radiating hairline fracture.	Tubercles on ribs 11-12 and costal facets on T11-12.
Sk74	?	Ado	12–16		Moderate	Moderate	ES, hands crossed over pelvis		W–E	Calculus, 2/25 teeth hypoplastic defect		
Sk75	?	OC	6–10		Moderate	Good	ES, hands crossed over pelvis		NW–SE	Calculus, 1/7 teeth hypoplastic defect		
Sk76	?	OC	6–10		Moderate	Moderate	ES, arms crossed over chest		W–E	1/8 teeth hypoplastic defect		
Sk77	?	A	18+		Moderate	Very Poor	ES		W–E		Chronic infection, osteomyelitis R leg?	
Sk78	M	YMA	25–30	169.2 (Fe)	Good	Good	ES, arms crossed over chest		W–E	Calculus and periodontitis	Healed non-specific infection	
Sk79	F	OA	50–60	157.8 (Hu)	Good	Moderate	ES, arms crossed over chest	Dsk 14 placed over body from Sk 82?	NW–SE	Calculus and periodontitis, 2/17 sockets AMTL, 8/17 teeth hypoplastic defect, 3/17 teeth caries	Healed non-specific infection; DJD T1-9, T11 and L acetabulum (hip joint)	Supernumery vertebra L6
Sk80	?	YC	4–6		Moderate	Moderate	ES, hands crossed over pelvis		W–E	Calculus		
Sk81	?	OC	5–8		Good	Poor	ES, hands crossed over pelvis		NW–SE			
Sk82	?F	A	18+	159.3 (Fe)	Good	Poor	ES		NW-SE		Healed non-specific infection	
Sk83	?	YC	1–2		Good	Moderate	ES, arms crossed over chest		NW–SE			

ID	Estimated Sex	Estimated Age Category	Estimated Age Range (years)	Estimated Stature in cm (bone)	Preservation	Completeness	Burial Position	Grave Anomalies	Orientation	Dental Pathology	Pathology & Trauma	Developmental Anomaly
Sk84	?M	A	18+		Moderate	Poor	ES, hands crossed over pelvis		W–E		OA L wrist and bilateral knee joints	
Sk85	?	A	18+	M164.7 or F160.8 (Hu)	Moderate	Moderate	ES, hands crossed over pelvis		NW–SE		DJD T4, T8-9, SN T10 and T12	
Sk86	?	YMA	25–29	M169 or F 165.5 (Hu)	Moderate	Moderate	ES, hands crossed over pelvis		NW–SE	Calculus		
Sk87	?	OC	5–8		Moderate	Very Poor	ES		NW–SE			
Sk88	F	YA	20–25		Moderate	Moderate	ES, hands crossed over pelvis		W–E	Calculus		
Sk89	?	YMA	25–35		Very poor	Poor	ES, hands crossed over pelvis		NW–SE		Bilateral spondylolysis of pars interarticularis L5	
Sk90	M	YA	20–25	172.6 (Fe)	Good	Moderate	ES, hands crossed over pelvis		NW–SE	Calculus, 1/24 teeth hypoplastic defect, non-masticatory wear pattern	Healed non-specific infection	
Sk91	M	MA	30–40		Moderate	Moderate	ES, hands crossed over pelvis	Iron staining on cranium	NW–SE	Calculus and periodontitis, non-masticatory wear pattern	SN T12, L1-3	
Sk92	M	OMA	35–45	170.6 (Fe)	Good	Moderate	ES, hands crossed over pelvis		NW–SE		Bilateral MSM upper and lower limbs; DJD T4 and bilateral shoulder, elbow and hips, SN T7, T11-12; Bilateral spondylolysis of pars interarticularis L5, healed FX R T3 lamina	Spina bifida occulta
Sk93	?	Ado	10–14		Good	Moderate	ES, arms crossed over chest		W–E	Calculus		
Sk94	?F	MA	30–45		Poor	Moderate	ES, arms crossed over chest		W–E	Calculus and periodontitis	OA neck C1, C3-6, DJD bilateral shoulder (glenohumeral joint)	

ID	Estimated Sex	Estimated Age Category	Estimated Age Range (years)	Estimated Stature in cm (bone)	Preservation	Completeness	Burial Position	Grave Anomalies	Orientation	Dental Pathology	Pathology & Trauma	Developmental Anomaly
Sk95	F	OMA	35–45		Poor	Moderate	ES, hands crossed over pelvis		W–E		DJD L4	
Sk96	?M	YMA	25–35		Poor	Moderate	ES, hands crossed over pelvis		NW–SE			
Sk97	?M	YMA	25–35	166.9 (Ul)	Poor	Moderate	ES, hands crossed over pelvis		NW–SE	Calculus and periodontitis	MSM bilateral forearm	
Sk98	?M	OMA	35–45		Good	Moderate	ES, arms extended at side	Scallop shell, ear muff?	NW–SE	Calculus and periodontitis, 1/32 sockets abscess, 2/29 teeth caries		
Sk99	F	YA	20–25	166.8 (Ra)	Good	Moderate	ES, arms crossed over chest		W–E		MSM bilateral thighs	
Sk100	?	OC	6–9		Good	Very Poor	ES		NW–SE			
Sk101	?	YC	3–4		Moderate	Moderate	ES, arms crossed over chest		W–E	Calculus	Bilateral cribra orbitalia	
Sk102	?M	MA	25–45	164.5 (Fe)	Good	Good	ES, arms crossed over chest		W–E	Calculus and periodontitis, 1/14 sockets AMTL, 1/15 teeth caries, 1/15 teeth hypoplastic defect	MSM R arm; bilateral active non-specific infection; OA T3-9, L elbow, L wrist, bilateral hip joints, SN T8, T11-12, L1-5	
Sk103	?	YC	2–4		Good	Moderate	ES, 1 arm extended, 1 arm flexed		W–E	1/5 teeth hypoplastic defect		
Sk104	?	OC	8–12		Good	Good	ES, arms crossed over chest		W–E	Calculus; shovel-shaped incisors		
Sk105	?F	MA	30–45	165.3 (Fe)	Moderate	Moderate	ES, arms crossed over chest		WSW–ENE	Calculus and periodontitis	OA T2-11, ribs, L hip, R foot.	
Sk106	?	YC	3–6		Good	Moderate	ES, hands crossed over pelvis		W–E			

ID	Estimated Sex	Estimated Age Category	Estimated Age Range (years)	Estimated Stature in cm (bone)	Preservation	Completeness	Burial Position	Grave Anomalies	Orientation	Dental Pathology	Pathology & Trauma	Developmental Anomaly
Sk107	M	YA	17–20		Good	Moderate	ES, hands crossed over pelvis		W–E		MSM torso and hands; bilateral healed non-specific infection	Spina bifida occulta
Sk108	M	OMA	35–45	173.3 (Fe)	Good	Good	ES, hands crossed over pelvis	Scallop shell on chest	W–E		Bilateral osteitis of tibiae, OA C4-7, T9, L2 and L4; SN T10	partial lumbarisation of T11-12
Sk109	?F	A	18+		Moderate	Very Poor	ES		W–E			
Sk110	?	YC	2–4		Moderate	Moderate	ES, hands crossed over pelvis		W–E		Active cribra orbitalia; active non-specific infection	
Sk111	?	I	0-1 month		Moderate	Poor	ES		NW–SE			
Sk112	?	Ado	11–13		Good	Good	ES, hands crossed over pelvis	Ear muff?	W–E			
Sk113	?M	MA	25-45	161.4 (Fe)	Poor	Poor	ES, hands crossed over pelvis		W–E			
Sk114	M	OA	45–49	181.4 (Hu)	Moderate	Moderate	ES, hands crossed over pelvis		W–E	Calculus and periodontitis, 3/22 sockets AMTL, 2/18 teeth caries; non-masticatory wear pattern	DJD C3-4, T5-6; SN T11-12 and L1-4; Healed FX distal R ulna and min. 4 posterior R ribs; osteochondritis dissecans distal R humerus	
Sk115	?	OC	8–11		Good	Poor	ES, arms extended at side		NW–SE	Calculus, 1/20 teeth hypoplastic defect	Healed bilateral cribra orbitalia	
Sk116	?	YC	3–5		Moderate	Moderate	ES, arms extended at side		W–E			
Sk117	M	YA	17–20	182.1 (Fe)	Good	Good	ES, hands crossed over pelvis		W–E		Chronic systematic infection; bilateral spondylolysis of pars interarticularis L4 and L5	Flattened metacarpal heads and rib heads, absent rib tubercle

ID	Estimated Sex	Estimated Age Category	Estimated Age Range (years)	Estimated Stature in cm (bone)	Preservation	Completeness	Burial Position	Grave Anomalies	Orientation	Dental Pathology	Pathology & Trauma	Developmental Anomaly
Sk118	?M	A	18+		Good	Poor	ES		W–E		Healed non-specific infection	
Sk119	F	YA	17–25		Moderate	Moderate	ES, arms crossed over chest		W–E	Calculus, 1/30 teeth caries		
Sk120	M	YMA	30–34	174.5 (Fe)	Good	Moderate	ES		W–E		Slight DJD L hip	
Sk121	M	OMA	35–45	168.5 (Fe)	Good	Good	ES, 1 arm extended, 1 arm flexed		W–E	Calculus and periodontitis, 5/29 sockets AMTL, 2/27 teeth caries, 9/27 teeth hypoplastic defects	MSM hands; DJD bilateral acromioclavicular joint; Healed FX R anterior rib and associated infection	
Sk122	?	A	17+		Poor	Poor	ES		W–E		MSM lower limbs, healed non-specific infection	
Sk123	?M	A	17+		Good	Very Poor	ES		NW–SE		MSM lower limbs, healed non-specific infection	
Sk124	M	YA	17–25	169.2 (Fe)	Good	Good	ES, hands crossed over pelvis		W–E	Calculus and periodontitis	MSM upper limbs; healed hairline FX anterior L tibia	Slight ridge along fused metopic suture
Sk125	?	YC	3–6		Moderate	Poor	ES		W–E			
Sk126	?M	A	17+	170.9 (Fe)	Good	Poor	ES, R arm extended		W–E		Non-specific infection; healed FX R 5th finger	
Sk127	?	A	17+		Moderate	Very Poor	ES		W–E		Osteitis L leg?	
Sk128	?	A	17+		Moderate	Very Poor	ES		W–E			
Sk129	?M	OA	45+	176.4 (Hu)	Moderate	Moderate	ES, hands crossed over pelvis		SW–NE	Calculus and periodontitis, 1/5 sockets AMTL	DJD C1–2, C6; OA L acromioclavicular joint	
Sk130	M	YA	17–25	176.4 (Hu)	Good	Moderate	ES, arms crossed over chest		W–E	Calculus and periodontitis, 1/30 teeth caries; non-masticatory wear pattern	SN T6–12 and L1–2; MSM forearms	
Sk131	?F	A	18+		Moderate	Poor	ES		W–E		Healed non-specific infection	

	imated Sex	imated Age tegory	imated Age nge (years)	imated Stature cm (bone)	eservation	mpleteness	rial Position	ave Anomalies	ientation	ental Pathology	thology & auma	evelopmental nomaly
Sk132	?M	A	18+		Moderate	Very Poor	ES		W–E			
Sk133	?	YC	2–3		Moderate	Poor	ES		W–E			
Sk134	?M	OMA	35–45	179.9 (Ra)	Moderate	Moderate	ES, R hand under chin, L hand on chest	unusual hand position	W–E	Calculus and periodontitis, 1/19 teeth caries, 1/19 sockets periapical abscess	MSM bilateral upper limbs; OA C1, C6-7, T10-11	
Sk135	?	YC	2–4		Poor	Very Poor	ES		W–E			
Sk136	F	MA	30–40		Moderate	Poor	ES		W–E		Healed non-specific infection	
Sk137	?	A	18+		Poor	Poor	ES, arms crossed over chest		W–E		MSM bilateral upper limbs	
Sk138	M	YMA	25–35	169.7 (Ra)	Good	Good	ES, arms crossed over chest		W–E	Calculus and periodontitis, 3/29 teeth caries, 5/29 teeth hypoplastic defect	Chronic non-specific infection; SN T6-8 and L2; FX 4th R finger, misaligned	
Sk139	?	OC	6–9		Moderate	Poor	ES, hands crossed over pelvis		W-E			
Sk140	?	YC	1–2		Moderate	Poor	ES, arms crossed over chest		W-E			
Sk141	?	OC	6–9		Good	Good	ES, hands crossed over pelvis		W-E	Calculus and periodontitis	Bilateral cribra orbitalia	
Sk142	?	OC	8–10		Good	Good	ES, hands crossed over pelvis		W-E	Calculus, 2/15 teeth caries, 3/15 teeth hypoplastic defect	Cribra orbitalia	
Sk143	?	A	18+		Moderate	Very Poor	ES		W–E			
Br 12*	M	OA		170	Good	Moderate			W–E	29/32 sockets AMTL	OA C1-L5 and ribs; DJD hips, shoulders, L elbow, wrists, SN, sternoclavicular joints	
Br 13*	M	OA		184	Moderate	Moderate			SW–NE	2/5 sockets AMTL	DISH - fusion of T6-12 and ribs; MSM upper arms; SN; Healed FX body T12	L5 sacralized
Br 22*	M	OMA		177	Good	Good			W–E	1/21 teeth caries	OA L1-5	

ID	Estimated Sex	Estimated Age Category	Estimated Age Range (years)	Estimated Stature in cm (bone)	Preservation	Completeness	Burial Position	Grave Anomalies	Orientation	Dental Pathology	Pathology & Trauma	Developmental Anomaly
Br 27*	M	A		164	Moderate	Moderate			W–E			
Br 45*	F	MA		158	Good	Good			W–E	2/23 sockets AMTL, 2/14 teeth hypoplastic defects, periodontitis; 3 teeth congenitally absent	OA T4-9 and 1 rib, SN; DJD shoulders; healed FX 5th finger	
Br 46*	M	OMA		165	Good	Good			W–E	1/19 teeth caries; 1 tooth congenitally absent	OA T4-6, T12, L3, ribs and elbows; DJD shoulders; SN T5-12; healed non-specific infection; Spondylolysis L5; osteochondritis dissecans R prox. ulna	
Br 47*	F	OMA		149	Moderate	Good			W–E	2/19 teeth hypoplastic defect and periodontitis; 1 tooth congenitally absent	OA T11-12	
Br 48*	F	YA		152	Good	Good			W–E	1/13 teeth hypoplastic defect		
Br 49*	?	OC	4–8		Moderate	Moderate			W–E			
Br 50*	M	YMA		165	Good	Good			W–E	1/32 sockets AMTL, 2/26 teeth caries, 14/26 teeth hypoplastic defect, 1/32 sockets abscess	SN T6-12, L1 and L3; arachnoid pits endocranial surface; compression T12 body	
Br 51*	M	YMA		173	Good	Good			SW–NE	2/30 sockets AMTL, 4/27 teeth caries, 13/27 teeth hypoplastic defects, 1/30 sockets abscess and periodontitis	OA C5-7, T5-8, L1-3; SN T8-12; compression L4 body	
Br 52*	?	YC	6		Poor	Poor			W–E			
Br 53*	F	YMA		165	Moderate	Moderate			W–E		OA T1-2, T4, L5, SN T3, T5, T6, L2-4	
Br 54*	F	MA		153	Moderate	Moderate			W–E		SN T9-10; Healed FX mid-shaft L femur and assoc. MSM	
Br 55*	?	YC	3–5		Poor	Poor			NW–SE			
Br 56*	?	OC	10–12		Moderate	Moderate			NW–SE			
Br 57*	F	OA		161	Good	Good			W–E	12/24 sockets AMTL, 2/24 sockets abscess	OA C1-7, T1-2, T5, T9-10 and first rib heads; DJD hips, R shoulder, L elbow	
Br 58*	M	MA		174	Good	Good			NW–SE	3/23 teeth caries, 5/23 teeth hypoplastic defects	OA C1-7, T1-5; MSM L leg; DJD shoulders and Rib 12 (fusion to vertebra)	

APPENDIX 6.2. PREVALENCE OF NON-METRIC TRAITS AT ST THOMAS'S ABBEY

Cranial	L	R
Ossicles at Lambda	11.9% (4/42)	
Ossicles in Lambdoid	15% (6/40)	16.7% (7/42)
Ossicles at Bregma	0% (0/39)	0% (0/39)
Ossicles in Coronal	0% (0/41)	2.4% (1/42)
Metopic Suture	3.6% (2/56)	
Auditory Torus	0% (0/52)	0% (0/51)
Palatine Torus	0% (0/38)	0% (0/38)
Mandibular/ Maxillary Torus	0% (0/61)	0% (0/60)
Infra-Cranial	**L**	**R**
Sternal Foramen	0% (0/15)	
Septal Aperature	8.8% (5/57)	9.1% (6/60)
Supracondyloid Process	3.3% (2/61)	3.1% (2/65)
Poirer's Facet	14.3% (7/49)	10.9% (5/46)
Hypertrochanteric Fossa	0% (0/58)	1.8% (1/55)
Third Trochanter	15.4% (8/52)	17.3% (9/52)
Vastus Notch	0% (0/9)	9.1% (1/11)
Vastus Fossa	0% (0/9)	0% (0/11)
Emarginate Patella	0% (0/9)	0% (0/10)
Med. Tibial Squatting Facet	2.2% (1/45)	5.1% (2/39)
Lateral Tibial Squatting Facet	38.6% (17/44)	37.5% (15/40)

APPENDIX 6.3. COMPARATIVE DENTAL PATHOLOGY IN MEDIEVAL POPULATIONS

Site (Source)	Period	Caries		AMTL		Calculus		Abscess		Hypoplasia*		Periodontal	
		%T	%I	%S	%I	%T	%I	%S	%I	%T	%I	%S	%I
Ballyhanna, Donegal (McKenzie & Murphy 2018)	8–17th C.	5.4% (319/ 5,855)	36.6% (122/ 333)	5.4% (441/ 8145)	35.7% (127/ 356)	90.8% (5667/ 6238)	96.1% (342/ 356)	2.8% (179/ 6506)	26.4% (94/ 356)	-	21.8% (82/ 367)	-	52% (185/ 356)
Ardreigh, Kildare (ibid.)	11–15th C.	9.7% (1079/ 11173)	66.6% (345/ 516)	10.4% (1375/ 13280)	51.9% (268/ 516)	-	96.3% (497/ 516)	1.6% (211/ 13280)	22.7% (117/ 516)	-	-	-	41.2% (213/ 516)
St Thomas's abbey (Tobin 2021; Buckley 2003)	**11–13th C.**	**5.5% (54/ 989)**	**40.7% (22/54)**	**7.9% (85/ 1078)**	**42% (21/50)**	**72.9% (601/ 824)**	**90.7% (49/54)**	**1% (11/ 1078)**	**20% (10/50)**	**6.4% (87/ 1366)**	**35% (26/92)**	**45.9% (373/ 813)**	**78% (39/50)**
Aungier/ Stephen St, Dublin (Coughlan 2021)	12–16th C.	6.1% (182/ 3003)	44.4% (64/ 144)	8.4% (292/ 3476)	52.2% (72/ 138)	74% (2223/ 3003)	97.2% (139/ 143)	2.4% 83/ 3476	28.3% (39/ 138)	2.3% (81/ 3471)	14.7% (21/ 143)	50.5% (1430/ 2830)	79% (109/ 138)
Augustinian friary, Dublin (Ó Donnabháin and Cosgrove 1994)	12–16th C.	9.5% (36/ 378)	52.6% (10/19)	6.1% (28/ 457)	-	-	78.9% (15/19)	6.1% (28/ 457)	26.3% (5/19)	-	69% (20/29)	-	-
Dominican priory, Drogheda (Halpin & Buckley 1995)	13–14th C.	6.5% (29/ 515)	46.7% (14/30)	5% (28/ 550)	30% (9/30)	-	-	2% (11/ 550)	30% (9/30)	-	-	-	20% (6/30)
Tintern abbey, Wexford (Ó Donnabháin 2000)	13–15th C.	13.7% (87/ 635)	68.75% (22/32)	16.9% (151/ 894)	-	-	93.7% (30/32)	3.1% (28/ 892)	93.7% (30/32)	-	30.6% (15/49)	-	74.1% (23/33)

(adult only data except *sub-adults and adults)
Key: %T = percentage of teeth; %S = percentage of sockets; %I = percentage of individuals affected)

BIBLIOGRAPHY

Aufderheide, A.C. and Rodriguez-Martin, Conrado 1998 *The Cambridge encyclopedia of human palaeopathology*. Cambridge.

Beaumount, Julia and Montgomery, Janet 2016 'The Great Irish Famine: identifying starvation in the tissues of victims using stable isotope analysis of bone and incremental dentine collagen'. PloS ONE 11 (8), e0160065.

Berry, A.C. and Berry, R.J. 1967 'Epigenetic variation in the human cranium'. *Journal of Anatomy* 101, 361–79.

Brickley, Megan and McKinley, Jacqueline 2004 *Guidelines to the standards for recording human remains*. IFA Paper No.7. BABAO and Institute of Field Archaeologists. Southampton.

Brothwell, Don and Zakrzewski, S.R. 2004 'Metric and non-metric studies of archaeological human bone'. In Brickley and McKinley 2004, 27–33.

Buckley, Laureen 2003 'Health status in medieval Dublin: analysis of the skeletal remains from the abbey of St Thomas the Martyr'. In Seán Duffy (ed.), *Medieval Dublin IV*, 98–126. Dublin.

Buikstra, J.E. and Ubelaker, D.H. (eds) 1994 *Standards for data collection from human skeletal remains*. Arkansas Archaeological Survey Research Series 44. Arkansas.

Clarke, H.B. 2015 'King Sitriuc Silkenbeard: a great survivor'. In H.B. Clarke and Ruth Johnson (eds), *The Vikings in Ireland and beyond: before and after the Battle of Clontarf*, 253–67. Dublin.

Clyne, Miriam 1990 'A medieval pilgrim: from Tuam to Santiago de Compostela', *Archaeology Ireland* 4 (3), 21–2.

Collins, Tracy 2021 *Female monasticism in medieval Ireland: an archaeology*. Cork.

Coughlan, Jennie 2021 'Osteological analysis of the human skeletal remains from Aungier Street/Stephen Street, Dublin'. Unpublished specialist report. IAC Archaeology.

Cunningham, Bernadette 2018 *Medieval Irish pilgrims to Santiago de Compostela*. Dublin.

Daniell, Christopher 1997 *Death and burial in medieval England, 1066–1550*. London.

Donnelly, Colm and Murphy, Eileen 2008 'The origins of cillíni in Ireland'. In Eileen Murphy (ed.), *Deviant burial in the archaeological record*, 191–222. Oxford.

Duffy, Paul 2021 'Saints and skinners: excavations along the northern precinct of the abbey of St Thomas the Martyr, Dublin'. In Seán Duffy (ed.), *Medieval Dublin XVIII*, 194–242. Dublin.

Finnegan, Michael 1978 'Non-metric variation of the infracranial skeleton', *Journal of Anatomy*, 125, 23–37.

Fitzpatrick, Martin 2010 'Pilgrimage to Santiago de Compostela', *Archaeology Ireland*, 24:4, 14–17.

Foley, Áine 2017 *The abbey of St Thomas the Martyr, Dublin*. Dublin.

Geber, Jonny 2010 'Osteological report'. In John Lehane and Finn Delaney, 'Final archaeological excavation report Owenbristy, Co. Galway (Reg. No. E3770). Unpublished report. Eachtra Archaeological Projects.

Gilchrist, Roberta 2020 *Sacred heritage: monastic archaeology, identities, beliefs*. Online: Cambridge University Press. https://doi.org/10.1017/9781108678087

Gichrist, Roberta and Sloane, Barney 2005 *Requiem: the medieval monastic cemetery in Britain*. Museum of London Archaeology Service. London.

Halpin, Andrew and Buckley, Laureen 1995 'Archaeological excavations at the Dominican priory, Drogheda, Co. Louth', *PRIA*, 95C (5), 175–253.

Hillson, Simon 1996 *Dental anthropology*. Cambridge.

Knudson, K.J, Ó Donnabháin, Barra, Carver, Charisse, Cleland, Robin and Price, T.D. 2012 'Migration and Viking Dublin: paleomobility and paleodiet through isotopic analyses', *Journal of Archaeological Science*, 39:2, 308–20.

Larson, C.S. 1997. *Bioarchaeology: interpreting behaviour from the human skeleton.* Cambridge.

Lee-Thorpe, J.A. 2008 'On isotopes and old bones', *Archaeometry* 50:6, 925–50.

Leigh Fry, Susan 1999 *Burial in medieval Ireland, 900–1500*. Dublin.

Lyons, Susan 2015 'Food plants, fruits and foreign foodstuffs: the archaeological evidence from urban medieval Ireland', *PRIA* 115C, 111–66.

Mays, Simon 2006 'The osteology of monasticism in mediaeval England'. In Rebecca Gowland and Christopher Knusel (eds), *The social archaeology of funerary remains*, 179–89. Oxford.

McKenzie, C.J. and Murphy, Eileen 2018 *Life and death in medieval Gaelic Ireland: the skeletons from Ballyhanna, Co. Donegal*. Dublin.

McKenzie, C.J., Murphy, Eileen and Donnelly, Colm (eds) 2015 *The science of a lost medieval Gaelic graveyard: the Ballyhanna research project*. Dublin.

McKenzie, C.J., Murphy, E.M., Guiry, Eric, Donnelly, C.J. and Beglane, Fiona 2020 'Diet in medieval Gaelic Ireland: a multiproxy study of the human remains from Ballyhanna, Co. Donegal', *Journal of Archaeological Science*, 121, pp 105–203.

Moloney, Colm, Baker, Louise, Millar, Jonathan and Shiels, Damian 2016 *Guide to the excavations at Ardreigh, County Kildare*. E-publication produced by Rubicon Heritage Ltd. Cork.

Murphy, Eileen and Donnelly, Colm 2018 'Together in death: demography and funerary practices in contemporary multiple interments in Irish medieval burial grounds'. In Grete Lillehammer and Eileen Murphy (eds), *Across the generations: the old and the young in past societies*, 119–42. AmS-Skrifter 26; SSCIP Monograph 8. Stavanger.

Murphy, Margaret and Potterton, Michael 2005 'Investigating living standards in medieval Dublin and its region'. In Seán Duffy (ed.), *Medieval Dublin VI*, 224–56. Dublin.

Ó Donnabháin, Barra 2000 'The human remains'. In Ann Lynch (ed.), *Tintern abbey, Co. Wexford: Cistercians and Colcloughs. Excavations 1982–2007*, 105–25. Dublin.

Ó Donnabháin, Barra and Cosgrove, Úna 1994 'The bioarchaeology of the cemetery at Temple Lane, Dublin'. Unpublished specialist report. Dublin: Margaret Gowen and Co. Ltd.

Ó Donnabháin, Barra and Hallgrimsson, Benedikt 2001 'Dublin: the biological identity of the Hiberno-Norse town'. In Seán Duffy (ed.) *Medieval Dublin II*, 65–87. Dublin.

Ogden, A.R. 2008 'Periapical voids in human jaw bones'. In Megan Brickley and Martin Smith (eds), *Proceedings of the eighth annual conference of the British Association for Biological Anthropology and Osteoarchaeology*, 51–6. BAR International Series 1743. Oxford.

Ó Riain-Raedel, Dagmar 1998 'The Irish medieval pilgrimage to Santiago de Compostela', *History Ireland*, 6:3, 17–21.

Ortner, D.J. 2003 *Identification of pathological conditions in human skeletal remains*. 2nd ed. Washington DC.

Power, Catryn 1995 'A medieval demographic sample'. In M.F. Hurley and C.M. Sheehan (eds), *Excavations at the Dominican priory of St Mary's of the Isle, Cork*, 66–83. Cork.

Read, Christopher 2010 'Remembering where the bishop sat: exploring perceptions of the past at the Bishops's Seat, Kilteasheen, Co. Roscommon'. In Thomas Finan (ed.), *Medieval Lough Cé: history, archaeology and landscape*, 41–66. Dublin.

Roberts, Charlotte and Manchester, Keith 2005 *The archaeology of disease*. 3rd ed. Stroud.

Scheuer, Louise and Black, Sue 2004 *The juvenile skeleton*. London.

Stuart-Macadam, Patty 1992 'Porotic hyperostosis; a new perspective'. *American Journal of Physical Anthropology*, 87, 39–47.

Waldron, Tony 2009 *Palaeopathology*. Cambridge.

Walsh, Claire 2000 'Archaeological excavations at the abbey of St Thomas the Martyr, Dublin'. In Seán Duffy (ed.), *Medieval Dublin I*, 185–202. Dublin.

Whittaker, D.K. 2000 'Ageing from the dentition'. In Margaret Cox and Simon Mays (eds), *Human osteology in archaeology and forensic science*, 83–99. London.

Whitty, Yvonne 2012 'An Iron Age ring-ditch complex at Holdenstown 1, Co. Kilkenny'. In Chris Corlett and Michael Potterton (eds), *Life and death in Iron Age Ireland in the light of recent archaeological excavations*, 313–26. Bray.

Dublin 1190–1290: provincial capital or capital city?

BRUCE M.S. CAMPBELL

By 1790 Dublin was unquestionably the first city of an integrated all-Ireland urban system.[1] It was the political capital of a now-unified country, the residence of the lord lieutenant, permanent seat of the Irish parliament, and location of the civil service. Here sat the country's four highest courts and the king's inns housed the headquarters of the Irish legal profession. The latter's academic counterpart, Trinity College, was Ireland's sole university, albeit exclusively for protestants. Dublin's archbishops, both Roman Catholic and Anglican, were primates of Ireland and second only in rank to the archbishops of Armagh (the primates of All Ireland). The city was the most important banking centre in Ireland and since 1783 had been home to the Bank of Ireland. Until then it was through the Dublin White Linen Hall that linen manufactured in the north was marketed nationally and internationally and much of the country's domestic and half of its overseas trade were likewise handled by the city. Dublin was the hub of a developing national road network and terminus of what were intended to become the two most important cross-country canals.[2] With a large resident professional and mercantile middle class, and as the country's social capital and seasonal resort of the landed classes, the concentration of consumer spending power within the city was second to none. Given these unrivalled advantages it is unsurprising that, in accordance with the rank-size rule, Dublin, with a population of *c.*170,000, was more than double the size of the next largest city, at that time Cork, with a population numbering *c.*75,000.[3] In fact, within the kingdom of Great Britain and Ireland,

I am grateful to Steve Rigby for his helpful comments on an earlier version of this paper and for the invitation from Seán Duffy to present it at the 2021 Friends of Medieval Dublin Symposium. 1 David Dickson, 'The place of Dublin in the eighteenth-century Irish economy' in T.M. Devine and David Dickson (eds), *Ireland and Scotland, 1600–1850* (Edinburgh, 1983), pp 177–92; David Dickson, Dublin: the making of a capital city (Cambridge, MA, 2014), pp 152–87. 2 The Grand Canal, begun in 1757, had reached Athy by 1791 but was not completed to Shannon Harbour (Co. Offaly) on the River Shannon until 1803/4; work on the Royal Canal commenced in 1790 and reached Cloondara (Co. Longford) on the River Shannon in 1817. 3 Jan de Vries, *European urbanization, 1500–1800* (London, 1984), p. 271, gives population estimates for Cork of 58,000 in 1750 and 75,000 in 1800, and corresponding estimates for Dublin of 90,000 and 168,000. The 'rank-size rule' is based upon empirical observation and states that the population of a given city tends to be equal to the population of the largest city divided by the rank of the given city. In other words, the population of Dublin, as the premier city, should have been double that of Cork, the second city. Note that in colonial situations the largest city is often much larger than would fit the rule: Xavier Gabaix and Yannis M. Ioannides, 'The evolution of city size distributions', *Handbook of Regional and Urban*

London alone was larger, its population of *c.*865,000 making it the largest city in Europe.[4]

The hegemonic status achieved by Dublin by the end of the eighteenth century had long been in the making and was contingent in large part upon the advance and consolidation of English rule in Ireland. Following the invasion of 1169, it was Henry II who, in 1171, in recognition of the Hiberno-Scandinavian city's political and strategic importance, made the city the capital of his newly acquired lordship of Ireland.[5] In demonstration of that fact, it was here, over the bitter winter of 1171–2, that he held court. Over the next hundred years, as English power and institutions – a financial exchequer, shires and sheriffs, the common law and law courts, feudal tenures and manorialization, chartered boroughs, and a sterling currency – were rolled out across the conquered portions of Ireland, the city's political status was enhanced and it was confirmed as the largest and most important city in Ireland.[6] The fee farm of 200 marks that it paid at the exchequer was double the sum for which Waterford and Drogheda were each liable.[7] Nevertheless, with a population at peak of between 10,000 and 15,000, Dublin remained absolutely small and ranked below at least five English cities.[8] Its provisioning needs of food, fuel and raw materials could readily be met from a relatively

Economics, 4 (2004), 2,341–78. 4 De Vries, *European urbanization*, p. 270. 5 F.X. Martin, 'Allies and an overlord, 1169–72' in Art Cosgrove (ed.), *A new history of Ireland*; ii, *Medieval Ireland, 1169–1534* (Oxford, 1987), pp 89, 94–5; Seán Duffy, *Ireland in the Middle Ages* (Basingstoke, 1997), p. 69; Dickson, *Dublin*, pp 16–21. 6 J.F. Lydon, *The lordship of Ireland in the Middle Ages* (Dublin, 1972), pp 82–97; F.X. Martin, 'John, lord of Ireland, 1185–1216' in Cosgrove (ed.), *New history of Ireland*; i, pp 134, 143–5; Michael Dolley, 'Coinage to 1534' in Cosgrove (ed.), *New history of Ireland*; i, pp 818–19; Duffy, *Ireland in the Middle Ages*, pp 82–4, 94–8; Josiah Cox Russell, *Medieval regions and their cities* (Newton Abbot, 1972), pp 137, 139; Bruce M.S. Campbell, 'Benchmarking medieval economic development: England, Wales, Scotland, and Ireland, *c.*1290', *Economic History Review*, 61:4 (2008), 911, 913. 7 Eamonn McEneaney, 'Mayors and merchants in medieval Waterford city, 1169–1495' in William Nolan and Thomas P. Power (eds), *Waterford history and society: interdisciplinary essays on the history of an Irish county* (Dublin, 1992), pp 153, 169. For the urban topographies of Dublin, Waterford and Drogheda, see Clarke, *Dublin, Pt 1* (IHTA); John Bradley and Andrew Halpin, 'The topographical development of Scandinavian and Anglo-Norman Waterford' in Nolan and Power (eds), *Waterford history and society*, pp 105–29; John Bradley, 'The topography and layout of medieval Drogheda', *Journal of the County Louth Archaeological and Historical Society*, 19:2 (1978), 98–127 (republished as John Bradley, *The topography and layout of medieval Drogheda* (Drogheda, 1997)); Ned McHugh, *Drogheda: IHTA 29* (Dublin, 2019). 8 Estimates as high as 20,000 and 25,000 have been suggested: Margaret Murphy and Michael Potterton, *The Dublin region in the Middle Ages: settlement, land-use and economy* (Dublin, 2010), p. 30; David Dickson, 'Dublin' in S.J. Connolly (ed.), *The Oxford companion to Irish history* (Oxford, 2nd ed, 2002), p. 169; Russell, *Medieval regions*, pp 136–7, proposed a late thirteenth century population of 11,000; the same figure is given by Clarke, *Dublin, Pt 1* (IHTA), p. 12, thereby placing Dublin below London, York, Bristol, Lincoln and Norwich (Campbell, 'Benchmarking', p. 908); 250 years later its population has been estimated at about 8,000, making it 'the sixth largest city in the British Isles': Steven G. Ellis, *Tudor Ireland: crown, community and the conflict of cultures, 1470–1603* (London, 1985), p. 37.

narrow hinterland and had limited impact upon the wider Irish economy.[9] Nor, to judge from the circumscribed distribution of imported pottery, did its manufactures and imported goods yet command anything remotely resembling a national market.[10] In fact, its share of general overseas trade was modest. At the peak of the Irish export trade in the 1280s Dublin contributed only a tenth of Irish customs receipts and was eclipsed in the revenues that it generated by the south-coast ports of New Ross, Waterford and Cork.[11] Thus, in the late thirteenth-century, at the high-tide of English power in Ireland, Dublin was a long way from achieving the position of unrivalled national importance that it would enjoy five centuries later. The lordship's other major walled port cities, notably Waterford, Cork, Limerick and Galway, and their extensive hinterlands, still remained substantially autonomous of Dublin's influence and control, although not that of the English crown which retained all four as part of the royal demesne.[12]

Extant sources that might shed light upon Dublin's local, regional, national and international standing as a city and its place in the evolving urban networks of Ireland and Britain during the first century of English rule are few.[13] One, however, the Dublin Guild Merchant Roll (*DGMR*) of *c.*1190–1265, is of outstanding interest and potential. Along with lists of those admitted as freemen of the city between *c.*1230 and 1249, it has been transcribed, edited, indexed and published in both hardcopy and searchable electronic versions.[14] For 60% of those admitted to the merchant guild a

9 Murphy and Potterton, *Dublin region*, pp 481–6. For the correspondingly greater, but nonetheless geographically selective, provisioning hinterland of London, see Bruce M.S. Campbell, James A. Galloway, Derek Keene and Margaret Murphy, *A medieval capital and its grain supply: agrarian production and its distribution in the London region, c.1300* (n.p., 1993); James A. Galloway, Derek Keene and Margaret Murphy, 'Fuelling the city: production and distribution of firewood and fuel in London's region, 1290–1400', *Economic History Review*, 49:3 (1996), 447–72. 10 Murphy and Potterton, *Dublin region*, pp 456–7; Clare McCutcheon and Rosanne Meenan, 'Pots on the hearth: domestic pottery in historic Ireland', *PRIA*, 111C, *Special issue: Domestic life in Ireland* (Dublin, 2011), pp 96–9. 11 Campbell, 'Benchmarking', pp 914–15. 12 Goddard H. Orpen, *Ireland under the Normans* (Dublin, 2005 ed.), p. 570. 13 For alternative rankings of English towns based upon a range of criteria but especially their taxable wealth, see Alan Dyer, 'Appendix: ranking lists of English medieval towns' in D.M. Palliser (ed.), *The Cambridge urban history of Britain I: 600–1500* (Cambridge, 2000), pp 747–70. 14 Philomena Connolly and Geoffrey Martin (eds), *The Dublin guild merchant roll, c.1190–1265* (Dublin, 1992) [henceforth *DGMR*], electronic version available at http://databases.dublincity.ie/dmgr/browse.php. Because the electronic version of this text does not always capture all the individuals named as coming from a particular place, the results presented here are based exclusively upon a database created from the published hard copy. When there are several alternative identifications of a place individuals are divided equally between each of the alternative places, even when this involves the allocation to a place of a fraction of a guildsman. For example, there are three possible 'Barrows' – in Lancashire, in Somerset, and in Suffolk – from which Elias Carpentarius de Barewe and Willelmus of Barewe may have come in 1190–1221; each of these three places is therefore scored as having sent 2 ÷ 3 (0.666) guildsmen. For alternative methodological solutions to the ambiguities created when

place-of-origin is recorded, which shows that guildsmen came to Dublin from far and wide. They joined the guild, as Geoffrey Martin observes, because membership 'brought access to the market, as well as the support of fellow guildsmen, to those who were not necessarily resident in the city'.[15] Thus, numbers of Normans from Rouen who regularly came to Dublin to exchange wine for hides found it expedient to join the merchant guild, as did Bretons bringing iron from Dinan and Gascons bearing salt and wine from Bordeaux.[16] Visiting Flemings from Bruges and a succession of Englishmen from Dunwich, arriving from opposite shores of the North Sea, likewise joined the merchant guild, while much closer to home men from across the Liffey in Dublin's transpontine suburb of Oxmantown saw advantage in obtaining admission to it.[17] Presumably the same was true of many others from both extramural Dublin and its immediate provisioning hinterland but whose stated places-of-origin are either ambiguous or omitted.[18]

Freemen, in contrast to members of the guild merchant, enjoyed full rights of citizenship, including the right to attend the annual election of the mayor and provosts (later bailiffs) and to serve as officers, albeit with all the financial and political obligations that such service entailed.[19] By royal charter granted

several different places-of-origin bore the same name, see Peter McClure, 'Patterns of migration in the late Middle Ages: the evidence of English place-name surnames', *Economic History Review*, 32:2 (1979), 168–73. Previous studies which have made selective use of the information contained in the *DGMR* are J.A. Watt, 'Dublin in the thirteenth century: the making of a colonial capital' in P.R. Coss and S.D. Lloyd (eds), *Thirteenth-Century England, 1: proceedings of the Newcastle-upon-Tyne Conference, 1985* (Woodbridge, 1986), pp 155–6; Robert Bartlett, *The making of Europe: conquest, colonization and cultural change, 950–1350* (London, 1994), pp 181–3; Elmar Eggerer, 'The guild merchant of Dublin' in Seán Duffy (ed.), *Medieval Dublin VI* (Dublin, 2005), pp 144–59; Murphy and Potterton, *Dublin region*. **15** Geoffrey Martin, 'Introduction' in *DGMR*, p. xiv. The classic study of the guild merchant is Charles Gross, *The gild merchant, a contribution to British municipal history*, vol. 1 (Oxford, 1890), pp 1–76. **16** Kevin Down, 'Colonial society and economy in the high Middle Ages' in Cosgrove (ed.), *New history of Ireland*; i, p. 489; Wendy Childs and Timothy O'Neill, 'Overseas trade' in ibid., pp 507–8; Timothy O'Neill, *Merchants and mariners in medieval Ireland* (Dublin, 1987), pp 44–7, 84–5, 90; *DGMR*. **17** For example, Thomas of Dunwich was admitted in 1232–3, Geoffrey of Bruges in 1233–4, and Robert Smith of Villa Ostmannorum in 1236–7: *DGMR*, pp 65, 66, 71. Emer Purcell, 'The city and the suburb: medieval Dublin and Oxmantown' in Duffy (ed.), *Medieval Dublin VI*, pp 215, 222–3. **18** In addition to the 26 guildsmen recorded as coming from Dublin and Oxmantown, a further 43 are described as coming from Eastgate, '*de porta*', '*de ponte*', *parvo ponte*', '*Vico pontis*', *Vico* St Patrick, St Audoen's, St James's, St Kevin's/Kelvin's, St Mary's, St Olave's, St Paul's, St Sepulchre's, St Thomas's, St Trinity (alias Christ Church cathedral), the Hospital of St John, '*abbacia/abbatia*', and '*monasterio/monasteriis*'. If all are places close to Dublin, almost 70 of those admitted to the merchant guild came from greater Dublin, with another 29 coming from Kilmainham less than 3km away: calculated from *DGMR* with religious dedications from Clarke, *Dublin, Pt 1* (IHTA). **19** The distinction between guildsmen and freemen is discussed by Gross, *Gild merchant*, pp 61–76. For the distinction at Leicester, see Mary Bateson (ed.), *Records of the borough of Leicester, being a series of extracts from the archives of the corporation of Leicester, 1103–1327* (London, 1899),

by Henry II in 1171–2 and confirmed *c.*1174, they were guaranteed freedom to trade without charge throughout the king's dominions in Ireland, Wales, England, and Normandy.[20] Typically they were permanently domiciled in the city and, as elsewhere, although the rolls are silent on this, probably gained their entry into the freedom in a variety of ways.[21] Some will have inherited the places of their fathers, for others it may have been a reward bestowed by the city on influential outsiders, apprenticeship offered another potential route, but in the newly established colonial capital of Dublin the greater number were probably newcomers, admitted, like the guildsmen, upon payment of an unspecified but presumably substantial entry fine. Over a century later those purchasing the freedom paid fines of £1 at Exeter, 2 marks (26*s.* 8*d.*) at Chester, £2 at Grimsby, and, in some instances, as much as £3 at Bristol, York and London.[22] Presumably the fines levied at Dublin were of a comparable order of magnitude and certainly well above the fines levied for admission to the lesser privilege of membership of Dublin's merchant guild.

By the 1220s the entry fine for those admitted as guildsmen had settled at a flat rate of 9 shillings (when an unskilled English male labourer typically earned no more than 1½ pence a day).[23] Individuals with quite humble occupations – butchers, bakers, carters, cooks, fishermen, potters and many others who toiled to make a modest and honest living – evidently deemed it worthwhile to stump up this 9-shilling fee in order to qualify for the trading rights within the city's precincts that were contingent upon guild membership.[24] The revenues thereby generated were substantial: between 1230 and 1249 when, on average, respectively 114 guildsmen and 28 freemen were admitted per year, the combined sum annually received in entry fines is likely to have averaged at least £100. Although some guildsmen progressed to

pp xxvii–xxxviii. **20** Seán Duffy, 'Town and crown: the kings of England and their city of Dublin' in Michael Prestwich, Richard Britnell and Robin Frame (eds), *Thirteenth Century England X. Proceedings of the Durham Conference 2003* (Woodbridge, 2005), pp 95–117; H.B. Clarke, 'The 1192 charter of liberties and the beginnings of Dublin's municipal life', *DHR*, 46:1 (1993), 8–9; Eggerer, 'Guild merchant', p. 146. **21** Cf. Exeter: Maryanne Kowaleski, *Local markets and regional trade in medieval Exeter* (Cambridge, 1995), pp 96–7. **22** Kowaleski, *Local markets*, p. 98; S.H. Rigby and Elizabeth Ewans, 'Government, power and authority 1300–1540' in Palliser (ed.), *Cambridge urban history, I*, p. 301; S.H. Rigby, *Medieval Grimsby: growth and decline* (Hull, 1993), p. 86; Christian D. Liddy, *Contesting the city: the politics of citizenship in English towns, 1250–1530* (Oxford, 2017), p. 47. **23** Fines for entry to the guild merchant as low as 4½ and 5 shillings are recorded in the first six membranes but thereafter effectively disappear: *DGMR*, pp 1–23. These may represent the first instalment of two, totalling 9–10 shillings. From membrane 12d./A recorded entry fines correspond, with only slight variation, to a flat rate of 9 shillings: *DGMR*, p. 44. **24** The occupations are indexed in *DGMR*, pp 157–9, and https://databases.dublincity.ie/dmgr/occupations.php. S.H. Rigby, *English society in the later Middle Ages: class, status and gender* (Basingstoke, 1995), pp 161–2. For the use of coercion to compel poor workmen to join the merchant guilds at Oxford and Lincoln, see R.B. Dobson, 'Admissions to the freedom of the city of York in the later Middle Ages', *Economic History Review*, 26:1 (1973), 21.

become freemen, most found that belonging to the merchant guild matched their modest means, met their professional requirements, and spared them the obligation incurred by freemen to pay scot and lot or to serve in civic office.[25] Hence the fact that in the 1230s and 1240s, when records of those admitted as guildsmen and as freemen are both extant, the former outnumbered the latter by four to one.[26] Note, however, that it is unclear whether, given the several alternative routes to citizenship, the freemen's roll is fully comprehensive of all admissions.

Of the 8,477 individuals named in the *DGMR* between *c.*1190 and 1265, and 526 individuals named in the roll of free citizens between *c.*1230 and 1249, respectively 60% and 61% are described as having come from a named place (table 7.1), of which at least 90% can be identified with a degree of certainty.[27] Robert of Ratoath (Co. Meath), Robert of Rouen (*Ratomag'*, France), John Spicer of Chester, Robert of Manchester, William of London, Peter Palmer of Trim (Co. Meath), Bernard of Rocamadour (*Rochemadur*, France), and John of Neath (Wales), all admitted to the merchant guild in 1222–3 and paying 9 shillings each for the privilege, are characteristic examples.[28] A dozen years later William White of Drogheda North, Nicholas Palmer of Lichfield, Adam of York, tanner, Thomas Breard of Normandy, Richard White of Wicklow, Thomas of Exeter and Richard Baker of Oxmantown (transpontine Dublin) were enrolled as freemen.[29] As these examples illustrate, guildsmen and freemen were recruited from a wide area, encompassing Ireland, Britain and neighbouring parts of Europe. The relevant numbers are summarized in table 7.1. Here is invaluable evidence of the extent and intensity of Dublin's extensive commercial connections when the economic fortunes of the lordship of Ireland were in the ascendant and Europe's remoter regions were being drawn into closer and more regular contact with its commercial core.[30]

It would be convenient if those for whom a place-of-origin is given are representative of those for whom it is not (for some of whom an occupation is

25 R.H. Britnell, 'The economy of British towns 1300–1540' in Palliser (ed.), *Cambridge urban history, I*, p. 333; Gross, *Gild merchant*, pp 53–60; Niall Ó Súilleabháin, 'Mórmaors, mayors and merchants: the early development of municipal government in Ireland' in Seán Duffy (ed.), *Medieval Dublin XIII* (Dublin, 2013), p. 115. **26** The first 135 freemen's admissions are undated but probably immediately postdate the civic charter of 1229 and relate to the 4 years 1230–34. **27** Guildsmen and freemen admissions were almost exclusively male. The only women recorded as having been admitted in their own right were Felicia of Hinckley (Leics.) in 1227–8, Alice of Haverfordwest (Pembs.) in 1240–1, and Susanna widow of Henry Clerk of Arklow (Co. Wicklow) in 1243–4: *DGMR*, pp 58, 77, 81. Of the men admitted, 21 are described as the sons or other close relations of women. Philomena Connolly's locational identifications given in the hard copy have been accepted, subject to a few minor revisions and additions. **28** *DGMR*, p. 48. **29** *DGMR*, pp 114–15. **30** Lydon, *Lordship of Ireland*, pp 97–102; Andrew J. Dugmore, Christian Keller and Thomas H. McGovern, 'Norse Greenland settlement: reflections on climate change, trade, and the contrasting fates of human settlements in the North Atlantic islands', *Arctic Anthropology* 44:1 (2007), 16–18; Bruce M.S. Campbell, *The great transition: climate, disease*

Table 7.1 Recorded places-of-origin of those admitted to the *DGMR*, *c.*1190–1265, and as freemen of the city, *c.*1230–49

	Guildsmen				Freemen
	*c.*1190–1222	1222–45	1245–65	*c.*1190–1265	*c.*1230–49
Total legible entries	3,570	2,719	2,188	8,477	526
Approx. admissions per year	119	124	109	113	28
% giving place-of-origin	*48.7*	*64.3*	*73.3*	*60.1*	*61.0*
% of places unidentified	*8.1*	*6.2*	*8.5*	*7.6*	*9.7*
Ireland as % of known	*14.2*	*28.0*	*28.6*	*23.5*	*21.6*
Scotland* as % of known	*4.3*	*4.1*	*6.2*	*4.8*	*3.2*
England as % of known	*55.1*	*46.8*	*42.2*	*48.2*	*64.7*
Wales as % of known	*11.6*	*6.8*	*7.9*	*8.8*	*4.2*
Europe as % of known	*6.8*	*8.1*	*6.7*	*7.2*	*6.6*

Note: * Scotland includes the Isle of Man

given instead), but it is reasonable to suppose that those from outside Ireland and far away were more likely to have their place-of-origin recorded than those from within Ireland and near at hand.[31] This might explain why those coming to Dublin from named places in Ireland account for such modest proportions of the total, as well as why the Irish share of the total doubled from 14% to 28% after 1222 when the proportion of individuals with place-of-origin information rose from 49% to 64% (table 7.1).[32] Certainly, a specific place-of-origin is rarely provided for those described as Irish (*Paganus Hibernicus de Connacia* [Connacht], admitted in 1227–8, is a partial exception), bearing a conspicuously Irish name (as in the case of Gillemuri O Loan and Molroin O Keregan admitted as guildsmen in *c.*1190–1222 and 1238–9), or named after Ireland's national saint, Patrick (a forename also favoured by Welshmen).[33]

Probably many of those without a stated place-of-origin were already residents of Dublin and its extramural suburbs. Butchers, who fattened and slaughtered their animals outside the city and then traded the meat within its precincts, are a case in point. Over fifty of them are recorded in the guild roll, half of them with a place-of-origin, of whom eighteen came from no further away than Castledermot (Co. Kildare) and Trim (Co. Meath), with locations

and society in the late medieval world (Cambridge, 2016), pp 85–133. **31** Cf. McClure, 'Patterns of migration', p. 175. I hope to discuss the occupational information in a later volume in this series. **32** In 1275–6 the share of the total issues of the guild merchant contributed by men from Ireland was a modest 16%, compared with 22% contributed by those coming from overseas and 62% by those from England: James Lydon, 'Dublin in transition: from Ostman town to English borough' in Seán Duffy (ed.), *Medieval Dublin II* (Dublin, 2001), p. 136. **33** *DGMR*, pp 29, 57, 75.

within easy provisioning range of Dublin – Bray, Clonee, Kilmainham, Naas, Oxmantown, Palmerstown, Santry, Swords and St Patrick's highway – predominating.[34] Were place-of-origin information given for all butchers, probably this Dublin-focused pattern would be reinforced and the same probably applies more generally. Further, when butchers are described as coming from Aylesbury (Bucks.), Hereford and Weobley (Heref.), Nottingham (Notts.), and Ludlow and Shrewsbury (Salop.), this possibly reflects the colonial origin of those now practising this trade within Dublin's hinterland.

Fuller place-of-origin information would therefore undoubtedly reinforce the importance of the Dublin region. In most other respects the representativeness of this evidence can probably be trusted. Certainly, the coherence of the picture that it reveals, and which is corroborated by that conveyed for the 1230s and 1240s by the freemen admissions, is convincing, with its clear evidence of post-conquest colonial settlement in Ireland, marked geographical pattern of distance-decay from Dublin both within and beyond Ireland, strong focus on the network of maritime connections that characterized the wider Irish Sea region, and well-articulated hierarchical relationships between Dublin and urban centres elsewhere likely to have had and sought close commercial dealings with it. Foremost among the latter were the English royal and commercial capital of London, to which Dublin was politically and financially accountable, and the major Irish Sea port of Bristol. The latter's maritime links with Dublin's had long been particularly strong and in 1172 it was to the men of Bristol that Henry II had explicitly granted Dublin 'to inhabit and to hold of him with all the privileges and free customs which they enjoyed in Bristol'.[35] Here, therefore, is revealing information about the recruitment of tradesmen and craftsmen to Dublin during a formative stage in the city's development. Whence and in what numbers came those admitted as guildsmen and freemen reflect, on the one hand, the city's standing and sphere of influence within Ireland and, on the other, its connections and interactions with the more developed urban system of England and the wider commercial world beyond.

THE GEOGRAPHICAL PROVENANCE OF DUBLIN GUILDSMEN AND FREEMEN

Although, as was characteristic of late-medieval migration, those who enrolled as Dublin guildsmen and freemen came from near and far, numbers decreased

34 *DGMR*, p. 157, and https://databases.dublincity.ie/dmgr/freesearch_out.php?text_input=%22Carnifex%22. 35 Martin, 'Introduction' in *DGMR*, p. xv; Aubrey Gwynn, 'Medieval Bristol and Dublin', *IHS* 5:20 (1947), 275–86; Clarke, '1192 charter of liberties', 8–9; Lydon, 'Dublin in transition', pp 128–9, 140; Grace O'Keeffe, 'The merchant conquistadors: medieval Bristolians in Dublin' in Seán Duffy (ed.), *Medieval Dublin XIII*

with distance as the frictional effect of travel increased.[36] From within walking distance of the city came men from Ballyfermot, Carrickbrennan, Castleknock, Clondalkin, Clontarf, Coolock, Donnybrook, Dunsink, Finglas, Howth, Lucan, Palmerstown, Raheny, Saggart, Santry, Swords, Tallaght, and the immediate Dublin suburbs of St Kevin's, St Thomas's, St Sepulchre's and Oxmantown. Joining the merchant guild gave them the right to do business within the liberties of the city within whose sight they lived.[37] From the opposite extreme came Londoners in great numbers, men from the great Rhineland city of Cologne, Flemings from Antwerp, Bruges, Dixmude and Ypres, Frenchmen from Picardy, Normandy, Brittany and Gascony, a handful of Iberians from Portugal and from Cordoba, Santiago and Pamplona in Spain, and, from south of the Alps, Italians from the papal city of Rome and the thriving mercantile cities of Pisa, Lucca, Prato, and Florence.[38] Upon Dublin they all converged, at this melting point in time, with their many different languages, dialects and accents. Here, in the city's marts and warehouses, might be found and purchased the wares obtained via the interlinked system of commerce that connected Dublin to the Mediterranean, Levant and beyond, as manifest in the presence of this international array of guildsmen.[39]

Thriving commerce naturally nurtured the recruitment of guildsmen and freemen, whereas its underdevelopment inhibited it, especially when there were also cultural and political obstacles to be overcome. Thus, un-urbanized Welsh Wales, closer to Dublin than most other regions but at war for most of this period with the English crown, was an unimportant source of guildsmen. Likewise, migration from the more distant parts of England was typically greater than that from the more proximate parts of the independent but less commercialized Scottish realm. At this juncture in time there was no escaping the fact that Dublin was the colonial seat of English royal power in Ireland or that many of those enrolled in the guild roll were seizing the opportunities that creation of this new overseas colony presented.

Table 7.2 and figs 7.1 and 7.2 demonstrate quite clearly the influence of these contrasting frictional and enabling effects upon those admitted to the

(Dublin, 2013), pp 116–19. **36** McClure, 'Patterns of migration', pp 174–82; D.J. Keene, *Survey of medieval Winchester: Winchester studies 2* (Oxford, 1985), vol. 1 part 1, pp 375–8. **37** These places are mapped at https://databases.dublincity.ie/dmgr/map.php, while https://databases.dublincity.ie/dmgr/places.php gives links to many, but not all, of the relevant entries. All are indexed in the *DGMR*. **38** Church dedications to St Werburgh, St Martin, St Olave, and St Nicholas testify to the presence within the city of external national groups from England, northern France, Scandinavia and, probably, the Rhineland: Clarke, *Dublin, Pt 1* (IHTA), p. 5; Anngret Simms, 'St Nicholas's churches in medieval Irish towns in a European context: a challenge for the historian as detective' in Terence Doley, Mary Ann Lyons and Salvador Ryan (eds), *The historian as detective. Uncovering Irish pasts: essays in honour of Raymond Gillespie* (Dublin, 2021), pp 34–6. For the Italians in Ireland, see M.D. O'Sullivan, *Italian merchant bankers in Ireland in the thirteenth century* (Dublin, 1962). **39** Janet L. Abu-Lughod, *Before European hegemony: the world system, AD 1250–1350* (Oxford, 1989); Campbell, *Great transition*, pp 32–4.

Table 7.2 The regional origins of Dublin guildsmen, *c.*1190–1265, and freemen, *c.*1230–49 (densities per unit area indexed on the respective overall mean densities of Great Britain and Ireland

Country & region	Indexed density per unit area			
	Guildsmen			Freemen
	*c.*1190–1230	1230–65	*c.*1190–1265	*c.*1230–49
Ireland:				
Co. Dublin	910	1,933	1,471	1,399
Pale counties	418	672	557	359
Irish east coast	90	237	170	223
South Leinster	78	94	87	79
Rest of Munster	21	29	25	20
Connacht	21	22	22	14
Rest of Ulster	4	10	7	14
All Ireland	70	124	99	87
Scotland:				
Highlands & Islands	2	4	3	10
Lowlands & Borders	60	76	69	23
All Scotland	19	25	22	14
England:				
Northwest	140	165	154	75
Marches	435	322	373	399
Southwest	243	116	173	307
Midlands	175	125	148	219
Eastern cos	83	72	77	114
South	106	86	95	71
All England	155	119	135	165
Wales:				
Welsh Wales	50	64	57	18
South Wales	410	356	381	154
All Wales	181	170	175	67
GREAT BRITAIN & IRELAND	100	100	100	100

Notes: Densities per unit area calculated for each region are indexed on those for Great Britain and Ireland as a whole. The regions, defined according to their component historic cos, are as follows: 1. Co. Dublin; 2. Counties Kildare, Louth, Meath, Westmeath; 3. Counties Antrim, Down, Wexford, Wicklow; 4. Counties Carlow, Kilkenny, Waterford; 5. Counties Cork, Kerry, Laois, Limerick, Offaly, Tipperary; 6. Counties Clare, Galway, Leitrim, Longford, Mayo, Roscommon, Sligo; 7. Counties Armagh, Cavan, Donegal,

Fermanagh, Londonderry, Monaghan, Tyrone; 8. Counties Angus, Argyll, Bute, Perth & all counties to the north; 9. Isle of Man, Ayr, Berwick, Clackmannan, Dumfries, Dumbarton, East Lothian, Fife, Kinross, Lanark, Kirkcudbright, Mid Lothian, Peebles, Renfrew, Roxburgh, Selkirk, Stirling, West Lothian, Wigtown; 10. Cheshire, Cumberland, Lancashire, Westmorland; 11. Gloucestershire, Herefordshire, Shropshire, Worcestershire; 12. Cornwall, Devon, Somerset; 13. Bedfordshire, Buckinghamshire, Derbyshire, Hertfordshire, Leicestershire, Northamptonshire, Nottinghamshire, Oxfordshire, Rutland, Staffordshire, Warwickshire; 14. Cambridgeshire, Durham, Essex, Huntingdonshire, Lincolnshire, Middlesex and London, Norfolk, Northumberland, Suffolk, Yorkshire; 15. Berkshire, Dorset, Hampshire, Kent, Surrey, Sussex, Wiltshire; 16. Anglesey, Brecknock, Caernarvon, Cardigan, Denbigh, Flint, Merioneth, Montgomery, Radnor; 17. Carmarthenshire, Glamorganshire, Monmouthshire, Pembrokeshire.

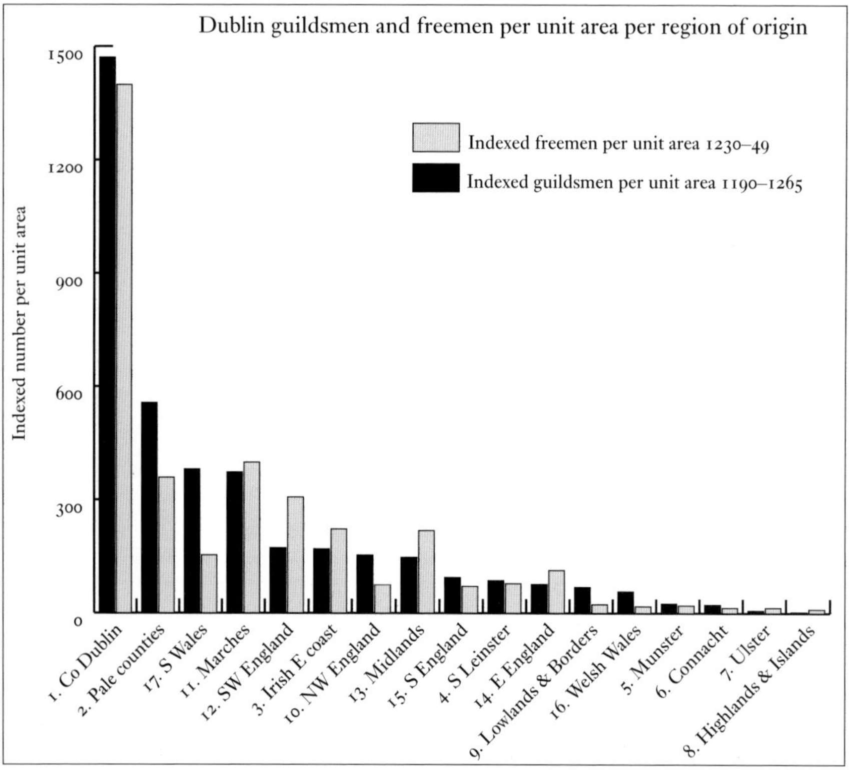

7.1 Densities of Dublin guildsmen per unit area, *c.*1190–1265, and of Dublin freemen per unit area, *c.*1230–49, per region of origin

(*Notes:* For regional definitions based upon the historic counties see notes to Table 7.2. Densities per unit area calculated for each region are indexed on those for Great Britain and Ireland as a whole.)

merchant guild and/or freedom of the city. For convenience of analysis and presentation, the recorded places-of-origin within Ireland and Great Britain from which these individuals came have been divided into seventeen regional groups based upon the historic counties (table 7.2). The numbers of guildsmen

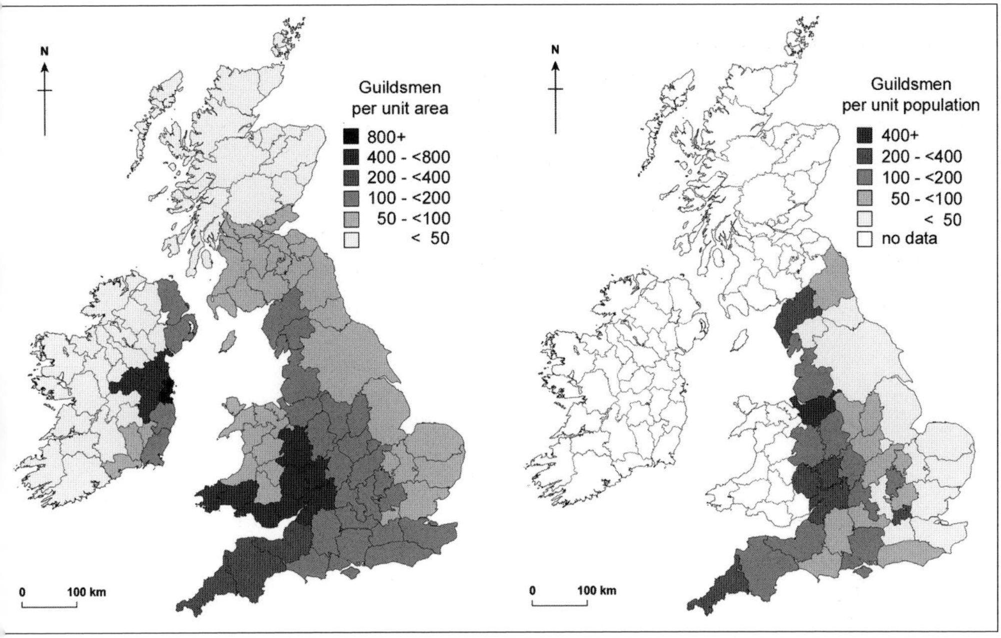

7.2 Indexed Dublin guildsmen *c.*1190–1265 per unit area and per unit population.

Notes: the regional groupings of historic cos are those given in the notes to Table 7.2. Guildsmen per unit area are indexed on the mean density of Great Britain and Ireland. Guildsmen per unit population are indexed on the mean ratio of England as a whole. The base population estimates used are those for *c.*1290 given in S. Broadberry, B.M.S. Campbell, A. Klein, M. Overton and B. van Leeuwen, *British economic growth, 1270–1870* (Cambridge, 2015), 25–6.

and freemen originating from within each region have then been expressed per unit area of those regions, and the results indexed on the corresponding figures for Great Britain and Ireland as a whole. In table 7.2 this exercise is repeated for the two sub-periods – *c.*1190–1230 and 1230–65 – as well as for the entire period *c.*1190–1265 and for the shorter period of *c.*1230–49 spanned by the separate roll of freemen admissions. Figure 7.1 charts the overall results for guildsmen and freemen while Figure 7.2 maps guildsmen admissions per unit area for each of the seventeen grouped regions and, for comparison, per head of population for each of the historic English counties using population estimates for *c.*1290.

Within Ireland a steep gradient emerges between areas whence came guildsmen in some numbers, where interaction with Dublin was persistent and strong, and those with weaker links to Dublin which sent far fewer guildsmen (figs 7.1–2). The former, lying well within Dublin's established sphere of influence, encompassed barely a quarter of the country and were concentrated on Ireland's eastern seaboard. The rest of the country, irrespective of whether it was under English control, lay outside that developed hinterland. From west of the River Shannon came scarcely any guildsmen at all. It is a pattern of recruitment that is regional rather than national in scope.

As is to be expected, no region was more closely integrated into Dublin's provisioning, manufacturing and commercial economy than County Dublin itself which, accordingly, contributed more guildsmen and freemen per unit area than any other (table 7.1). Its lead over other parts of Ireland was greater after 1230 than before and greater in the case of freemen than guildsmen (table 7.1). In order of importance, the neighbouring counties of Louth, Kildare, Meath, and Westmeath were the next most significant Irish source of guildsmen and freemen and collectively comprised a hinterland with a radius of approximately 80km from the city.[40] Dublin could be reached from all parts of this predominantly lowland area by road, augmented, in Co. Louth's case, by coastal shipping. It encompasses the zone identified by Margaret Murphy and Michael Potterton from a combination of historical and archaeological evidence to have been most intimately and regularly engaged in contact with the city and most heavily involved in supplying Dublin with victuals, fuel and other provisions.[41] Inland districts at the greatest distance are likely to have specialized in livestock production, since animals could be walked to market and their products – butter, hides, skins, fleeces and wool – were better able to bear the costs of overland transport than bulky grain or fresh produce – fruit and vegetables, meat and fish – prone to deterioration if delayed in transit.[42] The rural–urban relationship was reciprocal, for these counties provided the most immediate and accessible market for the goods and services supplied by that city. Enterprising dealers in the small towns developing in these inland areas – Ardnurcher, Kells, Loughsewdy, and Mullingar – extending as far west as Athlone on the River Shannon and the new borough of Rindoon, chartered in 1227, on the Co. Roscommon shore of Lough Kee, will have come to Dublin to stock up with some of the merchandise which they then retailed in their local markets.[43]

40 Using the evidence of place-name surnames, McClure ('Patterns of migration', p. 178) found that in the early fourteenth century 90% of migrants to Norwich, 73% of migrants to York, and 57% of migrants to London came from within 50 miles (80km) of these cities. The respective proportions originating from within 25 miles (40km) are 78%, 59% and 29%. In the case of Winchester, 74% came from within 50 miles and 54% from within 25 miles: Keene, *Survey of medieval Winchester*, pp 376–7. 41 Potterton and Murphy, *Dublin region*. Close relations between this region and Dublin were long established: Mary Valante, 'Dublin's economic relations with hinterland and periphery in the later Viking age' in Duffy (ed.), *Medieval Dublin I*, pp 69–83. 42 Murphy and Potterton, *Dublin region*, pp 478–80. 43 Kieran O'Conor and Brian Shanahan, *Rindoon Castle and deserted medieval town: a visitor's guide* (Roscommon, 2018), pp 16–20. John Norris, Robert the Mariner, William of Hereford and Ivor of Rindun, all came from Rindoon and were admitted as guildsmen between 1232 and 1237: *DGMR*, pp 66, 71.

From the 1220s, once subinfeudation and colonization of this core tract of the English lordship had bedded down and stable political and commercial relationships became established throughout it, this incipient Pale, led by Co. Dublin, consistently surpassed all other regions in the densities of guildsmen and freemen originating from it (table 7.2 and figs 7.1–2).[44] Understandably, recruitment per unit area was strongest from adjacent Co. Kildare and coastal Co. Louth and notably lower from inland Co. Meath and, especially, Co. Westmeath. Some of these guildsmen, like the freemen, may have been permanently relocating to the city but more were seeking the surety provided by guild membership that they could visit Dublin as and when required and transact their regular business there without let or hindrance. Their admissions reflect an intensity of interaction unsustainable at any greater distance and were clearly integral to the provisioning and functioning of the city.

To the north and south, an active coastal trade extended Dublin's commercial hinterland to include most of Ireland's east coast, extending from the conquered and colonized coastlands of the earldom of Ulster in the north to the settled grainlands of Co. Wexford in the south.[45] This maritime-dependent region was early subdued and occupied by the English and men from it were regularly admitted as guildsmen of Dublin, albeit, due to the greater distances involved, at a lesser rate than those from the five counties closest to Dublin. Grain dealers and fishermen from this favoured coastal strip found a ready market for their produce in Dublin which, in turn, provided the merchandise that probably formed the cargoes on the return trip. Approximately 20% of guildsmen and 30% of freemen came from these four coastal counties compared with respectively 60% and 50% from the five counties that constituted Dublin's core hinterland. Collectively, 80% of all guildsmen and freemen originating from within Ireland came from these nine eastern counties (table 7.1). This underlines how great was the constraint of distance upon movement within Ireland, which lacked a legacy of engineered Roman roads, awaited the bridging of many rivers, and where the towns with taverns and inns that facilitated movement were at an early stage of development.[46] Without the benefit of a developed transport infrastructure, Dublin's commercial reach remained circumscribed and the recruitment of guildsmen to Dublin declined steeply with overland distance from that city.

44 Cf. McClure, 'Patterns of migration'. 45 For later evidence of the coastal links between Ulster and Louth, see Brendan Smith, *Crisis and survival in late medieval Ireland: the English of Louth and their neighbours, 1330–1450* (Oxford, 2013), pp 160, 167. 46 For fords, ferries and bridges in Ireland and England, see Peter O'Keeffe and Tom Simington (revised by Rob Goodbody), *Irish stone bridges, history and heritage* (Newbridge, Co. Kildare, rev. edn 2016); David Harrison, *The bridges of medieval England: transport and society, 400–1800* (Oxford, 2004); Bruce M.S. Campbell and Ken Bartley, *England on the eve of the Black Death: an atlas of lay lordship, land and wealth, 1300–49* (Manchester, 2006), pp 299–300. The British network of roads, settlements and towns depicted on the later fourteenth-century Gough Map is analysed in Keith D. Lilley and Christopher D. Lloyd (with Bruce M.S. Campbell), 'Mapping the realm: a new look at the Gough Map of Great Britain

Beyond a radius of 100–150km from Dublin the falloff in the rate of recruitment of guildsmen and freemen was immediate and dramatic.[47] From Counties Carlow, Kilkenny and Waterford, early subdued and settled by the English, rates per unit area were only half those of the neighbouring coastal counties of Wicklow and Wexford (table 7.2). Further south and west only a trickle of guildsmen came from the English-settled lowlands of counties Tipperary, Cork and Limerick with their developing manorial economies and many rural boroughs.[48] Between *c.*1190 and 1265 these three counties were the origin of only 10% of Dublin guildsmen and an even smaller share of freemen, notwithstanding that in the final decade of the thirteenth century they contributed 31% of the £10,468 raised by the lay subsidy granted in 1292 and a decade later the southwestern dioceses of Ossory, Waterford, Lismore, Cashel, Emly, Cloyne and Limerick accounted for 30% of assessed Irish ecclesiastical wealth.[49] Outside the major walled towns of Kilkenny, Waterford, Cork and Limerick, so weak were the commercial links with Dublin that only rarely did anywhere from across this wide region send guildsmen to that city and never in any number.[50] It was not that the region was uncommercialized but rather that its commercial ties were with the south-coast ports and, via them, with the more developed economies of England, France and Flanders.[51] Connections with Dublin were of lesser importance.

West of the Shannon ties with Dublin were altogether more tenuous and outside of Galway City, source of 16 guildsmen and freemen, and maybe Athenry, this was a barren recruiting area for both guildsmen and freemen.[52] Whether by sea or land, the region remained geographically too remote from Dublin to be drawn within that city's regular sphere of influence. There had, of course, been determined English attempts to conquer Connacht but these had met with only partial success and had failed to create the commercial

(*c.*1360)', *Imago Mundi*, 61 (2009), 1–28. 47 Dublin's Irish catchment area was nonetheless significantly wider than the catchment areas of comparable English cities: McClure, 'Patterns of migration', p. 177. 48 B.J. Graham, 'The high Middle Ages: *c.*1100–*c.*1350' in B.J. Graham and L.J. Proudfoot (eds), *An historical geography of Ireland* (London, 1993), pp 63, 75, 84; John Bradley, 'The medieval towns of Tipperary' in William Nolan and Thomas G. McGrath (eds), *Tipperary: history and society: interdisciplinary essays on the history of an Irish county* (Dublin, 1985), pp 34–59; Adrian Empey, 'The Norman period: 1185–1500' in Nolan and McGrath (eds), *Tipperary*, pp 76–83. 49 Calculated from Mark Hennessy, 'Making Ireland English in the thirteenth century: the evidence of the Irish lay subsidy of 1292' in P.J. Duffy and William Nolan (eds), *At the anvil: essays in honour of William J. Smyth* (Dublin, 2012), p. 86 (the corresponding contribution from counties Dublin, Kildare, Meath, Westmeath, and Louth was 38%); Campbell, 'Benchmarking', p. 903. 50 https://databases.dublincity.ie/dmgr/ map.php. 51 Campbell, 'Benchmarking', pp 906, 915–17. By the end of the fifteenth century, Bristol conducted an active trade with all these south-coast ports and Waterford had replaced Dublin as Bristol's chief Irish trading partner: Childs and O'Neill, 'Overseas trade', pp 495, 514; Childs, 'Ireland's trade with England', pp 26–9; Susan Marie Flavin, 'The development of Anglo-Irish trade in the sixteenth century' (MA, Bristol, 2004), pp 26, 31–2, 34. 52 This is contingent upon the identification of *Archen'*, *Arthchen'* and their variants as Athenry.

conditions conducive to the recruitment of guildsmen.[53] Territories still under Gaelic control were hardly likely to have had close or friendly dealings with the capital of the English lordship. This was especially true of remote and largely townless Ulster outside of the earldom of Ulster, which sent almost no guildsmen to Dublin. Most, and maybe all, of the sixteen men described as coming from Ulster were probably denizens of the earldom rather than the wider province and, in total, the western half of Ireland supplied barely 5% of Dublin guildsmen and 8% of freemen, hardly surprising since Dublin's *de facto* authority and influence remained limited there.

Recruitment of guildsmen from within Ireland was skewed to the east. Across the Irish Sea, in contrast, the whole of England, the English lordships of South Wales and, to a lesser extent, the lowlands and borders of the independent kingdom of Scotland responded to Dublin's gravitational draw (figs 7.1–2). Men known to have come to Dublin from Britain outnumbered those known to have come from Ireland by approximately three to one (table 7.1). This ensured the predominance of English culture in post-conquest Dublin. These English guildsmen came from all parts of the kingdom and were undeterred by the fact that to reach Dublin they had to cross the Irish Sea. Sometimes treacherous, with a fair wind and calm sea, as demonstrated by the experience of those who in May 1169 had spearheaded the English invasion, that crossing was comparatively straightforward.[54] In fact, in contrast to the overland journey across Ireland, the availability of maritime transport appears to have expedited movement. Thus, those coming from the English east- and south-coast ports – from Lynn via Yarmouth, Dunwich, Ipswich, Sandwich, Dover, Winchelsea, Hastings, and Southampton, round to Exeter, all of which contributed guildsmen in some numbers – are likely to have made the entire journey by sea. Most landsmen, however, will have begun their outward journey by travelling overland to Bristol or Chester or one of the many lesser west-coast or south-Welsh ports that plied a regular trade with Dublin. Traffic along these routes was undoubtedly constant and substantial, as it was, in season, on the longer shipping routes that linked Flanders, Normandy, Brittany, Gascony and Iberia with Bristol and Dublin.[55]

Naturally, nowhere in England could match the impressive rates of recruitment sustained by Dublin's immediate hinterland, although initially the Welsh Marches and South Wales ran Dublin's wider hinterland close (table 7.2). It was, of course, men from the Anglo-Norman lordships of these areas who in 1169 had led the original invasion of Ireland and in their successful wake came others intent upon colonization and exploitation of the new commercial opportunities opened by the conquest. In an expansive age,

53 J.F. Lydon, 'The expansion and consolidation of the colony, 1215–54' in Cosgrove (ed.), *New history of Ireland*; i, pp 161–6. 54 Lydon, 'Expansion and consolidation', p. 170. 55 O'Neill, *Merchants and mariners*, pp 44–51; Childs and O'Neill, 'Overseas trade', pp 493–8.

those coming to Dublin were hoping to make their fortunes, or at the very least improve their lot, by either moving there or trading there. Townspeople from the Marcher counties were particularly active in enrolling as freemen whereas admission to the merchant guild held more appeal to men coming to Dublin from less urbanized South Wales (table 7.2). Reaching that destination from the many small ports that punctuated the coast of South Wales was relatively easy and for the mariners who regularly sailed these waters the crossing, weather permitting, would have been routine.[56]

Whether measured per unit area or, especially, per head of population (fig. 7.2), it was the counties of England's Irish Sea littoral that supplied guildsmen to Dublin at the greatest rate. Poor, thinly peopled and relatively weakly urbanized as was the northwest of England at this time, it was nonetheless an active participant in Irish Sea commerce and its leading port of Chester enjoyed strengthening links with Dublin, a port whose trade with Britain it would eventually dominate.[57] Owing to its lack of major towns (Chester, the largest, had a thirteenth-century population at peak of less than 4,000), the northwest was a more active supplier of guildsmen than freemen.[58] In fact, sparsely populated Cheshire led the country in the number of guildsmen per head of population that it sent to Dublin (fig. 7.2), a sure sign of the close ties that were developing between this region and Dublin. For similar reasons mountainous Cumberland, which was even less populous, was not far behind. The small border and fortress town of Carlisle was remarkably active in sending guildsmen to Dublin and surprising numbers were also furnished by the Furness region of north Lancashire. This Irish Sea axis of movement and exchange extended northwards, across the border and up the Scottish coast via the west coast ports of Kirkcudbright, Ayr, Irvin, and Greenock, as far as the Clyde, thereby underlining how well established and busy were Dublin's maritime connections with the whole of this northern section of Britain's coast.

Equally strong were the connections between Dublin and the facing coasts of South Wales and England's southwest peninsula, especially during the first half-century or so of English rule. Ties between Dublin and the Severn

56 Matthew Frank Stevens, *The economy of medieval Wales 1067–1536* (Cardiff, 2019), pp xiii, 60–1, 62–3. 57 Campbell and Bartley, *England on the eve of the Black Death*, pp 320–49; Bruce M.S. Campbell and Lorraine Barry, 'The population geography of Great Britain *c.*1290: a provisional reconstruction', in Chris Briggs, Peter Kitson and Stephen Thompson (eds), *Population, welfare and economic change in Britain, c.1290–1834* (Woodbridge, 2014), pp 53–68; H.J. Hewitt, *Medieval Cheshire: an economic and social history of Cheshire in the reigns of the three Edwards* (Manchester, 1929), pp 133–8. In *c.*1175 Henry II confirmed to the men of Chester the right to buy and sell in Dublin which they had exercised since the time of his grandfather, Henry I: Lydon, 'Dublin in transition', p. 140. Childs and O'Neill, 'Overseas trade', pp 368, 495, 514. 58 Campbell, 'Benchmarking', p. 908; Hewitt, *Medieval Cheshire*, pp 133–8; D.T. Williams, 'Medieval foreign trade: western ports' in H.C. Darby (ed.), *An historical geography of England before AD 1800* (Cambridge, 1948), pp 282–4, 295–6.

Estuary's chief port of Bristol were especially close and this region channelled large numbers of men to Dublin, sending more per unit area than the Irish east coast counties of Antrim, Down, Wicklow and Wexford combined. The whole of the southwest peninsula was also a major recruiting ground for Dublin guildsmen and freemen, those sailing from the south coast ports of Cornwall and Devon having to circumnavigate Land's End to get there. Strikingly, these three south-western English counties were consistently more active suppliers of guildsmen and freemen to Dublin than the export-orientated hinterlands of Ireland's south-coast ports from New Ross west to Cork (table 7.2). Very likely the links of Devon and Cornwall with Waterford and the other Irish south-coast ports, to which in nautical distance they were closer, were equally strong. At this time these two counties comprised one of the poorest and most thinly peopled parts of England and their poverty and underdevelopment may have encouraged people to quit them for the new opportunities opening across the sea in Ireland.[59] Strong cultural and environmental affinities between this region and Ireland may have further reinforced the flow. The exodus of prospective guildsmen per head of population was therefore particularly impressive and well above the national average (fig. 7.2), as was the exodus per unit area of prospective freemen (fig. 7.1).

Where England's western and southwestern coastal counties led, the rest of the country, without exception, followed. Significant numbers headed to Dublin from the Severn Valley counties of Gloucestershire, Herefordshire, Worcestershire and Shropshire, no doubt availing themselves of the established trade links to Dublin from the estuarine ports of Gloucester and Bristol. It was the departure for Dublin of significant numbers from Bristol and the county towns of Gloucester, Hereford, Shrewsbury and Worcester (table 7.4) that helped boost the significance of these Marcher counties as a source of guildsmen and, especially, freemen and in that respect elevated this region above most parts of Ireland (table 7.2 and fig. 7.1). Men from England's landlocked midland counties also joined the flow and did so in greater numbers than men from Ireland's own midland counties. The exodus per unit area and per head of population was lowest at the greatest distance from Dublin in the eastern counties that bordered the North Sea but, even so, exceeded the rates from almost the whole of the south and west of Ireland. These were populous counties with a substantial potential supply of would-be guildsmen and colonists and many were no doubt lured west by the economic opportunities that were opening in Ireland at a time when they were narrowing at home in England.[60] Men from the increasingly overcrowded east of England therefore accounted for one in nine of all those with a known place of origin admitted to Dublin's merchant guild and one in six of those who became freemen.[61] Once

59 Campbell and Bartley, *England on the eve of the Black Death*, pp 320–49; Campbell and Barry, 'Population geography'. 60 Campbell, *Great transition*, pp 160–72. 61 By 1290,

set in motion this westward outflow acquired a self-perpetuating momentum of its own. Across England there was certainly a pronounced west–east gradient in the relative scale of the movement to Dublin but crucially no part of the country was so distant that it was excluded from the flow.

The ease with which the English moved to Dublin was not, however, shared by the natives of Welsh Wales and Highland Scotland. The names of men from these regions do feature on the guild roll but are few and far between. In the case of west Wales and North Wales (Ceredigion and Gwynedd) this was the more remarkable for no other region of Britain was geographically so close to Dublin. Then as now the shortest and most direct Irish Sea crossing of all was between Anglesey and Dublin or, if the unbridged Menai Straits were an obstacle, from Caernarfon.[62] In the mid-thirteenth century, as the tempo of economic change quickened in much of native North Wales, a handful of men from Holyhead, Bangor and Caernarfon did travel to Dublin and were admitted to its guild, as did no less than nine men from the small but flourishing borough of Nefyn (alias Nevin) on the northwest coast of the Llŷn Peninsula, which faced Dublin 125km away across the Irish Sea.[63] But these were trifling numbers compared with the corresponding scale of movement from the South Wales counties of Pembrokeshire, Carmarthen, Glamorgan and Monmouth, all at a significantly greater nautical distance from Dublin. The difference, of course, was because Ceredigion and Gwynedd constituted the cultural and political core of the independent principality of Wales which throughout the period spanned by the guild roll existed in a state of ceaseless hostility with the neighbouring English Marcher lords, and ultimately the English crown.[64] Further, as an overwhelmingly rural and pastoral region and, as yet, unconquered by the English, it lacked the established urban centres whence would-be commercially active prospective Dublin guildsmen, and especially freemen, might have come.[65] Rural Welsh-speaking Welshmen from this extensive mountainous area would neither have been welcomed nor felt at home in the king of England's royal city of Dublin.

In contrast, the port town of Cardigan on the southern coast of Cardigan Bay plied an active trade with Dublin and, by 1265, 46 of its townspeople had become Dublin guildsmen. Few of these men bore conspicuously Welsh names

rural population densities in the block of eastern counties comprising Suffolk, Norfolk, Cambridgeshire, Huntingdonshire, Bedfordshire, Northamptonshire, and Rutland were 50% above the national average, with Lincolnshire not far behind: Campbell and Barry, 'Population geography', pp 56–7. Parts of these counties were already densely population in 1086: H.C. Darby, *Domesday England* (Cambridge, 1977), pp 87–94. **62** The distance from Holyhead to Dublin is 110km, which is roughly half that from either Chester or Pembroke. **63** R. Rees Davies, *Conquest, coexistence and change: Wales, 1063–1415* (Oxford, 1987), pp 163–4, 144–5; Stevens, *Economy of medieval Wales*, p. 58. **64** Davies, *Conquest, coexistence and change*, pp 213–332; Stevens, *Economy of medieval Wales*, p. 66. **65** Foundation of the planned and fortified boroughs of North Wales followed the English conquest of 1274: Maurice Beresford, *New towns of the Middle Ages: town plantation in England, Wales and*

or are described as Welshmen and the bulk of them were admitted as guildsmen after 1230 by which time the town was firmly back under English control.[66] Otherwise, the greater part of Welsh Wales was largely indifferent to the commercial and gravitational draw of Dublin. Densities per unit area of guildsmen and freemen originating from this area are among the lowest of any part of Great Britain and Ireland and below even those of the southern half of the independent kingdom of Scotland (table 7.2 and fig. 7.1). Political and cultural constraints overrode the region's geographical proximity to Dublin, where Scots from the Lowlands and Borders were more likely to be encountered than native Welshmen.[67]

Since at this period in time political relations between England and Scotland were largely peaceful, Scots are likely to have been readier in visiting Dublin than Welshmen and no doubt were encouraged to do so by the growth of Scottish trade and commerce.[68] As already noted, the Irish Sea was a notable artery of Scottish maritime trade that found expression in the admission of men from southwest Scotland to the Dublin merchant guild. There, they were joined by a trickle of east-coast Scots from Dundee, Perth, Edinburgh, Musselburgh and Berwick and others from the central lowlands who may have crossed Scotland at its narrow waist and then taken ship down the Irish Sea, the alternative being to sail around the north of Scotland or south of England to get there. Such voyages were not without peril and hence, unsurprisingly, the numbers who made them were small. Highland Scotland, in contrast, was a virtual blank and like western Ulster and for very similar reasons – its geographical remoteness, reinforced by its cultural and political separateness and limited commercial development – men from this region were rarely admitted as Dublin guildsmen.[69] Flemings, Normans, Bretons and Gascons were all more common.

No guildsmen came from a greater distance than the Italians who, for commercial reasons, were no strangers to international travel and the business opportunities to which it gave access. In the early 1260s, at a time when Italian

Gascony (Gloucester, 1988), pp 35–51. **66** Davies, *Conquest, coexistence and change*, pp 218, 226, 293, 304. **67** Welshmen from Welsh Wales who became Dublin guildsmen were outnumbered two to one by Scots from the Lowlands and Borders. 44 guildsmen are described as Welshmen or from Wales, six bore the distinctively Welsh surname element 'Map' (as in the case of John Map David Goch of Nefyn admitted in 1246–7), eight bore the Welsh forename Ivor, five the forename Madoc/Madog/Madok, and there were three Llewelyns. A search for other distinctively Welsh names would undoubtedly reveal more. Although almost 100 guildsmen bore the name David, not all were from Wales. **68** G.W.S. Barrow, *Kingship and unity: Scotland, 1000–1306* (Edinburgh, 1981), pp 92–7, 146–55. **69** Guildsmen who came from north of Scotland's central lowlands included Robert of Salan (Salen, Isle of Mull), William of Morref (Moray), and John of Hoirk (Dunnet Head, Caithness) admitted before 1222, Richard of Lochloch' (Loch Lochy, Inverness) admitted 1226–7, David of Tillakfergus (Tullyfergus, Angus) admitted 1246–7, Nicholas of Raford (Rafford, Moray) admitted 1247–8, William Not of Portloman (Port Lamont, Renfrewshire) admitted 1252–3: *DGMR*, pp 13, 24, 39, 55, 76, 78, 79, 81, 84, 85, 88, 91, 93.

merchants and bankers were becoming increasingly active in Ireland, three men from Lucca and two from Florence, including the merchants John of Lucca and Jacob Lombard of Florence, were admitted as Dublin guildsmen.[70] To reach Ireland they probably began by heading north over the Alpine passes to the Channel coast where they had the choice, either, of sailing directly to Dublin via one of the Dublin-bound Flemish or French merchantmen which seasonally sailed that maritime route, or of crossing the Channel and continuing by road to one of the English or Welsh Irish Sea ports.[71] Such long and arduous journeys were not unusual in this age of crusade, pilgrimage and increasing long-distance trade, but they were not to be undertaken lightly and, on the evidence of the admissions to the Dublin merchant guild, the numbers who embarked upon them were comparatively small and confined to those from high-status places. Their migration was, in fact, hierarchical – from one high-ranking city to another.

THE URBAN ORIGINS OF DUBLIN GUILDSMEN AND FREEMEN

Distance was not the only factor shaping the recruitment of guildsmen to Dublin. Since the bulk of those who came were townspeople, the size and rank of their towns of origin were also influential. This meant there was always a strong hierarchical dimension to the recruitment process. As the gravity-model of migration predicts, subject to the modifying effect of distance, inter-urban migration should increase as the importance of one, or both, of the urban locations increases.[72] Other things being equal, the closer in rank towns were to Dublin the more regular and intense should have been the interactions between them. This applied both to the nascent urban hierarchy that Dublin headed in Ireland and the developed urban hierarchy in England to which, from 1171, it had effectively become appended. The towns from which Dublin recruited its guildsmen and freemen and the numbers recruited, thus provides a telling commentary upon Dublin's place within the interconnected urban systems of England and post-conquest Ireland. They also help to define the extent and degree of integration the urban system that Dublin headed in Ireland.

70 M.D. O'Sullivan, 'Italian merchant bankers and the collection of papal revenues in Ireland in the thirteenth century', *Journal of the Galway Archaeological and Historical Society* 22:3/4 (1947), 132–63; M.D. O'Sullivan, *Italian merchant bankers in Ireland in the thirteenth century (a study in the social and economic history of medieval Ireland)* (Dublin, 1962); *DGMR*, pp 104, 107, 108. **71** Italian merchants were using the trans-Alpine route to visit the Champagne fairs in northern France from the 1170s. This overland route enjoyed a cost advantage over the direct sea route, to which regular resort was not made until the late thirteenth century: Campbell, *Great transition*, pp 89–90, 128, 139–41. **72** E.L. Ullman, 'The role of transportation and the bases for interaction' in John Blunden, Peter Haggett, Christopher Hamnett and Philip Sarre (eds), *Fundamentals of human geography: a reader* (London, 1978), p. 174; Peter Haggett, *Geography: a modern synthesis* (London, 1972), pp 329–32.

Table 7.3 Shares of Dublin guildsmen, *c.*1190–1265, and freemen, *c.*1230–49, originating from the highest ranking Irish and English towns

Place-of-origin	% of guildsmen			% of freemen
	*c.*1190–1230	1230–65	*c.*1190–1265	*c.*1230–49
Top 5 Irish towns	*15.9*	*14.7*	*15.1*	*12.8*
Top 10 Irish towns	*21.3*	*24.5*	*23.5*	*28.8*
All places in Ireland	*100.0*	*100.0*	*100.0*	*100.0*
Top 5 English towns	*12.0*	*15.2*	*13.6*	*13.9*
Top 10 English towns	*15.3*	*18.2*	*16.7*	*19.8*
Top 25 English towns	*26.6*	*29.2*	*27.8*	*39.0*
Top 60 English towns	*46.6*	*46.6*	*46.6*	*59.9*
All places in England	*100.0*	*100.0*	*100.0*	*100.0*

Note: the top ten Irish towns and top sixty English towns are those listed in B.M.S. Campbell, 'Benchmarking medieval economic development: England, Wales, Scotland, and Ireland, *c.*1290', *Economic History Review*, 61:4 (2008), 908–9 and 911. By 1290 the top 10 Irish towns contained an estimated 2.6–3.1% of Ireland's population, and the top 10 and top 60 English towns respectively 6.9% and 8.5% of England's population.

Although townspeople made up relatively small proportions of the populations of England and Ireland during the period spanned by the guild roll, they comprised a majority of those admitted as guildsmen and freemen of Dublin. Those who made their livings from crafts, trades and the provision of services were far more likely to be attracted by the opportunities offered by the city than those whose occupations were agricultural. Bailiffs, franklins, gardeners and fishermen feature on the guild roll but not husbandmen, ploughmen, cowherds, shepherds or others who made their living from farm work. Merchants, vendors of assorted goods and chapmen came, as did carriers, carters, waggoners and mariners. Craftsmen, manufacturers and construction workers of many types and in some numbers signed up, and so too did clerks, cooks, taverners, porters and an array of other service-sector workers.[73] These were the occupations at the core of urban employment in towns of any size in Britain and Ireland at this time.[74] They convey the clear impression that those coming to Dublin at this time were exchanging one urban environment for another: 'they were townsmen moving to a new town, not rural emigrants'.[75] For many this will not have been their first such move,

73 *DGMR*, pp 157–9 and https://databases.dublincity.ie/dmgr/occupations.php. 74 Compare the occupations of the men admitted to Leicester's merchant guild between 1196 and 1225: Bateson, *Records of the borough of Leicester*, pp xxix–xxx. Derek Keene, 'Continuity and development in urban trades: problems of concepts and the evidence' in Penelope J. Corfield and Derek Keene (eds), *Work in towns, 850–1850* (Leicester, 1990), pp 3, 7; Britnell, 'Economy of British towns', pp 121–3. 75 Bartlett, *Making of Europe*, p. 182.

nor was it necessarily their last.[76] Often it was purely temporary. Men on the make, then as now, tended to be mobile.

Table 7.3 brings out this strong urban bias to the recruitment of guildsmen; it is a bias even more pronounced among freemen, who were taking up civic responsibilities. Thus, although the top ten Irish towns probably contained less than 4% of Ireland's population, they contributed respectively 24% and 29% of those Dublin guildsmen and freemen whose recorded places-of-origin were Irish.[77] Similarly, the top ten English towns contributed 17% of the guildsmen and 20% of the freemen who hailed from England.[78] The names of these high-ranking places are listed in table 7.4 and show up repeatedly in the *DGMR*. Approximately two out of five guildsmen and three out of five freemen came from towns with at least 2,000 inhabitants. When account is taken of the plethora of lesser towns from which Dublin's guildsmen and merchants came, including numbers of the new towns of the age, it is plain that inter-urban migration was the predominant pattern of movement, with individuals moving up, across, and down the urban hierarchy as well as geographically through space.[79]

For men of ambition coming from the numerous petty boroughs and small towns that were such a characteristic feature of the British and Irish urban systems at this time – places like Berkhamsted and Ware (Herts.), Henley-on-Thames (Oxon.), Ardee (Co. Louth), and Castledermot (Co. Kildare) – a permanent move to Dublin was a big step up the urban hierarchy, to a populous city of international renown with a substantial internal market and access to a comparatively extensive hinterland.[80] Here such standard craft activities listed among the occupations of guildsmen as cloth-making, textile-working, leather-working, metal-working and pottery-making could be undertaken on a larger scale and with a greater division of labour. The presence of high-end consumer demand also meant that Dublin could accommodate such niche activities as bookselling, glass-selling, comb-making,

76 William of Hereford of Rindoon (Co. Roscommon), admitted as a Dublin guildsman in 1233–4, is one example, David the Welshman of Arklow (Co. Wicklow), admitted in 1245–6, is another: *DGMR*, pp 66, 84. **77** Campbell, 'Benchmarking', pp 911, 931. **78** Ibid., pp 908, 911, 931. **79** English and Irish places with borough status are listed in M.W. Beresford and H.P.R. Finberg, *English medieval boroughs, a hand-list* (Newton Abbot, 1973); B.J. Graham, 'The definition and classification of medieval Irish towns', *Irish Geography*, 21 (1988), 20–32; Geoffrey Martin, 'Plantation boroughs in medieval Ireland, with a handlist of boroughs to *c*.1500' in David Harkness and Mary O'Dowd (eds), *Historical Studies, XIII: The town in Ireland* (Belfast, 1981), pp 23–53. The 15 guildsmen from *Nova Villa* could have come from any of the many newly founded and chartered boroughs in England, Wales and Ireland. **80** Beresford and Finberg, *English medieval boroughs*, pp 124, 126, 148; Mark Bailey, 'The economy of towns and markets, 1100 to 1500' in Nigel Goose and T.R. Slater (eds), *Hertfordshire towns: the development of Hertfordshire's urban landscape to 1800* (Hatfield, 2008), pp 46–66; Noel Ross, 'The walled town of Ardee: selected extracts', *Journal of the County Louth Archaeological and Historical Society*, 27 (2011), 339–65; Christopher Dyer, 'Small towns 1270–1540' in Palliser (ed.), *Cambridge urban history*, p. 523.

parchment-making, scabbard- and shield-making, lock-smithing, copper-smithing and gold-smithing, which dealt in or worked with high-value raw materials.[81] Since Dublin outranked all other Irish towns and was larger than any Welsh or Scottish town, this upward hierarchical movement was the predominant experience of those coming to it from those regions. The same was true of those hailing from the northwest and southwest of England, whose largest cities – Chester and Exeter – had only a third as many inhabitants as Dublin.[82] The effect of Dublin's superior size and status was to magnify its gravitational attraction and extend its geographical reach.

Small towns and petty boroughs, however, were incapable of contributing more than small numbers of guildsmen or of doing so on a regular basis. They lacked the necessary threshold populations and the need for close and regular interactions that came with a higher urban rank. Towns sending at least 25 guildsmen and freemen to Dublin between *c.*1190 and 1265 were typically both large and relatively high-ranking. They are listed in rank order in table 7.4, where information is given for the sub-periods *c.*1190–1230, 1230–65, and *c.*1230–49 (for freemen), as well as for the entire run of years and for guildsmen and freemen combined. Whereas some towns, such as Bath, Tiverton, Cardiff, Cardigan, Trim and Carrickfergus, feature on only one of these lists, others, owing to their high urban rank and the closeness of their ties with Dublin, appear on all of them. Chief among these were the English cities of London, Bristol, Gloucester and Chester.

That many of those admitted to Dublin's merchant guild came from London should be no surprise. It was the seat of English government, the highest-ranking city in England's well-articulated urban network, a national and international centre of commerce and, after Paris, probably the largest European city north of the Alps.[83] From 1171 its political, administrative, financial and commercial vested interests in Dublin ensured a fairly constant traffic between the two cities and ensured that they remained in close contact notwithstanding the physical distance between them. Until 1230 Londoners dominated guildsmen admissions and, by 1265, 124 of them had been admitted as guildsmen and, between *c.*1230 and 1249, 11 as freemen. Some – probably all the freemen and many of the guildsmen – were moving to Dublin for good, others will have been visiting with a view to exploring what commercial opportunities were available there.

Bristol alone, which overtook London after 1230, sent more guildsmen. Its direct access to the Bristol Channel and thence the Irish Sea was very much to its advantage. It was a regional capital and England's leading west-coast port and at the end of the thirteenth century ranked third in England's urban hierarchy. Dublin was an established trading partner well before the conquest.

81 *DGMR*, pp 157–9 and https://databases.dublincity.ie/dmgr/occupations.php. 82 Campbell, 'Benchmarking', pp 908, 911. 83 Derek Keene, 'London from the post-Roman period to 1300' in Palliser (ed.), *Cambridge urban history*, pp 190–96, 203–16.

Bristol's support of that costly venture was rewarded by Henry II's grant of privileged rights in Dublin to the men of Bristol. This cemented the close trading relationship between the two cities and guaranteed that, once established, a large number of Bristolians would be admitted to Dublin's merchant guild.[84] It was a number that no Irish town or city could rival. Rather, Bristol's closest rivals were the English provincial cities of Gloucester and Chester at the respective tidal heads of navigation of the Severn and Dee estuaries and therefore strategically placed to trade directly with Dublin and send men to join the colonial enterprise.

Gloucester and Chester were both former Roman walled cities. Each served a wide hinterland, although that of Gloucester was more populous, urbanized and developed than that of Chester. Given that neither ranked in the top ten of English towns, *pro rata* they probably supplied more guildsmen than either London or Bristol.[85] Of the two, Chester enjoyed the benefit of the shorter and more direct sea crossing to Dublin and hence, although it was barely a quarter to a third the size of Bristol and not in the same urban league, by the end of the period men from Chester were increasingly well represented in Dublin's merchant guild.[86] This connection, like those that London and Bristol had with Dublin, proved strong and enduring and formed one of the links which effectively integrated Dublin into an extension of England's own developing and expanding urban system.

For the highest-ranking English cities, want of direct access to the Irish Sea was no impediment to the admission of significant numbers to Dublin's merchant guild. Men from York, for example, England's second city and effective capital of the north of England, were prominent in Dublin from an early date and 31 were eventually admitted as guildsmen and four as freemen.[87] These were enough to put York in the top 25 of contributing towns (table 7.4) and eclipse the modest contribution of Ireland's own joint-second city of Waterford, which sent just 16 guildsmen and a solitary freeman.[88] Winchester,

84 Gwynn, 'Medieval Bristol and Dublin'; Martin, 'Allies and an overlord', p. 94; Marie Therese Flanagan, *Irish society, Anglo-Norman settlers, Angevin kingship: interactions in Ireland in the late twelfth century* (Oxford, 1989), pp 68, 70, 75–6; Clarke, '1192 charter of liberties', 8–9; Lydon, 'Dublin in transition', pp 128–9, 140; David A. Hinton, 'The large towns 600–1300' in Palliser (ed.), *Cambridge urban history*, p. 232. Note that Bristolians were not exempted under the terms of Henry II's earlier grant from the requirement to join the merchant guild and pay the relevant fine for admission. 85 Campbell, 'Benchmarking', p. 908. 86 Hewitt, *Medieval Cheshire*, pp 133–8; Williams, 'Medieval foreign trade', pp 282–4, 295–6; Lydon, 'Dublin in transition', p. 140. By the fifteenth century Chester had superseded Bristol as Dublin's chief British trading partner: Wendy Childs, 'Ireland's trade with England in the later Middle Ages', *Irish Economic and Social History*, 9:1 (1982), 26–9; Childs and O'Neill, 'Overseas trade', pp 368, 495, 514. 87 Campbell, 'Benchmarking', p. 908. For variant spellings of York's name see *DGMR*, p. 156; https://databases.dublincity.ie/dmgr/places.php#Y. 88 Based upon its fee farm of 100 marks, McEneaney, 'Mayors and merchants', p. 153, believes that 'Waterford had, after Dublin, the greatest density of settlement and probably population in the colony'. Nevertheless, the twin Drogheda

Table 7.4 Rank order of places sending guildsmen and freemen to Dublin, *c.*1190–1230, 1230–65, *c.*1230–1249 and *c.*1190–1265

Rank	*c.*1190–1230		1230–65		*c.*1190–1265		*c.*1230–49		*c.*1190–1265	
	Place	Guilds-men	Place	Guilds-men	Place	Guilds-men	Place	Free-men	Place	G + F men
1	London [E]	74	Bristol [E]	103	Bristol [E]	156	London [E]	11	Bristol [E]	162
2	Bristol [E]	53	Chester [E]	59	London [E]	124	Coventry [E]	11	London [E]	135
3	Gloucester [E]	53	London [E]	50	Chester [E]	92	Hereford [E]	10	Chester [E]	96
4	Cardiff [W]	52	Ayr [S]	46	Gloucester [E]	86	Exeter [E]	10	Gloucester [E]	92
5	Worcester [E]	37	Drogheda [Ir]	46	Cardiff [W]	61	Naas [Ir]	7	Cardiff [W]	61
6	Chester [E]	33	Greater Dublin [Ir]	*c.*35	Ayr [S]	57	Wexford [Ir]	7	Coventry [E]	60
7	Carlisle [E]	27	Cardigan [W]	33	Haverfordwest [W]	57	Wicklow [Ir]	7	Exeter [E]	59
8	Exeter [E]	27	Gloucester [E]	33	Drogheda [Ir]	55	Shrewsbury [E]	7	Ayr [S]	57
9	Haverfordwest [W]	26	Haverfordwest [W]	31	Kells (Ir)	54	Bristol [E]	6	Haverfordwest [W]	57
10	Winchester [E]	26	Kells [Ir]	29	Greater Dublin [Ir]	*c.*52	Gloucester [E]	6	Drogheda [Ir]	57
11	Bedford [E]	25	Arklow [Ir]	28	Coventry [E]	49	Perth? [S]	5	Hereford [E]	56
12	Kells (Ir)	24	Down [Ir]	27	Exeter [E]	49	Worcester [E]	5	Greater Dublin [Ir]	*c.*55
13	Shrewsbury [E]	24	Hereford [E]	27	Hereford [E]	46	Kilmainham [Ir]	4	Kells (Ir)	54
14	Northampton [E]	23	Coventry [E]	26	Cardigan [W]	46	Chester [E]	4	Worcester [E]	50
15	Coventry [E]	22	Wexford [Ir]	26	Worcester [E]	45	Lincoln [E]	4	Shrewsbury [E]	50
16	York [E]	20	Castledermot [Ir]	24	Carlisle [E]	43	York [E]	4	Cardigan [W]	46
17	Hereford [E]	19	Bordeaux [Fr]	22	Shrewsbury [E]	43	Leicester [E]	4	Winchester [E]	45
18	Leicester [E]	19	Carrickfergus [Ir]	22	Winchester [E]	42	Caermarthen [W]	4	Carlisle [E]	43
19	Lichfield [E]	19	Exeter [E]	22	Castledermot [Ir]	38	Oxmantown, Dublin [Ir]	3	Naas [Ir]	40
20	Naas [Ir]	19	Ross [Ir]	≤22	Down [Ir]	37	Tiverton [E]	3	Wexford [Ir]	40
21	Greater Dublin	*c.*17	Dundalk [Ir]	21	Northampton [E]	36	Winchester [E]	3	Castledermot [Ir]	40
22	Bath [E]	15	Shrewsbury [E]	21	Carrickfergus [Ir]	34	Bury St Edmunds [E]	3	Leicester [E]	38
23	Dunwich [E]	15	Nottingham [E]	18	Leicester [E]	34	Derby [E]	3	Down [Ir]	37
24	Kildare [Ir]	15	Rouen [Fr]	18	Naas [Ir]	33	St Albans [E]	3	Northampton [E]	36
25	Kilmainham [Ir]	15	Carlisle [E]	17	Wexford [Ir]	33	Lichfield [E]	3	York [E]	35
26	Trim [Ir]	15	Coleraine [Ir]	16	York [E]	31	Stafford [E]	3	Carrickfergus [Ir]	34
27	Castledermot [Ir]	14	Kilkenny [Ir]	16	Arklow [Ir]	30			Arklow [Ir]	31
28	Oxford [E]	14	Winchester [E]	16	Bedford [E]	30			Bedford [E]	31

Notes: [E] = England; [Fr] = France; [Ir] = Ireland; [S] = Scotland; [W] = Wales.

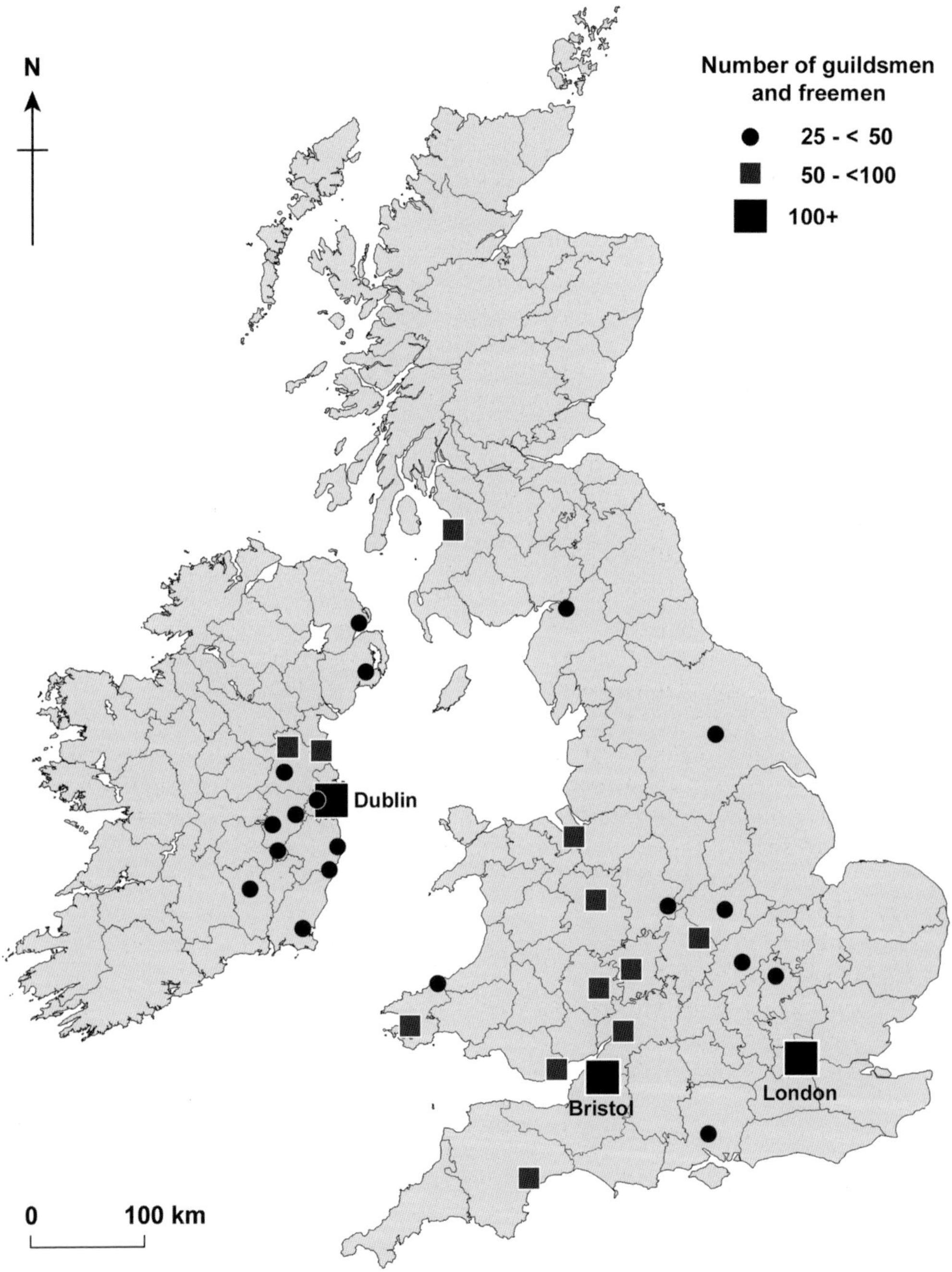

7.3 Places sending a combined total of at least 25 guildsmen and freemen to Dublin, *c.*1190–1265.
Source: table 7.4 and *DGMR*.

England's former southern capital, supplied an even larger combined contingent of 42 guildsmen and three freemen. The host of the annual international St Giles's fair and conveniently served by the developing port of Southampton, Winchester enjoyed a commercial importance all its own.[89] The contrast with the neighbouring but lower-ranking episcopal and county town of Salisbury is striking. The oak timbers used to construct the roof of Salisbury's new cathedral may have come from Ireland but this did not induce it to send more than a few guildsmen to Dublin.[90]

Other county and episcopal towns were more energetic in developing connections with Dublin. From the leading southwestern port of Exeter came 49 guildsmen and ten freemen, over 100 originated from Hereford and Worcester, Carlisle sent 43, and the landlocked midland towns of Leicester, Northampton, and Bedford each contributed over 30 (table 7.4). All were mostly a rank or so below Dublin and within their respective regions performed many of the same central-place functions. For men from these towns the move to Dublin was not such a big step and it was the closeness in rank of these towns to Dublin that encouraged movement, especially by those who thought that Dublin was on the way up and hoped to better themselves by moving there. Feedback information from those who had successfully made the move may then have initiated a sustained outflow of hopeful migrants, confident of finding friends and family to receive them upon arrival in Dublin. That, no doubt, is one reason why these particular towns, in contrast to some others, are named so repeatedly in the Dublin roll (table 7.4).

Information about the opportunities available in Dublin seems to have been widely shared among a group of towns inland and upstream of Gloucester. Collectively, 183 guildsmen and 33 freemen came from Coventry, Hereford, Worcester and Shrewsbury (fig. 7.3), with numbers more hailing from the many smaller towns of the region, Tewkesbury (Glos.), Leominster and Weobley (Heref.), Ludlow (Salop.), Warwick (Warks.), and Evesham (Worcs.). The presence in Dublin of so many men from this one region brought that city within this region's cultural orbit, as manifest in the decision taken, it is now thought *c.*1234, by the canons of Christ Church cathedral in Dublin to give the commission to design and construct a new gothic nave to masons from this area.[91] The result was a building which, architecturally, would have looked equally at home whether in the valley of the Severn or the Liffey.

boroughs paid a combined fee farm that was the same and from it Bradley, *Topography and layout*, p. 28, inferred a population of *c.*6,600. In England, Lincoln and Norwich were the next highest-ranking towns after York and Bristol and the recorded origin of, respectively, 9 and 13 Dublin guildsmen. **89** C.H. Vellacott, 'Winchester: fairs and trades' in William Page (ed.), *A history of the county of Hampshire: Volume 5* (London, 1912), pp 36–40; Keene, *Survey of medieval Winchester*, pp 88, 94–5, 101–3. **90** Tim Tatton-Brown, 'The roofs of Salisbury cathedral', *Spire: Annual Report of the Friends of Salisbury Cathedral*, 71 (2001), 18–23. **91** Michael O'Neill, 'Design sources for St Patrick's cathedral, Dublin, and its

From towns large and small right down Britain's west coast, from the Clyde in the north to the Exe in the south, men converged on Dublin and were admitted to its merchant guild, thereby testifying to the strength and intensity of the connections that extended across the Irish Sea and the centrality of Dublin within that maritime network. From the north came men from the Scottish ports of Greenock, Irvin and Ayr, and from the English city of Carlisle. Greater numbers crossed to Dublin from Chester, a route which, because of its shortness, gained steadily in popularity. A few made the shortest crossing of all from the minor ports of northwest Wales, although far more came from the English-controlled ports of Cardigan, Caermarthen, and Cardiff in South Wales. The busiest route of all syphoned men from Bristol, Gloucester, and the towns of the Severn Valley via the Bristol Channel to both Dublin and, no doubt, the other towns located on Ireland's east and south coasts.[92] Finally, a regular traffic connected the lesser ports of the southwest peninsula and the regional capital of Exeter to Dublin.[93] There they were joined by men from a string of ports down Ireland's east coast: Coleraine and Carrickfergus, Carlingford, Dundalk and Drogheda, Wicklow and Arklow, Wexford and Ross (fig. 7.3). Like Venice, Dublin's hinterland, at this stage in its development, extended further by sea than it did by land.

The Irish towns that contributed guildsmen to Dublin were altogether more restricted in distribution than their English counterparts (figs 7.5–6). Of course, Irish towns were mostly smaller and younger than those in England and hence few were in a position to supply as many migrants. Nor was migration from them impelled by the same colonial imperative. It was also the case that until *c.*1230 places-of-origin were less likely to be recorded for guildsmen from Ireland than from England. Consequently, whereas seven English, two Welsh and one Scottish town each sent a combined total of over 55 guildsmen and freemen to Dublin (table 7.4), among Irish towns Drogheda alone did so. Newly founded as it was, it enjoyed the double advantage of being both a port and located 50km from Dublin and was readily able, therefore, to access the city by both sea and land.[94] With a population approximately half that of Dublin and more Dublin guildsmen admissions than any other Irish

relationship to Christ Church cathedral', *PRIA*, 100C:6 (2000), 223–7; Roger Stalley, 'The construction of the medieval cathedral, *c.*1030–1250' in Kenneth Milne (ed.), *Christ Church cathedral Dublin: a history* (Dublin, 2000), pp 68, 70, 74. O'Neill, p. 226, cites Hereford cathedral's lady chapel, Pershore abbey's choir, and the parish churches of Droitwich and Overbury, as sources of the design. For Stalley, p. 71, 'the roots of the Christ Church design lie … in Worcestershire'. **92** By the fifteenth century, Bristol's commercial connections with Waterford were closer than those with Dublin and ships from Cork, Youghal, Dungarvan and Wexford were regular visitors to Bristol: Childs, 'Ireland's trade with England', p. 26. **93** J.P. Allan, *Medieval and post-medieval finds from Exeter 1971–1980*, Exeter Archaeological Reports, 3 (Exeter, 1984), p. 15. Shortly after Henry II departed from Dublin, Richard de Clare, acting on behalf of the king, granted a burgage in the city to a man from Exeter: Lydon, 'Dublin in transition', p. 138. **94** McHugh, *Drogheda*, pp 1–4, 12.

town, it clearly functioned as the second city within the geographically circumscribed urban hierarchy that Dublin headed.[95] In 1253 it was in recognition of this co-dependency that representatives from Drogheda-in-Louth and Dublin met to discuss matters of mutual concern.[96] A further 30 Irish towns sent at least ten guildsmen to Dublin, all but four of them concentrated into the ten-county area – counties Antrim, Down, Louth, Meath, Westmeath, Dublin, Kildare, Kilkenny, Wicklow and Wexford – that constituted Dublin's core hinterland within which an integrated urban network may be deemed to have operated. Key components of that network included Carrickfergus (Co. Antrim), Down (Co. Down), Kells (Co. Meath), Naas and Castledermot (Co. Kildare), Arklow (Co. Wicklow), and Wexford (Co. Wexford), all of which were the recorded place-of-origin of at least 30 Dublin guildsmen. Significantly, Waterford, Cork, Limerick, and Galway, which ranked among Ireland's ten largest towns, all sent fewer.[97]

Waterford, like Dublin, was well established at the time of the English invasion and when the latter's guild roll began it was Ireland's second largest town.[98] It was less than 150km from Dublin by land and not much further by sea. At this distance and given its size and importance, had it been integrated into a developed and hierarchical urban system headed by Dublin, it should have been a significant contributor of guildsmen to that city. Yet, over a 75-year period, it is named as the source of just 16, all but one of whom were admitted between 1224 and 1248 when the fortunes of Dublin and the English lordship were at their zenith and relations between the two cities may have been closest. Those who made that move over this 25-year period were nevertheless outnumbered by men from the lesser town and port of Wexford and the small inland town of Castledermot (Co. Kildare), located, respectively, close to the maritime and overland limits of Dublin's regular reach. As far as the Dublin merchant guild was concerned, the English cities of Coventry and Exeter each supplied three times as many members as Waterford notwithstanding the far longer and more arduous journeys entailed in getting there. By implication, both conducted a more active trade with Dublin than Waterford and each, in fact, contributed more guildsmen than Waterford, Cork and Limerick put together. This is a reminder that not only were Dublin's patterns of urban interaction within Ireland more characteristic of those of a provincial city than a capital city, but also that within England it was with cities of provincial rank that Dublin's interactions were strongest.

As one of Ireland's busiest exporting ports, Waterford's ties were necessarily stronger with the overseas cities with which it traded than with Dublin, with

95 Bradley, *Topography and layout*, p. 28, has proposed a population of 5,000–6,600, based upon Drogheda's built-up area and fee farm payment; for Dublin, Clarke, *Dublin, Pt 1* (IHTA), p. 12, gives a figure of 11,000. 96 McEneaney, 'Mayors and merchants', p. 168, citing Gilbert (ed.), *Hist. & mun. docs*, p. 130. 97 Campbell, 'Benchmarking', p. 911. 98 Bradley and Halpin, 'Scandinavian and Anglo-Norman Waterford', pp 105–29.

which it evidently had much less cause to do business.[99] Like all substantial provincial cities, it was the head of its own network of towns (places like Carrick, Clonmel, Fethard, Cashel and Callan) spread through the settled interior of east Munster, few of which sent more than one or two men to join Dublin's merchant guild.[100] It was a region largely within the bounds of the English lordship but well outside Dublin's own regular urban sphere of influence, which is why fewer Waterford men were admitted to Dublin's merchant guild than the gravity-model of migration would suggest. Within Ireland it ranked equal-second in size but, with Coleraine (Co. Derry), Ardee (Co. Louth) and Mullingar (Co. Westmeath), joint twenty-first as a named source of guildsmen. The same must undoubtedly have been true of lower-ranking Cork, Limerick and Galway, which similarly functioned as largely autonomous port cities, answerable to the lordship's Dublin-based administration but with closer ties to towns outside Ireland than those within. To Dublin they were less important than Rouen in Normandy, Dinan in Brittany and Bordeaux in Gascony, with all three of which it traded regularly and from which larger numbers of men were admitted to the merchant guild (table 7.4). Their greater numbers are a further reminder of how much more important to Dublin were these overseas connections than those with all but the most immediately adjacent parts of its Irish hinterland.

CONTINUITY AND CHANGE *c.*1190 TO 1265

These patterns of admission to Dublin's merchant guild display more continuity than change over the 75 years spanned by the *DGMR*, although it is only from 1222 that the admissions are dated annually. Throughout this period consistently more of the new guildsmen originated from England than from Ireland, over half of those admitted came from the Irish Sea region broadly defined, rates of recruitment per unit area declined with distance from Dublin (steeply in Ireland but less steeply in England), townspeople accounted for a disproportionate share of these admitted, and London, Bristol, Gloucester, and Chester headed the league-table of towns sending guildsmen to Dublin (tables 1–4 and fig. 7.1). Thus, although changes did occur in the annual rates of admission, the relative contributions of different regions, the scale of movement from individual towns, and the numbers from Ireland admitted to the merchant guild, these were changes of degree rather than of kind. Dublin itself was growing and changing over this period, as was the English lordship of Ireland, of which it was the political and administrative centre, and the wider commercial environment within which its guildsmen and freemen

99 Campbell, 'Benchmarking', p. 915. **100** Bradley, 'Medieval towns of Tipperary'; Graham, 'Definition and classification'; Ellis, *Tudor Ireland*, p. 38.

operated.[101] The observed shifts of scale, of focus and of balance in the numbers and origins of those becoming guildsmen were a response to these developments.

By the 1190s, when the *DGMR* seems to begin, Dublin had been in English hands for twenty years.[102] Since Henry II's visit, most of Leinster, easternmost Ulster and much of Munster had been conquered, subdued and subinfeudated, a substantial influx of colonists had begun, and Henry's youngest son John had become lord of Ireland.[103] It was John who granted Dublin its first full charter of privileges in 1192 in which he explicitly licensed the establishment of guilds.[104] Probably it was that charter which led to formal constitution of the Dublin merchant guild, although Geoffrey Martin and James Lydon believe that something akin to it may have existed for some time, and it is to *c.*1190 that Martin and Connolly date the earliest entries enrolled in *DGMR*.[105] Commencement of this remarkable record coincides with the onset of a boom time for the city which lasted for the next 30–40 years. Over this period Dublin served as a gateway for the steady flow of colonists coming to north Leinster and, of course, the wave of newcomers who settled in the city and hastened its transition from a bastion of Hiberno-Norse to one of Anglo-Irish culture with a strong west of England flavour. Dublin's rapid expansion was physically manifest in the progressive extension and strengthening of the city's defences.[106] Meanwhile, at John's command, between 1204 and 1230 a mighty stone castle was constructed, a mint set up and the newly-established Irish exchequer given a permanent home.[107] The city's churches and religious houses were further endowed and adorned, in 1204 a two-week annual fair was founded, and a guild hall for the merchants was erected.[108] Undoubtedly, these developments enhanced the city's reputation, stimulated its commerce, both domestic and overseas, boosted employment, and attracted an influx of construction workers, craftsmen, dealers and traders from near and far.

Throughout this period, as the city's physical and institutional infrastructures were upgraded, admissions to the Dublin merchant guild clearly ran at a high rate. Frustratingly, until 1222 (and membrane 14 of the 43 that are extant), none of the admissions are dated, not all are legible, and some are

101 Clarke, *Dublin, Pt 1* (IHTA), pp 6–8; Lydon, 'Expansion and consolidation', pp 65–86, 121–30. **102** Martin, 'Introduction', pp xviii–xix. Martin, 'Allies and an overlord', pp 89–90; Flanagan, *Irish society*, pp 168–72; 202–3. **103** For accounts of these well-known developments, see Cosgrove (ed.), *New history of Ireland*; i, pp 98–155, 441–5. **104** Martin, 'Introduction', pp xv–xvi; Clarke, '1192 charter of liberties', 9; Clarke, *Dublin, Pt 1* (IHTA), p. 12. **105** Martin, 'Introduction', pp xviii–xix; Lydon, 'Dublin in transition'. **106** Linzi Simpson, *Dublin city walls and defences* (Dublin, 2006); Clarke, *Dublin, Pt 1* (IHTA), p. 6, 20–2. **107** Seán Duffy, 'Part 1: the medieval period' in Seán Duffy, John Montague, Kevin Mulligan and Michael O'Neill, *Dublin Castle: from fortress to palace, volume 1, Vikings to Victorians. A history of Dublin Castle to 1850*, ed. Ann Lynch and Conleth Manning (Dublin, 2022) pp 1–68; Clarke, *Dublin, Pt 1* (IHTA), pp 6, 22, 23. **108** Clarke, *Dublin, Pt 1* (IHTA), pp 23, 27.

missing.[109] The extant and legible entries number 3,570, giving an average of 112 a year, although were the record complete and fully legible that annual figure might be as much as 10% higher. Presumably, as in later years, numbers varied a great deal around that average. Of those new guildsmen with an identified place-of-origin, 16% came from Ireland, 5% from Scotland, 60% from England, 12% from Wales, and a further 7% from Continental Europe.[110] The English would always dominate guildsmen admissions, although only in this initial period, when the crown's influence was paramount, were they led by Londoners, at least sixty of them, followed by almost forty men from Bristol. Guildsmen originating from South Wales were also more prominent than would later be the case, encouraged thither no doubt by the relative shortness of the sea crossing and by feedback from the men of this region who had played a prominent role in the original invasion and conquest.[111] Their numbers would fade as the influence of this first generation of invaders diminished.

At this relatively early stage in the development of the lordship of Ireland, only one in six of the new guildsmen is recorded as having come to Dublin from elsewhere in the country. Their numbers may be under-recorded but it must also have been the case that few of the lordship's newly established manors and boroughs were yet in a position to start developing their connections with Dublin.[112] The twin boroughs of Drogheda in Meath and Drogheda in Louth, from which many guildsmen would eventually be drawn, had only been founded in the 1170s and by 1222 are recorded as having supplied only three guildsmen.[113] The city of Kilkenny, which was eventually Ireland's most important inland town, did not receive its foundation charter until 1207 and by 1222 just eight of its townspeople had been admitted to the Dublin merchant guild.[114] In later years, as fledgling towns like these began to grow and prosper, more men from Ireland would seek admission to Dublin's merchant guild. Thus, 52 men from Drogheda and 18 from Kilkenny city became guildsmen between 1222 and 1265 (table 7.4), the difference reflecting the higher urban rank of Drogheda and greater distance of Kilkenny from Dublin.

By the second quarter of the thirteenth century the lordship of Ireland and its capital, Dublin, had entered a halcyon period. Behind the lordship's still

109 *DGMR*, pp xii–xiii, 1–48. **110** For the comparable domination of Welsh towns by English immigrants, see Stevens, *Economy of medieval Wales*, pp 62–4. **111** Flanagan, *Irish society*, pp 137–60. **112** Gearoid Mac Niocaill, *Na Buirgéisí XII–XV aois*, 2 vols (Dublin, 1964), i, pp 72–321, documents more first borough charters during the opening quarter of the thirteenth century than at any other time between 1171 and 1300. **113** Ibid., pp 172–3, 184–5. Drogheda in Meath received its foundation charter in 1194, the law of Breteuil was then conferred by King John on both boroughs in 1213: Bradley, *Topography and layout*, pp 10–11; McHugh, *Drogheda*, pp 1–4, 12. **114** John Bradley, *Kilkenny: Irish historic towns atlas 10* (Dublin, 2000), pp 1, 9.

contested borders manorial structures were bedding down and tenancies were being taken up by a steady influx of colonists, attracted by the availability of land on generous terms in Ireland and pushed by its mounting scarcity in England.[115] Dendrochronological evidence of sustained woodland clearance implies that the lordship's population was expanding, thereby raising output and stimulating demand.[116] Numbers of the boroughs and towns that were an intrinsic part of the colonial venture were putting down roots and, lubricated by an increasing output of coins from the Irish mints, commerce was beginning to prosper.[117] Meanwhile Ireland was becoming drawn into stronger currents of expanding European commerce, exchanging grain, fish, lumber, wool, skins, hides and other primary raw materials for wine, salt, iron, manufactured goods and luxury wares.[118] The building industry continued to boom since, although the post-conquest surge of monastic foundation, which had peaked in the opening decades of the thirteenth century, was drawing to a close, the ambitious scale and protracted nature of many of these projects sustained an ongoing high level of construction activity.[119] Attention also began to shift to erection of the first of the new mendicant houses, mainly in towns, beginning in 1224 with the Dominican friaries in Drogheda and Dublin.[120]

The city was on a roll and undoubtedly its population was increasing. A municipality of sorts had been in existence since *c.*1170 and in 1215 this was formally acknowledged when John granted Dublin's citizens the fee farm of the city and, with it, the right to appoint the provost or reeve (an office which was soon split into two).[121] Within seven years the names of the provosts (later bailiffs) would head the annual lists of those admitted to the merchant guild, which implies that by then the guild merchant was being regulated by the citizens.[122] Then, in 1229, a raft of new royal charters confirmed existing privileges and formally allowed the election of a mayor, to whom the provosts/bailiffs were subordinate and who headed a municipal council of twenty-four.[123] Full civic self-government had arrived and, with it, the need to

115 'it is clear that over wide areas along the east and south coasts, and far inland, there had been, probably in the first two generations after the conquest, a substantial immigration of a genuinely peasant population of English, or sometimes Welsh, origin': A.J. Otway-Ruthven, *A history of medieval Ireland* (New York, 1993), p. 114; Graham, 'High Middle Ages', pp 73–7. For the land-hunger that had developed in England by the end of the thirteenth century, see Campbell, *Great transition*, pp 182–9. **116** Bruce M.S. Campbell and Francis Ludlow, 'Climate, disease and society in late-medieval Ireland' in James Kelly and Tomás Ó Carragáin (eds), *PRIA*, 120C, *Special issue: Climate and society in Ireland: from prehistory to the present* (2021), 188–201. **117** Martin Allen, 'The first sterling area', *Economic History Review*, 70:1 (2017), 82–3, 87–8, 90–1. **118** Childs and O'Neill, 'Overseas trade', pp 498–509. **119** Aubrey Gwynn and Richard Neville Hadcock, *Medieval religious houses: Ireland: with an appendix to early sites* (London, 1970), pp 102–207, 307–43. **120** Gwynn and Hadcock, *Medieval religious houses*, pp 218, 224–5; at about the same time the Franciscans settled in Youghal and Cork: ibid., pp 236, 246–7, 261. **121** Duffy, 'Town and crown', pp 102–7; Lydon, 'Dublin in transition', pp 130, 139; R. Dudley Edwards, 'The beginnings of municipal government in Dublin', *DHR*, 1:1 (1938), 6. **122** Ibid., p. 6. **123** Ibid., pp 6–7;

maintain a list of those newly admitted as citizens and therefore eligible both to stand for election and vote. Presumably, it was into the municipality's coffers that their entry fines and those paid by new guildsmen now flowed. Certainly, a transcript of a now-destroyed pipe roll confirms that by 1275–6 it was the city's bailiffs who were responsible for accounting for the issues of the guild merchant.[124]

From 1221 regular murage grants enabled completion of the extension and strengthening of the city's walls, towers and gates and parallel work on the castle was nearing completion, culminating with the building of a hall and chapel.[125] Several prestigious new ecclesiastical building projects were also initiated. Around 1224 work began on the new Dominican friary of St Saviour, followed in 1227 by erection of a new church for the Augustinian priory of St Thomas and then, from 1233, construction of a house of Franciscan friars.[126] The single most ambitious project, however, was the razing of the old church of St Patrick and its replacement with an episcopal church in the new Gothic style on a scale and with the splendour that befitted its recent elevation (in 1191) to cathedral status.[127] Dedication of the new building took place in 1254. In anticipation of, and in rivalry with, that event, around 1234 the chapter of the older cathedral of Christ Church commissioned a master mason from the Severn Valley to provide their cathedral with a new and enlarged nave of the most up-to-date design and thereby transform it into 'the most distinguished piece of Gothic architecture in Ireland'.[128] None of these endeavours would have been embarked upon without command of substantial financial and material resources, the availability of a skilled workforce and considerable confidence in the future.[129] It can be no coincidence that masons, tilers, joiners, carpenters, glaziers and painters are enumerated among the building workers recorded as having been admitted to the merchant guild around this time.[130] The multiplier effects of work on these major building projects must have stimulated the city's economy and their progress would have been the talk of the town. Visually, they proclaimed Dublin's status as the premier city of a lordship whose future prosperity must have seemed assured. The record of admissions to the Dublin merchant guild reinforces that impression.

From 1222–3 onwards entries in the *DGMR* are dated annually. For the next twenty years or so enrolment remained at a high level, averaging over 119

Mac Niocaill, *Na Buirgéisí*, pp 86–9; Martin, 'Introduction', p. xvi; Clarke, *Dublin, Pt 1* (IHTA), p. 12. **124** Lydon, 'Dublin in transition', p. 136. **125** Clarke, *Dublin, Pt 1* (IHTA), pp 12; Duffy et al. (eds), *Dublin Castle: from fortress to palace*, pp 31–6. **126** Clarke, *Dublin, Pt 1* (IHTA), p.19; Gwynn and Hadcock, *Medieval religious houses*, pp 224, 248. **127** Clarke, *Dublin, Pt 1* (IHTA), pp 12, p. 18; O'Neill, 'Design sources for St Patrick's cathedral', 207–8. **128** Ibid., 225–7; Stalley, 'Construction of the medieval cathedral', p. 70. **129** Eltjo Buringh, Bruce M.S. Campbell, Auke Rijpma and Jan Luiten van Zanden, 'Church building and the economy during Europe's "Age of the Cathedrals", 700–1500 CE', *Explorations in Economic History*, 76:C (2020). **130** *DGMR*, pp 157–9 and https://databases.dublincity.ie/dmgr/occupations.php.

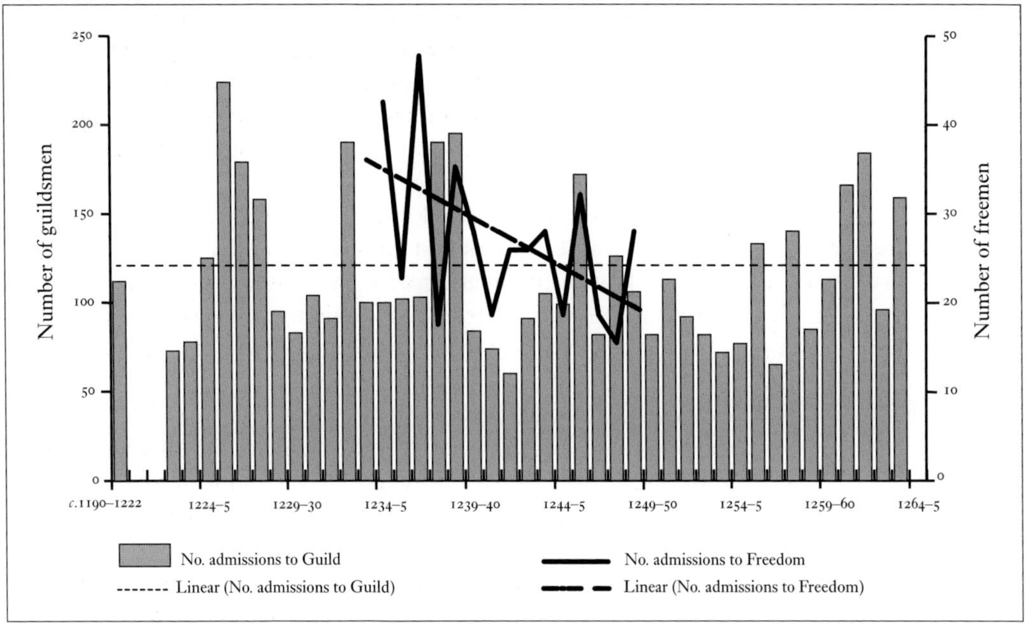

7.4 Admission numbers of Dublin guildsmen, 1222–65, and freemen, 1234–49. *Source: DGMR*, p. 121.

a year, with peaks, never to be exceeded, of 224 in 1225–6, 190 in 1232–3, and 190–5 in 1237–9 when the city's episcopal building boom was in full swing (fig. 7.4). In these peak years either immigration was surging or, more likely, the civic authorities were cracking down on those trading without guild membership within the city's limits. Either way, such elevated numbers of admissions imply that commercial optimism must have been running at a high level. Numbers, however, subsided in the early 1240s and sank to a recorded minimum of 60 in 1241–2. Freemen admissions were also down. The record of these runs from *c.*1230 until 1249, although they are not annually dated until 1234–5. From an annual average of over 30 in the 1230s and absolute peaks of 41 in 1234–5 and 46 in 1236–7, freemen admissions declined to an average of 23 in the 1240s and just 15 in 1247–8 (fig. 7.4). Evidently, becoming a Dublin freeman was losing its appeal. Maybe the expense of becoming a citizen was beginning to outweigh the benefits, especially given that membership of the merchant guild offered a more affordable and less onerous alternative, although its appeal was also waning. Probably, too, the city was losing some of its early dynamism. The major building campaigns of earlier decades were now mostly finished or nearing completion and the erection, starting in 1243, of an imposing new King's Hall in the castle was the sole notable new initiative.[131] Of more general benefit was the city's investment in providing the essential public utility of 'an adequate and continuous supply of fresh water' to the walled city, a project largely completed by 1245.[132] This brought to an end the era of great urban infrastructure improvements. Thereafter, even if Dublin's population was still increasing the numbers joining its merchant guild were not (fig. 7.4).

Place-of-origin information is recorded for a higher proportion of the 1222–45 cohort of guildsmen than those admitted between *c.*1190 and 1222; 64% as opposed to 49% (table 7.1). The equivalent proportion for the freemen admissions is 61% and in both cases over 90% of the recorded places can be identified with some degree of confidence (table 7.1). With the greater availability of locational information, more persons from Irish places-of-origin become visible. Nevertheless, they still constituted a minority of all those admitted – 30% of guildsmen and 22% of freemen – and continued to come overwhelmingly from within a radius of 100–120km from Dublin (table 7.2). Respectively, 83% of guildsmen and 82% of freemen now came from the ten eastern counties that encompassed Dublin's core hinterland. The corollary was that only 6% of guildsmen and 10% of freemen came from Ireland's south and southwest, where its busiest exporting ports were located, with the remainder hailing from the less developed west and north.[133]

Except for Waterford, the dozen most important Irish places sending guildsmen and freemen to Dublin – Wicklow and Wexford to the south, Drogheda, Downpatrick and Carrickfergus to the north, Kilmainham, Naas, Kildare, and Castledermot, inland and to the southwest, and Kells inland and to the northwest – were located within this eastern ten-county hinterland area. Unless this distribution is the product of recording bias, it suggests that whereas Dublin's ability to recruit from its wider hinterland was strong, its capacity to attract prospective guildsmen from the lordship as a whole was weak. This was in direct contrast to the mother kingdom of England, from all parts of which men continued to be admitted to Dublin's merchant guild in significant numbers. In fact, in the case of freemen, Englishmen outnumbered Irishmen by three to one (tables 7.1–2). Men from South Wales were less prominent than formerly, as that region's involvement in the original English invasion and conquest receded, but Germans, Flemings, Frenchmen, Iberians and Italians continued to constitute a small but conspicuous group of those becoming guildsmen or freemen. They, like the English, were representatives of the wider European economy, which in the second quarter of the thirteenth

131 Roger Stalley, 'Irish Gothic and English fashion' in James Lydon (ed.), *The English in medieval Ireland: proceedings of the first joint meeting of the Royal Irish Academy and the British Academy, Dublin, 1982* (Dublin, 1984), pp 74–5; Duffy et al. (eds), *Dublin Castle: from fortress to palace*, pp 33–6. 132 H.F. Berry, 'The water supply of ancient Dublin', *JRSAI*, 21 (1890–91), 557–73. 133 Campbell, 'Benchmarking', pp 908, 916.

century was thriving and into whose orbit, evidently, Dublin was now fully integrated.[134]

The record of admissions to Dublin's merchant guild abruptly ceases in 1265.[135] Until then the established patterns of recruitment more or less prevailed. The city itself underwent no fundamental changes and no significant improvements were made to its institutions, fabric or infrastructure such as might have stimulated renewed growth.[136] Instead, maintenance and consolidation of the *status quo* were the order of the day. Far from rising, admissions to the merchant guild subsided from an annual average of 124 for 1222–45 to 109 for 1245–65 (table 7.1). Admissions were at a particularly low ebb in the early 1250s, with just 65 admissions in 1256–7, the second lowest number on record. The consequent decline in revenues from entry fines may have spurred renewed efforts to enforce guild membership upon those trading within the city, for the 1260s brought a notable recovery and by 1261–2 admissions were back up to numbers last recorded in the 1230s. Marked as were these short-term fluctuations, as is clear from fig. 7.4, they were superimposed upon a long-term trend that until 1265 remained essentially flat. Within ten years, however, the issues of the guild merchant had slumped to £7 14*s*. 8*d*., which implies that either entry fines had been slashed or admissions had shrunk to less than twenty.[137]

Across this period the zone from which Dublin recruited its guildsmen was becoming more sharply focused on the Irish Sea region and upon the city's immediate terrestrial hinterland (fig. 7.5). After 1230 recruitment from England's southwest peninsula, the Welsh Marches, and from South Wales waned. Tellingly, too, London slipped as a leading source of guildsmen, as the commercial interest in Dublin initially taken by men from the English capital diminished (table 7.4). This suggests that the once strong Dublin–London axis was weakening. In fact, in the case of England, only from the north-western counties of Cheshire, Lancashire and Cumberland was there a modest net increase in migration, driven in the main by strengthening movement between Chester and Dublin. The trickle of men heading to Dublin from North Wales and the Lowlands and Borders of Scotland also increased somewhat, borne there by the rising tide of maritime commerce within the northern half of the Irish Sea. Nevertheless, the greatest gains of all were made by Dublin's

134 Robert S. Lopez, *The commercial revolution of the Middle Ages, 950–1350* (Englewood Cliffs, 1971); Campbell, *Great transition*, pp 85–130. 135 *DGMR*, pp 109, 121. 136 Subsequent urban additions included houses of the Friars of the Sack (*c*.1268), Carmelite friars (1270) and Augustinian friars (c.1282): Clarke, *Dublin, Pt 1* (IHTA), p. 19. 137 Lydon, 'Dublin in transition', p. 136: in 1275–6 Dublin was in the king's hands and the account of the bailiff and two others detailing the issues of the guild merchant was enrolled on the pipe roll of 4 Edward I. The original roll was destroyed in 1922 but a transcript was made by Walter Harris in the eighteenth century. Note that the sum enrolled is not an exact multiple of a standard entry fine of 9 shillings. Whether it represented the income from a

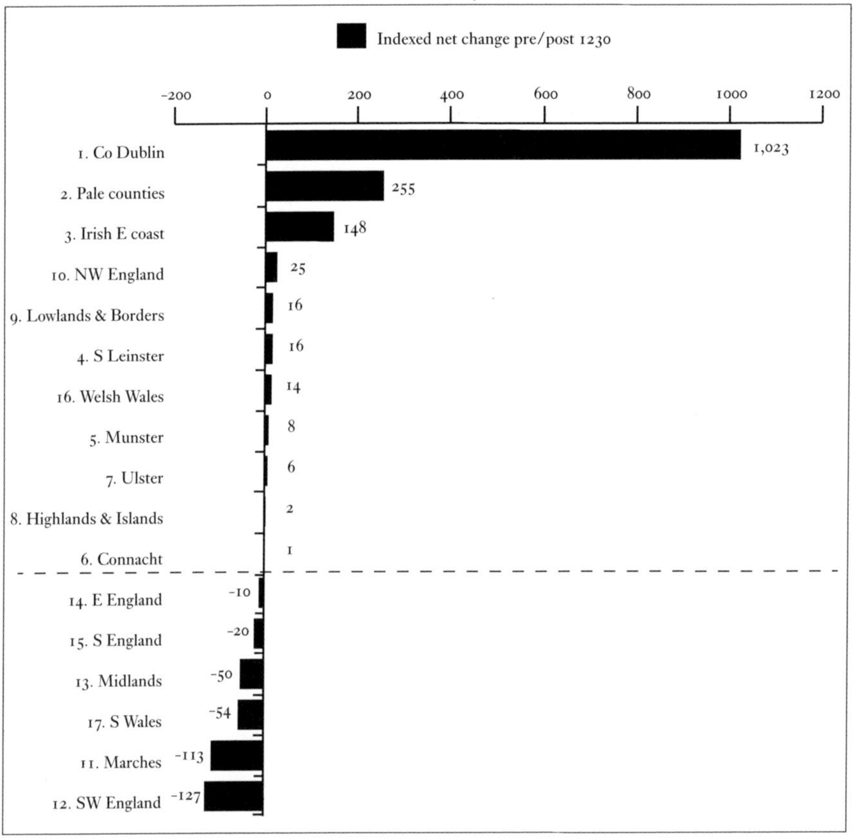

7.5 Regional changes in the recruitment of Dublin guildsmen, pre and post 1230. *Source:* table 7.1.

immediate hinterland within Ireland. Recorded recruitment from Co. Dublin soared, that from the four adjacent counties of Louth, Meath, Westmeath and Kildare, increased significantly, and lesser gains were registered by the east-coast counties of Antrim, Down, Wicklow and Wexford, as these areas responded to the strengthening gravitational attraction of Dublin. In stark contrast, beyond a radius of 75–100km from that city, gains in recruitment were negligible. The rest of the lordship and greater part of the country continued to lie outside Dublin's regular sphere of influence. Admission to its merchant guild of men from Munster, Connacht and Ulster consequently remained as uncommon as before. Recruitment from Germany, the Low Countries, France, Iberia, and Italy continued to be greater, as European commerce experienced an Indian summer of prosperity.[138]

full accounting year is uncertain. **138** Increasing Italian involvement in Irish financial and commercial affairs is possibly indicated by the admissions of Bonisius of Florence in

None of these developments is consistent with a city gaining in metropolitan status and asserting its dominance over the whole of the English lordship and beyond. Rather, they are characteristic of a city which, in common with those with which it most regularly interacted, was consolidating its essentially provincial sphere of influence. Vital to its prosperity and that of the provincial urban system that it headed was its key role within an Irish Sea nexus of commerce triangulated by the three provincial capitals of Dublin, Bristol and Chester and of which Drogheda was a major beneficiary.[139] In this age of sail, the Irish Sea united more than it divided and consistently well over half of those admitted as guildsmen and freemen came from the Irish Sea region broadly defined.[140] Traversing Ireland was evidently more of an obstacle than crossing the Irish Sea with the result that Dublin was more strongly orientated to the east than to the west, with far more guildsmen and freemen coming to it from Britain than from Ireland. For as long as men from elsewhere in this interconnected maritime region saw advantage in being admitted to Dublin's merchant guild, the city's economic success and that of the region that it served were likely to be assured. It was, however, an orientation that worked more to England's advantage than Ireland's, whose urban system headed by Dublin remained underdeveloped.

DUBLIN 1190–1290: A CAPITAL IN WAITING

It was Henry II who in 1171–2 established Dublin as the seat of English power in Ireland. For the next 50–70 years Dublin was a growing city in a land of economic opportunity at a time when men of an entrepreneurial disposition across Britain and Europe were seeking the means of improving their lot, and powerful centrifugal demographic and economic forces were drawing men and their families outwards towards Europe's commercial periphery.[141] It was via the dense, complex and overlapping regional, national and international networks of exchange in which the late twelfth-century city had become enmeshed that information about these opportunities was widely disseminated and acted upon by those whose names are entered in the *DGMR*.[142] In this commercially dynamic and expansive age, it should therefore be no surprise

1261–2, John of Lucca, merchant, in 1262–3, and James the Lombard, merchant of Florence, Persewall' of Lucca and John of Lucca in 1263–4 (*DGMR*, pp 104, 107, 108): O'Sullivan, *Italian merchant bankers*, pp 44–51. **139** For the commercial orientation of Drogheda, see Bradley, *Topography and layout*, pp 23, 26–7; Smith, *Crisis and survival*, pp 169–70; McHugh, *Drogheda*, p. 4. **140** Smith, *Crisis and survival*, p. 169. **141** Edwin S. Murray and James M. Murray, *A history of business in medieval Europe, 1200–1550* (Cambridge, 1999), pp 31–122, discuss the revolution in business methods which began at around this time. R. Rees Davies, *Domination and conquest: the experience of Ireland, Scotland and Wales, 1100–1300* (Cambridge, 1990), pp 5–13. **142** Valante, 'Dublin's economic relations'; Benjamin T. Hudson, 'The changing economy of the Irish Sea

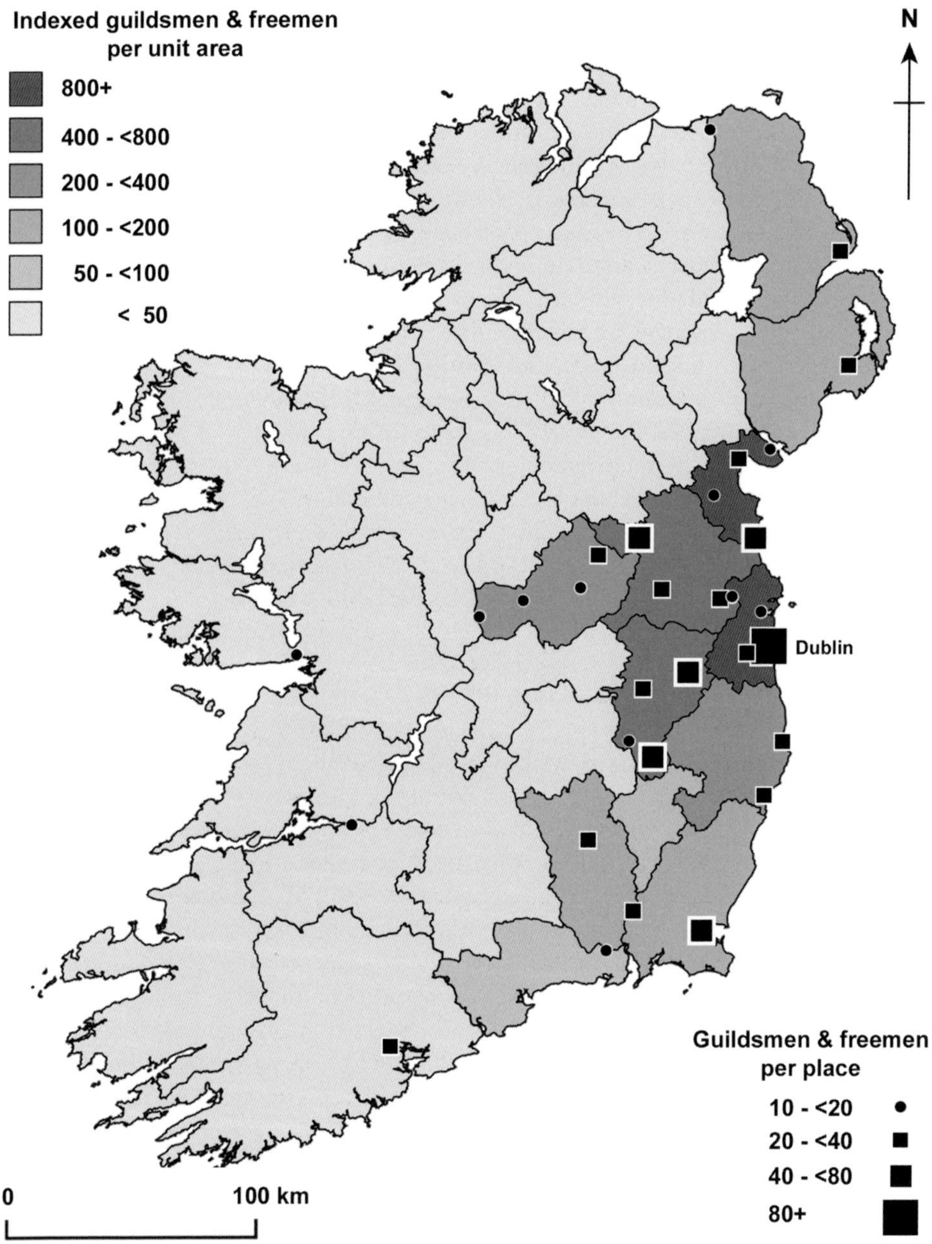

7.6 Ireland: indexed guildsmen and freemen admissions per unit area and places sending a combined total of at least 10 guildsmen and freemen to Dublin, *c.*1190–1265. *Source: DGMR* database.

that the bulk of those who became guildsmen or freemen of Dublin came to the city from a wide geographical spread of places, great and small, extending far beyond Ireland's own shores.[143]

Notwithstanding Dublin's location at the administrative heart of the lordship, it is difficult to resist the conclusion that within Ireland its own sphere of influence failed to penetrate very far. Only within a hinterland rarely extending more than 100km beyond the city does it appear, on the evidence of guildsmen admissions, to have succeeded in establishing itself at the head of an integrated and hierarchical urban system (fig. 7.6). Towns at a greater remove, especially the walled port cities of the south and west, enjoyed a high degree of autonomy and remained largely indifferent to Dublin's commercial allure. When, belatedly, in 1286, Waterford, Cork, Limerick and Drogheda entered into a compact with Dublin 'for the maintenance of their liberties', the first of the triennial meetings that were scheduled to take place was held at the geographically intermediate and non-royal venue of Kilkenny.[144] Self-evidently, Dublin was unable to assert its own primacy and demand that the meeting be held there. Moreover, this experiment in cooperation proved short lived for within another twenty years, in response to the deteriorating political and security situation, Waterford's financial accountability to the government in Dublin had been suspended as it was allowed greater jurisdiction over its own affairs.[145] In due course the same applied to the other walled port towns located 'beyond the Pale'.

Rather than promoting the creation of a developed Irish urban network embracing the lordship as a whole, the effect of conquest was to extend westwards England's own well-articulated urban system to incorporate the individual port cities of Ireland and their respective hinterlands. In Dublin's case the relevant links were hierarchically with London and geographically with Bristol, Gloucester and Chester (table 7.4 and fig. 7.3). The origins of Dublin guildsmen and freemen imply that the city had closer ties with these English cities than with any of the next tier of Irish towns with the notable exception of Drogheda (table 7.4), the only one of them to be located within its immediate hinterland.[146] It, not Waterford, was the second city within the provincial urban hierarchy headed by Dublin. These interactions place Dublin on a par with the second tier of English provincial cities, below York but

province: AD 900–1300' in Brendan Smith (ed.), *Britain and Ireland, 900–1300: insular responses to medieval European change* (Cambridge, 1999), pp 52–66. **143** See the map https://databases.dublincity.ie/ dmgr/map.php. The only thing that is remarkable about this is the survival in the municipal archives of Dublin of the guild merchant roll of 43 parchment membranes and roll of free citizens of three parchment membranes which together contain the personal information that reveals this picture so clearly: Martin, 'Introduction', pp x–xi. **144** Orpen, *Ireland under the Normans*, p. 570; McEneaney, 'Mayors and merchants', p. 168. **145** Ibid., pp 159–60. **146** After Dublin, however, Drogheda's strongest commercial dealings were with Bristol: Smith, *Crisis and survival*, pp 169–70.

similar in rank, scale and functions to Bristol, Lincoln and Norwich, and above such shire towns and episcopal cities as Gloucester, Exeter, Salisbury, Winchester and Canterbury.[147] Whereas London's influence was felt throughout the realm, Dublin's impact within Ireland was altogether more circumscribed: tellingly, three-quarters of its guildsmen and freemen were recruited from within a radius of 150km and those extensive parts of the north and west still under Gaelic control sent almost none (tables 7.1–2 and fig. 7.6).[148]

English rule had endowed thirteenth-century Dublin with the trappings and functions of a capital city. Its city walls, towers and gates, royal castle, two cathedrals (St Patrick's the largest and Christ Church the finest in the land) and constellation of churches and religious houses proclaimed its status as a city of some wealth, standing and importance. It was the nerve centre of the lordship's government. Here was located the exchequer with its staff of barons, chamberlains and clerks, where mayors from the royal boroughs paid their annual farms and account was taken of the revenues collected by the sheriffs in those shires which had so far been created. From mid-century it was joined by the chancery and, later, by the court of common pleas (the first of what eventually were to become the four courts). The justiciar, the treasurer, the justices, the escheator and the coroner, although itinerant, often spent time here and the council and, in due course, parliament not unusually met here.[149] Nevertheless, Dublin's ability to capitalize upon these embryonic governmental and administrative functions was constrained by the itineracy and uneven reach of these officials, the corresponding itineracy of the courts, council and parliament, and the incompleteness of the English conquest.[150]

Under these circumstances Dublin could never be more than a partial capital nor exercise its influence throughout the lordship with the result that outside its own east-coast hinterland it was a capital in little more than name. It is the small numbers of individuals who came to Dublin from the major Irish port towns of Waterford, Cork, Limerick and Galway that is one of the most striking features of the guildsmen and freemen listings, especially when compared with the impressive numbers originating from their British counterpart towns of Carlisle, Chester, Cardiff, Gloucester, Bristol and Exeter,

147 Campbell, 'Benchmarking', pp 908–11. 148 Derek Keene, 'Metropolitan values: migration, mobility and cultural norms, London 1100–1700' in Laura Wright (ed.), *The development of standard English, 1300–1800: theories, descriptions, conflicts* (Cambridge, 2000), pp 93–114. 149 Clarke, *Dublin, Pt 1* (IHTA), p. 23; Otway-Ruthven, *Medieval Ireland*, pp 152–90. 150 'there was no fixed centre of government. The chief governor, though he might remain fixed at Dublin for considerable periods, was constantly journeying through the country, attended by the council, by the "court which followed the justiciar", the later chief place or court of king's bench, and often by the chancery. Justices acting under the various commissions held sessions throughout the country. Though the exchequer was fixed, its officials were not, and were constantly being sent out "to hasten the levy of the king's debts", or on other exchequer business': Otway-Ruthven, *Medieval Ireland*, p. 160.

let alone those from Bordeaux, Dinan and Rouen (table 7.4). The high degree of autonomy enjoyed by this quartet of second-tier Irish towns, all geographically at some remove from Dublin, meant that, contrary to the predictions of both the rank-size rule and, in the case of Dublin guildsmen, the gravity-model of migration, inter-urban migration to Dublin did not necessarily increase as the importance of one or both of the urban locations increased.[151] Drogheda, alone among the largest Irish towns, conformed to both predictions and therefore stands out as functionally the second city to Dublin.

Notwithstanding Dublin's status as the nominal capital of the lordship of Ireland, its circumscribed sphere of influence within both the lordship and Ireland as a whole is more characteristic of a provincial city (fig. 7.6). The dynamism displayed by the city during the opening decades of the thirteenth century, when increased guildsmen recruitment from Galway, Limerick, Cork and Waterford indicates that a geographically more extensive urban hierarchy might have been developing, was not sustained into the second half of that century. The opportunity for Dublin to extend its influence and expand its hinterland passed. Only centuries later, when the political and administrative obstacles to Dublin's growth had been removed and the financial, commercial and transport infrastructures appropriate to a capital city had been put in place, would Dublin successfully mirror London and, on one hand, eclipse in scale, influence and importance the largest of England's provincial cities and, on the other, establish its primacy over the provincial cities of Ireland.[152] Building upon institutional foundations laid following the English conquest, it was the creation during the seventeenth century of a fully integrated Irish urban system that enabled Dublin to achieve the hegemonic status it had attained by 1790 and, conversely, the lack of such a system that in 1290 denied it that status.[153] That the opposite was so clearly the case in England is evidenced by the fact that by 1290 London was already the national capital in both name and function, with a reach that since at least 1190 had extended as far as Dublin.[154] The enrolments in the Dublin Guild Merchant Roll thus provide a tantalizing glimpse of, on the one hand, a well-articulated English urban and commercial network and, on the other, a corresponding Irish network in the making but not yet fully evolved.

151 Gabaix and Ioannides, 'Evolution of city size distributions'; Ullman, 'Role of transportation', p. 174; Haggett, *Geography*, pp 329–32. 152 On the emergence of London as the indubitable capital and primate city of England, see Keene, 'London', pp 211–16; Caroline M. Barron, 'London 1300–1540' in Palliser (ed.), *Cambridge urban history*, pp 395, 438–40. The estimates by de Vries (*European urbanization*, pp 270–1) indicate that by 1700 Dublin had overtaken all other British and Irish cities to become the second in size after London. 153 Dickson, *Dublin*, pp 152–200. 154 Campbell, 'Benchmarking', pp 908–9; Keene, 'London', pp 211–16.

'Suitable men of good repute' and a 'public fornicator': the many priors of St John's hospital in Dublin

GRACE O'KEEFFE

INTRODUCTION

> 'It happens now that those in charge of hospices, leperhouses, almshouses or hospitals disregard the care of such places and fail to loosen the hold of those who have usurped the goods, possessions and rights of these places. They indeed permit them to slip and be lost completely and the buildings to fall into ruin.'

Such was the proclamation of the Council of Vienne of 1311–12. In an effort to stop, and presumably reverse, this decline it recommended that they 'should compel the persons in charge to receive the poor people and maintain them in accordance with the resources and revenues of the places' and that these institutions were to be 'governed by prudent suitable men of good repute'.[1] It ends with a declaration that these recommendations were not intended to apply to the 'hospices of military or religious orders', which suggests that a recognized difference existed between these latter institutions and the leper-houses, almshouses and hospitals listed in the opening paragraph of the statute; the hospices were merely reminded that they were to abide by the discipline of their superiors and observe the rules of their order. Such a comprehensive reprimand can only have been prompted by reports reaching the papacy of the mismanagement of those charitable houses under its ultimate jurisdiction.

From the fourteenth century, and probably earlier, not only were questions being raised about the quality of those in charge of the hospitals, but the standard of care offered, and indeed the bona fides of those presenting themselves to these houses of charity increasingly came under scrutiny. A sixteenth-century literary source depicts the difficulties faced by hospitals in determining between those beggars and infirm arriving at the door who were genuine and those who were 'idle slouches' and 'deceivers of people'.[2] In 1536 St John the Baptist's in Dublin, once the source of donations from the wealthiest and most prominent of Dublin's citizens, was considered to serve no purpose and to be of no good.[3] A year later, when John Alen was recommending

1 *Decrees of the ecumenical councils*, ed. Norman P. Tanner (2nd ed., 2 vols, Washington, DC, 1990), i, no. 17, pp 374–5. 2 Robert Copland, 'The highway to the spital-house' in A.V. Judges (ed.), *The Elizabethan underworld* (2nd ed., London, 1965), pp 1–25. 3 *Letters and papers, foreign and domestic, Henry VIII* (21 vols, London, 1862–1932), xi, no. 1416, p. 564.

the suppression of St Thomas's abbey, All Hallows and St John's, it was again reiterated that in these were places 'where is nother greate hospytalytie kept, nor yet ther nedyth greatly'.[4] Those assessing these religious houses in the heady period prior to the Dissolution may have had their own personal and financial reasons for recommending their closure. However, that there were only three pensions issued to the hospital on its demise, presumably as there were only three brothers still living in the house (the final prior, Thomas Everard and brothers Robert Sex and Walter Cartan), would suggest a corresponding low number of domestic staff, as well as of those for whom the hospital had initially been founded, the poor and sick. It seems that by this point it no longer held its position as the largest house of charity in Dublin.

The hospital of St John the Baptist was the first known foundation in Ireland of the *Fratres Cruciferi* (crutched friars), regular canons under the rule of St Augustine. Located outside the Newgate, in the western suburb of medieval Dublin, it was in existence by *c.*1188 and was suppressed in 1539 as part of Henry VIII's dissolution of the monasteries. The site of the hospital is today largely occupied by the Augustinian church of SS Augustine and John on Thomas Street. The hospital was founded by Ailred Palmer and his wife; they also donated to it their burgage plot in the city of Dublin.[5] As head of the priory and hospital the priors must then come under scrutiny. Although no evidence of the minutiae of hospital administration has been unearthed, as the figurehead of the largest charitable institution in the city, the quality of leadership provided by the prior, his family, contacts, perhaps even his political allegiances cannot be ignored.

How can we assess whether, as has been assumed, the hospital entered a period of decline in the fourteenth century, and how much responsibility for this was down to the heads of the house? The clearest method of assessing this decline is by examination of the hospital's finances. In her study of St Giles's hospital, Norwich, Carole Rawcliffe noted that 'the administrative structure … followed a model traditionally adopted on most lay estates of any kind … [as each] of the hospital's appropriated rectories, manors and other substantial properties was placed under the control of a bailiff, reeve, rent collector or farmer, who answered, in turn, to the receiver general'.[6] Unlike St John's, the muniments of St Giles's allow for a relatively detailed financial analysis. Rawcliffe further warns against 'sweeping generalisations about indifference and lack of vocation' when assessing hospitals whose archives were either not managed well or destroyed following suppression. To that end, the conclusions reached here about any deterioration of service provided by St John's, and the

4 *State papers, Henry VIII* (11 vols, London, 1830–52), ii, p. 484. 5 *Vetera monumenta Hibernorum et Scotorum historiam illustantia quae ex Vaticani, Neapolis ac Florentiae tabularis depromsit et ordine chronologico diposuit, 1216–1547*, ed. Augustinus Theiner (Rome, 1864), p. 215. 6 Carole Rawcliffe, *Medicine for the soul: the life, death and resurrection of an English medieval hospital, St Giles, Norwich,* c.*1249–1550* (Stroud, 1999), p. 67.

merits of its priors, will be made by examining those sources which mention the hospital and an attempt will be made to determine trends in donation or quality of management.

This contribution will attempt a prosopographical examination of the priors. It is not a conclusive exercise, and indeed some of what follows is speculative, occasionally several individuals are offered as possibilities when the current available evidence does not clearly point to one individual. It will however offer some insight into the political and familial connections of men operating at this level of society in medieval Dublin. It will demonstrate the impact of English settlers in Ireland, but will also show that the Irish were not entirely excluded from such prestigious positions. The exciting work of Joseph Harbison and René Gapert (in this volume, above) on the crania found on the site of the former hospital is a reminder that more can and will be uncovered about the hospital's practices.

THE REGISTER AND THE LISTS

The main source for information on the hospital is its register, or cartulary. The register of St John the Baptist's in Dublin carries no scribal autograph that would help to define the period of time during which the main clerk was at work transcribing the original muniments in the hospital's possession. However, a note from Sir James Ware, who briefly had possession of the manuscript, would seem to indicate that the prior responsible for commissioning the cartulary was one of the late fourteenth-century holders of that office, William Gerard.[7] If Ware is correct in this assertion, it might possibly have been related to the complaints being made about the mismanagement of the hospital, perhaps an attempt to gather together all the surviving deeds of the hospital and make a transcription should disputes about the hospital's right to lands or rents arise in the future. Gerard may have been attempting to counter the claims made against him: it is known that priors and other head of houses 'who hoped to exploit a potentially lucrative source of income at the expense of staff and patients, moved quickly to confiscate documents of title, statutes and … common seals'.[8] This may have been Gerard's attempt to prove that he at least had done no wrong. It may even be the case that he was not himself responsible for setting the scribes their task and that the creation of the register came about as a result of Archbishop Minot's investigations. The head of a religious house did not always of course commission a cartulary for

7 This manuscript, MS Rawlinson, B.498, is currently housed in the Bodleian Library, Oxford. This is the MS on which *Register of the Hospital of St John the Baptist*, ed. Eric St John Brooks (Dublin, 1936), a transcription and examination of the MS, was based (hereafter *Reg. St John*). 8 Carole Rawcliffe, 'Passports to paradise: how English medieval hospitals and almshouses kept their archives', *Archives*, 27:106 (2002), 14.

negative reasons – fear of theft, fire or legal disputes – as such a record could also be a source of pride for a house, the opportunity to demonstrate the many acquisitions made by it. In this capacity it might have functioned almost as a brochure for prospective benefactors, who might see at an easy glance the illustrious citizens whose souls were being prayed for by the infirm within the hospital.

In his edition of the register, Eric St John Brooks provides a list of the priors that combines both James Ware's list (attached to the manuscript) with his own investigations.[9] Where he could, St John Brooks provided the probable dates for each of the listed priors. Given the patchy nature of the sources, many of these dates are only suggestions and there are many gaps in his succession list. One of the difficulties with the list is how best to interpret the gaps in dates. Some might mean that several years lapsed between the death of one prior and the election of his successor, while others may simply be due to a lack of evidence for those years. St John Brooks's list overlooks two men who were named elsewhere as priors, a John Walsh who, it was claimed, held the office in 1322 and a John Onextiffe who supposedly held the office the following year.[10] These will be dealt with in further detail below.

Ailred, founder and first prior

Ailred Palmer has been the cause of much speculation, because of his name (forename and surname). Could he have been an Hiberno-Norse citizen of Dublin who remained in the town following its capture by the English?[11] Had he been on pilgrimage, hence earning the 'Palmer' sobriquet/ surname?[12] Possibly, just as it is also possible that he was English by birth, given that he bore an Anglo-Saxon name.[13] The search for him began in the most comprehensive source for the nomenclature of a certain swathe of medieval Dubliners, the Dublin guild merchant roll. Far from being one of a kind, this search quickly throws up evidence of many Ailreds, or other variants such as Alured, Eilward. Additional difficulties lie in the fact that there is even more than one Ailred Palmer listed. An Eilward Cornubiensis Palmer, Eilward Palmer, Ailwardus Frater and Ailward (and Alfwine) Palmer are all present in the roll.[14] Ailred

9 *Reg. St John*, pp xx–xxi; all subsequent references to St John Brooks's dating of the priors refers to the list supplied on these two pages, additional information unearthed through research otherwise fully footnoted. 10 Archdall, *Monasticon Hibernicum: or, an history of the abbies, priories, and other religious houses in Ireland* (London and Dublin, 1786), p. 202; repeated in John Warburton, James Whitelaw and Rrobert Walsh, *History of the city of Dublin* (2 vols, London, 1818), i, p. 347; the date given for Onextiffe would appear to be wrong: see below. 11 *Reg. St John*, p. v. 12 See Catherine Swift, 'Palmers as ex-crusaders in Irish urban environments? The evidence of the Dublin guild merchant roll' in Edward Coleman, Paul Duffy and Tadhg O'Keeffe (eds), *Ireland and the Crusades* (Dublin, 2022), pp 70–5 (and her discussion of the term *palmerus* in this volume, above). 13 William George Searle, *Onomasticon Anglo-Saxonicum: a list of Anglo-Saxon proper names from the time of Beda to that of King John* (Cambridge, 1897), pp 46–8. 14 *DGMR*, p. 6 (2nd column),

could conceivably be any of those listed in the roll of the merchants' guild, such as Alured de Kermerdin (Carmarthen).[15] In the very earliest days of the English invasion an Alured of Lincoln and an Alured of Poitou are known to have sent goods from England to Ireland, probably as part of the preparation for the landing of Henry II.[16] He could possibly be the Alured of Wendover who with Reiner Palmer and Ralph of Norwich was granted a piece of land outside the western gate of the city by a W, styled clerk of Hamwoda.[17] Given the fluidity of naming practices at that time, an Ailred who was a merchant could also have been Ailred, a former pilgrim.

Not only do many Ailreds appear as part of the Dublin merchant scene, so too do several individuals listed as 'son of' Ailred. In previous scholarship it was believed that Ailred and his wife were childless, and hence the donation of their burgage plot to the hospital. It is not implausible however that they had raised a family and that once any children of theirs had reached maturity both parents wished to devote their life to God, in this instance inspired by the succour of the poor and sick. Ailred, the founder, is believed to have died *c.*1202. Taking *c.*1185–8 as the foundation date, it is clearly possible that he had adult children at that time. Nicholas Palmer, son of Aillarid, William, son of Aldred and Robert de [...] son of Alewardi could all be possible candidates.[18] The earliest extant date for an Ailred Palmer is as a witness to a charter of Earl Richard, or Strongbow, to Hamund Mac Turcaill (*c.*1174).[19] That this was in fact the Ailred Palmer of St John's is strengthened by some of his fellow witnesses, especially Roger, brother of Hern, who is probably the man more usually known as Roger, brother of Haim, listed among those whose donations had been received by the hospital by 1188.

Osbert de Colesell

The second prior listed by St John Brooks is Osbert de Colesell whose dates are given as *c.*1217–*c.*1220. There are several aspects of existing research into Osbert, and his dates as prior, that are still uncertain. The evidence presented here is for all suitable candidates, and none of the possibilities will be ruled out until it can be definitive. St John Brooks points to a charter in the Register of St Thomas's abbey which could suggest that until *c.*1217 the hospital was in fact without a prior,[20] while nonetheless dating one charter which named

p. 10 (2nd column), p. 20 (1st column) and p. 27 (2nd column). **15** Ibid., p. 26 (2nd column). **16** *CDI*, i, nos 2, 28 and 30. **17** *Reg. St Thomas*, no. 438, pp 384–5; by calling the gate Western, rather than New, the charter can probably be dated to the 1180s: for the dating of this and the expansion of this new area of medieval Dublin, see Cathal Duddy, 'The western suburb of medieval Dublin: its first century', *Irish Geography*, 34:2 (2001), 159. **18** *DGMR*, for Nicholas see p. 13 (1st column) who is listed after a Robert *gener* Aillard, for William see p. 14 (1st column) and same for Robert. **19** *CCD*, no. 1. **20** *Reg. St Thomas*, no. 371, part 3, p. 322; in a deed in Gilbert's publication, no. ii, pp 321–2, Osbert de Colesell is named as prior of the hospital. The manuscript of this publication is housed in the Bodleian Library, Oxford. In a later transcript of this, Osbert is named as Osbert de

Osbert as prior to *c.*1210.[21] Another charter dated to the same year (*c.*1210) was witnessed by 'O' as prior.[22] The confusion also extends to the date Osbert left office. The charter given as evidence for the 1220 date of his priorship (Osbert appears as one of the witnesses) is a charter to Holy Trinity from Strongbow's daughter, Isabel de Clare, for the salvation of her father's soul and that of her husband, William Marshal.[23] The editor of the charter, H.J. Lawlor, dated it not to 1220 but to *c.*1210 with an explanation suggesting that the date can be no later than 1212. The calendared edition of the Christ Church deeds dates the same deed as *c.*1200.[24]

Unfortunately, the witness list is of limited assistance as those named with their official positions held them for well over a decade, such as Simon, bishop of Meath, the first witness, who held his position 1192–1224,[25] and S[imon], abbot of St Thomas, who was abbot for probably much of the first two decades of the thirteenth century.[26] Even William, baron of Naas, could refer to William fitz Maurice (d. 1199) or his son, William fitz Willam (d. 1227). Other Dublin notables such as Audoen Brun and Gilbert de Livet were also active citizens in the early thirteenth century. That Isabel died in 1220 and Marshal a year earlier, may suggest that St John Brooks ignored Lawlor's dating and instead placed the grant, which was partially for the salvation of Marshal's soul, between the death of William and Isabel.[27] However this is not the earliest reference in Ireland to an Osbert de Colesell, nor indeed do the references refer solely to his religious activities.

Coleshill in Warwickshire was one of the manors home to the Clinton family, where one of the earliest of the family, Geoffrey de Clinton, was an administrator in Henry I's treasury in the 1120s.[28] The Clintons were also cousins of the de Verduns and it is in this capacity that they appear in Ireland, more particularly in Co. Louth where they were tenants of both the de Verduns and Pipards.[29] Prior to 1191 an Osbert de Coleshull (assumed here to be the

Colchester (RIA 12 D 2, fol. 33v); a copy of RIA 12 D 2 also repeats the Colchester toponym (RIA 12 D 38, fol. 33v). Without having the opportunity to check the Bodleian MS on which Gilbert based his publication, it seems preferable to follow both Gilbert and St John Brooks's rendering of this name rather than that of a late copy of the original. **21** *Reg. St John*, no. 13. **22** Ibid., no. 443. Even if this speculative date is incorrect, the charter is issued by Donat O'Lonergan, archbishop of Cashel, who held the position 1208–16 which, if 'O' is Osbert, would support an earlier date than 1217 for his position as prior; F.J. Byrne, 'Bishops, 1111–1534' in T.W. Moody, F.X. Martin and F.J. Byrne (eds), *A new history of Ireland, ix: maps, genealogies, lists* (Oxford, 1984), p. 290. **23** H.J. Lawlor, 'Calendar of the *Liber Niger* and *Albus* of Christ Church, Dublin', *PRIA*, 27C (1908–9), 18–19. **24** *CCD*, no. 13, p. 38. **25** Byrne, 'Bishops', p. 285, Simon Rochfort. **26** Aubrey Gwynn, 'Early history of St Thomas's abbey', *JRSAI*, 84:1 (1954), 18–20. **27** For a synopsis of Isabel's life, see M.T. Flanagan, 'Clare, Isabel de, suo jure countess of Pembroke (1171x6–1220)', *Oxford dictionary of national biography* (Oxford, 2004) [hereafter *ODNB*] online ed., September 2010; for William, see David Crouch, 'Marshal, William (I), fourth earl of Pembroke (*c.*1146–1219)', *ODNB* online ed., May 2007. **28** David Crouch, 'Clinton, Geoffrey of (*d.c.*1133)', *ODNB* online ed., May 2007. **29** Brendan Smith,

later prior Osbert) began granting land to St Thomas's in Dublin.[30] One deed in particular demonstrates the early date of his settlement in Louth; he granted to the canons all the tithes of the land of Heoth Mac Uballether and one carucate in the land of Macunekuleth and one other carucate of land of his conquest in Uriel, with the promise that if he failed to conquer this land he would provide an alternative for the house elsewhere.[31] Among the witnesses to his grant were Agatha, his wife, and Alexander, his son. In a separate grant Osbert had initially granted St Thomas's tithes of only the vill of Macubalother,[32] and it is from the confirmation of this by the bishop of Louth, Christian (or Gilla Críst Ua Mucaráin), that Osbert's activities in Ireland can be dated prior to 1191 as the grant was witnessed by Eugene, bishop of Clonard, who held the position 1177–91.[33]

Meanwhile in Coleshill itself, another Osbert was, in 1207, granted royal approval for a weekly market and an annual fair in the manor of Coleshill.[34] This same Osbert sided with the barons against King John but was restored to his lands by Henry III,[35] and following his death in 1222 his son Thomas and wife Elysant survived him. Records of this Osbert make no mention of his holding any lands or having ambitions or a life outside England, while the Osbert de Coleshill who became part of his extended family's settlement in Louth would, based on the personal names of his wife and son, appear to have exclusively resettled in Ireland, leaving whatever possessions he had in Warwickshire to the care of others. How closely could they have been related? Hagger's reference to Osbert de Clinton of Coleshill as the grantor of land in 1195 to St Thomas's abbey mentions also that he was Bertram de Verdun's cousin. This is the Bertram de Verdun whose Dublin home, known as Bertram's Court, lay opposite the hospital. Osbert was a common name among

Colonisation and conquest in medieval Ireland: the English in Louth, 1170–1330 (Cambridge, 1999), p. 38; for the later history of the Clintons of Co. Louth, see J.B. Leslie, 'The Clinton family in County Louth', *County Louth Archaeological Journal*, 2:4 (1911), 398–412. **30** Mark S. Hagger, *The fortunes of a Norman family: the de Verduns in England, Ireland and Wales, 1066–1316* (Dublin, 2001), p. 199. **31** *Reg. St Thomas*, no. 60, pp 49–50; Hagger dates this charter to 1195 (*The fortunes of a Norman family*, p. 199). **32** *Reg. St Thomas*, no. 39, p. 39. **33** Ibid., no. 314, pp 267–8. See Byrne, 'Bishops', p. 285 for Eugene's dates. Christian held his bishopric 1187–93 (ibid., p. 274). Other notables on the list include Ralph, archdeacon of Meath, who later became bishop of the same, 1227–30 (ibid., p. 285); Aubrey Gwynn has also indicated that one of the other witnesses on this list, a Robert of Ardee, may be the same as Robert, parson of Ardee, and as such an indication of the Pipard organization of parish life in their new settlement of Ardee (Aubrey Gwynn, 'Ardee in the Middle Ages', *County Louth Archaeological Journal*, 11:2 (1946), 82). **34** *The Victoria history of the counties of England: a history of Warwick*, eds various (8 vols, London, 1904–69), iv, p. 50. **35** *Rotuli litterarum clausarum*, ed. Thomas Duffus Hardy (2 vols, London, 1833), i, p. 311 (a). In addition to various members of the de Verdun family, the same list also mentions Henry of Wotton, also a de Verdun tenant in Ireland. In 1238 Henry de Wotton was appointed as attorney to Roesia de Verdun (*CDI*, i, no. 2446, pp 356–6); Hagger, *The fortunes of a Norman family*, p. 199 suggests that Bertram had granted land to the de

the Warwickshire Clintons in the twelfth and thirteenth centuries and, while the Louth Osbert, probably the later prior of the hospital, was certainly from Coleshill, which branch of the Clintons he represented cannot be stated with certainty. If he was born outside marriage, there is no record of an exemption being granted to allow his elevation to religious orders.

The de Verdun connection with St John the Baptist's in Dublin is not as strong as that of many of the earlier English families who came to own land in Dublin, as is also the case with the Pipard family, the other Clinton cousins. Despite this, Roger Pipard, younger brother of Gilbert who came to Ireland with the Lord John in 1185, is the ascribed founder in 1207 of a priory and hospital of crutched friars in Ardee, also dedicated to St John the Baptist.[36] In Dundalk, the foundation of the priory and hospital of St Leonard, also of the order of crutched friars, is attributed to the de Verduns, either Bertram or his son Nicholas. Considering that he then had family connections with the Ardee and Dundalk foundations it is perhaps surprising that Osbert came to be prior of the Dublin hospital. Conversely, it could be expected that under Osbert the three hospitals would have had some level of interaction, or that St John's in Dublin would have had a greater volume of donations from Louth-based magnates, which based on extant evidence is not the case.[37]

Daniel

Osbert was succeeded in his post by Daniel, whose dates are *c.*1220 to *c.*1248. In addition, Daniel was the first of several priors who was also elected to a bishopric while simultaneously holding his position as prior. Before April 1238 Daniel was elected as bishop of Emly in the province of Cashel, but he was unsuccessful in getting possession of the temporalities.[38] One piece of evidence to suggest an earlier date than 1220 for his appointment as prior is a charter dated to November 1219 in the cartulary of the Augustinian abbey of Oseney in Oxfordshire where Daniel, prior of St John's in Dublin, is named as one of the witnesses.[39] Certainly Daniel was one of several heads of religious houses called upon by papal mandate to mediate in a dispute between Richard Warminster, a canon of St Patrick's in Dublin, and St Mary's abbey, regarding tithes.[40] A decade later an anomaly appears in a charter detailing an agreement made between the Augustinian priory of Llanthony Prima and Adam de Cusack concerning land in Killeen, Co. Meath. It mentions that it was made in

Wottons, based on the existence by 1191 of a *Wotonrathe* in Dundalk. **36** Gwynn, 'Ardee in the Middle Ages', p. 82; Aubrey Gwynn and R. Neville Hadcock, *Medieval religious houses: Ireland* (London, 1970). **37** Twelve charters concern areas within Co. Louth, three of which are grants made by the hospital (*Reg. St John* nos 234, 235, 236, 237, 238, 239, 240, 241, 242, 243, 244 and 245). The last is undated by St John Brooks and no. 235 is fourteenth-century, the remainder are all thirteenth. **38** Byrne, 'Bishops', p. 297; Archdall, *Monasticon Hibernicum*, p. 200. **39** *Cartulary of Oseney abbey*, ed. H.E. Salter (6 vols, Oxford Historical Society, vols, 89–91, 97–8, 101), v, 612 B, pp 128–9. **40** Arlene Hogan, *The priory of Llanthony Prima and Secunda in Ireland: lands, patronage and politics* (Dublin,

the presence of, amongst others, a 'B' as prior of the hospital and, given that this was dated 1233–44, it would appear to be in the middle of Daniel's time as prior. This either represents a break in priors, and the only known reference to this 'B', or this was in fact Daniel, and a scribal error at some point when a *D* was mistaken for a *B*.[41]

Walter de Southwell

Although the latest date for Daniel in the role of prior is *c.*1248, the next prior, Walter de Southwell, does not appear as his successor until 1251.[42] Four years later Walter was elected as bishop of Waterford.[43] There may have been some confusion within the papacy as Pope Alexander IV's letter of confirmation names William, rather than Walter, as the bishop-elect.[44] The error was corrected as a bull of Alexander's issued in 1257 clearly names Walter as the bishop.[45] Like other ecclesiastical leaders, Walter was involved in acting on behalf of the papacy in dispute settlement, and at times causing such disputes, like that between the dioceses of Waterford and Lismore regarding their respective claims to lands.[46]

Jordan

If the earliest date of the next prior, Jordan, *c.*1269–*c.*1276, is correct, it would appear that Walter did not relinquish his role as prior upon assuming the office of bishop of Waterford. Jordan's imprint on records is slight, largely confined to a series of grants to him and from him, and a number of legal disputes, in his capacity as prior of the hospital.[47]

Bartholomew

Bartholomew, prior *c.*1278–90, may have been a brother in the hospital before becoming prior: in one of the two wills in the register a brother Bartholomew was appointed as co-executor to the will of Gilbert le Decer, who requested burial in the hospital.[48]

John Scot

John Scot served as prior *c.*1297–1311. Aside from the register, Scot was also named in a deed in the Ormond collection, which also appears in the Oseney cartulary. He may possibly be the same John Scot who in 1293 was given letters of attorney to cover Ireland and England on behalf of Cambinus del Pape, clerk.[49]

2008), p. 131. 41 Ibid., no. LXXXVIII, pp 304–5. 42 *Reg. St John*, no. 502. 43 Byrne, 'Bishops', p. 297. St John Brooks, based on Ware, gives the date of de Southwell's death as *c.*1268 whereas *NHI* gives *c.*24 March 1271. 44 *Pontificia Hibernia*, ed. Maurice Sheehy (2 vols, Dublin, 1962–5), ii, no. 401, pp 230–2. 45 *CStM*, ii, no. 15, pp 120–2. 46 Assumpta O'Neill, 'Waterford diocese, 1096–1363', *Decies: Journal of the Old Waterford Society*, 45 (Spring 1992), 36–7. 47 *Reg. St John*, nos 39, 149, 150, 215, 216, 220, 444. 48 *Reg. St John*, no. 66. 49 *Calendar of Ormond deeds*, ed. Edmund Curtis (5 vols, Dublin,

John Palmer

Scot was followed by John Palmer, *c.*1317–*c.*1324–31. In 1321 Palmer, on behalf of the hospital, granted Herbert de Marisco 'ninety-five acres of land and a mill in "le Milleton" in the tenement of Cloghir'.[50]

William Gerard / Thomas de Landa

The precise date at which Palmer's time as prior ends and that of the next prior, William Gerard, begins is unclear. In 1331 Thomas de Landa was appointed prior, following Gerard. The record of de Landa's appointment is the only evidence that Gerard had in fact ever held the position at this time.[51] It states that 'William Gerardi has resigned the said office, to which he was elected on the death of John called "Palmer"'. De Landa in turn was dead by 1340 at which point William Gerard was apparently back in the role of prior.[52] How successful that was is doubtful: in April 1363 the archbishop of Dublin, Thomas Minot, was ordered to investigate 'rents, lands, vineyards, rights and goods thereof, which Prior William and his predecessors are said to have alienated and wasted, to the injury of the men, women, and orphans living therein' and to remove the prior if he was found guilty.[53] Who brought the charge to the attention of the papacy is not recorded in this, a single and highly important insight into the inner workings of the hospital, and is also the last date for Gerard. Complaints against priors regarding the mismanagement of their houses can be found in other areas in Ireland: the mid fifteenth-century archbishop of Armagh, John Mey, investigated the prior of the house of St Leonard outside Drogheda (also a hospital run by the crutched friars) on charges of having neglected 'to care for the sick and needy in accordance with the purpose of the foundation of his house', after which its prior, Clynton, suffered a sentence of deprivation.[54]

John

We hear nothing further of Prior William Gerald following the 1363 investigation into his property dealings, and the hospital's register appears to contain no mention whatever of his successor, named simply as John, other than, ironically, a 1380 conveyance by him on behalf of the hospital of a property-plot in the parish of St John of Bothe Street to a certain John Blaknay and his wife Alice.[55]

1932–41), i, no. 452, p. 177; *Oseney cartulary*, v, no. 618 B, p. 138; *CDI*, iv, no. 20, p. 8. **50** *Calendar of Ormond deeds*, ii, no. 555, p. 230. **51** *CPL*, ii, p. 343. **52** *Reg. St John*, no. 577 (1341) and no. 578 (1346). **53** *CPL*, iv, p. 87. Minot is not named in the letter; see Byrne, 'Bishops', p. 310 for his name and dates. **54** *Registrum Iohannis Mey: the register of John Mey archbishop of Armagh, 1443–1456*, eds W.G.H. Quigley and E.F.D. Roberts (Belfast, 1972), nos 341–2, pp 359–60. **55** *Reg. St John*, no. 145.

Henry Randolph

Happily, the next prior, Henry Randolph, left more of an impression in surviving records despite what would appear to have been a short tenure in office. In October 1381 he secured letters of attorney for Adam Oheth and John Motyng.[56] This is the earliest reference to Adam who was himself prior before the end of the fourteenth century.[57] Four years later Henry was again granted letters of attorney, this time under the names John Rede and William Bernard.[58] Much like his predecessor William Gerard, Henry Randolph got himself embroiled in some personal legal issues. In 1384 he was apparently accused, along with Robert Grandon (called one of his monks, presumably meaning that he was a brother of St John's), of taking £200 worth of money and goods from a Thomas Gifford and his wife Maud.[59] The prior's defence seems to have been based on a technicality in how he was named in the writ.[60] He was still prior in late 1385 and according to Ware he remained so in 1386 and hence perhaps his defence was a successful one.[61]

Richard/Adam O'Hethe (Ua Haeda)

His successor is named only as 'Richard' by St John Brooks, and only the year 1395 is supplied. As Richard appears to have regained his position when Adam O'Hethe ran into difficulties the two will be considered together. Adam's surname, O'Hethe/Ua hAeda points to an Irish heritage, which, in a house at the heart of the English colony in Ireland, might seem surprising. This is all the more odd since '[t]he Irish parliament made attempts as early as 1310 to exclude Irish clerics from holding benefices in the English colony, and in contrast to much anti-Irish legislation, there is evidence that there were relatively frequent efforts made to enforce these prohibitions'.[62] A clue to how he was able to attain the position may lie in a 1381 concession to 'Odo, William, John and Edmund O'Hethe that they and all their issue may be of free status and use English law in the same manner in which the English in Ireland enjoy it'.[63] This was a month after O'Hethe had been appointed attorney for the then prior, Henry Randolph. In 1398 Adam was still being called a brother in St

56 *CIRCLE*, PR 5 Rich. II, §37. 57 Archdall, quoting King's *Collectanea* as his source, states that Adam O'Hethe was prior and in this year received a pardon for crimes. This would appear to be an incident which occurred *c.*1400 and is the only reference to Adam being prior on this date (*Monasticon Hibernicium*, p. 203), an error repeated in Warburton, Whitelaw and Walsh, *History of the city of Dublin*, i, p. 348. 58 *CIRCLE*, PR 9 Rich. II, §143. 59 Archdall, *Monasticon Hibernicium*, pp 203–4, based on National Library Ireland MS 13, vol. 13, p. 55; TCD MS 579/2, 77r. 60 'The defence the prior set up was, that in the writ he was named prior of the house of St John without Newgate, and not prior of the house of St John the Baptist.' 61 In November 1385 Henry had letters of attorney under the names of brothers John Rede and William Bernard (*CIRCLE*, PR 9 Rich. II, §143). 62 Sparky Booker, 'Irish clergy and the diocesan church in the "four obedient shires" of Ireland, *c.*1400–*c.*1540', *IHS*, 39:154 (2014), 186. 63 *CIRCLE*, PR 5 Rich. II, §22.

John's,[64] but by April 1400 Adam had been appointed prior and was afforded protection for travel to England. He may have been responsible for securing by July of that year indulgences granted by the papacy to those who would visit the hospital and 'give alms for the conservation of the church, and for the conservation of the poor'.[65] He was granted letters of attorney in the names Nicholas White of Clonmel and Richard Walsh and also of Brothers John Watir and John Cormok (presumably members of the congregation at St John's, the latter also native Irish, to judge from his surname).[66]

Even more interesting is the mention of a licence for Adam 'passing to the curia in Rome in the service of James Butler, earl of Ormond'.[67] This could perhaps indicate that he was somehow involved in the agreement made in 1399 between James and the bishop of Cloyne, Gerald Caneton, to act on Butler's behalf in Rome to secure a papal dispensation for a marriage between him and Katherine of Desmond, the mother of four of his children, a marriage that never transpired.[68] Adam's involvement with Ormond may have been the reason behind the complaints made against him, which led to him being deprived of his office in 1401, having been found guilty of 'dilapidation, homicide and perjury'.[69] It was at this point that Richard Eirot, described as a brother of the house, was assigned the priory. As this Richard makes no other appearance, and as Adam was later restored as head of the house, it is possible that this Richard Eirot was the same Richard who preceded Adam.

The nomination of James Coytyff and Nicholas White as attorneys acting on behalf of the prior unfortunately fails to name the prior in question.[70] The entry, though, does prove an invaluable insight into difficulties the Dublin-based hospital administration faced in attempting to manage the resources of the hospital. The prior claimed that he was unable personally to attend to his business in Munster, Kilkenny and Wexford not only due to other business of his house in lower Leinster (*in inferiore Lagenie*), but also because of the danger of the roads. James and Nicholas were then appointed as attorneys to represent the prior in these three areas. They in turn had power to appoint other attorneys to attend to the hospital's affairs. These concerns can be found echoed in the 1392 complaints by Thomas Butler (illegitimate son of the same

64 *CPL*, v, p. 134; the description is 'Adam Ohette, brother of the Augustinian hospital of St John Baptist without the new gate, Dublin, priest, of the diocese of Dublin'. 65 *CPL*, v, p. 303. 66 *CIRCLE*, PR 1 Hen. IV, §§26, 27; John Watyr was also a future prior of the hospital. 67 *CIRCLE*, PR 1 Hen. IV, §28. 68 C.A. Empey, 'Butler, James, third earl of Ormond (*c.*1360–1405)', *ODNB*. For Caneton's dates see Byrne, 'Bishops', p. 294. For the agreement made between James Butler and Gerald Caneton, see *Calendar of Ormond deeds*, ii, no. 337, pp 239–40. 69 *CPL*, v, p. 372. In what could entirely be coincidence, a John and Odo Ohech, brothers and clerks in the diocese of Lismore, were in 1400 given a dispensation, in addition to a dispensation they had already received, to enter holy orders. The circumstance of their birth was the reason a dispensation was required as they had been born to an unmarried woman and a 'priest religious of the order of St Augustine' (*CPL*, v, p. 302). 70 *CIRCLE*, PR 3 Hen. V, §41 (with thanks to Dr Peter Crooks for assistance with

James Butler, third earl of Ormond, who had employed Adam O'Hethe) that areas within the Ormond barony in Munster had been 'wasted by Irish and English malefactors … so that the passage of merchants had been disrupted'.[71] However, Adam was certainly prior of the hospital again by 1407–8.[72]

John Watyr/James Coytif

By 1412 Adam had been replaced by one of the brothers, John Watyr, who had previously acted as his attorney. St John Brooks points to a date of 1414 for John but two years previously he had received letters of protection for travel to England.[73] St John Brooks also speculates that, based on the evidence of a deed in the Ormond collection, John Water may have temporarily replaced his successor, James Coytif, as prior.[74] In the latter, in 1440 John, prior of the hospital, presented to John Hedian, seneschal of the liberty of Tipperary, various deeds which had been granted in 1437 to several persons in Tipperary concerning lands in the county.[75] Ware places Coytif's earliest date as prior in 1425, and this is confirmed by a rent negotiation dated 20 January 1425 by James regarding land in St Nicholas Street.[76] He was certainly prior in 1435.[77] His time as prior was not without controversy, however, as a 1441 papal mandate depicts a prior considered far from the ideal. William River, the prior of St John's in Drogheda, also a crutched friars hospital, would appear to have informed the papacy that James Coytif 'has dilapidated the goods of the said priory and, being a public fornicator, has begotten offspring and cherished it', prompting the papacy to respond that William was to summon James and accuse him in front of a named canon of Dublin, and if all found James to be guilty of this behaviour, he was to be deprived of his office and replaced by his accuser, River.[78] If River was in some way motivated by ambitions to become prior in Dublin his ambitions would seem to have been frustrated as Coytif was again acting as prior in 1443.[79]

this entry). 71 C.A. Empey, 'The Butler lordship in Ireland, 1185–1515' (2 vols, PhD, TCD, 1970), i, p. 71. Empey also explains how attacks by the Irish in the Kilkenny region in these same years meant that 'the last land route between Dublin and Munster was seriously impeded' (ibid., pp 215–16). 72 *CIRCLE*, PR 9 Hen. IV, §80. 73 *CIRCLE*, PR 13 Hen. IV, §106. 74 *Calendar of Ormond deeds*, iii, no. 351, p. 387. 75 Other pleas in the same year (1440) name the seneschal of the Liberty of Tipperary as Peter Hedian. The Hedian family appear widely in political and ecclesiastical records in Munster; as one of the family was prior of St John's in the fifteenth century they will be examined in detail below. 76 *The Dublin city franchise roll, 1468–1512*, ed. Colm Lennon and James Murray (Dublin, 1998), pp 64–5. 77 *Reg. St John*, no. 146; *CCD*, no. 286, p. 88. James was also involved in the sale of lands in Tipperary to various persons; the date is unclear but as it is the same group as in the previous reference it is probably 1437–40 (*Calendar of Ormond deeds*, iii, p. 388). 78 *CPL*, ix, pp 221–2. This would appear to also refer to the death of John Watyr. 79 J.G. Smyly, 'Old (Latin) deeds in the library of Trinity College', *Hermathena*, 70 (1947), no. 154, 13–14; this is part of a collection in *Hermathena* which also includes 66 (1945), 24–39; 67 (1946), 1–30; 69 (1947), 31–48; 70 (1947), 1–21; 71 (1948), 36–51; 72 (1948), 115–20; 74 (1949), 60–7 (hereafter Smyly, 'Old Latin deeds').

William Talbot

The next two priors were no less contentious, and there were further claims of sexual impropriety. William Talbot had succeeded Coytif by the late 1440s as a Brother William, prior of St John without the Newgate, is named in a charter of the barber-surgeons, dated 18 October 1446.[80] In 1451 he was granted leave to be absent for one year.[81] The Talbot name had a long association with Dublin. Henry II had bestowed Malahide on Richard Talbot 1184–5 and subsequently the Talbots became a prominent political and ecclesiastical family in the Dublin region and administration. In the fifteenth century the Talbot name was a particularly prominent one in the political governance of Ireland and the ecclesiastical governance of Dublin. Richard Talbot, son of the fourth Lord Talbot of Herefordshire and younger brother of John Talbot, first earl of Shrewsbury, was consecrated archbishop of Dublin in 1418 and held the office until his death in 1449.[82] His brother John Talbot made a particularly lasting impression on the political scene courtesy of his feud with the Ormond Butlers.[83] Other Talbots who held similar positions in the fifteenth century were Nicholas Talbot, abbot of the nearby St Thomas's abbey in 1420,[84] and Brother Thomas Talbot of the Hospitallers in Kilmainham.[85]

Richard Hedian

William Talbot was contentiously replaced by Richard Hedian by October 1462,[86] but it is only from the papal records of 1464 that the reason for the antipathy between them emerges. Here William, named as prior of the hospital, argued that 'although he has always studied to be of good life and conversation, and has not been defamed of any crime', this was not heeded as 'the present pope, circumvented by the false report of Richard Hediane, clerk, of the diocese of Cashel, to the effect that William had perpetrated a number of excesses and crimes then expressed, ordered the dean of Leighlin, his name not being expressed, if Richard accused William before the said dean, and if he found the said statements to be true, to deprive and remove William, and collate and assign the priory to Richard'.[87] One of William Talbot's main complaints about this procedure appears to have been the meeting-place

80 Henry F. Berry, 'The ancient corporation of barber-surgeons, or gild of St Mary Magdalene, Dublin', *JRSAI*, 33 (1903), 218. 81 *CIRCLE*, PR 30 Hen. VI, §2. 82 Byrne, 'Bishops', p. 311. For Richard's varied and controversial career, see Elizabeth Matthew, 'Talbot, Richard (d. 1449)', *ODNB* [http://www.oxforddnb.com/view/article/26939, accessed 15 November 2016]; John Henry Bernard, 'Richard Talbot, archbishop and chancellor (1418–49)', *PRIA*, 35 (1918–20), 218–29. 83 Peter Crooks, 'Factionalism and noble power in English Ireland, *c.*1361–1423' (PhD, TCD, 2007), pp 319–49, examines the causes of the dispute and the motives of those involved. 84 Archdall, *Monasticon Hibernicium*, p. 49. 85 M.C. Griffith, 'The Talbot-Ormond struggle for control of the Anglo-Irish government, 1414–47', *IHS*, 2:8 (1941), 389. 86 Noel Donnelly, 'Incumbents of Killadreenan and archdeacons of Glendalough in the fifteenth century. With extracts from the Roman archives', *JRSAI*, 23 (1893), 135. 87 *CPL*, xii, p. 209.

chosen for the hearing, claiming that 'said place was not safe for him', but the dean of Leighlin refused to accede to any changes. The abbot of St Thomas's and the prior of All Hallows in Dublin were then to decide whether William's claims were correct and, if so, to call Richard Hedian and William before them and judge the complaints of both men.

We hear nothing further of this case until, in 1469, Richard Hedian, now prior of the hospital, referred to a dispute arising between himself and William Talbot in relation to the office of prior.[88] In the five years between this and the previous record it would appear that several hearings had taken place, in front of various judges, two hearings having been favourable to Richard and one to William, 'which however was null'. One settlement reached was to the effect that Richard was to 'receive and levy the fruits etc. of all the prior's benefices and goods etc. in the province and dioceses of Cashel and Leighlin for a period of seven years'. It also refers to Richard setting out on a journey to the Roman court. Although from this it would appear that Richard had been the victor in the dispute, William Talbot again appears acting as prior in 1473.[89] In 1474, Brother William, named as prior, was listed in a charter of the smiths' guild, whose chantry was on the grounds of the hospital.[90] Presumably he had either successfully regained the position through an eventual settlement of the dispute in his favour, or had temporarily replaced Richard following the latter's death.

The only reference to the cause of the dispute was that it was 'about the said priory', although even something as vague as that could be a cover for a more personal or politically motivated disagreement.[91] The Hedians (Uí Éidigheáin) were part of an ecclesiastical dynasty, or erenagh family, centred around the province of Cashel and closely aligned to the Ormond Butlers. In 1403–4 a Richard son of Richard Ohedian was mentioned in connection with the prior of the hospital.[92] In 1432 a Richard O'Hedian, cleric, received the right to hold the chapel (*capella*) of Holy Trinity of Cork (*sce Trin de Cork*).[93] This was in fact probably a confirmation by Henry VI of a grant of the same to another Richard, cleric, in August 1414.[94] In 1406 Richard O'Hedian (Risteárd Ó hÉidigheáin) was consecrated as archbishop of Cashel, a position he held until his death in 1440.[95] Prior to his elevation to the bishopric O'Hedian had been archdeacon of Cashel.[96] In 1439 a William O'Hedian, canon of Lismore, can be found in Rome acting in a dispute that arose over a vacancy in Killaloe.[97] In 1429 a Uilliam Ó hÉidigheáin was provided to the bishopric of Elphin in the

88 *CPL*, xii, pp 324–5. In April 1469, a William, named as prior of the hospital, was admitted to the franchise of the city (*Dublin city franchise roll*, p. 1). 89 *Reg. St John*, no. 428. 90 T.B. Le Fanu, 'A note on two charters of the smiths' guild of Dublin', *JRSAI*, 60 (1930), p. 151. 91 *PL*, xii, p. 324. 92 *CIRCLE*, PR 5 Hen. IV, §111: the prior at the time was most likely Adam O'Hethe. 93 *CIRCLE* PR 10 Hen. VI, §96. 94 *CIRCLE* PR 2 Hen. V, §65. 95 Byrne, 'Bishops', p. 291. 96 *Calendar of Ormond deeds*, iii, no 175, pp 166–7. 97 *CPL*, ix, p. 50.

province of Tuam,[98] before being transferred in October 1449 to the bishopric of Emly, in the province of Cashel, which he held until his death in 1475.[99]

In a book written on behalf of Edmund macRichard Butler, nephew of James Butler, fourth earl of Ormond, known as the White Earl, can be found a blessing for the soul of Archbishop O'Hedian, 'for by him the owner of this book was fostered'.[100] The close family ties between the Gaelic archbishop and the Ormonds were not without repercussion. In the 1421 parliament in Dublin, O'Hedian found himself accused by the English bishop of Waterford-Lismore, John Geese (deprived of the office 1414–22), of 'prejudice against clerks of English origin and of harbouring an ambition to make himself king of Munster'.[101] As the White Earl was then the lieutenant for Ireland and in that capacity presided over the parliament, publicizing the strong links between the Gaelic O'Hedians and the Butlers, while also implying links between Archbishop O'Hedian and the Desmonds, traditional rivals to the Ormonds, Geese clearly opted for maximum impact. If his intention was to gain the temporalities of Waterford-Lismore he was successful.[102]

The archbishop's namesake, Richard O'Hedian, was archdeacon in 1425 and most likely from 1437 until 1463.[103] As the 1464 description of the Richard Hedian involved in the dispute with William Talbot describes him as 'of the diocese of Cashel' it seems likely that the Richard who became prior of the hospital in the 1460s was at the time archdeacon of Cashel. In 1464, John, earl of Ormond, son of James le Botiller (Butler), late earl of Ormond, appointed Peter Neille to be keeper of his beds in the hospital.[104] This may simply have been a continuation of the family's connection with the hospital, going back to the thirteenth-century grant of one carucate to provide for the maintenance of thirteen patients, but it may also have been reinforced by the close connections of the new prior, O'Hedian, with the Butlers.[105]

The decision to allow Richard O'Hedian to farm the prior's benefices in Cashel was not without its repercussions and his somewhat-controversial legacy continued. In 1484 Richard Butler, of the diocese of Cashel, laid some serious claims against O'Hedian, which would suggest that he might not entirely have been the innocent party in his dispute with Talbot. Butler claimed that 'from time immemorial a number of rectories of parish churches

98 Byrne, 'Bishops', p. 326. **99** Ibid., p. 298. **100** Myles Dillon, 'Laud Misc. 610', *Celtica*, 6 (1963), 151. **101** Peter Crooks, 'Representation and dissent: "Parliamentarianism" and the structure of politics in colonial Ireland, *c.*1370–1420', *English Historical Review*, 125:512 (2010), 14–15. **102** Ibid., pp 15–16. **103** *Calendar of Ormond deeds*, iii, pp 166–7; Henry Cotton, *Fasti ecclesiæ Hibernicæ: the succession of the prelates and members of the cathedral bodies in Ireland* (5 vols and supplement, Dublin, 1847–78), i, part 2, p. 53. In 1463 a John O'Hedian replaced Richard as archdeacon of Cashel, until 1479 when he became bishop of Ossory: Cotton, *Fasti ecclesiæ Hibernicæ*, i, part 2, pp 53–4; Byrne, 'Bishops', p. 318 (Seán Ó hÉidigheáin) and *CPL*, xiii, part 2, pp 667–8. John O'Hedian was for a time archdeacon of both Cashel and Ossory (*CPL*, xiii, part 1, p. 208). **104** TNA, London, C 47/10/28. **105** *Reg. St John*, no. 222.

and arable lands in divers dioceses and in the province of Cashel' had been in the possession of the hospital, but that some had begun 'to fall into ruin through neglect of their holders'.[106] His particular complaint was that the worst offender was Richard Hedian who, having been given 'a life grant to farm, or yearly pension … of a number of the said rectories', was then allowing them to fall into disrepair. Butler, who 'alleges that he is by both parents of noble birth', promised that if granted the churches he would use both his own resources and those of the church to repair them. He had more serious claims about Hedian though, saying that he 'has committed simony, both in the obtaining of the said rectories, and also with divers other ecclesiastical persons and with the said prior, and is a notorious fornicator, perjurer and apostate'.[107] That Butler was clearly eager to gain possession of these churches may have encouraged him to exaggerate some of Hedian's faults, and certainly they cannot be automatically accepted as true. That said, the presentation in 1484 of a Robert Edian (*recte* O'Hedian) as archdeacon of Ossory might provide a clue as to the basis of Richard Butler's complaints about Richard O'Hedian. In April of that year, the archdeacon of Cashel, the precentor of Waterford, and Richard Eluarde (Aylward), a canon of Cashel, were ordered to collate and assign to Robert Edian, clerk of the diocese of Ossory, the archdeaconry of the same diocese.[108] The bishop of Ossory at the time was John O'Hedian, presumably a relative. This might further explain why Robert had been given a dispensation by the bishop, despite his illegitimacy, 'as the son of the then archdeacon of Cashel and an unmarried or a married woman, to be promoted to all minor orders, and who in virtue thereof has been made a clerk'. The archdeacon of Cashel must have been one of the O'Hedians, either Richard or John. If it refers to John, then the bishop of Ossory was providing an archdeaconry for his son.[109] If the Richard O'Hedian who was archdeacon of Cashel was also the same man who became prior, then the prior of the hospital had a son, and Butler accusing O'Hedian of fornication might not be as unsubstantiated as would first appear.[110]

106 *CPL*, xiii, part 1, p. 180. **107** The claims were to be investigated and if found true the churches were to be transferred to Butler, if it was considered to the benefit of the hospital and the various rectories. **108** *CPL*, xiii, part 1, p. 169. **109** John certainly 'kept a certain unmarried woman and had offspring by her', maintaining her from the archdeaconry of Cashel. John was himself the child of unmarried parents. To receive dispensation and to 'purify his conscience' John even travelled to Rome in 1474–5: *CPL*, xiii, part 1, pp 393–4. **110** Richard would not have been the only O'Hedian in religious orders to have fathered a child. In 1474–5 a papal order commanded that an Edmund O'Hedian, clerk of the diocese of Emly, was no longer allowed to hold a benefice in the church, as dispensation had not been granted to him. Such a dispensation was required as Edmund was the son of the bishop of Emly and of an unmarried woman. The bishop at the time was one William O'Hedian. Edmund's successor was David de Burgo, son of a canon regular and of an unmarried woman (*CPL*, xiii, part 1, p. 387). A year later similar complaints were still being made against him (ibid., part 2, p. 478). A Peter Hedian, son of a priest holding a dignity and of an unmarried woman, was in 1478–9 granted dispensation to be a clerk and hold the

John Onextiffe / Walter Ludlow

As previously mentioned, William Talbot appears to have regained office in the 1470s, being named as a witness in the 1474 charter of the smiths' guild. His successor by St John Brooks's list is Walter Ludlow. However, there may have been a John Onextiffe who briefly held the position between Talbot and Ludlow. Ware reports Talbot's death as *c.*1475,[111] and the earliest date located for Ludlow's time as prior is April 1477, so that Onextiffe's term must have been very brief.[112] Although Archdall gives Onextiffe's dates as 1323, quoting *Collectanea de rebus Hibernicis* as his source, the actual entry in this collection which mentions Onextiffe points to a date immediately prior to Ludlow.[113] In 1478 Nicholas Gaydon complained that although he had formerly held the office of the miller of St John the Baptist's mill by its cemetery, and as part of this office had the right to a third of the toll of the produce ground in the mill, he had been deprived of this by Walter Ludlow, prior of the hospital. Gaydon had apparently been appointed by Prior John Onextiffe.[114] In 1486 Ludlow granted an acre of meadow called St John in Coolock to a Richard Ludlow, merchant and presumably also a family member.[115]

The disputes between priors over the previous few decades would also seem to have taken their toll on the hospital. Within a short time of becoming prior, Talbot seems to have decided to make a full appraisal of the financial conditions of the hospital and attempted to regain some control over the resources of the institution for which he was then responsible. He complained

treasurership of Cashel (*CPL*, xiii, part 2, p. 670). For calculations of how widespread this phenomenon was in Ireland, see Henry Jefferies, *The Irish church and the Tudor reformations* (Dublin, 2010), pp 28–30. 111 *Reg. St John*, p. xxi. Talbot appears in September 1447 (Thursday next before the feast of St Michael the Archangel, in the 26th year of the reign of King Henry VI) as witness to a charter of the guild of barber-surgeons whose chantry was on the hospital's grounds: Berry, 'The ancient corporation of barber-surgeons', 218. 112 Richard Caulfied, 'Early charters relating to Kinsale', *The Gentleman's Magazine and Historical Review* (February 1863), 185. Acting as prior, Ludlow granted various lands of the hospital in Kinsale to local merchants. 113 NLI MS 13, vol. 13, p. 56 (Harris, *Collectanea de rebus Hibernicis*). The National Library of Ireland copy is based on two volumes (MSS 25 & 26) in the Cashel diocesan library. This in turn is based on TCD MS 579/1 & 579/2. Both the Trinity College original and the National Library copy suggest a date for Onextiffe immediately preceding Ludlow. 114 TCS MS 579/2, 73v; NLI MS 13, vol. 13, p. 56. Perhaps the same Nicholas Gaydon who was mayor of Dublin 1532–3. See Jacqueline Hill, 'Mayors and lord mayors of Dublin from 1229' in T.W. Moody, F.X. Martin and F.J. Byrne (eds), *A new history of Ireland*, ix: *maps, genealogies, lists* (Oxford, 1984), p. 554. 115 *Reg. St John*, no. 581. Walter Ludlow may have been well integrated in Dublin society before his time as prior: in 1462 a Walter Ludlow, chaplain, was granted a house and garden in Oxmantown: John L. Robinson and E.C.R Robinson, 'On the ancient deeds of the parish of St John, Dublin', *PRIA*, 33 (1916–17), 200 (a receipt of *c.*1477 mentions the rents paid by Ludlow for these properties, pp 201–2). In 1471 a Walter Ludlow, chaplain, was bequeathed a blue gown and 20*s.* silver by John Wylde, merchant. In 1474 a Sir Walter Ludlow was owed 5*s.* by Dame Margaret Nugent and in the same year Walter Ludlow is noted as owing Nicholas Lok 4*s.* 8*d.* (H.F. Berry (ed.), *Register of wills and inventories of the diocese of Dublin in the time of Archbishops Tregury and Walton, 1457–1483* (Dublin, 1898), pp 16, 79 and 114).

that 'whereas the said house or hospital and the house in which the poor and sick remain, by the negligence and bad government of the priors of the same are so ruinous, in default of repair made before this time, that 100 pounds will not suffice to or for their repair'.[116] So many of the possessions of the hospital had been granted and alienated that 'divine service and hospitality must cease there and the aforesaid house or hospital forthwith fall to the ground, unless they be suitably remedied at this time'. To that end all the grants and leases made by William, the late prior, presumably William Talbot, to James Cotyiffe, Brothers William Sewell and Thomas Broun of the said hospital and also to Richard Hedian, were to be restored to Walter Ludlow as prior, to 'enjoy henceforth according to his title and right'. The statute does not explicitly state that once restored to Ludlow the value of the lands and leases was to be used to repair the fabric of the hospital and provide maintenance to the sick and infirm, and, given the complaints made of it by the assessors some sixty years later, it is possible that they were at least partly correct about mismanagement.

William Fowle/Robert Nangle/John Theodoricus/James Osbert/ Thomas Nangle
William Fowle was prior from the late fifteenth into the early years of the sixteenth century, the last years in which the hospital existed as an Augustinian institution.[117] From 1516 to 1520 four priors held office: Robert Nangle,[118] John Theodoricus,[119] James Osbert and Thomas Nangle: Ware gives Osbert only one date, 1518, and Nangle only 1520.[120] A lease in May 1520 by a James Osborne as prior of the hospital would suggest that the James Osbert of Ware's list is the same man as Prior James Osborne named in the Talbot collection deed. Osborne granted a James Rere of Dublin, merchant, a messuage in Rochelle Lane for fifty-one years.[121] This would make Thomas Nangle's time as prior particularly short-lived.[122]

116 *Statute rolls of the parliament of Ireland, twelfth and thirteenth to the twenty-first and twenty-second years of the reign of King Edward the Fourth*, ed. James Morrissey (Dublin, 1939), pp 505–6. **117** Ware gives Fowle's dates as 1496–1516 (*Reg. St John*, p. xxi); in 1487 a William Fowle, chaplain, granted to Holy Trinity a messuage and land in Roganstown, Swords (*CCD*, no. 1084, p. 219). In April 1516 William Fowle, noted as prior, was listed in the Kildare rental for the hospital's lands in Grange Clare (*Crown surverys of lands 1540–1, with the Kildare rental begun in 1518*, ed. Gearóid Mac Niocaill (Dublin, 1992), pp 238–9). **118** TCD MS 579/2, 77r (16 October, 8 Henry VIII). **119** *Reg. St John*, p. xxi. He was dead by 1520 (Donnelly, 'Incumbents of Killadreenan', p. 138). **120** *Reg. St John*, p. xxi. **121** Brian C. Donovan and David Edwards, *British sources for Irish history, 1485–1641: a guide to manuscripts in local, regional and specialised repositories in England, Scotland and Wales* (Dublin, 1997), p. 236 (Bodleian: MS Talbot c. 96/4). **122** These two Nangles were not the only holders of this name to hold office as prior in Dublin in the sixteenth century: Richard Nangle was the last prior of the Augustinian friary (the hermits of St Augustine) situated in the eastern suburb of the city: Seán Duffy and Linzi Simpson, 'The hermits of St Augustine in medieval Dublin: their history and archaeology' in John Bradley, Alan J. Fletcher and Anngret Simms (eds), *Dublin in the medieval world* (Dublin, 2009), p. 217.

Patrick Collyn/Thomas Weston

Thomas Nangle's replacement, Patrick Collyn (Pádraig Ó Cuilín), was yet another prior who was also a bishop. Appointed as bishop of Clogher in 1517 he held this position both before and after he became prior of the hospital, which he held from 1520 to 1531.[123] He was followed by Thomas Weston, whose most notable action as prior was to renounce its exemption from the jurisdiction of the archbishops of Dublin. In July 1531 when it was becoming clear that the independence of the hospital from diocesan control was no longer feasible, Weston, along with James Travers, sub-prior, and four others, was forced by the archbishop of Dublin, John Alen, to surrender to him all 'liberties, immunities and apostolic privileges'.[124] In asserting his jurisdiction over the hospital Archbishop Alen was following a policy that saw him take several houses in Dublin under his personal control, perhaps acting in a similar vein to the way in which he had in England during the suppressions of the 1520s when his 'roughshod methods gained him notoriety'.[125] Echoes of the early fourteenth-century pleas to the crown following the destruction wrought on the western suburb can be found in a petition sent by the civic representatives to Henry VIII in the wake of the 1534 Silken Thomas revolt.[126] It speaks of ruin and decay, of the damage done to towers, bridges and houses. But rather than simply request vague financial assistance, the mayor and citizens had themselves decided how best to manage their difficulties. The hospital of St John the Baptist, valued by them at 110 marks 10*s*., or the priory of All Hallows, valued at 84 marks, were considered ample compensation and the transfer of one of them to city ownership was touted as a possible means of recuperation of losses. It was the latter which was eventually to become city property and before the century was out had become the site of Trinity College. As will be seen, the site on which St John the Baptist's stood was to have a much less salubrious history.

Thomas Everard

The final prior, Thomas Everard, who finally surrendered the hospital on 22 February 1539, had perhaps sensed that change was on the way and several grants made by him through the 1530s were given on long leases. As early as 1532, probably only within his first year as prior, he negotiated a twenty-one year lease with Nicholas Hancoke and William Newman, merchants of Dublin, regarding the tithes of Straffan in Kildare.[127] In March 1536 Everard leased a

123 Byrne, 'Bishops', p. 275. The only other reference unearthed for his decade as prior is an agreement made between him and a merchant in Dublin, Nicholas Hancock, regarding tithes: Smyly, 'Old Latin deeds', 72 (1948), no. 212, 119–20. In 1507 a Patrick Culnyn was prior of another Augustinian house in Dublin, that of the hermits of St Augustine: Robinson and Robinson, 'On the ancient deeds of the parish of St John', no. 149, p. 205. 124 *Reg. Alen*, p. 276. 125 Brendan Bradshaw, *The dissolution of the religious orders in Ireland under Henry VIII* (Cambridge, 1974), p. 43. 126 *CARD*, i, pp 500–1. 127 Smyly, 'Old Latin deeds', 74 (1949), no. 218, p. 64; TCD MS 1207/277. According to Smyly a

messuage in Rochelle Lane in Dublin to a merchant named John Candell for sixty-one years.[128] In June of the same year he leased to Piers Butler, earl of Ossory, and his wife Margaret, a portion of the profits of two parsonages in Co. Tipperary.[129] Everard's activities in Tipperary may have been carried out with two purposes: acting as prior he may have been attempting to protect the possessions of the hospital but as a member of a Tipperary family he may also have had an eye on how best to provide for himself and those associated with the Everards. Bradshaw suggests that Piers's son James, the future earl of Ormond, was just back from court and

> was close enough to Cromwellian circles, both in London and in Dublin, to be mildly protestant in sympathy, and to be aware of the direction in which policy was moving. There may very well be a link, therefore, between Prior Everard's property transactions from the summer of 1536 onwards, Pier's Butler's interest in the Tipperary possessions of the monastery, and the inclusion of St John's in suppression proposals by members of the Cromwellian group in the first half of 1537.[130]

Based primarily around Fethard, Co. Tipperary, from at least the early fourteenth century, the Everards can, perhaps inevitably, be found engaged with the Butlers.[131] The history of the family in Ireland may be connected to King John's visit in 1185.[132] As early as 1515 Thomas Everard, cleric, can be found acting as witness to John Everard of Fethard in a grant to St Canice's cathedral in Kilkenny.[133] In 1525 John Everard of Knokanstalyn, possibly the same as John Everard of Fethard, was one of the witnesses to a writ of Piers Butler.[134] In 1544 a Nicholas Everard of Fethard (perhaps a nephew of Thomas) admitted himself bound to James, earl of Ormond, for £30, and bound to abide by the decision of both the justice of the liberty of Tipperary and Thomas Everard, vicar of Fethard, concerning payment.[135] Following what

receipt for the initial payment for these tithes is in Everard's handwriting: 74 (1949), no. 219, pp 64–5; TCD MS 1207/278. Signed as *per me Thomas Euard Priorem predictum*, other signatures are in a different hand. One of those was Walter Cartan who was still a brother of the house on surrender and received a pension. This lease is mentioned in the extent of the hospital's possessions in Co. Kildare made in November 1540: *Extents Irish monastic possessions, 1540–1541*, ed. Newport White (Dublin, 1943), p. 62. **128** Donovan and Edwards, *British sources for Irish history*, p. 236 (Bodleian: MS Talbot c. 96/5). **129** *Irish monastic and episcopal deeds*, ed. Newport B. White (Dublin, 1936), pp 251–2. **130** Bradshaw, *The dissolution of the religious orders*, p. 85. **131** Richard H.A.J. Everard, 'The family of Everard', *The Irish Genealogist*, 7 (1986–9), 328–48, 505–42. For Fethard as a medieval settlement and the Everards in context, see Tadhg O'Keeffe, *Fethard*, Irish Historic Towns Atlas, 13 (RIA, Dublin, 2003). **132** Everard, 'The family of Everard', 329. Two main branches emerged in the fourteenth century, one in Co. Meath, one in Co. Tipperary, especially Fethard, and a junior line in Co. Waterford. **133** *Calendar of Ormond deeds*, iv, no. 31, p. 22. In the fifteenth century, a Richard Everard was a canon in Cashel. **134** *Calendar of Ormond deeds*, iv, no. 116, p. 101. **135** Ibid., no. 314, part 3, p. 259.

amounted essentially to his resignation as prior of the hospital, Everard clearly returned to his native Fethard and was maintained both by his pension from the hospital and from the joint lease with Walter Cowley of the rectories of Fethard and Grange.[136] Indeed, although crown officials such as Thomas Cusack and John Alen had expressed concerns about religious institutions in Ireland in the 1530s selling their possessions or leasing them over many years, that Everard would appear to have engaged in this practice was clearly no impediment to his participation in conducting an extent of the hospital's possessions in Tipperary, held in Clonmel on 15 January 1541.[137]

Over a decade after he surrendered the hospital, Everard found himself embroiled in a controversy about some of the decisions he had made in the last years of the hospital. Nicholas Bennett held the three vills of Palmerstown, Cottrelstown and Jordanstown for £15 12*d*. He was challenged in 1553 to prove that he did in fact hold a lease for the three vills. Not only had this to be proven but three further conditions had to be satisfied: that he had acquired that lease from Thomas Everard, that he had presented the lease at court in Palmerstown and whether he had received rent from any tenants prior to suppression.[138] Alison Davy was named in the extent as the holder of one messuage and 130 acres. The queries concerned her receipt of the lease, the place, the witnesses and its author. Had she received the lease in June of 1538 and had an ante-date been applied? Bennett was found to have made suit at Palmerstown and received the rent while Davy's lease was considered to have been made by the prior for her but around Lammas Day (1 August). Everard then confirmed that Bennett's lease had been sealed prior to Davy's. The crux of the case seems then to have been whether Bennett or Davy held the lease first, the outcome here certainly indicating that it was Bennett, although she 'was long their farmer before'.[139] As will be seen, Bennett's support from the former prior may have been influenced by the many leases held by Bennett.

Although it has not been possible to determine why it was that any of the priors were chosen for the position, or whether there was ever serious competition between any contenders for the role, in this instance Thomas Everard would probably have been aware of the early links between the hospital and Fethard. The foundation of the town itself was as a result of the settlement in the southeast of Ireland by the new English arrivals. It was certainly sufficiently settled by *c.*1208 when William de Braose, for his soul,

136 *Extents Irish monastic possessions*, p. 67. Cowley and Everard appear as witnesses together in 1543 (*Calendar of Ormond deeds*, iv, no. 288, p. 242). In 1607 Sir John Everard was instrumental in securing a second royal charter for Fethard (the first in 1552–3 designated it a corporation) which was intended to attract more settlers to the town and increase its commercial appeal: Tadhg O'Keeffe, 'Townscape as text: the topography of social interaction in Fethard, County Tipperary AD 1300–1700', *Irish Geography*, 32:1 (1999), 15. 137 *Extents Irish monastic possessions*, pp 63–4. 138 *Calendar of the patent and close rolls of chancery in Ireland of the reigns of Henry VIII, Edward VI, Mary and Elizabeth*, ed. James Morrin (Dublin, 1861), no. 45, pp 311–12. 139 Ibid.

that of his wife Matilda and his son, also William, made a substantial grant to the hospital. In this, de Braose impropriated the church in Fethard to the hospital, the tithes of his two mills there, as well as the mill of Adam de Abereskir in the *theodum* or tuath of Fethard. He also gave one messuage and twelve acres of land *in burgo meo*.[140] The hospital retained the benefice for the next century until it came under the jurisdiction of the archbishopric of Cashel and the archbishop of the time, Maurice Mac Cearbhaill.[141] O'Keeffe suggests that the grant of the benefice of the church in Fethard to the hospital, thus making it responsible for the supply of clergy to the church, indicates that de Braose was attempting to organize the parochial settlement of his borough. The architectural style of the parish he contends would 'not be inconsistent with a date in the first decade of the thirteenth century'.[142]

CONCLUSION

As scarce as the surviving information about the priors of St John the Baptist's is in places, this is even more pronounced for the brothers and sisters of the hospital. No mention at all is made of the domestic staff who, when the hospital was caring for 155 people, must have constituted a significant number. Occasionally a name does appear in the sources; for instance, a Geoffrey is named as chaplain of the hospital, in the late twelfth century.[143] A John Cordon, of the poor hospital of St John, was, in 1357, granted plenary remission by the papacy, but no further information is given to distinguish his ecclesiastical or lay status.[144] While our knowledge of the domestic staff of the hospital is of course hampered by the lack of any housekeeping records, such as account rolls for the kitchen, or details about the laundering of the bedclothes from the infirmary, it is perhaps more surprising that our knowledge of some of the priors is so scarce. Had more of the hospital's own records survived, a more complete understanding of the holders of this office, and indeed the office itself, could be achieved. Despite the uncertainty, it is clear that the priors of the hospital of St John the Baptist were men of varied backgrounds and abilities. Some were certainly of good repute; the fornicator's case is still to be heard.

140 *Reg. St John*, no. 463. St John Brooks suggests a 1208–10 date. De Braose's Tipperary lands were confiscated by the crown in 1208, his son William and Matilda being imprisoned by 1210. **141** Ibid., no. 459. **142** O'Keeffe, *Fethard*, 'Topographical development', p. 1. One of the witnesses, Adam le Bret, was himself a grantor of benefices in Co. Tipperary earlier in the same decade (*Reg. St John*, no. 483). De Braose was not the first to grant the hospital ecclesiastical rights in Fethard (*Reg. St John*, no. 465). Fethard and surrounding areas were part of a network of parochial organization in Tipperary at this time. For an examination of this, and the hospital's part in this, see Mark Hennessy, 'Parochial organisation in medieval Tipperary', in William Nolan (ed.), *Tipperary, history and society: interdisciplinary essays on the history of an Irish county* (Dublin, 1985), pp 60–70. **143** *Reg. St Thomas*, no. 338, pp 291–2. **144** *CPL*, iii, p. 587.

The annals of John de Pembridge as a source for the history of Dublin and its hinterland

BERNADETTE WILLIAMS

The Dublin annals of Prior John de Pembridge OP and his continuator (also a Dublin Dominican) were written in medieval Latin in the first half of the fourteenth century. John de Pembridge wrote the first and major section, ceasing in 1348. The annals were then continued by the second author until 13 September 1370. These two Dominican friars lived in the Dublin priory called St Saviour's, situated where the Four Courts building is today, that is, on the north side of the Liffey across the river from Holy Trinity (Christ Church cathedral). The entire work covers the period 1162–1370. Sadly, the original manuscript is no longer extant but, very fortunately, two medieval copies survive, one in Trinity College Dublin (TCD MS 583) and the other in the Bodleian Library in Oxford (Laud Miscellaneous MS 526).[1]

Pembridge displays no significant knowledge of any area outside the greater environs of Dublin. His interest is firmly Dublin-centred. Pembridge also displays no significant knowledge of the Irish nation apart from the Irish living in the Dublin mountains. Pembridge's reports about the Irish nation are spasmodic, and he displays no personal familiarity with individuals. As regards more distant parts, he knows only about major military battles against the Irish. Indeed, even his account of the famous Bruce invasion of Ireland has less material relating to the native Irish than one might expect. Pembridge's main interest is in noting incursions onto the archbishop of Dublin's lands by the Irish of the Dublin mountains.[2] Pembridge also has information about suspected heresy among these same people. His overall impression of the Irish nation is difficult to assess accurately because, first, the earlier section of the annals is derived from an earlier source and, second, he is describing military circumstances where the Irish are usually, but not exclusively, the aggressors.

PEMBRIDGE ON THE IRISH OF THE MOUNTAINS

In Pembridge's time, Dublin saw the Irish of Leinster become increasingly more aggressive as they attacked the thickly populated, fertile and extensively

1 A new edition and translation is in preparation by the writer. 2 For the condition of lands, see *Reg. Alen*, pp 170–2, 180–2, 194–6; Robin Frame, 'The defence of the English lordship, 1250–1450' in Thomas Bartlett and Keith Jeffery (eds), *A military history of Ireland* (Cambridge, 1996), pp 76–98; J.F. Lydon, 'Medieval Wicklow: "a land of war"' in Ken Hannigan and William Nolan (eds), *Wicklow: history and society: interdisciplinary essays*

colonized area surrounding Dublin: this was a time of famine, which inevitably was the cause of increased raids. Dublin was, in effect, on the fringe of a military zone and news of incursions would quickly reach Dublin. Despite Pembridge's comparative lack of information about the Irish in his annals, the Dublin Dominicans were certainly familiar with some of the Irish especially the O'Tooles (Uí Thuathail). Pembridge does demonstrate some familiarity with individual names of the Uí Thuathail, beginning with the first entry naming Blessed Laurence (Lorcán Ó Tuathail). The first major upheaval reported was in 1209 when the Dubliners were feasting at Cullenswood (near Ranelagh) on Whit Monday and the Uí Thuathail came down from the mountains, slaughtered three hundred and carried off men, women and children as hostages for ransom.[3] This animosity between the Dubliners and the Uí Thuathail was exacerbated by the fact that the archbishop of Dublin's episcopal manors of Saggart and Tallaght were adjoining the Irish of Leinster; this meant that whenever the Irish, especially in times of famine, needed stock or food they raided those manors. However, the story was not clear-cut and both English and Irish tenants on the manor of Saggart petitioned the king (1275–84) asking for his help. Saggart and Tallaght were under constant attack and the rustling of livestock from the archbishop's manors was virtually endemic with Saggart being referred to as being 'beside the land of war' in 1274/5.[4]

Then, in 1303, the Uí Thuathail burned Castlekevin, and it escalated from then on with more attacks on the archbishop's manors. As early as 1307 extra forces were allowed to guard against the Uí Thuathail and this was a yearly recurring theme, with Pembridge reporting items such as 'thieves, namely the O'Byrnes and O'Tooles, attacked Saggart and Rathcoole'.[5] In 1308, Pembridge reports that Castlekevin was burnt and guards killed by William Macbaltor (William son of Walter Ó Tuathail) and Cuygnismio Ó Tuathail and his accomplices. A possible identification of Walter is that he was the father of that Adam Dubh Ó Tuathail, the heretic who met his end in College Green in 1327.[6] The next entry in the same year states that Courcouley was burnt by the same malefactors.[7] Naturally, the Bruce invasion, plus the appalling famine

on the history of an Irish county (Dublin, 1994), pp 151–89. 3 Declan Johnston, 'Black Monday: the power of myth in medieval Dublin' in Seán Duffy (ed.), *Medieval Dublin XIII* (Dublin, 2013), pp 139–49. 4 *Reg. Alen*, pp 170–2; 180–96. 5 For a full analysis of the situation, see Lydon, 'Medieval Wicklow'; James Mills, 'Notices of the manor of St Sepulchre in the fourteenth century', *JRSAI*, 19 (1889), 33–4; James Lydon, 'The defence of Dublin in the middle ages' in Seán Duffy (ed.), *Medieval Dublin IV*, pp 70–1; James Mills, 'Tenants and agriculture near Dublin in the fourteenth century', *JRSAI*, 4th ser., 21 (1890–91), 54–63; Áine Foley, *The royal manors of medieval County Dublin* (Dublin, 2013), pp 175–6. 6 'Felimidh's brother, Balthair or Walter, was the father of that Adam Dubh O'Toole': P.L. O'Toole, *History of the clan O'Toole (Uí Thuathail) and other Leinster septs* (Dublin, 1890), pp 149, 165–6. 7 Called Courcowley by Thaddeus Dowling, Richard Butler (ed.), *The annals of Ireland by Friar John Clyn and Thady Dowling, together with the*

with which it coincided, exacerbated the situation. Pembridge relates that in 1316 the Uí Thuathail and the Uí Bhroin (O'Byrnes) burnt Arklow, Newcastle Mackynegan, Bray and all the adjacent vills.[8] And in the same year the Uí Thuathail, Uí Bhroin, Archebolds and the Harolds conspired together, and they devastated the town of Wicklow with all the countryside.[9] Fear of the Irish of the mountains was very real, especially during harvest time, and in 1344 the account roll of the priory of Holy Trinity records a payment for two men 'watching upon the tops of the mountains through fear of the Irish', but only for two nights at a cost of two pence per night, perhaps just to safeguard the harvest until it could be removed.[10]

THE 'HERESY' OF ADAM DUBH Ó TUATHAIL

In 1327 we get a more serious view of two individuals from among the Uí Thuathail. The first was David Ó Tuathail, captured by John de Wellesley.[11] David was called a powerful thief, enemy of the king, burner of churches and destroyer of people, and was executed quite ruthlessly by the justices of the common bench.[12] The second was Adam Dubh, son of Walter Dubh from Leinster, of the *cognomine* (surname) of Uí Thuathail, who was convicted of very serious heresy and blasphemy. He was accused of denying the Incarnation and the Resurrection and saying that the Virgin Mary was a harlot and the sacred scriptures were fables. In a 1331 letter from the justiciar and the council of Ireland to the pope, he is described as 'a certain Irishman Aduk Duff Octohyl, properly convicted of heretical depravity, relapse and blaspheming against his spiritual judge, and for this reason abandoned to secular court for punishment, his perverse preaching and doctrine and erroneous information he held contrary to the holy catholic faith, resulted in many souls among the Irish being lost (to the faith) and damned'.[13] The result was, not surprisingly, that by decree of the church in March 1328 he was burned at Hoggen Green in

annals of Ross (Dublin, 1849), p. 18; Courcouley could be '*Villata de Coule*', property of the Cistercian abbey of Dunbrody (*CStM*, ii, p. 211). 8 Emmett O'Byrne, 'A much disputed land: Carrickmines and the Dublin marches' in Seán Duffy (ed.), *Medieval Dublin IV* (Dublin, 2003), pp 229–52; idem, 'Cultures in contact in the Leinster and Dublin marches, 1170–1400' in Seán Duffy (ed.), *Medieval Dublin V* (2004), pp 111–48. 9 Mills, 'Manor of St Sepulchre', 39; O'Byrne, 'Carrickmines and the Dublin marches', p. 237. 10 James Mills (ed.), *Account roll of the priory of the Holy Trinity, Dublin, 1337–1346* (Dublin, 1891; reprinted Dublin, 1996), p. 64; *CCD*, p. 78. 11 In 1327 John de Wellesley and Milo de Rocheford, knights, were witnesses to a Christ Church grant (*CCD*, p. 75). 12 Bernadette Williams, 'Heresy in Ireland in the thirteenth and fourteenth centuries' in Seán Duffy (ed.), *Princes, prelates and poets in medieval Ireland: essays in honour of Katharine Simms* (Dublin, 2013), p. 347; O'Byrne, 'Cultures in contact', p. 133; *CCD*, pp 140–1. 13 *Sorcery trial of Alice Kyteler*, p. 88; O'Toole, *History of the Clan O'Toole*, p. 149.

Dublin.[14] So, one Ó Tuathail was executed as a heretic and the other as an enemy of the king.

But although the situation of Dublin and the Uí Thuathail was fraught with hostility, we cannot write off the burning of the alleged heretic Adam Dubh Ó Tuathail, or the execution of David as a thief, as simply reflecting animosity against the Uí Thuathail. There was clearly no need to trump up a charge of heresy to get rid of any troublesome Uí Thuathail. Regarding Adam, the question to be asked is whether this was a genuine case of heresy. The only other person of that name to be found in the medieval records is Brother Adam O'Toole, a Cistercian, who in 1302 was appointed by the abbot of Dunbrody (daughter house of St Mary's Dublin) to represent him during his absence.[15] Whether there is any connection between the heretic Adam Dubh Ó Tuathail and Dunbrody is mere speculation, but nevertheless a valid problem. If this was indeed Brother Adam, then it might explain why the full force of legal and ecclesiastical retribution was levied against him. Also if Adam was a Cistercian, Pembridge might not want to report such a distressing fact, as the Cistercians of St Mary's abbey were benefactors of St Saviour's Dominican priory and, of course, they lived side by side. Yet one would have thought that if Brother Adam was the heretic Ó Tuathail he would have claimed benefit of clergy.[16] The fact is that this case of heresy was viewed with such concern by the Dublin administration because they perceived it as part and parcel of the Irish discontent with English rule. In the 1331 letter mentioned above, it also appears that some people of 'English origin' are among those heretics who agree with the Irish rebels, and, while this appears to refer specifically to the heresy, it is also possible that it could be interpreted as meaning that they support the Irish in their rebellion.[17]

DOMINICAN GO-BETWEENS

It is illuminating to find the names of several Dublin Dominicans who were paid by the administration to liaise with the Irish. It should be kept in mind that the *Generalissimum* (the Dominican special general chapter of 1236)

14 Hoggen Green, now College Green; Williams, 'Heresy in Ireland', pp 346–8; *CJRI*, i, p. 271. 15 *CStM*, ii, p. lxxxvi; 'William, abbot of Dunbrody … appoints brother Adam O'Thothyl and William [Kerdiff] as his attorneys' (*CIRCLE*, PR, 31 Edw. I, no. 51). 16 In 1294 a lay brother of St Mary's abbey was hanged for robbery (E.B. Fitzmaurice and A.G. Little, *Materials for the history of the Franciscan province of Ireland 1230–1450* (Manchester, 1920), p. 60) but when, in 1320, one of his monks was accused of murdering two fellow monks, the abbot of St Mary's was emphatic that no one but he could punish him (*CStM*, i, pp 6–7). 17 The pope is then requested to grant a crusade (*crucesignationem*) or a just war (*bellum licitum*) unless they recant and return to the church; this letter adds weight to a vague possibility of a heretical sect in the Dublin mountains (Williams, 'Heresy in Ireland', pp 347–8; *Sorcery trial of Alice Kyteler*, pp 87–9).

commanded friars in every province and priory to learn the language of those living in their neighbourhood.[18] One of these Dublin Dominicans was Friar Richard Ó (sometimes Mac) Cormacáin, who was prior of the Dublin Dominicans in 1327 when Adam Dubh Ó Tuathail was accused of heresy.[19] In 1331 Friar Richard was paid for his expenses in going to the Uí Thuathail for the third time; this time it was to pronounce sentence of excommunication against Adam and his accomplices, 'enemies and rebels of the king'.[20] Ó Cormacáin was not the only Dublin Dominican in close contact with the Irish. In 1335, the Dublin Dominican, Friar Henry Holywode, had 'by order of the justiciar and council' gone as king's messenger on several occasions to 'Oconeghur, *princeps* of the Irish in Connacht'.[21] At around the same time Friar William Jordan, another Dublin Dominican, was sent to treat with Ó Conchobhair on the state of Ireland, and he was also ordered to talk to Edmund, son of Richard de Burgh late earl of Ulster, on certain important matters touching the king.[22] Also in 1335 another Dublin Dominican, Friar Andrew Lawless, was sent by the justiciar and council to Ulster 'with the king's writ addressed to Henry Mandeville to further certain arduous business'.[23] Pembridge's annals are missing for the years 1334, 1335 and 1336 and so unfortunately we cannot see a reflection of these journeys in the annals. Some years later, in 1337–9, Friar Ó Cormacáin was still active as he was sent to treat and parley with certain Irish concerning the observation of peace and tranquillity between the king's people and themselves.[24] The actions of these Dominicans give an insight into how the Dominicans could be used for political reasons. One might presume that Ó Cormacáin could speak Irish and it is perhaps logical to assume that Holywode, Lawless and Jordan had at the least some knowledge of Irish. This knowledge of Irish in the Dublin priory might explain the Irish verse found in marginalia in the same hand and ink on the bottom of the page under the year 1337; although, of course, we cannot know whether it was written in 1337 by Pembridge or was a later addition by the copist.

THE BRUCE INVASION

It is quite clear that the Irish used the period of the Bruce invasion to their own advantage and, in the first entry concerning the arrival of the Scots in Co.

18 *Monemus quod in omnibus provinciis et conventibus fratres linguas addiscant illorum quibus sunt propinque, Acta*, i, p. 9; Galbraith, *The constitution of the Dominican order, 1216 to 1360* (Manchester, 1925), pp 109–10. **19** Ó Cormacáin (McCormegan, McCormogan, Ocormaken, Ocornegan), see Philomena Connolly (ed.), *Irish exchequer payments, 1270–1446*, p. 693. **20** Ibid., pp 337, 339, 347, 392. **21** Ibid., pp 379, 623. **22** Ibid., pp 379, 623. **23** Ibid., pp 379, 623; for 'Alex Lawless OP Dublin sent with citizens of Dublin to Ulster' (Charles McNeill, 'Harris: Collectanea De Rebus Hibernicis', *AH*, 6 (1934), 345. **24** Connolly (ed.), *Irish exchequer payments*, p. 392.

Louth in June 1315, Pembridge reports that it was a combination of the Scots and the Irish who burnt the church at Ardee and later that the Irish of Ulster were again allied with the Scots when in 1316 the church of Bright in Co. Down was burnt. From Pembridge we hear of the Irish also out in force against the English of Ireland in Connacht, Munster, and Leinster and we hear especially when incidents occur nearer to Dublin. Around late 1315 or early 1316 Pembridge tells us that, not only did Ó Tuathail and Ó Broin burn Arklow, Newcastle Mackynegan, Bray and adjacent vills, but the Uí Mhórdha burnt and devastated Laois, although the then justiciar Edmund Butler retaliated and brought almost eighty heads to Dublin Castle.[25] More than twelve heads arrived at Dublin Castle when William Comyn, custodian of the peace, and his *sequaces* killed Donnchadh Ó Broin. It was William Comyn, with the men of Dublin, who attacked David Ó Thuathail when they found him in Cullenswood in September 1316.[26] We also hear that same year that when the Irish of Imaal attacked Tallaght around 400 of the Irish were killed, and heads were sent to Dublin.[27] Then Pembridge relates that 'wonders were afterwards seen there because the dead arose and in turn they fought and cried out their signal *Fennok Abo*', the war cry of the Uí Thuathail.[28] Pembridge once again demonstrates his predisposition to believe tales of wonder, or perhaps he is merely echoing the siege mentality that may have been evident in Dublin at this time. The war cry of the Uí Thuathail certainly evoked fear and we have a histrionic account elsewhere of a group of English robbers in 1312 who rushed into a town and shouted in a loud voice, '*Fennok abo, Fennok abo*', and 'by this cry of malice made all the men and women of the town fly out of their houses, and this done, robbed the said town'.[29]

FAMINE

The Irish are, to some degree, seen as peripheral in these annals, but nevertheless annals do afford an insight into the situation on the ground. In 1337, the Franciscan annalist Friar Clyn, writing in Kilkenny, gives a vivid picture of a country suffering dire weather conditions, and reports disastrous floods 'such as had not been seen for forty years', so that from the beginning of November to the end of March 'there was rain, snow or frost … and ploughing

25 On 6 Jan. 1316 'there was a great massacre of the Irish, namely of the Uí Mhórdha, and about three hundred of those men were killed near Balilethan' (Bernadette Williams (ed.), *The annals of Ireland by Friar John Clyn* (Dublin, 2007), p. 162). **26** Mills, 'Manor of St Sepulchre', 34. Johnston, 'Black Monday'. **27** The manor of Tallaght covered 14,330 acres (A.J. Otway-Ruthven, 'The medieval church lands in county Dublin' in J.A. Watt, J.B. Morrall and F.X. Martin (eds), *Medieval studies presented to Aubrey Gwynn* (Dublin, 1961), p. 57). **28** Around 1 July 1316 'there was a great slaughter of the Irish near the abbey of Baltinglass where around three hundred were killed' (*Annals of Clyn*, p. 164; *CStM*, ii, p. cxiv n3). **29** *CJRI, 1308–14*, p. 244.

ceased because of snow and ice that at that time was continuously abundant … oxen and cows perished and sheep especially were almost wiped out'.[30] Pembridge reported that the Liffey froze. The annals of Ulster likewise reported 'a great plague of snow and frost'.[31] The result of these weather conditions meant that the food supply was drastically depleted and not surprisingly war broke out in many places as a consequence. Pembridge reports the truly horrendous weather of 1338–9, as does Clyn in Kilkenny.[32]

Famine, often as a result of bad weather, was a regular and harrowing occurrence. There was a bad famine in 1271, noted throughout Ireland, and Pembridge reports 'plague, famine and death by the sword' and adds that it was greatest in Meath.[33] The comment in the annals of Inisfallen was that even 'the rich suffered hardship'. The great northern European famine that accompanied the Bruce invasion saw the Scots suffer, and 'they were so weakened, both from hunger and from travel, very many of them died'.[34] Pembridge also tells us that it was reported that some evildoers were so hungry that they took bodies from the graves and cooked the flesh in the skulls for food, and women ate their own children through starvation. Dublin was also in great distress in 1331 due to a 'great and worsening famine' but 'God's mercy caused around 500 whales to beach at the mouth of the River Dodder'. Normally, a stranded whale was the property of the crown but the justiciar allowed the Dubliners to kill and take away about 200 of them.

PEMBRIDGE ON THE IRISH KINGS

Pembridge, being ultimately of English extraction and a loyal subject of the English king, has little good to say of the Irish. He does however use the title king in reference to particular Irish noblemen. The first such occurrence in the annals distinguishes between being a *princeps* and a *rex* when he refers to Ruaidhrí Ó Conchobhair, prince of Connacht, becoming 'king and monarch of Ireland' (*Rothericus Oconghir, princeps Connacie, rex et monarcha Hibernie factus est*). In this earlier section of the annals, from 1167 to 1315, the word *rex* is frequently used.[35] In 1316 Pembridge mentions four Irish kings in Connacht

30 *Annals of Clyn*, pp 168, 224. 31 *AU*, p. 463. 32 *Annals of Clyn*, p. 224. 33 Noted by most annals (e.g., 'great scarcity in Ireland and many men died because of hunger' (*Annals of Clyn*, p. 148); *AI*, p. 371). 34 As Pembridge puts it; see Margaret E. Crawford (ed.), *Famine: the Irish experience 900–1900: subsistence crises and famines in Ireland* (Edinburgh, 1989); William Chester Jordan, *The great famine: northern Europe in the early fourteenth century* (Princeton, 1996); Ian Kershaw, 'The great famine and agrarian crisis in England, 1315–1322', *Past and Present*, 59 (1973), 3–50. 35 1167, Ua Ruairc, *rex* Meath; 1168, Donnchadh, *rex* Uriel; 1200 and 1202, Cathal Crovderg, *rex* Connacht; 1290, Ó Molaghelyn, *rex* Meath; 1305 Muircheartach Ó Conchobhair, *rex* Offaly; 1306, Ó Briain, *rex* Thomond; Donald Ruffus, *rex* Desmond; 1308 Aodh Ó Conchobhair, *rex* Connacht; 1315 Felim Ó Conchobhair, *rex* Connacht. All these items are clearly from an earlier source.

and Feidhlim Ó Conchobhair, king of Connacht, but interestingly he refers to Ó Ceallaigh with 'many other *reguli* ('kinglets')'. After 1316 there are only two mentions of the word *rex* in relation to the Irish. The tone has changed by 1327 when the Irish of Leinster 'made a certain king', namely Domhnall son of Art Mac Murchadha, who then ordered his banner to be placed two miles from Dublin, and afterwards to cross through all the lands of Ireland. Perhaps like Friar John Clyn, he saw that the earlier kings were not claiming to be king of Ireland, that is until 1327 when Mac Murchadha was going to itinerate 'through all the lands of Ireland'; this hints at usurping the authority of the king of England. Pembridge relates that 'God, seeing his pride and malice', allowed him to be captured and 'much misfortune fell upon the Irish of Leinster'. In 1347 Pembridge tells us that 'Domhnall Mac Murchadha, son of Art Mac Murchadha, *rex* of Leinster, was treacherously killed by his [men]'. But he was *rex* of Leinster, not of Ireland.[36]

FIRES IN THE CITY

Although the Dublin Dominicans did not actually live within the city walls, they lived just across the river and to all intents and purposes were fully part of the town. From Pembridge and the continuator, we get an insight into many aspects of Dublin medieval life from items of news which they report, both large and small.[37] One aspect is the matter of the not-infrequent fires which broke out there. Obviously, any fire in the crowded environs of the walled city of Dublin was extremely dangerous. The law in Dublin concerning fires was that if a house went on fire and the flames spread, the fine was 20 shillings, but only as long as the fire caused no damage to a neighbour. However, if a servant caused the fire, he was to be cast into the fire if he could be caught, otherwise a search was made for him. If the fire was intentional he was hanged.[38]

In the earlier section of the annals we are merely informed that Dublin was burned in 1191, but in 1283, when the Dominicans were in residence in Dublin, we hear that on Monday 3 January 'the city of Dublin was partly burnt including the campanile of the church of Holy Trinity'.[39] This would have been clearly visible from the north bank of the river and indeed the river must

36 Clyn also uses *rex* in reference to the Irish. However, these kings were not claiming to be king of Ireland, as Edward Bruce did in 1315 ('inflicting himself as king of Ireland') and 1318 ('usurping the name and making his men call him king of Ireland'); they were kings of areas within Ireland (*Annals of Clyn,* pp 85–6). 37 For a general understanding of how Dublin was ruled, see '"The laws and usages of Dublin": a complete translation of *Les leys et les uagesde la cite de Diveline*', eds Phyllis Gaffney and Yolande de Pontfarcy Sexton, in Seán Duffy (ed.), *Medieval Dublin XVII* (Dublin, 2019), pp 174–203. 38 'The laws and usages of Dublin', p. 193. 39 On 2 Jan. 'within the walls' (*Annals of Clyn,* p. 152). In 1285 'after the burning of the city' (*CARD*, i, p. 106).

have been a great source of comfort as a barrier against a fire in the city. Again on Friday 3 June 1301, it was the more populous south of the river which suffered when the church of St Werburgh was damaged with 'the greater part of the city of Dublin'.[40] But it was the turn of the north side of the river on Monday 8 June 1304 when 'the greater part of Dublin was burnt, namely Bridge Street with a great part of the quay and the church of the friars preachers, and the church of the monks [St Mary's Cistercian abbey] with a great part of the monastery'. Repairs must have started immediately as, remarkably, it was less than a year later, on Friday 5 February 1305, that Eustace le Poer laid 'the first stone of the choir of the friars preachers'. It is therefore not surprising that in 1329 when Arnold le Poer died in Dublin Castle, he 'lay for a long time with the Preachers without burial'. But he had been left unburied 'in accordance with the fifteenth article in the constitutions of Bishop Ledrede, which declares that anyone who (*inter alia*) "impedes the jurisdiction of the bishop" shall not receive ecclesiastical burial, and if buried in ignorance they should be exhumed and cast on a dunghill'.[41]

The fire in February 1317 was a deliberate action. The citizens decided to burn Thomas Street, on the west of the city, 'for fear of the Scots' who were within view at Castleknock. However, fire is notoriously difficult to control and 'the church of St John [the Baptist] with the chapel of Blessed Mary Magdalen by misfortune was consumed by fire. And all the suburbs were burned, together with the monastery of Blessed Mary [St Mary's del Dam], and the church of St Patrick was destroyed'. This conflagration must have been easily visible to Bruce at Castleknock. More difficult to understand is the bald statement that on Monday 21 February 1317, after the earl of Ulster was captured in St Mary's Cistercian abbey and taken to Dublin Castle, 'the chamber in which he was kept was burnt and seven of the men of the same earl were killed there'. Perhaps the fire in the chamber was an accidental adjunct to the capture of the earl or perhaps they smoked him out. In 1343, Thomas Street was again burnt but the report states that the fire was spontaneous and did not spread. When we come to the continuator, he mentions two fires. We are told the name of the culprit responsible for the fire of Wednesday 6 April 1362 that destroyed St Patrick's; he was named as John Sexton. Sexton can be an identification of a position held or a surname. Here it is probably a surname as a John Sextyn/Sextyne was a tenant in Patrick Street and New Street. The continuator also reports a fire in Trim where St Mary's Augustinian friary was burnt, both church and monastery.

40 In 1301 'a great part of Dublin, with St Werburgh's church was burnt' (H.J. Lawlor, 'A calendar of the *Liber Niger* and *Liber Albus* of Christ Church, Dublin', *PRIA*, 27 (1907–9), 1–93, at p. 53. 41 H.J. Lawlor, 'Calendar of the *Liber Ruber* of the diocese of Ossory', *PRIA*, 27 (1907–9), 168.

BREAD

There were also strict rules concerning bread, a staple of the medieval diet. Bread production was taken extremely seriously and the ordinances of the city of Dublin declared that bakers had to stamp their bread with their own names, unstamped breads to be forfeited and the bakers fined. If a baker made 'faulty bread' he would be fined 15*d.*, then 30*d.*, and for the third infringement he was to stand on the pillory and subsequently leave the city for a year and a day. The baker was also responsible for the misdeeds of his servants. The ultimate punishment was 'life and limb'.[42] Pembridge records that 1310 was a year of great shortage of grain in Ireland and a crannock was selling for 20*s.* and more.[43] This item is immediately followed by the notice that 'the bakers of Dublin, for their false weight of bread, have received a new kind of torment at that time not seen before, because on the feast day of St Samson, bishop [Tuesday 28 July], they were drawn upon hurdles at horses' tails through the streets of the city'.[44] This was the law in action.

DESTRUCTIVE WEATHER

Another great hazard was weather, also a deadly and destructive force, albeit milder in the city than in the countryside. In the countryside farming suffered, in the city buildings suffered, as for example on Friday 19 November 1316 when 'a great storm of wind and rain' did great damage on land and sea, demolished many houses and the campanile of Holy Trinity at Christ Church. The friars must have heard of, or indeed seen, ships affected. Both Holy Trinity and Dublin Castle must have dominated the view from the Dominican priory just across the river. As weather is only mentioned sparsely, when mention is made it must indicate a serious incident. In 1325 a reference is made to a 'great wind', on the night of the Epiphany which must indicate a fairly major storm. In November and December 1330 bad weather was reported in different places in Ireland. Clyn reported that Kilkenny experienced 'a violent and dreadful wind' which 'dispersed haycocks, destroyed houses and caused much damage'.[45] In Dublin the wind threw down part of the de Verdun house collapsing on the wife and the daughter of Lord Milo de Verdun and Pembridge claims that 'such a wind had never been seen in the land of Ireland'.

42 'The laws and usages of Dublin', pp 179–80. 43 Ware fragment says 20 shillings and more (*CStM*, ii, p. 295). 44 Ware fragment (*CStM*, ii, p. 295); *CARD*, i, pp 219, 221, 224; 'The laws and usages of Dublin', pp 179–80; Mills, 'Manor of St Sepulchre', 32–3. 45 *Annals of Clyn*, p. 200.

After the atrocious weather of 1330, Pembridge tells us that the Boyne was also badly affected by floods with all the bridges, both stone and wood, being utterly breached. It is informative to note that there were both stone and wooden bridges and that Babe Bridge survived. Also, Pembridge relates that mills were swept away, and the Franciscan friaries of Trim and Drogheda were demolished. The result was a great shortage of grain and 'a crannock of wheat was selling for twenty shillings … a crannock of oats for eight shillings; peas, beans and barley one crannock for eight shillings'. Pembridge tells us that this scarcity happened because of great abundance of rainwater so that the great part of the grain harvest was not able to be gathered before Michaelmas. Not surprising then that we hear of warfare between the English of Meath and the Mic Eochagáin who burnt and sacked fifteen small vills, and of course the inevitable reprisal ensued. And as stated above there was the very extreme weather report in 1338 and Pembridge gives the dates as from Wednesday 2 December to 10 February 1339, and declaring that this type of weather 'was unheard of in this age and had never been known in Ireland'.

Pembridge gives us a wonderfully evocative picture of some pleasure among the grimness of that extreme frost when he informs us that

> in parts of Ireland the frost was so intense that the Dublin river, the Anna Liffey, thoroughly froze over in such a way that many were dancing, playing with a ball, and running upon the ice of the same river. Then, upon the same ice, they kindled a hearth of wood and peat and they roasted herrings upon the hearth.[46]

Even though Pembridge does not give the dramatic picture of farming suffering as the result of atrocious weather that Clyn in Kilkenny affords us, the effect of any bad weather would automatically result in food shortage for the following season and then most probably an attack on outlying areas by the Irish, especially if their food supply had been similarly depleted. Mention must be made of the ominous report concerning the arrival of a new chief governor, Ralph Ufford, in Ireland in 1343, that 'an abundance of very heavy rain and copiously bad weather followed' and then two years later the information that 'on his death the floods and wild air ceased'. Perhaps this weather report can be taken with a pinch of salt as a kind of prophetic fallacy. On 15 January 1362 the continuator reports a great storm which damaged various trees, spires, chimneys, and other buildings and among the campaniles damaged was that of the Dominicans, built by Kendrick Sherman, which was flung to the ground.

46 For a description of extraordinary weather, see *Annals of Clyn*, p. 224.

BUILDINGS

These annals can also be useful for information on Dublin buildings, and occasionally other places, in this period. An entry under the year 1231 confirms that by this year the choir of the Dominicans in Kilkenny was fully functional when the recently deceased lord of Leinster, William Marshal the younger, was buried there. The year 1308 is interesting as this was when the Dublin mayor, John le Decer, at his own expense, erected the marble cistern to receive water from the aqueduct in the city of Dublin. John le Decer was evidently a man interested in buildings and in 1313 he built a bridge with arches on the way to Clontarf, which was unfortunately destroyed by a heavy rainfall. Decer also constructed a bridge over the Liffey near the priory of St Wolfstan. Decer was a Dominican benefactor and did 'many good things for the convent'; he also gave 'one stone column in the church and one broad stone upon the high altar with its ornaments'.

Then of course in 1316 when part of the priory was appropriated by the mayor and citizens to protect Dublin against attack by Bruce, we are afforded a valuable insight into the priory itself. Reading the Dominicans' petition to the king in 1317 asking for restitution, it appears to have been an aggressive destruction of the priory which included breaking windows, cutting down the trees in the garden and taking corn and other foodstuffs.[48] The Dominican campanile must have been a later addition as we are then told that when the former Dublin mayor mentioned above, Kendrick Sherman, died in the friary in 1351 he was buried under the Dominican campanile which he had built. Colmán Ó Clabaigh thinks it likely that he retired to the monastery infirmary as his end approached and died there. The bell tower or campanile generally marked the division between the choir and nave in Irish mendicant churches. A door in the north wall of the cloister beneath the bell tower provided internal access for the friars from the friary to the church. Turning left they could enter the choir, turning right, the nave. By being buried here Sherman was ensuring that the friars were reminded of him each time they entered the church for prayers or to preach. It also memorialized him beneath the most prominent architectural feature of the church, which he had sponsored, and meant that he was buried just underneath the rood.[49]

Sherman had also contributed in some way to the roof and had glazed the window in the chapter choir. Professor Roger Stalley (pers. comm.), commenting on the use here of 'window' in the singular, opines that 'it was more likely to be the main east window; by the early fourteenth century these were getting quite elaborate in terms of window tracery (see Kilkenny Dominicans)'. Interestingly, we have a record of a 'William, the glassmaker of

48 G.O. Sayles (ed.), *Documents on the affairs of Ireland before the king's council*, IMC (Dublin, 1979), p. 87. 49 Colmán Ó Clabaigh, *The friars in Ireland, 1224–1540* (Dublin,

Dublin' who got lands in Oxmantown in 1319.[50] We also hear that Maurice Doncref, who died in 1361 and was buried in the Dominican cemetery, had also contributed forty pounds to glaze the church. Glazing appears to be in progress in this period as Archbishop John de St Paul (1349–62) who built the 'long quire' of Holy Trinity is also listed as erecting three windows. The sad aftermath is that, unfortunately, on 15 January 1362 a huge storm hit Dublin and 'spires, chimneys and other more eminent [edifices], trees beyond number, and various campaniles, and the campanile of the friars preachers, Dublin was flung to the ground'.

FEASTS

Feasts must have made a lovely diversion whenever they occurred. Pembridge reports when feasts were given in the city and one assumes that, at the very least, the Dominican prior would be invited to such gatherings.[51] The first report by Pembridge was in 1305 when in Holy Trinity, Dublin, the chancellor Thomas Cantok was consecrated as bishop of Emly, and 'all the great noble born of Ireland attended at this consecration with such a generous feast of a kind unheard of in Ireland in times past, [for] first the rich ate and afterwards the poor'. The years 1328 and 1329 were years of Dublin feasts. The former saw the great vindication of the crown minister Roger Outlawe where 'everyone said that he [Roger] was an upright man and faithful and zealous supporter of the faith and prepared to die for the faith' and to celebrate this acquittal Outlawe 'formally held a great feast for all who wished to come'. And in the latter year, 1329, on Saturday 25 March the magnates of Ireland came to a parliament at Dublin, the list including the earl of Ulster, the earl of Louth, Lord Maurice fitz Thomas, and William Bermingham, and peace was established between the earl of Ulster and fitz Thomas. As a result, a plethora of feasts were held: the earl of Ulster held a great feast at Dublin Castle and the next day Maurice fitz Thomas held a great feast in St Patrick's cathedral and on the third day Brother Roger Outlaw, justiciar of Ireland, held a great feast at the priory of the knights hospitallers in Kilmainham. The Outlawe feast is included twice by Pembridge, perhaps because it was more local; we are told it was 'for all who wished to come' to celebrate Outlawe's 'great purgation', so it must have been an occasion of great joy. When Thomas Butler died in Ardnurcher he was taken to the Dublin Dominicans and then carried by the citizens with great honour and buried at friars preachers and then his wife held a feast. This statement appears to imply that Thomas's burial with

2012), pp 110–12, 235–41. **50** *CCD*, p. 140. **51** Especially if at least 50 men of the city were invited: 'If the mayor and bailiffs and the 24 were invited to a feast they must bring with them 24 young men from the city to follow them and learn courtly behaviour' ('The laws and usages of Dublin', p. 201).

the Dominicans was at the request of the citizens. A feast that is of great interest, as being more unusual since the food that was served is recorded, is that of Robert Savage in 1360 who prepared a feast for an anticipated victory over the Irish near Antrim. Before the battle, each Englishman was given either wine or ale. Then for after the battle, Savage had ordered to be killed sheep and oxen, fowl, fattened poultry, flying birds of the skies, and hunting stags. Clearly, he was a man to be admired in his time. Clyn has a similar comment in his eulogy for his great hero Fulk de la Freigne: 'He was a great-hearted man … a bountiful man and … he was lavish in giving feasts, closing his door to no one.'[52]

PEMBRIDGE ON THE DUBLIN ELITE

Sadly for us, Pembridge was not interested in the Dublin oligarchy. He only mentions three mayors and those incidentally. Those three are John le Decer, who was a great benefactor to both the city and the Dominicans, Philip Craddock, because of the incident of the whales in Dublin, and Robert Nottingham who captured the earl of Ulster in the Cistercian abbey. The continuator, similarly, mentions only two mayors who coincidentally were also Dominican benefactors, Kendrick Sherman and John Taillour. The continuator further notes the death of Maurice Doncref, an eminent citizen of Dublin, and also a great benefactor.

52 *Annals of Clyn*, p. 252.

William Hogeson, mayor of Dublin, *fl.* 1493–1519

RANDOLPH JONES

The will of William Hogeson,[1] mayor of Dublin, can be found today among the Bellew of Barmeath papers, deposited in the Public Record Office of Northern Ireland in 1937.[2] It is not known how this document came to be in this family's archive, but it may have come with others relating to a Dublin property later inherited or purchased by the Bellews. Surviving wills for Dublin's former mayors are rare, particularly for the late medieval period. This example is doubly valuable as it enhances our knowledge of Hogeson's personal and professional life, as he has left very little trace in the surviving record. It also sheds light on a section of Dublin's society based in the transpontine suburb of Oxmantown during the early decades of the sixteenth century, a period poorly served, thanks to the loss of the city's assembly and franchise rolls.

The document is written on a single sheet of parchment, beginning with an inventory of Hogeson's goods made on 12 May 1519, followed by a list of debts, both of them in Latin.[3] There then follows a will and testament drawn up at 'Coutrey' on 27 July 1519, followed by another made at St Bridget's church 'near Dunboyne', Co. Meath, on 5 May 1519. Both wills are written in English, except for the final clause in the first will, in which the two executors are named, and the date on which it was drawn up, both of which are in Latin. The text is written on one side of the document, except for the probate clause which is written in a neat block of Latin text on the reverse. Probate was granted by Thomas Darcy, the principal officer of the court of the Metropolitan of Dublin, on 18 December 1519.[4] The remains of his official seal are still appended. The whole document is a certified copy and may have been the one the administrators were obliged to present to the mayor and bailiffs within a year and a day of the testator's death. It was then proclaimed for three days at the High Cross of Dublin, followed by an inspection by a jury

1 The surname is spelt as 'Hogisson' in the inventory and 'Hoygisson' in the will itself. In the Dublin assembly rolls, it is rendered as 'Hogeson', in which form it also appears in the Dublin franchise roll as well as in the extended form of 'Hoggesson'. The Dublin chronicle however has 'Hogssone' and 'Hogsone'. All these variants appear to be early renditions of the modern surname 'Hodgson'. 2 Deputy Keeper's report NI 1937. 3 PRONI, D 430/59. Unless otherwise stated, the information contained in this article comes from the will itself, which is given in the appendix. 4 Thomas Darcy, rector of Howth, was appointed clerk or keeper of the rolls of chancery on 7 July 1522: 'Calendar of Fiants of King Henry VIII' in *Rep. DKPRI*, no. 7 (Dublin, 1875), p. 33. Darcy was elected dean of St Patrick's cathedral, Dublin, in April 1528 and died on 8 February in the following year: William Monck Mason, *History and antiquities of the collegiate and cathedral church of St*

of twelve citizens to determine whether the testator had good title to any of the lands and rents within the franchises of the city that he had bequeathed. If there were no irregularities, the city's sergeant was ordered to make execution.[5]

The structure of the will suggests that Hogeson made one before departing Ireland but was obliged to update it after falling ill while away from home. His death was noted in the Dublin chronicle during the mayoral year of John Loghan (1518–19). Other notables who succumbed in the same year were Nicholas Roche, mayor in 1510–11, and Richard Skyrrett, prior of Christ Church, Dublin, together with others, all of whom probably died of the plague.[6] Both Roche and Skyrrett seem to have predeceased Hogeson, for mention is made in the latter's will of four nobles (£1 6*s.* 8*d.*) worth of ale provided for Roche's exequies, whereas the Christ Church martyrology mentions that Skyrrett died on 5 March 1518/19.[7]

Hogeson's family came originally from England. His father may have been Thomas Hoggesson of Wakefield, one of several English merchants mentioned in a statute passed by the Irish parliament in November 1486. This protected them from a licence granted to the citizens of Dublin, who were empowered to seize the goods of any English merchants trading in Ireland in compensation for merchandise taken by the men of Lancaster, Cheshire and Yorkshire, when some of their own colleagues were trading in England.[8] During the reign of Henry VII, a Thomas Hogeson was sued in the English Chancery by William Fryston for detaining deeds relating to messuages and lands in Wakefield.[9] William's will also mentions that he had two sisters living in the same Yorkshire town. William's English origin is also suggested by a bequest he made in his will of twenty-six pounds of wax to 'our lady chapell at the brig fote'. This chapel was on the stone bridge (at the site of the modern Fr Mathew Bridge) and was where the fraternity or guild of English merchants trading in Ireland was based, dedicated to the Blessed Virgin Mary.[10] The guild was established in 1460 by letters patent granted by Richard, duke of York, and led the Dublin city assembly to refuse the franchise to any English merchant and the loss of this privilege to any Dublin freeman who joined it, as well as a

Patrick near Dublin (Dublin, 1820), pp li, lxxxii, and 146. 5 *CCD*, no. 336; Colm Lennon and James Murray (eds), *The Dublin city franchise roll, 1468–1512* (Dublin, 1998), pp 66–7, 74–5. 6 Trinity College Dublin MS 543/2/14, as printed in Alan J. Fletcher, 'The earliest recension of the Dublin chronicle: an edition, with commentary' in John Bradley, Alan J. Fletcher and Anngret Simms (eds), *Dublin in the medieval world* (Dublin, 2009), p. 401. The annals of Loch Cé mention that in 1519 there was 'Pestilentia magna, in hoc anno; and a great number of the Foreigners of Ath-cliath died of this plague.': William M. Hennessy (ed.), *ALC*, ii, p. 229. 7 Raymond Refaussé with Colm Lennon (eds), *The registers of Christ Church cathedral, Dublin* (Dublin, 1998), p. 48. 8 David B. Quinn, 'The bills and statutes of the Irish parliaments of Henry VII and Henry VIII', *AH* 10 (July 1941), 79–80; Dublin White Book https://databases.dublincity.ie/chainwhite/white.php?image_order=89. 9 TNA C 1/134/47, 1486–93 or 1504–15. 10 See John T. Gilbert, *A history of the city of Dublin*, 3 vols (Dublin, 1854–9), i, pp 323–5.

fine of ten pounds.[11] The patent of the English merchants' guild was frequently voided by several acts of resumption passed by the Irish parliament, only to be re-established each time after much trouble and expense. It was permanently re-established by the same parliament in 1480, with a guarantee that it would not suffer again from any further acts of resumption.[12]

Hogeson became a freeman of the city of Dublin on 25 October 1493, his first appearance in surviving records. This was due to his marriage to Joan Blake, who only acquired this status herself on 3 May, being the daughter of Thomas Blake.[13] Little is known about Hogeson's father-in-law, other than that he lived in Oxmantown, where he was appointed one of the constables for that parish during the years 1465 and 1470. He was also overseer of the city's works in the latter year. In 1476, he was listed as one of the founding members of religious guild of the Blessed Virgin and St Sythe, based in the parish church of St Michan.[14] It seems that Hogeson became a member of the same guild, for he mentions in his will that he owed money and wax to the chapel of St Mary in the same church. Blake also rented a messuage from the mayor and commonalty of Dublin in Mary's Lane, on the northern bank of the Liffey (running between modern Capel Street and Church Street).[15]

Before Joan died, she had several children by William, four of whom were still living by the time he passed away himself: Katherine, Janet, Martin and Joan. The first two were adults by the time he died and were probably married, possibly to James Shelton and James Browne, both of whom are also mentioned in the will.[16] John Shelton or Shilton is mentioned several times: he brought Hogeson from Flanders a silver goblet with a cover weighing twenty-three ounces, which Hogeson bequeathed to his daughter Janet, as well as a bequest to Shelton himself of a gown lined with fox and another of scarlet. The will contains the earliest mention of Shelton in connection with Dublin, whose differenced coat of arms indicates that he belonged to a cadet branch of the same family from Norfolk.[17] Shelton no doubt acquired the franchise of the city thanks to his connection with Hogeson. He was subsequently one of Richard Talbot's two bailiffs during his year as mayor in 1525–6, one of the 'masters of works' in 1533, and mayor himself in 1536–7. His eponymous

11 *CARD*, i, pp 305–6. 12 *Stat. rolls Ire. Edw. IV*, ii, (Dublin, 1939), pp 769–85. 13 *Dublin city franchise roll*, p. 29. 14 Colm Lennon, 'The foundation charter of St Sythe's guild, Dublin', *Archivium Hibernicum*, 48 (1994), 9. 15 *CARD*, i, pp 321, 341, 343, and 387. 16 NLI GO MS 48, *Visitations in Dublin city and county containing arms and short pedigrees*, vol. II, 1607–1610. On folio 18 it is mentioned that John Shelton was married to a lady with the surname 'Hodge': Colm Lennon, *The lords of Dublin in the age of reformation* (Blackrock, 1989), p. 269; Mildred Campbell Whitaker, *A history of the Shelton family of England and America* (St Louis, Missouri, 1941), p. 74. 17 Azure, a cross or, in the dexter chief an escallop ar: Sir Bernard Burke, Ulster King of Arms, *The general armory of England, Scotland, Ireland, and Wales; comprising a registry of armoral bearings from the earliest to the present time* (London, 1884), p. 920, quoting a herald's visitation to Dublin in 1607.

grandson was also elected to the same office in 1604.[18] James Browne was admitted to the franchise in 1509 and became a bailiff during James Fitz Simon's mayoralty in 1522–3 but never became mayor.[19] In 1533 and 1534 he was appointed one of the city's two 'masters of works'.[20]

After Joan Blake's decease, William married Agnes Thonder, who was his spouse at the time of his death. Together with William's daughter Katherine, Agnes was also the executor of his will. William had five children by Agnes, none of whom are named and were quite young when he died. It also suggests that the couple were married during the first decade of the sixteenth century, for Agnes was the widow of John Mastoke of Kilmainham, husbandman, who was dead by 1503, when some of his lands in Crumlin passed to the abbey of St Thomas the Martyr and others to St Mary's abbey.[21] There are also two sets of documents in the Bellew family collection in which Agnes alienated messuages and lands in Kilmainham to James Eustace in 1497 and 1498.[22] It is not known who Agnes's parents were. A Christina Thonder was admitted to the freedom of city in 1483 and a Thomas Thonder, merchant, likewise in 1494.[23] There was also a branch of the family established in Drogheda.[24]

Hogeson's mother is also mentioned in the will, but her name is not given. She was alive the year before Hogeson died, but it is not clear whether she lived in Dublin. Hogeson's brother Thomas is also mentioned on the same occasion. Whether this Thomas is the same person as Thomas Tei, who is also described in the will as Hogeson's brother, perhaps his brother-in-law, is not known. The latter person was probably Thomas Tw, the apprentice of William Tw, who was granted the freedom of the city on 26 October 1498.[25] He was later one of Thomas Bermyngham's bailiffs during his year as mayor in 1511–12.[26] Thomas was elected mayor himself in 1520–1.[27] The Tew family were likewise based on the north bank of the Liffey. William had been one of the constables for the suburb of Oxmantown.[28] He was also one of the founder members of the fraternity or guild of St Sythe based in the parish church of St

18 *CARD*, i, pp 248–9, 397, 400–1. 19 BL Add. MS 4791, fol. 199v (Exch. Mem. Roll 15 Hen. VIII, mem. 1. Easter term). Fletcher, 'Dublin chronicle', p. 402. In 1505–6 a James Browne was involved in the transfer of lands in Crumlin, from John Mastoke of Kilmainham to the abbot and convent of St Thomas the Martyr, Dublin (see n. 21 below). 20 *CARD*, i, pp 397–8. 21 Agnes seems to have married Mastoke sometime before 1490. RIA MS 12 D 38, fols 15–18 (Register of the Abbey of St Thomas, Dublin, 1526); College of Arms, London, MS Ph 15175, p. 333 (Exch. Mem. Roll 21 Hen. VII, mem. 20); PRONI D430/49–50. 22 PRONI D430/31a, b, and c; D430/32; D 430/42 and 43. 23 *Dublin city franchise roll*, pp 19 and 30. 24 BL Add. MS 4793, fol. 159; NLI MS 761, fol. 333; BL Add. MS 4791, fol. 194. The Thunder coat of arms, 'argent a chevron engrailed between three trumpets sable', once appeared in a window in St Peter's church, Drogheda: John Guillim, *A display of heraldie*, 3rd ed. (London, 1638), p. 331. 25 The surname is also rendered in contemporary sources as Tyve, Tywe, Tu, Tw, Tue and Twe. 26 *Dublin city franchise roll*, pp 34, 46. 27 BL Add. MS 4791, fol. 199 (Irish Exchequer Memoranda Roll 12 Hen. VIII, m. 11a); Fletcher, 'Dublin chronicle, p. 402. 28 *CARD*, i, pp 33, 343, 351, 358, 375–6.

Michan.[29] He was master of the same religious guild in October 1490.[30] After holding the mayoralty in 1488–9, William was slain on St Margaret's Eve 1493, together with other prominent citizens, during an altercation with the earl of Kildare's men on Oxmantown Green.[31] In 1526, a Thomas Tyve was holding land and a garden in Oxmantown, lying to the west of the bridge across the Liffey.[32]

Nothing further is heard of Hogeson until Michaelmas 1501, when Hugh Talbot chose him as one of his two bailiffs for his year in office as mayor. At the city's assembly meeting held on 22 October 1501, Hogeson was granted the same messuage in Mary Lane, previously held by his father-in-law Thomas Blake, for an annual rent of 4*d*. This was a significant reduction from the 9*d*. or 15*d*. paid by previous tenants. In this same year, two of Hogeson's apprentices, Thomas Hossey and John Cowper, acquired the freedom of the city. As an apprenticeship usually lasted seven years, it suggests that all three were taken on shortly after Hogeson acquired the franchise himself. In the same year, Philip Laynarth, clerk, and Walter Kelly, a weaver, also acquired the same franchise thanks to Hodgson's sponsorship.[33] On 4 May 1509, a Bell Hogeson was also admitted to the franchise at the instance of the mayor, who was then Thomas Philip.[34] The relationship between Bell and William is not known, but Philip is mentioned in the inventory of Hogeson's goods, holding one or more mazers in pledge, weighing fifty ounces, and valued at £11. Philip also had Oxmantown connections, being one of the two bailiffs of the guild of St Sythe in St Michan's in October 1490.[35] A William Philip, possibly Thomas's son, is also named in the will as Hogeson's godson. Hogeson bequeathed William Philip a 'gret Nutt of sylver gylt' to sell, from which he was to give £8 in Irish currency to St Michan's.

Hogeson was chosen as one of the twenty-four jurats or aldermen of the city sometime after Michaelmas 1512. He was subsequently elected mayor for the year 1514–15, with Richard Talbot and Nicholas Hanse as his two bailiffs.[36] Unfortunately, the records of the city's assembly meetings from 1507–8 to 1529–30 are no longer extant, which means that we have no knowledge of what business was passed during his time in office.

In addition to the house on Mary's Lane, the remaining term on which he bequeathed to his wife Agnes, provided she did not remarry, William Hogeson rented four other houses in Dublin: the one in which he lived in himself, containing a hall, chamber, dining room and workshop, the remaining term on which he bequeathed to his daughter Katherine; the house next door, which he

29 Lennon, 'Foundation charter of St Sythe's guild', pp 6–9. 30 *CARD*, i, pp 140–1. 31 'Register of the mayors' in BL Add. MS 4791, fol. 141; Dublin City Archives, Gilbert MS 85, fol. 4; Refaussé with Lennon (eds), *Registers of Christ Church*, p. 63. 32 *CCD*, no. 417. 33 *CARD*, i, p. 387; *Dublin city franchise roll*, pp 37–8 and 72–3. 34 *Dublin city franchise roll*, pp 43–4. 35 *CARD*, i, pp 140–1. 36 BL Add. MS 4791, fols 196v and 197f (Irish Exchequer Memoranda Rolls for 5, 6 Hen. VIII, m. 15a and 7 Hen. VIII, m. 1a

bequeathed to his daughter Janet; and 'Master Philip's house', which he bequeathed to his wife Agnes. The fourth house was located within the grounds of St Mary's, Dublin, which appears to have been rented to Walter Hussey, at the time of the abbey's dissolution.[37] It is possible that Hogeson also held property in the country, where he raised livestock and crops, for listed among his goods and chattels are £21 13*s.* worth of grain and meat for the current year as well as the next, which suggest that the harvest had not yet been brought in by the time he died.[38] He also owed Anne Walsh six acres of grain and barley. Mention is also made of a term he held on 'Scharons park' as well as an orchard, although the latter could have been located in an urban space. Hodgson also rented a garden from the priest William Ball. Again, where these fields, park, orchard, and garden were located is not known. However, as his first will was made at St Bridget's church 'next to Dunboyne', the ivy-covered ruins of which still lie to the northeast of Kilbride, across the border in Baytown townland, these may have been located in Co. Meath.

Hodgson's will requested that he be buried in the church of Our Lady at 'Coutre' or 'Coutrey', the place where he drew up his second will. Identifying this place name has been a problem. The will itself suggests that 'Coutrey' is located outside of Ireland. Certainly, the debt of 40*s.* sterling Hodgson owed to Christopher Damport for his lodging, as well as the bequest to his hostess of a gold ring and a mark in money, 'for the easement of her house', indicates that he died some distance from home. It is possible that 'Coutrey' is an abbreviation of Coventry, where the Damport or Davenport family was established from 1500.[39] There also used to be a priory church and cathedral dedicated to St Mary in that city, until it was dissolved and demolished during the Reformation. Despite being based in Dublin, Hogeson's first will suggests that he was about to go on a journey abroad and made suitable arrangements should he fail to return home. He seems to have passed through Liverpool, where he left or kept a coffer. The mention in the second will of Alexander Beswick, to pay six pounds to a man in London, suggests that the capital may have been Hogeson's ultimate destination.[40] It is possible that his journey to

respectively); Fletcher, 'Dublin chronicle', p. 400. **37** Newport B. White (ed.), *Extents of Irish monastic possessions, 1540–41 from manuscripts in the Public Record Office, London* (Dublin, 1943), p. 2. **38** The Dublin chronicle mentions there was 'a great derthe' in Ireland this year, likewise in England because of a poor harvest. **39** Mary Dormer Harris (ed.), *The Coventry leet book: or mayor's register, containing the records of the city court leet or view of frankpledge, AD 1420–1555, with divers other matters. part III* (London, 1909), p. 796; Amzi Benedict Davenport, *A supplement to the history and genealogy of the Davenport family, in England and America, from AD 1086 to 1850* (Stamford, CT, 1876), p. 34. **40** Beswick is mentioned several times in the Chester local customs account of 1525–6: see K.P. Wilson (ed.), *Chester customs accounts, 1301–1566* (Liverpool, 1969), pp 133, 135, 136, 137,138, 140, 141, 142. He was one of the bailiffs of Dublin in 1527–8: BL Add MS 4791, fol. 202f (Exch. Mem. Roll 19 Hen. VIII, Easter term). He died in 1533 and was buried in St Audeon's church, Dublin. He had links with Manchester: Henry F. Berry, 'History of the religious

England could have been linked with that of Gerald fitzGerald, ninth earl of Kildare, deputy lieutenant of Ireland, who was summoned to England in January 1519 by Henry VIII, although he did not leave Ireland until September of that year.[41] There is no record of Hogeson previously being connected with Kildare, but he may have been part of an advance party to prepare for the earl's eventual arrival at court, but fell ill on the way and died.

Evidence of Hogeson's activities as a merchant can be gleaned from various commodities mentioned in his will. These include bequests of iron and salt made to certain individuals. Together with coal and wine, the supply of these commodities was tightly controlled by the Dublin guild of merchants, dedicated to Holy Trinity. This suggests that Hogeson was also a member of this guild, although when it was re-founded in 1438, members were not permitted to belong to any other except the religious ones of St Anne's and St George's. Hogeson's bequest to the chapel of St Mary at the Bridge (home of the guild of English merchants trading in Ireland) suggests otherwise, but he was able to circumvent this requirement, otherwise his progression to high civic office would not have been possible. On their arrival in the city, these four commodities could only be purchased by the four 'buyers' appointed for the year – the two guild masters themselves and two other guild members appointed by them. They then apportioned the stock according to the requirements of the individual guild members first, and then to any outsiders, if there was a surplus. The guild members could only sell these commodities on to others at a fixed price and were subject to fines if they failed to observe this.[42]

To bring his bulky goods in and out of Dublin, Hogeson owned a 'pykard' and a 'lavyer' valued together at £6. A picard or pickard was a single-masted vessel of 12–40 tons used as a lighter, loading and unloading from larger vessels lying at anchor outside the port. In the sixteenth century, larger seagoing vessels could not sail up to Dublin and discharge at the city quay because of silting at the mouth of the Liffey. They therefore discharged their cargoes into lighters at Dalkey or Howth, which were small enough to cross the bar at the estuary and sail into the city itself. It is not clear what is meant by a 'lavyer', but a 'crayer' was a slightly larger vessel of 25–50 tons, with a deck and two or three masts, suitable for transmarine work.[43] Hogeson may have

gild of S. Anne in S. Audeon's church, Dublin, 1430–1740, taken from its Records in the Halliday Collection, R.I.A.', *PRIA* 25C (1904–5), 50. 41 J.S. Brewer (ed.), *Letters and papers, foreign and domestic, Henry VIII, vol. 3, 1519–1523* (London, 1867), p. 5; Mary Ann Lyons, *Gearóid Óg ninth earl of Kildare* (Dundalk, 1998), p. 32. 42 Henry F. Berry, 'The records of the Dublin guild of merchants, known as the guild of the Holy Trinity, 1438–1671', *JRSAI*, 5th ser., 10 (1900), 53–4; Charles Gross, *The guild merchant: a contribution to British municipal history* (Oxford, 1890), ii, pp 69–71. 43 Alan McGowan, *The ship: tiller and whipstaff – the development of the sailing ship, 1400–1700* (London, 1981), p. 33; Timothy O'Neill, *Merchants and mariners in medieval Ireland* (Blackrock, 1987), pp 111–12.

used such a craft to convey his goods to and from Liverpool, where he seems to have kept business premises.

However, the mention of a workshop in his principal residence in Dublin suggests that Hogeson was also involved in manufacturing. In view of his status as a merchant, the products must have been of high value. Mention of jewels, gold rings, silver gilt, spoons, mazers, and scrap silver from which to make a salt seller suggests that he was a goldsmith by trade. By 1498, the Dublin goldsmiths were recognized as a separate craft, being charged with supplying the three kings of Cologne in the annual Corpus Christi pageant.[44] When they were incorporated as a separate fraternity or guild, dedicated to All Saints, is not known. In 1557, the goldsmiths stated that their charter of privileges, granted by Queen Mary's progenitors (unnamed), had been burnt. The city's assembly then confirmed their privileges. All goldsmiths working within Dublin were to be members of the guild and foreigners were prevented from exercising the craft within the city's franchise.[45]

In conclusion, Hogeson's family originated in Wakefield, establishing itself in Oxmantown in the 1480s. It quickly integrated with other prominent families living there, centred on St Michan's parish church and in particular the religious guild of the Virgin Mary and St Sythe. Hogeson was able to enter the ranks of the Dublin oligarchy thanks to his marriage to a freewoman of the city in the early 1490s. Thereafter he became bailiff in 1501 and mayor in 1514. His trading activities as a merchant seem to have been based on the restricted commodities of iron, salt, coal, and wine, although he diversified into manufacturing and food production. He was probably a goldsmith by trade. His mercantile connections outside of Ireland were based in Liverpool, in the northwest of England, although he may have traded further afield, even as far as Flanders. He was wealthy enough to own small vessels to convey and land bulky goods at Dublin. He was also able to convert some of this wealth into real estate, renting several houses in Dublin for himself and his family members, as well as estates in the surrounding country, possibly in Co. Meath. He married twice and was survived by several children, but his progeny in the male line at least does not seem to have survived his own death, with his legacy passing through the Shelton family.

APPENDIX

[The following transcript of the inventory and will is rendered into modern English, although most of the surnames and place names have retained their original spellings, plus those of any doubtful words. My thanks to Heather Falvey who kindly reviewed my initial transcript and for translating the Latin

44 *CARD*, i, pp 239–41. 45 Ibid., pp 465–7.

portions of the text. However, any errors or omissions in this version are mine alone.]

The inventory of all the goods of William Hogisson citizen and late mayor of the city of Dublin, made the 12th day of May AD 1519 and in the 11th year of the reign of Henry VIII.

Firstly, in jewels silver gilt 122 ounces, price the ounce 5s, total £30 10*s*.
Item, in precious objects silver, not gilt, 121 ounces, price the ounce 4*s*. 6*d*, total £27 4*s*. 6*d*.
Item, three mazers price, 40*s*.
Item, those with Katherine his daughter, a piece of plate and six silver spoons, 20 ounces in pledge, price £5.
Item, that with Thomas Fylipp of 50 ounces weight with him in pledge, £11.
Item, in grain and meat this year now current and in the next year coming, £21 13*s*.
Item, in salt two measures, price £5.
Item, in crushed salt loaf English and dry measure, £21 14*s*.
Item, in various other merchandise in the workshop, £17 11*s*. 8*d*.
Item a 'Pykard' & a 'lavyer', price £6.
Item, a horse with Thomas Legh, 40*s*.
Item, a great copper bowl, 6 marks.
Item, in the hall, the chamber and dining room in various items, price £41 7*s*. 4*d*.
Item, in a certain chest in the house, 24 ounces, price £5.
Item, those more in the same, that is 4 nobles.
Item, with Mathew £8.
Item, from Katherine Koke lady by Bartholomew Blanchvyle, £6.
Item, more in ale 4 nobles for the exequies of Nicholas Roche.
Item, ornaments of (his) body, £10.
Total of the goods declared, £200 40*s*.
Deceased's portion, 100 marks.

These are the debts that he owes.
Firstly, to the church of St Michee[n], £4.
Item, to the chapel of the Blessed Mary in silver, 46*s*. 8*d*.
Item, to the same chapel 16 lbs of wax.
Item, to John Philip £4 6*s*.
Item, to Walter Eustace of Dublin, merchant, for the pyx of the Blessed Mary, 20*s*.
Item, to Lord Dublin 10 marks.
Item, to the steward of Lord Dublin 50*s*., these countersigned for them.
Item, to Master William Cargyne, 10*s*.
Item, to Richard Talbote, 7*s*. 6*d*.

Item, to Ann Walsh, 6 acres of grain and barley.
Item, to Christopher Damport for his board, 40*s.* sterling.
Item, to Nicholas Herbard for 'le Werris' of Kylmaynane, 40*s.*
Item, to Agnes Hossey, 30*s.*
Item, to Sir Thomas Freman chaplain, 20*s.*
Item, to Sir William Ball for rent of the garden.
Item, for rent of my house in the monastery of the Blessed Virgin Mary, 20*s.*
Total of the debts which he owes, £32.
Clear debts which are owed by estimation, £43.

In the name of God Amen. In the year of our lord God 1519 and the 27th day of July, I, William Hoygisson, whole of mind and sick of my body, make my testament in this wise.

Firstly, I bequeath my soul to almighty God, his blessed mother St Mary and all the hallows of Heaven, my body to be buried in the church of our lady of Coutre.
Item, I bequeath to the reparation of the said church, 10*s.*
Item, I bequeath to Master Richard Picke, Vicar of the said Church, to pray for my soul, a horse that cost 20*s.*
Item, I bequeath to the said vicar 6*s.* 8*d.*
Item, I bequeath Sir Richard Hewes to pray for my soul, 6*s.* 8*d.*
Item, I bequeath to my hostess a gold ring and 13*s.* 8*d.* for easement of her house.
Item, I will that all such goods as I have at home shall be divided between my wife and my children save only a great nut of silver gilt and that I bequeath to my godson William Philip and he to give to St Michan's church £8 Irish.
Item, I will that Sir Richard Lang shall sing these two years for my soul and for the soul of John Philip and you to sell a salt seller of silver to pay him for his labours and if the price of the said salt seller extends not to him you to pay the over plus.
Item, I will that my son Martyne have my best clothes.
Item, I will that John Scheltowne have one of my furred gowns.
Item, I will that my servant Mathewe Archeboll have a gown furred with fox, and a wey of salt, a last of barrells, and a horse that he rides on.
Item, I will that there be given to the four orders of Friars each of them 6*s.* 8*d.*
Item, I will that my wife Agnes Thonder pay to my lord of Dublin 10 marks or £10.
Item, I will that Alexander Bexwyk be paid £5 for a man of London.
Item, I have in my keeping of Sir John Pers a nut and a piece of silver and spoons of silver that is with Kate and this parcel to be delivered to the said Sir John Pers and my wife to give to the said Kate spoons for them again.

Item, I will that the said Sir John has to pray for me a feather bed with two blankets and two sheets.

Item, I will that Richard Heke be crossed out of my book and he to have a recompense of four stones iron and four pecks salt.

Item, I will Dongnughe Oleghane has some recompense.

Item, there is in my coffer in Liverpool (*lerepoll*) sixteen ounces broken silver that I to make a salt seller of. I will that it be made in a chalice to St Michan's church.

Item, I will that the two sisters that I have in Wakefield have each of them 6*s.* 8*d.* to remember me.

There is an indenture in my coffer betwixt me and Jamys Dowdall of an orchard: I will that it be broken.

Item, I will that John Fench that bears me port has given to him five pecks malt and five pecks wheat.

Item, my lord of St Mary abbey owed me 20 marks: I will that five marks thereof be given to the said house.

Item, I will there be given to Our Lady chapel at the bridge foot 26 lbs wax.

And upon my blessing wise, be favourable to my debtors and be not too covetous on them nor none of my servants and see that they you do no poor man hinderance.

All this will was made in Coutrey.

Now follows a will made in Ireland.

Item, I will my goods be divided in three parts: one to my wife, another to my children five on her body gotten, and another third part to myself to be divided for my soul.

Item, I will my debts be paid of my whole goods.

Also, I will that my daughter Jenet have £10 of my goods and that £10 I delivered to my mother and my brother Thomas in her garden before May last past, and a goblet of silver with a cover weighing 23 ounces that John Schilton brought me out of Flanders, and a little maser with all such duteis[46] as is in my mother's hands and my brother Thomas Tei's hands, and she to be quit from any challenge of my goods unless I leave her in trust of my children's goods as it shall appear here after.

Also, if it shall please God to call her to his mercy or she be married I will these goods extend and come to profit of my other children.

Also, I will that my wife has her third part, clear without let or perturbance of any of my friends.

Also, I will my wife has the custody and keeping of my children's goods until they come to lawful age and discretion as long as she is sole widow. And if

46 Not clear what is meant here.

she be disposed to marry, I will she deliver my children's goods to my daughters Kateryn and Jenet's hands, and they to keep such goods till my children come to age. And if please God to call one or any of my children to his mercy I will the other part has it and so from one to other as it shall please God to order for them.

Also, I will my wife has the term of Scharon's park and term of my orchard as long as she is unmarried. And if she marries I will that my daughter Katerine and my daughter Jenet have the terms of the said park and orchard.

Also, I will my wife has term of my house in Mary Lane as long as she is unmarried upon this condition, she keep my annual mind in St Michan's church with five priests, five prickets burning every year; and if she marries, I will my daughters Kateryne and Jenet have the term upon condition above written. And if they fail any year to keep my foresaid mind, I will master Mayor and bailiffs enter into it and take it to the City's profit.

Also, I will if my part of goods will extend there be a priest found two years to sing for me. Master Philip Rose Stakboll and Master Roch, and this priest to sing three times in the week at Scala caeli in the Austyn friars.[47]

Also, I leave to every order of friars 6*s.* 8*d.* to pray for me.

Item, to the Poor House of St Stephen's 6*s.* 8*d.*

Item, to St James' house 5*s.* 1½*d.*

Item, to poor houses in Dublin 20s to be divided after the discretion of my wife.

Item, to daughter Kate my crimson gown.

Item to my daughter Jenett my murrey gown.

Item, to John Schilton my fox gown.

Item, to Mathewe my fox gown that Master Roch gave me.

Item, to my brother Tewe my velvet doublet that Master Roch gave me.

Item to my gossip Kateryn Chen' a pair great amber beads that is in the shop.

Item, to Sir John Pers a feather bed, a pair sheets and a pair blankets.

Item, I will that my wife has that best girdle she wears during her life unless she will of her gentleness to give it to Kayt'; and after her day I will she deliver it to Kate for it was Kate's mother gave it me.

Also, I will my daughter Kateryn have term of my house that I dwell in so that my wife enjoys Master Philipp's house. And if she be put from Master Philipp's house I will she have term of my house during her life and she marry not and if she marry I will Kayt have my term.

Also, I will my daughter Jenet have term of the next house to mine.

Also, I will there be 25 lbs wax in five tapers and 2 lbs in two prickets burning over my hearse.

47 *Scala caeli*, 'Stairway to heaven'.

Also, I will they spend at my burying 10 pecks wheat and 14 of malt, two kine, a pork and two mothorys[48] to be given to poor people and much at my month's mind after the discretion of my wife and children.

Also, I will that my daughter Jowan have Schiltons have [sic] my scarlet gown or five marks of money if she lives to be married at the discretion of my wife to take whether she will.

Also, I will when that £9 of money is received of St John's without Newgate they pay of that same money to Holywodd's wife five pounds.

Item, I have six gold rings, three in my purse and in my shop coffer, I will that my wife has two, Kateryn two and Jenet two.

I will that John Fynyn have four pecks salt and two stones iron and Thomas Fynyn as much.

Item, I ordain, make, and constitute executors of this testament Agnes Thonder my wife and Katherine my daughter, with the counsel of John Shilton and James Browne to dispose my other goods not bequeathed for the health of my soul as seems best to them.

Made in the church of St Bridget next to Donboyne, A.D. 1519 and the 11th year of reign of Henry VIII on the 5th day of the month of May [15]19, the end made and praise be to God, Amen.

[*Reverse side*]

This present within-written testament was proved before us, Thomas Darcy, principal officer of the court of the Metropolitan of Dublin and approved and favoured by us on 18 December A.D. 1519.

And administration of the goods was committed to the executors within written, [they being] sworn in form of law. Given under our official seal on the day and year above said.

48 Possibly from Irish *meadar*, 'wooden vessel, pail', found in Hiberno-English in the form 'mether', a 'wooden vessel used for measuring liquids; a square wooden drinking vessel, frequently used as a measure of liquor' (*OED*).

Christopher St Lawrence, seventh baron of Howth, and the identity of the Old English

LENORE FISCHER

Christopher St Lawrence, seventh baron of Howth (*c.*1510–89), was a controversial figure caught in the middle of cultural conflict between the Old English community that had formed in Ireland over the preceding four centuries on the one hand, and the new settlers being introduced under Queen Elizabeth's rule on the other. Like the new broom sweeping clean, the newcomers threatened to brush aside their forerunners and carve out a new and different future in this land. A regular attender of government sessions, Lord Howth was at first cooperative with the new government. By the 1570s, however, Lord Howth had become a leading figure in the opposition and had acquired a reputation for obstreperousness. Charges were brought against him for domestic violence in 1579: he was accused of beating his wife and servant and of causing the death of his 13-year-old daughter. After some nineteen weeks in prison and a fine of £500, Howth returned to politics and remained active in government until his death in 1589, at times opposing government measures, at other times fulfilling commissions or negotiating on behalf of the Old English.[1]

St Lawrence is best known today for his magnum opus, the Book of Howth (*BH*).[2] Work on this seems to have begun in the 1560s, well before his falling-out with the government. By 1572 he and his scribes had compiled the bulk of the manuscript, outlining the history of the Old English in Ireland. It was only after he had put this main section of the manuscript together that he turned to an introductory section in which he attempted to graft the Old English scion onto an Irish rootstock, providing his people with a mythic, quasi-Irish identity.[3] A number of studies over the past fifty years have addressed the subject of the Old English and their defining characteristics. Nicholas Canny paints a picture of the landowners of the Pale and their views based on their letters, tracts and petitions.[4] Aidan Clarke sums up their identity as resting 'upon two-fold desiderata: a common ancestral history and the common interests which were a product of that history'.[5] Colm Lennon investigates

1 A more thorough review of Howth's career may be found in Valerie McGowan-Doyle, *The Book of Howth* (Cork, 2011), pp 16–35; see also, Sparky Booker, 'The knight's tale' in Sparky Booker and Cherie N. Peters (eds), *Tales of medieval Dublin* (Dublin, 2014), pp 135–48. 2 S.J. Brewer and William Bullen (eds), *Calendar of the Carew manuscripts preserved in the archiepiscopal library at Lambeth*, 6 vols (London, 1871), v. 3 McGowan-Doyle, *Book of Howth*, p. 44. 4 Nicholas Canny, 'The formation of the Old English elite in Ireland', O'Donnell Lecture, UCG, 6 Sept. 1974 (National University of Ireland, Dublin, 1975). 5 Aidan Clarke, *The Old English in Ireland 1652–42* (Ithaca, 1966), p. 16.

Howth's contemporary, Richard Stanihurst; believing 'in the power of history to teach lessons and also in its role in helping to identify and cherish cultural roots', Stanihurst's 'Description of Ireland' and *De rebus in Hibernia gestis* provided a historical perspective for the Old English.[6]

But Howth went beyond simply describing his people or writing their history, he provided them with a mythic model as well. The work as a whole may be described as a document of cultural memory. It falls neatly into the category which, following on Jan Assman's *Das kulturelle Gedächtnis*, Dagmar Schlüter describes as formative as opposed to normative. Formative texts, according to this approach, are texts which answer the question, 'who are we?', while normative texts address the question 'what should we do?'. Formative texts include genealogies, tales of heroes and origin legends. They underpin a sense of identity; their accounts of experiences shared in the past foster the community's ability to act in a unified manner in the present.[7] A similar framework for examining the identity of community is provided by Anthony D. Smith in *The ethnic origins of nations.* Smith proposes that an ethnic community shares certain distinctive features, namely a collective name, a common myth of descent, a shared history, a distinctive shared culture, an association with a specific territory and a sense of solidarity:

> Myths combine cognitive maps of the community's history and situation with poetic metaphors of its sense of dignity and identity. [They] provide an overall framework of meaning for the ethnic community, a *mythomoteur*, which 'makes sense' of its experiences and defines its 'essence'. Without a *mythomoteur* a group cannot define itself to itself or to others, and cannot inspire or guide collective action.[8]

The story of the Kalevala provides a confirming instance of this, where the rediscovery of the Finnish epic myths so sparked a sense of national identity that it helped bring about Finland's declaration of independence from Russia in 1917.[9] As remarked by the Norwegian ambassador to Ireland: 'politics is about identity and identity is about history'.[10]

The supreme example of Smith's *mythomoteur* for the Old English community is Geoffrey Keating's *Foras feasa ar Éirinn*.[11] Since it was well known that the Anglo-Norman ancestors of the Old English had taken Ireland

6 Colm Lennon, 'Richard Stanihurst (1547–1618) and the Old English identity', *IHS*, 21 (1978), 121–41, at 137. 7 Assman's work on cultural memory forms a background for much of Dagmar Schlüter, *History or fable? the Book of Leinster as a document of cultural memory in twelfth-century Ireland* (Münster, 2010); see p. 22 in this context. 8 Anthony D. Smith, *The ethnic origins of nations* (Oxford, 1986), pp 22–30, at p. 24; see also, Katherine Cross, *Heirs of the Vikings: history and identity in Normandy and England,* c.*950*–c.*1015* (Woodbridge, 2018), pp 18–21, 214. 9 Described in Verlyn Flieger, 'Introduction' in J.R.R. Tolkein, *The story of Kullervo* (London, 2018), p. xi. 10 H.E. Kristine Fjelde Heimstad, addressing the Tionól session, DIAS, 14 Nov. 2019. 11 Geoffrey Keating, *Foras*

by conquest, it was not necessarily easy to provide them with a myth of descent that tied them to the land. Keating solved this problem by adroitly integrating the Anglo-Norman conquest within the invasion cycles of the *Leabhar gabhála Éireann*: his profound knowledge of Gaelic culture and history enabled Keating to liken the Anglo-Normans to the quintessentially Irish Tuatha Dé Danann and the later Milesians, each of whom had also in their turn been invaders from abroad.[12] Christopher St Laurence was not blessed with Keating's mastery of Irish *seanchas*. But he did have access to popular Irish lore, and he used this to provide quite a different origin myth for his people. His solution was to provide his own people with a paradigm of a kindred likeness to the people of the Fianna Éireann, who, he claimed, had been brought over from Denmark by the Irish kings in order to protect Ireland from external enemies. The opening sentence of *BH* reads 'the genealogy of Fin Herin came out of Denmark', and this is followed by nearly fourteen pages of Fianna lore.

His redaction falls into three main sections, as shown in table 11.1. First he gives us Fionn mac Cumhaill's pedigree down to its final member, Oisín, who told it to St Patrick. He then gives some seemingly unrelated snippets and describes at great length the battle of Gabhair (*Cath Gabhra* in Irish, title of a popular narrative from the Fenian Cycle of tales) in which the Fianna met

Table 11.1 Fianna lore in the Book of Howth

1a	Fionn's genealogy (p. 1)
1b	Three snippets: (p. 1)
	Zenobia – hardiest woman ever
	Meath – head of Ireland
	O'Neills, O'Donnells, Brian Boru
1c	Battle of Gabhair (pp 2–6)
1d	Harbour bases (pp 6–7)
2a	'The burning of Fionn's house' (pp 7–8)
2b	(Reallmondus brought these people) (pp 8–9)
2c	What Oisín missed most; baptism (p. 9)
2d	Fionn and the king of Denmark (pp 9–10)
2e	Clan Morna vs. Clan Baoiscne (p. 10)
2f	Giant lands at Howth (pp 10–11)
2g	Conn Cead Cathagh and the stone of kingship (p. 11)
3a	The battle of Ventry (pp 11–15)
3b	A queen jousts with the king of Connacht's son and marries him (pp 15–16)

feasa ar Éirinn: the history of Ireland, ed. and trans. David Comyn and P.S. Dinneen, 4 vols (London, 1902–14). 12 See the discussion of Keating's use of origin myths, in Bernadette Cunningham, *The world of Geoffrey Keating: history, myth and religion in seventeenth-century*

their downfall. This section finishes with a recounting of the harbours which the Fianna held in order to guard the coasts of Ireland. Section 2 consists of a series of stories, mostly told by Oisín to Patrick, and the final section is a lengthy version of the battle of Ventry (*Cath Fionntrágha*, another popular Fenian battle-tale), followed by another seemingly unrelated snippet.

It is not proposed here to discuss the Fianna lore itself in any detail, as that has been done elsewhere.[13] The purpose of this essay is rather to explore the manner in which Howth tried to make this material relevant to his audience. Leaving aside for the present the genealogy of Fionn (to which however we will return), we see that the Fianna lore both begins and ends with snippets of information which bear no obvious relation to the Fianna as such. The first of these is a reference to Zenobia 'the best and hardiest of women that ever was in martial feats of arms', and the last of these is a passage (3b, following the numbering laid out in table 11.1) about a woman doing battle with, and finally marrying, the son of the king of Connacht. After this the book then turns to the saints Patrick and Brigid before going on to Ireland's geography and history. Clearly these passages are intended as reflections of Queen Elizabeth. As a loyal subject of the crown, Howth establishes her presence in the text from the outset, bracketing his introductory lore with images reflecting her as a warlike and victorious sovereign.

Zenobia is followed by a brief anecdote about 'Tweltactor' explaining Meath as the metaphoric 'head' of Ireland. Howth then states that there were eighteen Nyellis (O'Neills) that were kings before the conquest, ten Donels (O'Donnels), and one Munsterman named Bren Bere (Brian Bóraimhe) 'of who the Brenis (O'Briens) took their surname, and five chyampynons [sic] out of Conoght; these was they that most account was made of in Ireland'. In second place to Queen Elizabeth, therefore, Howth establishes Meath as the focus of kingship in Ireland and attempts a summary of its main kings. The Meath story about Tuathal Techtmar ('Tweltactor') was drawn straight from the *Agallamh na Seanórach*,[14] of which several written versions were in existence by Howth's time.[15] Howth seems to have been well acquainted with its contents. His next section, 1c, outlines the battle of Gabhair, or Gareston as he calls it, a battle which likewise features as part of the opening story in the *Agallamh*. Howth begins the account of the battle thus:

Ireland (Dublin, 2000), pp 122–40. 13 Lenore Fischer, 'Fionn mac Cumhaill among the Old English: some comments on The Book of Howth', *North American Journal of Celtic Studies*, 3 (2019), 65–84. 14 See Maurice Harmon, *The dialogue of the ancients: a new translation of Acallam na senórach* (Dublin, 2009), p. 102. 15 *Agallamh na seanórach* survives in three fifteenth-century MSS: Laud 610, Rawlinson B 487 and the *Book of Lismore*. Versions of some of its material contained in the twelfth-century Book of Leinster, however, suggest that some form of it existed before the Anglo-Norman invasion; for more on the dating of the *fianagecht* corpus, see Kuno Meyer, *Fianaigecht* (Dublin, 1910, reprint 2006), pp xvi–xxxi; Gerard Murphy, *Duanaire Finn, The book of the lays of Fionn*, Part II (London, 1933), and Kevin Murray, 'Interpreting the evidence: problems with dating the

> In Ireland there was soldiers called Fyen-erryne, appointed to keep the sea coasts, fearing outward invasion ... These soldiers waxed bold ... and so strong that they did contrary to the orders and institutions taken by the kings of Ireland, their chief lords and governors, and became very strong and stout, and at length would do many things of themselves without licence of the kings of the land ... They charged all the commons of Ireland that they should not hunt no game without their special licence; and if they did, they should pay after this rate: for a hare's killing 20*d*.; for a water dog's [otter's] killing double as much, and so after that rate, doubling still as the game was, as the fox, the wolf, the deer, and all other pastimes.

Howth is describing a people here whom he regards as very similar to the Old English themselves: a non-native body of people running the country in defiance of the native kings, spiritual forerunners of the Old English. The material is in the main drawn directly from the *Agallamh* though in places much elaborated with detail.[16]

Following the battle of Gabhair, Howth lists the harbours that the Fianna were employed to guard. This functions as what Smith calls 'an alleged and felt symbiosis between a certain piece of earth and "its" community': a symbiosis which is one of his six essential features defining an ethnic community.[17] A list similar to Howth's crops up in eighteenth- and nineteenth-century versions of *Cath Fionntrágha* ('The Battle of Ventry').[18] These begin at Howth, naming thirty-eight harbours clockwise round the coast as far as Drumcliff just beyond Sligo. The list in *BH* begins instead at Dublin and goes clockwise right round the entire coast of Ireland, ending at Howth. Though the landholders named do not correspond, there is extensive overlap in the places named, as shown in table 11.2. It is scarcely conceivable that the eighteenth-century Irish sources drew their inspiration from Howth: Howth must have had access to an older source no longer extant. He was by this means able to provide the Fianna, here the paradigmatic forerunners of the Old English, with an intimate connection to the confines of the island, by inference staking the Old English claim to the entire territory defined by that boundary.

early *fianaigecht* corpus' in Sharon J. Arbuthnot and Geraldine Parsons (eds) *The Gaelic Finn tradition* (Dublin, 2012). 16 For comparative material on the battle of Gabhair, see Nicholas O'Kearney, 'The battle of Gabhra/Garristown in the county of Dublin, fought AD 283', *Transactions of the Ossianic Society*, 1 (Dublin, 1854), 50–1. Note that while he states on p. 48 that the poem is located on folio 109 of the Book of Leinster, this is in error, it is on folio 154a. 17 Smith, *Ethnic origins*, p. 28, with further expansion on this theme on pp 183–90. Schlüter, *History or fable?* also addresses the relationship between memory and places, pp 145–6. 18 Published by Kuno Meyer in *Cath Finntrága* (Oxford, 1885). See pp i, viii and 59–60. Meyer took British Library MS Egerton 149 as the base text for this list of harbours.

Table 11.2 List of harbours in BL MS Egerton 149 compared with *BH*. Egerton commonly lists two place names using the formula X *rea raidhtear* Y: 'X that is to say Y'.

BL MS Egerton 149	*Book of Howth*
Cairuig na cCurach/Binn Eaduir [Howth]	Howth
Inibher Lifeach / Aith Chliath [Dublin]	Doublynge
Inibher Breágh /Beárna Gaoithe [Windgates nr Bray]	Wyne-Gyattes
Inibher Da Glas/Cill Mheanntaín [Wicklow]	Wycklowe
Inibher Bheag/Inibher Mhor [Arklow]	Arclo
Caislín/Ghlasfairge [Glascarrig]	
Loch Faolcon/Loch Garmon [Wexford]	Wexford
Glaise an Bhanntracht/Cluain na m-Ban [?Bannow]	
Comuir na tTrí n-Uisge mar attéid Siuir 7 Feair 7 Bearbha a muir [Waterford Harbour, 10km south of New Ross]	Rosse
Ros Bruic/Dun Gabhaín [sic; Dungarvan]	Dongarvane
Tacmaín/Roinne Crú [Rincrew nr Youghal]	O'Keylle [Youghal]
	Corke
Fán an Tiobruide/Ceann t-Saile [Kinsale]	Kynsall
Uisge g-Caol/Tig Mholaíse [Timoleague]	
Garga na tTréd/Cárda ó cCarbre [nr Rosscarbery]	
Cluthar/Cuan Dorn [Glandore]	
Cuan na hInnsi/Cuan an Tighe Mhoir [?Roaringwater Bay]	
Innis Creagaín/Dún Baoi [Dunboy]	
Glascaruig/Sgellig Mhichil [Skellig Michael]	
na ttrí Inibhir Mong [?at Valentia]	
Tonn Toíme [?Glenbeigh]	
	Deyngne Koysse [Daingean Uí Chúis]
	Fentra [Ventry]
Tráighlí [Tralee]	Traley
Uisge Geal/Casán Ciaruighe [mouth of the Cashen?]	
	Lymnaghe
Inbhir na m-Barc /Innis Catha [Scattery Island]	Enyskaghe
	Corke
ó Leim Chongcullaind go Croímlinn [Loop Head to Crumlin, nr Black Head, Co. Clare]	Canborne [Ceann Boirne, Black Head, Co. Clare]
Dromann Trágha Bhaille/Dún Guare [Kinvarra]	Dourys Oveyragh [Durlas Guaire, Kinvarra]
Dún na tTrí cCaith	
Inbhir na bh-Fleadh/Muicinis	
Tiobruid Fála Beíne/Tír Iarthach	
Fuaran na Feíne/an Ghaillibh [Galway]	Galleway

BL MS Egerton 149	*Book of Howth*
Inibher Mhór / Portlárge	
Aís Dá Bhun Báoghlacha	
Inis Ríoghna / Inis Bó Finne [Inishbofin]	*Enis-bresyn [?Inishbofin]
Deirgiort / Oileain Bheaga	*Small Island [* in inverse order in *BH*]
Séanchoill na bh-Fiann / Cliarach [Clare Island]	Klere [Clare Island]
	Koymaghtbe
	Galley
Ros Broinn Duibh	
Inibhir uí Fhógurtaicc / an Mádh Méaghrach [?mouth of the Moy]	Moye [mouth of the Moy at Ballina?]
Trágha na Mná Marbhaidh / Trágha Eochuille [Ballysadare]	
Srathán an Tobuir Ghil / Slígeach	Sligoe
Druim Cliabh na hEirionn [Drumcliff]	
	Bondroys [Bundrowse]
	Asseroe [Assaroe]
	Dongall [Donegal]
	Fanyd [Fanad]
	Loghfoyll [Lough Foyle]
	Bon-bane [Benbane Head]
	Cnocfergos [Carrickfergus]
	Ard-olloe [Aird Uladh, the Ards]
	Ardglas [Ardglass]
	Dondourme [Dundrum]
	Karlynfourd [Carlingford]
	Dondalke [Dundalk]
	Trodathe [Drogheda]
	Gourmanston [Gormanstown]
	Erlandysey [Ireland's Eye]

Section 2 of the Fianna lore in *BH* consists of a series of stories told by Oisín to St Patrick. While at first reading they may appear to form a random collection of strange tales, closer study shows that they are very carefully chosen from an existing fund of Fianna lore and organized for a deliberate purpose. Several of the stories, namely 2a, 'The burning of Fionn's house', 2c 'What Oisín missed most'; 2e, the feud between 'Klan-ne-Morne and Klan-ne-Boysken' (the Clan Morna and Fionn's Clan Baoiscne), and 2g, 'Conn Cead Cathagh and the stone of kingship', are known from *Agallamh na Seanórach.*[19]

19 See E.J. Gwynn, 'The burning of Finn's house', *Eriu,* 1 (1904), 13–37; Harmon, *The dialogue,* pp 8, 31, 185. For a more detailed description of Howth's treatment of these, see Fischer, 'Finn mac Cumhaill', pp 73–7.

Howth includes an intriguing twist on the tale of Oisín's baptism in 2c, however, when he describes St Patrick driving his 'croyge or bahell' through Oisín's foot, who bears it patiently thinking it part of the ritual. This is patently lifted from the *Vita Tripartita* where it refers to St Patrick's baptism of the king of Munster at Cashel,[20] and is also present in latter-day folklore.[21] Howth may have had an ulterior motive for including this passage, for Patrick's staff, the Bachall Íosa, had been publicly burnt in 1538 on the orders of the English archbishop of Dublin George Browne, in the interests of Henry VIII's Reformation.[22] By weaving this emotive symbol of Ireland's patron saint into his story of the Fianna forerunners, Howth reinforced his identification of the Old English cause with the land and history of Ireland.

2b is a story flagged 'Realmondus' in the margin. It is not attributed to Oisín, but begins 'Those kind of people was brought into Ireland by Realmondus, King in Ulstyer, out of Denmark, as the old histories of Ireland testified'. A somewhat confused story follows in which a beautiful lady (stated to be the wife of the king of Connacht) was wooed by many, but said she would have none but he who could wrest tribute by force from abroad. King Realmondus succeeded and won the lady, but was banished to Denmark where 'he received great aid of soldiers, and so was his own; and their generation rested in Ireland, and served there in Ireland worthily till the field of Caghecauro, where as all these was slain; and so Feyn Ereyn all was destroyed'. Despite Howth's reference to the testimony of 'old histories', the story does not survive independently anywhere else today. It does however seem to provide the backstory to *BH*'s first line '[The genealogy of] Fin Herin came out of Denmark'. It is moreover a striking parallel to Diarmait Mac Murchada's contretemps with Derbforgaill (also a Connacht queen through marriage to Tigernán Ua Ruairc of Bréifne), subsequent banishment and appeal for assistance from Henry II. Howth's account thus presents Realmondus and the coming of the Fianna as the literary forebearers of Mac Murchada and the Old English. It would seem probable that the story is of Howth's own invention.

The story of the giant, number 2f, seems the least informative of the stories recited, and yet it too may have a purpose, for the giant lands at Howth, Christopher St Lawrence's own home, and it is Fionn who eventually brings

20 See Whitley Stokes, *The Tripartite Life of Patrick, with other documents relating to that saint*, Part I (London, 1887), pp 196–7. **21** See Joe Éinniú, *Stories about Fionn Mac Cumaill* (Galway, 2015), downloaded at www.joeheaney. org/ga/fionn-mac-cumhaill-1/ 12 Oct. 2018; Brian Mac Amhlaoibh, narrator, 'Oisín i ndiaidh na Féinne', Royal Irish Academy archive recording ID LA_1203d1, 1931, downloaded at www.doegen.ie/LA_1203d1-, 12 October, 2018; Douglas Hyde, *Legends of saints and sinners* (London, 1915), downloaded at www.aughty.org/pdf/legends_patrick_ oisin.pdf 12 Oct. 2018; Reider T. Christiansen, *The Vikings and the Viking-wars in Irish and Gaelic tradition* (Oslo, 1931), p. 13. **22** See Myles V. Ronan, 'St Patrick's staff and Christ Church', *DHR*, 5 (1943), 121–9. This point was brought to my attention in discussions at the Tudor and Stuart Ireland Conference (2015).

about the giant's downfall. Thus Fionn saves Ireland and in particular the baron of Howth's own homeland from destruction. The final story in this section, 2g, 'Conn Cead Cathagh and the stone of kingship', brings us back to the issue of kingship. Howth expands on the *Agallamh* version of the story by having Oisín relate how the kingship had been usurped but was restored when Cone Kede Caghe (Conn Cétchathach) slew the usurper and caused the stone to speak. Conn Cétchathach appears as a marginal figure in 2a and 2f as well.

The Fianna lore in the *BH* ends with 3a, 'the battle of Ventry', which takes up more than four pages. Though referred to only tangentially in the *Agallamh*, the battle survives in many other versions, the oldest of which occurs in the fifteenth-century Rawlinson B 487; there is a poetic version in the early sixteenth-century *Book of the Dean of Lismore*, and there are also many eighteenth-century and indeed more modern versions of the battle.[23] Howth's description differs significantly from all of these. He states that the trouble arose because Ireland had been levying tribute on Denmark, Argyll, Cornwall, Normandy, Germany and Spain and enslaving their people. The princes of these realms rebelled and agreed to attack Ireland from all sides. Howth lovingly and minutely describes the logistics and topography of the ensuing actions. The men of Denmark and Scotland landed in the north but were repulsed by Conn Cétchathach; the English Saxons and Norman French marched inland from Lambay and Skerries to Knock-ne-Kyan (*Cnoc na gceann*, 'hill of the heads'), named according to Howth from the quantity of Saxon and Norman heads heaped there after the battle. The survivors of these two battles then joined German and Spanish troops in an attempted landing at Ventry. Rawlinson B 487 has a different story. Here the 'high-king of the world' was seeking revenge for Fionn's elopement with the wife and daughter of the king of France. His attack landed at Ventry, to which the king of the world and his forces were guided by Glas son of Dreman, a traitor whose misdeeds had earned him expulsion from the Fianna. *BH* describes the foreigners as being repulsed there seven times, and only winning to land at Ventry through the treachery of an Irishman, Gyllemore, a man who, having been insulted by the Fianna, was looking for revenge.

Once landfall is made, Howth's version soon becomes a sort of prolonged tournament, lords and ladies of both sides feast and joust together and carry on love-affairs and battles of honour punctuated by truces lasting anything from a fortnight to a month. Thus the year whiled away until the treacherous Gyllemore, on returning from combat, ill-fatedly washed his bloodied hands in a cup of wine, which he then mistakenly drank. Such shame did the drinking of his own blood bring upon him that he confessed all his treacheries to his father. By his father's counsel they agreed with the invaders to bring things to a head, and they fought three days and nights without stopping. But while the

23 Meyer, *Cath Finntrága*, pp vii–viii.

Irish had constant reinforcements, the strangers had none: all Europe had been emptied to conquer Ireland, and in the end were all slain. The Irish version contains no such pleasantry and dalliance, being a grim year-long series of martial encounters. Its only love story is that of Ceide keening for her slain lover.

Looking at the production as a whole, it may seem odd that Howth begins his discussion of the Fianna with the story of their downfall at the battle of Gabhair, but in fact *Agallamh na Seanórach* does also.[24] Howth may moreover have had a purpose in mind: showing how the Fianna had become ungovernable and how the kings of the land dealt with them. The first of Oisín's stories likewise concerns a wild, ungovernable lot, where one of their number burns a group of women alive, laughs over their burnt bones, and is slain by his own son at Fionn's command. Significantly, this is followed immediately by the passage stating: 'Those kind of people was brought into Ireland by Reallmondus, King in Ulstyer, out of Denmark', intimating that such a wild bunch were not truly Irishmen, but had been introduced from abroad. Oisín is then baptized by St Patrick, the untamed and dangerous group of foreign rowdies becoming thus sanctified and incorporated into an Irish Christian milieu; the stories that follow are uniformly more respectable in nature.[25] The lengthy concluding tale of the battle of Ventry balances the opening story of the battle of Gabhair. But in contrast to the bitter grief of the battle of Gabhair, the battle of Ventry reads joyously, even ebulliently. Up until this point Howth seems, insofar as our existing sources permit us to judge, to have stuck fairly closely to native tradition, but here we may suspect Howth of conscious embroidery. No foreign elopements figure as causes for, since Oisín's baptism, all our stories have dispensed with such amoral adventuring; instead it is the Fianna Éireann's inordinate success at conquest abroad that occasioned the conflict. The event itself resembles an Elizabethan entertainment more than a battle: what in the heel of the hunt Howth really wants us to remember is all the jolly times they had with 'good sport and pastime for the love of ladies'.[26] The entire sequence thus illustrates the coming of a wild band from abroad who become intimately involved with the kingship of the land; with Christianization they become civilized and wind up, really, hardly different than the Old English themselves.

Whence came the idea that the Fianna came from Denmark? Mairtín Ó Briain has suggested that Dublin oral folklore, drawing on Ostman roots, may have already claimed the Fianna as their own Danish kin.[27] The Ostmen or Viking inhabitants in and around the old Viking settlements had, according to

24 Harmon, *The dialogue*, p. 1. 25 The importance of this Christianization is seen too in origin myths produced for tenth-century dukes of Normandy and Anglo-Saxon descriptions of Danish settlements in England: Cross, *Heirs of the Vikings*, pp 75–90. 26 Brewer, *BH*, p. 14. 27 Máirtin Ó Briain, 'Ginealach "Geinealach Oissín"' in Dónall Ó Baoill et al. (eds), *Saltar saíochta, samasíochta agus seanchais* (Dublin, 2013), pp 261–73, at

Aidan Clarke, 'mingled so closely with the newcomers [the Old English] as to become within a very few generations indistinguishable from them'.[28] Descriptions of the Fianna at times closely resemble the Viking 'foreigners' in the twelfth-century *Cogadh Gáedhel re Gallaibh*.[29] One source even lumps the two peoples together.[30] And though the Fianna usually ward off attacks by outsiders, all sources agree that the king of Denmark's son and his troops were brought in to support them against the kings of Ireland in their final battle. The idea that the Fianna were themselves Danish thus provided Howth with a parallel for the Old English, a group who had similarly come to Ireland and established themselves as masters, both at odds with and yet allied to the established owners of the land. Like Keating, Howth was thus able to create an identity for his own people, a myth of descent.

Keating had of course a vastly greater background in Irish lore than Howth did, and was able to make a much more persuasive and plausible case for his contention that the Anglo-Norman invasion was nothing new to Ireland, that in fact Ireland's own celebrated rulers were the descendants of similar invasions. Just what sort of background did Howth in fact have? He translates many of the place-names for us, and that he had some knowledge of Irish is highly probable, given that in his day English was scarcely used outside the Pale.[31] Irish was used on at least one occasion in parliament,[32] while a near neighbour of Howth's, Sir Christopher Nugent, ninth baron of Delvin, even compiled an Irish primer for Queen Elizabeth's use.[33] Though Richard Stanihurst admitted that his Irish was 'very simple', his remark that certain 'toothless old men of the English province' had no Irish whatsoever suggests that, indeed, most of the Old English had some familiarity with the language.[34] Howth twice explicitly refers to sources for his Fianna material,[35] works which can hardly have been written in English. Was Howth then able to read Irish himself? Perhaps so, but the genealogy of Fionn with which Howth begins his discussion of the Fianna (see table 11.3) turns out to conceal some intriguing information. Ó Briain discussed *BH*'s genealogy in detail and showed that it corresponded in many respects very closely with a text, *Geinealach Oisín*, published in 1825 in *Reliques of Irish poetry consisting of heroic poems, songs, elegies &c*:[36]

p. 267; my thanks to Peadar Ó Muircheartaigh for drawing my attention to this valuable reference. **28** Clarke, *The Old English*, p. 15. **29** *CGG*, pp 48–51. **30** O'Kearney, 'The battle', pp 136, 137. **31** Marc Caball and Kaarina Hollo, 'The literature of later medieval Ireland, 1200–1600: from the Normans to the Tudors: poetry' in Margaret Kelleher and Philip O'Leary (eds), *The Cambridge history of Irish literature* (Cambridge, 2013), p. 89. **32** Brian Ó Cuív, 'The Irish language in the early modern period' in T.W. Doody et al. (eds), *A new history of Ireland*, iii (Oxford, 1976), pp 507–45 at p. 510. **33** Ó Cuív, 'The Irish language', p. 511; see now, Denis Casey, *The Nugents of Westmeath and Queen Elizabeth's Irish primer*, Maynooth Studies in Local History 123 (Dublin, 2016). **34** Colm Lennon, 'Richard Stanihurst', pp 132, 129. **35** 'I find … in an old book' and 'this much I find in another book': Brewer, *BH*, p. 6. **36** Ó Briain, 'Ginealach', p. 261.

1. *Mac do Bhaoisgne, Goire na sluagh:*
   Mac do Ghoire, Conn na gcath mór:
   Mac do Chonn, Farlacht nár ghann:
   Mac d'Fharlacht nár ghann, Tréanmór.

2. *Mac do Thréanmor, Cumhall na bhfleadh:*
   Mac do Chumhall, Fionn faidh:
   Mac d'Fhionn an áigh mé féin:
   Beód bocht 'na ndiaigh a táim.

Additional material is supplied by sections of the *Duanaire Finn* XXVII, where Cú Rí, Baoiscne, Fiachaidh and Eochaidh are all described as sons of Dáire Donn mac Deadhaidh.[37]

Table 11.3 *BH*'s genealogy of Fionn compared with genealogies in *Duanaire Fionn* and *Geinealach Oisín*.

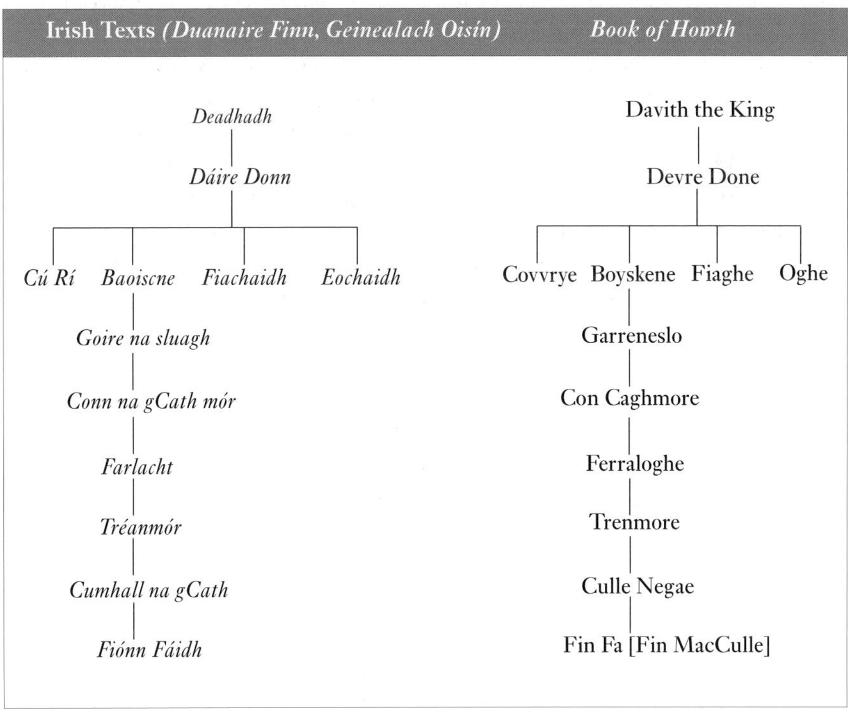

37 Eoin MacNeill, *Duanaire Finn: The book of the lays of Fionn*, Part 1 (Dublin, 1948), p. 133.

Ó Briain suggested that both *BH* and *Geinealach Oisín* derive from a lost or additional verse of the *Duanaire Finn*. That Howth had access to written sources of Fianna lore is clear. But the manner in which he treats chevilles such as 'na sluagh', 'na gcath mór' as though they were part of the proper name suggests that the names were at some stage of the transmission written down from oral sources: they were either being read aloud from a book or recited from memory.

HOWTH'S LEGACY

A final question relates to Howth's audience. Who was he intending to reach, and to what extent did he succeed? McGowan-Doyle's analysis of the political activities in which Howth was involved has shown that he was responding to the crisis within Ireland between the established community of the Old English and the *arrivistes* or New English. Zimmermann has pointed out that 'ethnic identity offering a sense of continuity and dignity is perceived as more crucially important when it seems under threat'.[38] Howth was seeking both to motivate the Old English community around him and to educate the New English with regard to the nature and values of that community. Within the scope of that readership, Howth seems initially to have achieved a certain measure of success. Sixteenth-century copies of his work preserved in the Trinity College Library collections and in Lambeth palace have led McGowan-Doyle to conclude that 'Howth's work enjoyed much livelier circulation in the decades following its completion than suggested by the relative obscurity into which it increasingly slipped over the ensuing centuries'.[39] Obscurity was to be his fate, however, and the only author to make any extensive mention of Howth's introductory Fianna lore prior to the publication of *BH* in 1871 was Meredith Hanmer.[40]

Although not published until 1663, Hanmer's *Chronicle of Ireland* seems to have been written sometime in the 1580s or 1590s, i.e., in the period when *BH* was still in active circulation.[41] He makes ample use of Howth's introduction, but his organization of the material reflects important changes, as shown in table 11.4.

38 George Denis Zimmermann, *The Irish storyteller* (Dublin, 2001) p. 311. 39 McGowan-Doyle, *Book of Howth*, p. 114. 40 Meredith Hanmer, *The chronicle of Ireland* (Dublin, 1663, reprint Amsterdam, 1971). 41 The description on the cover page of the 1809 version of his *Chronicle*, stating that his material was collected 'in the year 1571', is certainly incorrect, as Hanmer did not come to Ireland until perhaps as late as 1591, according to both Anthony Wood, *Athenae Oxonienses* (Oxford, 1815), p. 747 and Alan Ford, 'Hanmer, Meredith (1543–1604), church of England and church of Ireland clergyman and historian', *Oxford dictionary of national biography* (accessed 17 Feb. 2023).

Table 11.4 Hanmer's organization of Fianna material compared to Howth's.

Hanmer	Pages	*Book of Howth*
1a Realmond	46–7	**2b**
1b Genealogy of Fin Eryn	47–8	**1a**
1c Battle of Ventry	48–52	**3a**
1d Harbour bases	52–4	**1d**
1e The causes and battle of Gabhair	54–61	**1c**
2a Clan Morna vs. Clan Baoiscne	61	**2e**
2b Fionn and the king of Denmark	61–2	**2d**
2c A giant lands at Howth	62	**2f**
2d The burning of Fionn's house	62–3	**2a**

Hanmer was not a native of Ireland, and his ordering of the material broke free of the *Agallamh* tradition that Howth followed. Instead Hanmer chose to give us a sequential account of the Fianna, beginning with their introduction by Realmondus (following Howth's story, known from no other source), carrying on then with their genealogy, their great battle at Ventry and the harbours they kept, and ending with their destruction in the battle of Gabhair. This chronologically quite logical organization of the Fianna story is unique to Hanmer. He then follows with various of Howth's Fianna tales, ending with the lurid story in which the wives of the Fianna are burnt alive and, at Fionn's command, a son kills his own father in retribution and runs mad as a result: 'And the end of Fin Mac Coill was, that he dyed a beggar and in great miserie.'[42] If Hanmer was taking on Howth's paradigm of the Fianna as the precursors of the Old English, then he seems to be saying that the Old English were a doomed race.

Some memory of the idea that Fionn was Danish in origin seems to have stayed afloat, however, either deriving from Howth's description or perhaps surviving from earlier Ostman lore, as Thady Dowling (d. 1628) saw fit to incorporate a mangled story to that effect in his *Annales breves Hiberniae*, according to which a certain Stracatherus, member of a Danish army invading Ireland, received a head-wound, but so impressed the Irish with his enormous stature and ferocity that they called him Fin McCoyl (*sic*).[43] The giant Stracatherus seems to be drawn from Saxo Grammaticus's late twelfth-

42 Hanmer, *The chronicle*, p. 63. 43 Thaddeus (Thady) Dowling, *Annales breves Hiberniae*, Corpus of Electronic Texts, http://www.ucc.ie/celt, 2003, first published (Dublin, 1849), annal 1105.1. My thanks to Catherine Swift for assistance in translating the extremely tangled Latin text.

century *Danish history*, which relates how Starkad invaded Ireland and suffered a grievous wound to the head.[44] The story there of how Stracatherus visited terrible punishment upon Irish jugglers and buffoons may perhaps have prompted Dowling to associate the Danish hero with the story of the Fianna and their supposed Danish origin.

Hanmer's *Chronicle* was printed by James Ware in 1663, but Howth's own work was left untouched until 1871 when published by Brewer among the material collected by Howth's contemporary, Sir George Carew. Echoes of Howth's theory reappear at the turn of the eighteenth/nineteenth century in Edward Ledwich's *Antiquities of Ireland.* Fired by the growing British adulation of all things northern, Ledwich maintained that the name Fionn (Old Irish 'Finn') came from Finland:

> The districts seized by the Finns were named Bescha na Fene. [To] render these pirates useful the Irish intermarried with them, and of them formed a militia to protect the coasts against their marauding countrymen. This was the body of national forces, celebrated in Irish romantic history under the name of Fionn Eirionn.[45]

Ledwich, however, was operating in an entirely different context, one in which, for instance, Pinkerton was regarding all things Celtic as inferior to all things Nordic,[46] Beauford denigrating the ancient Irish as 'an aggregate of vagabonds',[47] and Vallancey insisting that the Irish language and monuments must be Phoenician in origin.[48] Although Ledwich went on in his *Antiquities* to derive the Tuatha de Danann from Denmark,[49] it is perhaps unfair to place undue emphasis on a connection between his theories and the information relayed via Hanmer from Howth.

Was Christopher St Lawrence the irascible domestic tyrant that his political opponents sought to make out? We shall never know if the charges brought against him for domestic violence were genuine or simply trumped up. Politically, however, he seems to have held a steadfast course, fulfilling government duties, negotiating when he saw room, staunchly opposing when he believed his principles to be at stake. His attempt to codify a framework of reference for the Old English was a heroic and highly innovative enterprise. For sources, he had some annals and Ralph Higden's fourteenth-century *Polychronicon*. He was already well started on his project when Edmund

44 Oliver Elton (trans), *The first nine books of the Danish history of Saxo Grammaticus* (London, 1894), pp 228–9. 45 Edward Ledwich, *The antiquities of Ireland* (Dublin, 1804), p. 25; the first edition of this work was published in 1791 under the name of Francis Grose. 46 John Waddell, *Foundation myths: the beginning of Irish archaeology* (Bray, 2005), p. 69. 47 Quoted in ibid., p. 80. 48 See Clare O'Halloran, *Golden ages and barbarous nations* (Cork, 2004), pp 42–4; also Joep Leerssen, *Mere Irish and Fíor-Ghael* (Notre Dame, 1997), p. 361. 49 Ledwich, *Antiquities*, pp 25–6.

Campion's *History of Ireland* came out in 1571, and Howth immediately set about mining this for material as well.[50] Otherwise there was very little literature being produced within the Anglo-Irish community. Certainly an intellectual community existed, best exemplified in Stanihurst's circle, among whom were one or more schoolmasters, lawyers, poets, antiquarians, philosophers and classical scholars,[51] but this community was evidently at this stage first finding voice in print. Howth had already embarked upon his project when Richard Stanihurst was invited to submit a contribution to Holinshed's *Chronicles of England, Scotland and Ireland*.[52] Edmund Campion and Meredith Hanmer were men born in Britain writing about Ireland, as was Edmund Spenser, whose *View of the present state of Ireland* came out in 1596. Stanihurst himself, though of Old English descent, had been much influenced by Campion, his tutor. Thus a major impetus for self-analysis and self-expression seems to have come from outside the community itself, underscoring the pioneering nature of Howth's work.

Howth does not seem in the end to have succeeded in providing the Old English with a viable foundation myth. Though Hanmer took up the paradigm, he evidently foresaw the oblivion to which the Old English were doomed, for Hanmer's version of Fionn brings him to a miserable end. Later authors dismissed Howth's work as whimsical nonsense, and in the end it was Keating who proved able to incorporate the Old English into the framework of an Irish *mythomoteur*.

50 MacGowan-Doyle, *Book of Howth*, pp 71–3. 51 Lennon, 'Richard Stanihurst', p. 131. 52 Ibid., p. 12.